Two Cocks on the Dunghill

William Cobbett and Henry Hunt: their friendship, feuds and fights

Penny Young

Twopenny Press

First published in the UK in 2009
reprinted 2010

Twopenny Press
2 The Old School South Lopham
Norfolk IP22 2HT
www.twopennypress.co.uk

ISBN 978-0-9561703-3-0

Typeset in Adobe Garamond, designed and produced by
Gilmour Print, www.gilmourprint.co.uk

To William Cobbett and Henry Hunt

Penny Young

23/3/2013

They walked down the mean streets but were neither tarnished nor afraid.

With thanks to Raymond Chandler

Contents

Acknowledgements

I am grateful to all the friends, family members and experts who helped me to research and write *Two Cocks on the Dunghill*. Peter Clark wonderfully introduced me to William Cobbett and Henry Hunt in the first place. Sue Waldram and Lisa Ausden kindly bought me a rare copy of John Belchem's political biography of Henry Hunt. My sister Jennifer Whyte provided the technical help to gather in the illustrations. Molly Townsend, the late chairman of the William Cobbett Society, and Robert Wallen kindly read the manuscript. Nick Stanley went through it with a penetrating but graceful toothcomb. His patient and painstaking work stopped me falling into many holes. Michael Russell of Wilby Hall in Norfolk gave excellent advice. Any mistakes are, of course, my own.

Cambridge University Library, The Library of Nuffield College, Oxford, and the British Library provided every facility, support and encouragement. Eye Library in Suffolk and Diss Library in Norfolk were also tireless in helping me find the books and material I needed. Ilchester Museum was kind enough to open especially for me. It is a mine of information. I am grateful too to the American universities, which make their valuable collections so easily available. I am also deeply obliged to Jennifer Ramkalawon, Curator of the Department of Prints and Drawings at the British Museum, who spent a lot of time so that I could include rare caricatures of Cobbett and Hunt from the museum's collection. I thank the Fighting Cocks pub in Winfarthing and Diss Museum for the pictures of the two fighting cocks.

The West Sussex Record Office, Joan Ham and Helen Whittle gave me the key to the identity of Mrs Vince and the Bisshopp family. Barbara Jacobson, whom I met by chance in the pouring rain near the site of Merlin's Cave on the former Spa Fields, gave me invaluable pieces for the jigsaw. Jonathan and Althea Bailey so generously kept me supplied with books, including a copy of the three-volume *Concise Dictionary of National Biography*. Its pages are now very well-thumbed. I am also very grateful to the Misses Olive and Gladys Bolderston for their generosity. Ted Burt has offered me every assistance over so many years to keep my computer working smoothly and my temper even. I would like to pay tribute to the work of my surgeon Mr Francis Wells, Dr Lauren Bate, Dr Clare Laroche and nurse Theresa Bage. Without them I would not have been here to write the book.

Gary Collier encouraged me throughout. When I flagged or got depressed, he reminded me that Cobbett and Hunt remained true to the cause right to the end.

This is the second printing of *Two Cocks on the Dunghill*. Typographical errors have been corrected. On page 177, we have retained the original caption as listed in the British Museum catalogue. Professor Michael Bush has suggested, however, that the figure of Tom Paine is in fact that of Richard Carlile. We are also grateful to James Sambrook for his comments.

Introduction

Two Cocks on the Dunghill is an account of the extraordinary relationship between two leading radical reformers of the early nineteenth century, who spent their lives fighting for justice, human rights and a reformed, democratic House of Commons. Both were imprisoned because of their beliefs, and both became fiercely independent members of parliament. The men were William Cobbett (1763-1835) and Henry Hunt (1773-1835). Cobbett was the greatest radical political writer of his times. His life is well documented and many biographies have been written about him. He is still celebrated today. By contrast, Henry Hunt remains largely unknown, yet he was the most famous radical public speaker and darling of the people. It was 'Orator' Hunt who was speaking on the platform on St Peter's Field in Manchester on 16 August 1819 when the yeomanry slashed their way into the crowds to put a stop to the meeting. The event went down in history as the Peterloo Massacre. Hunt features in biographies about Cobbett merely as one of the other reformers with whom Cobbett had dealings. There is only one biography of Hunt to have been written since 1836, John Belchem's excellent political study, published in 1985 and, sadly, out of print.

What nobody has written about in any depths before is the unlikely but very real political partnership and friendship between these two charismatic and inspiring men. Against all the odds, Cobbett the conservative radical, experienced and wily, became the closest of friends with Hunt the democratic radical, ten years younger and new to the game. There is plenty of material; the clues are there. They can be found in Hunt's *Memoirs* and *Addresses* and scattered through the numerous volumes of Cobbett's *Weekly Political Register*. The evidence is there in contemporary newspapers and diaries, and in letters including those from Cobbett to Hunt. Only two letters from Hunt to Cobbett appear to have survived. I believe they are the last two letters Hunt wrote to Cobbett. They are so important because they reveal why Hunt finally severed relations. As far as I know, the two letters have never been made public before. Nobody has chartered the course of the pair's relationship from close friendship to deadly enmity, with the peaks and troughs in between. It lasted in one way or another for more than thirty years until the deaths of both men in 1835, just four months apart. The events take place at a momentous time in history, in the run up to and the passing of the Reform Act of 1832. Hunt was an MP for Preston during the passage of the bill; Cobbett sat in the first reformed House of Commons as a member for Oldham.

It is a puzzle why their story has remained untold until now. Everybody knew these men. The relationship, with its ups and downs, was conducted in the full glare of the late Georgian public. It was all there in black and white for everybody to read. People feasted on what the one wrote about the other. Not only were there Cobbett and Hunt's colourful political activities, there was also Cobbett's wife, Nancy, with her violent hatred of Hunt and fury at her husband's friendship with that 'bad man'. There was Hunt's long-time mistress, his beloved and beautiful Mrs Vince, illegitimate granddaughter of a baronet. The press used Mrs Vince as a stick with which to beat Hunt, the would-be MP. The scandal of Hunt's life with a 'prostitute', as Mrs Vince was so hatefully called, was raised in the House of Commons and in the City of London's Court of Common Council. Legitimate tactics or press intrusion into private life? Cobbett stoutly defended Hunt, thus adding to his wife's fury. Yet everybody was able to read what Cobbett really thought of men who dumped their wives, and of women who slept outside the marriage bed, when he published his *Advice to Young Men* in 1829. There were also the scandals, including Nancy's attempted suicide and her unfounded accusation that her husband had a homosexual relationship with his secretary, and the later collapse of Cobbett's marriage. Cobbett's biographers have largely avoided these matters, maybe out of a desire to protect his reputation, or because they found them of no significance, or because they believed that the incidents were part of Cobbett's private life and off limits. Yet all these events sprang out of the relationship between William Cobbett and Henry Hunt and are of relevance in understanding what happened.

Not only is this a story about the personal and political relationship between two men at a crucial moment in history, but the issues, arguments and emotions resonate today. The questions raised are ever relevant. How should a government fight against a perceived foreign and home threat of 'Terror'? When, if ever, should human rights be suspended? What role does the press play? How much integrity can there be in politics and at what cost? *Two Cocks on the Dunghill* is a story about corruption and greed, compassion and morality. It tells of love, hate, jealousy and scandal and how human beings deal with them. It is also about the courage of individuals against an oppressive state and the triumph of will power and determination in adversity.

1
Roots

We hold these truths to be self-evident, that all men are created equal; that they are endowed by their Creator with certain unalienable rights; that among these are life, liberty and the pursuit of happiness.

Declaration of Independence, 4 July 1776

One hot summer's day in July 1805, a fashionably-dressed, good-looking man with a proud and confident step and his head held high might have been seen making his way through the crowded streets from Charing Cross in the west end of late Georgian London down Whitehall towards Westminster. He was on his way to one of the most important meetings of his life. The man was Henry Hunt. Few heads would have turned to watch him pass. At this moment in history, Hunt was largely unknown. In a few years' time, the situation was to be very different. Hunt would be the most famous radical orator in England, pulling in crowds of anything up to 100,000 people eager to listen to his fiery speeches advocating one man one vote, secret ballots and annual parliaments. Over the breeze floated the future shouts and cries of the famous meetings to come at London's Spa Fields and St Peter's Field in Manchester. The latter would go down in history as the Peterloo Massacre and would lead to the incarceration of Hunt in a prison cell for two and a half years. Governments would fear Henry Hunt and ministers would plot his death. On this July day in 1805, however, he was still able to walk through the London streets in comparative anonymity. On the other hand, the man Hunt was about to meet was very well known indeed by the highest in the kingdom to the lowest. He was William Cobbett.

By the summer of 1805, Cobbett, who was bred at the plough-tail and in the hop gardens of Farnham in Surrey, was established as one of the most famous or infamous political writers in the country. Three years previously, he had set up *Cobbett's Weekly Political Register*, the radical newspaper which pioneered the concept of the kind of political commentary written in our newspapers today. The *Political Register* was to continue on Saturdays with only a few interruptions until Cobbett's death in 1835, a feat indeed given the governmental heavy fist against the politically independent and subversive grass roots press.

The *Political Register* was launched when the main issue of the day was the war with revolutionary France, which had begun in 1793, and how the British government should deal with it. Cobbett opposed the peace treaty of Amiens signed on 27 March 1802, although the people welcomed it. The mob smashed in his windows when he refused to light them up with candles in celebration. He did not believe the treaty would contain France's expansion plans or its revolutionary fervour, and he was proved right. The treaty was no more than a truce. The war against France resumed in May 1803 and continued until the Battle of Waterloo in 1815. Cobbett supported the war although that did not stop him criticising the whitewashing of the military disasters and exposing the propaganda that put a glossy spin on events however disastrous. He also turned his persuasive pen towards domestic issues. He increased his attacks against endemic state corruption, backhanders, sleaze, jobs for the boys and lucrative pensions. He waged ceaseless war against the church and the tithes that the clergy had the right to seize every year from smallholders and farmers, everything from hens to sheep and cattle, and produce including corn, wheat and barley. He wrote about the harsh impact of the war against France on the lives of the people, the heavy taxation and the huge disparity in wealth between the upper classes and the mass of the poor.

Although Cobbett was no revolutionary, he also exposed the ruthless way in which the government exploited the fear of Jacobinism to crush any dissent. Jacobins were French revolutionaries. The name was given to anybody who wanted to change the status quo. It became a convenient term of abuse, to be freely used against anybody brave enough to challenge the system and call for parliamentary rights, justice and equality. Both Cobbett and Hunt were regularly accused of being Jacobins in spite of the fact that both believed and argued that a reform of parliament and more democratic voting procedures would prevent a revolution in England.

By the time Henry Hunt decided to call on Cobbett, whom he so admired for his 'able, clear and perspicuous expositions', Cobbett was on his way to becoming the most widely read political journalist of his time. In coffee houses, salons and bedrooms, kings, princes and emperors, prime ministers and presidents, politicians and poets, choked and chortled every week over the *Political Register*. It was, after all, the most infuriating and entertaining of political magazines with its diatribes against political corruption, ineptitude and nepotism, its lambasting of the judicial system and its sharp criticism of the mishandling of the economy and foreign affairs. Soldiers read it secretly under their bedclothes. Illiterate labourers listened in awe as Cobbett's *Register* was read aloud in smoky alehouses. Napoleon Bonaparte lodged a formal complaint. He would sit in his bath and get somebody to read him out extracts. 'It's a lie!' he would shout, banging on the side.

Whether they approved or disapproved, Cobbett's insults hurled against the tax eaters, stock jobbers, loan-mongering robbers and 'wen devils' (the latter Cobbett-speak for certain people who lived in London) and his clarion calls for 'a clean sweeping out of all the dirt', in short 'a complete *change of system*', had become compulsive reading. The essayist William Hazlitt considered Cobbett to be 'a kind of *fourth estate* in the politics of the country.' (The others were the King, the Lords and the Commons.)

In 1805, Cobbett was on the point of moving from the wen with his family to set up a farming business in the village of Botley in Hampshire. In the long hot summer of that year, he was still living in London in a rented terraced house in Duke Street, Westminster, close to Downing Street. (Duke Street was subsequently demolished and the area is now part of Horse Guards Road.) Cobbett was a busy man. He had many visitors, some of them leading members of the government. His house, on the south eastern edge of St James's Park on Birdcage Walk, was within easy walking distance of the Houses of Commons and Lords, and Westminster Hall, the principal home of the Courts of Justice. Across the park, was Pall Mall, St James's Palace and Carlton House, the extravagant mansion of George, Prince of Wales, 'Prinny' to his friends, heir to the throne of his sick father, George III, and soon to become Prince Regent. It was a world that could not have been further away from the one into which William Cobbett was born.

Cobbett was born on 9 March 1763 at the Jolly Farmer Inn (still a pub, but now called the William Cobbett) on Bridge Square in the fine stone-built town of Farnham on the North Downs of Surrey. Cobbett's grandfather was a labourer who worked for the same farmer for forty years. His son, George, managed to earn enough twopences driving the plough to pay his own way through the village evening school. George Cobbett's rudimentary education and enterprise meant that by the time his third son, William, was born, he had acquired enough land to run a small farm.

It was a good time to be alive – at least as William Cobbett remembered it. The Hanoverian King George III had just ascended the throne. His subjects numbered around seven million people. The countryside was green and fruitful, bursting with hops and billowing with corn. It was cultivated by yeomen – farmers who either owned small farms or leased them at unchanging annual rents from the big landowners. For the rest of his life Cobbett looked back to those times as the best of times when life was harmonious, the landowners (some of them) looked after their workers, and everybody brewed their own beer, kept their own livestock and could afford to enjoy a rasher or two of fat-rich bacon for breakfast.

In reality, life in rural England was at a turning point. Vast tracts of the countryside had already been enclosed. Now the landowners were turning their attention to the commons and wastelands. These were being fenced off and hedged in even though they were vital grazing and food-growing areas for the people. The hated so-called Speenhamland system of poor relief, which was greedily exploited by the farmers to keep wages at starvation levels, was soon to be introduced. New machines were being invented which would smash cottage industry and force people out of their villages into slave labour in hellish factories in new and expanding towns. On the horizon loomed the American War of Independence (1775-1781), the French Revolution (1789-1792) and the long costly war that followed between Britain and France.

As a small child, Cobbett was oblivious to the winds of change. Wearing his blue smock-frock, he joined his brothers working on his father's land, chasing away the rooks from the peas and weeding through the wheat, although he was so small he was hardly able to climb over the gates and stiles. He progressed from leading a single horse at harrowing barley to driving the team and holding the plough. Aged eleven, he was sent to clip the box shrubs edging the paths and weed the flowerbeds in the gardens of Farnham Castle, then part of the real estate owned by the Bishops of Winchester. As a treat, his father took him to the agricultural fair at Weyhill outside Andover where he was to go in future years to eye up the sheep with Henry Hunt. Cobbett loved field sports and often risked a beating to run after the horses and the hounds. In later years, he wrote and spoke about his childhood with deep nostalgia. Farnham was the most beautiful place in the whole world, he said, but at the time he had wanted more out of life than the lot of a ploughboy.

On 6 May 1783, Cobbett left home. He was going to Guildford Fair when, on impulse, he jumped on board the coach to London. His travels led him to Chatham in Kent where he enlisted, as he thought, in the marines. He had, in fact, joined the infantry as a soldier. During the year he spent based at Chatham Barracks, he set out to improve his education. His father had taught him to read and he already wrote 'a fair hand', which had won him the honour of being secretary to the garrison commander. He made many mistakes and was well aware of his own limitations. So, although he only received sixpence a day, he managed to save up to buy a grammar book and learned it by heart while on sentry duty. He practically starved to be able to buy pens and paper and wrote of one particular day when he lost the halfpenny he had saved to buy himself a red herring (the cheapest kind) to eat. 'I buried my head under the miserable sheet and rug and cried like a child!' he wrote.

In 1785, Cobbett's regiment sailed for Halifax in Canada. He spent the following six years in the county of New Brunswick, quickly gaining promotion to the rank of sergeant major. One winter, he spotted a young girl scrubbing out a washtub in deep snow. She was Ann Reid, just thirteen years old, daughter of a sergeant of artillery. 'That's the girl for me,' said Cobbett and married her in Woolwich five years later in 1791 after he returned to England and obtained his discharge. Nancy, or his 'dear little girl' as Cobbett so lovingly called her almost to the end, was to become the sworn enemy of Henry Hunt. Her hatred of him was to cause immense difficulties for both men.

Despite his shining track record as a soldier, Cobbett wanted to leave the army to have a free hand to expose the blatant dishonesty and corruption he had witnessed. He was appalled to discover that the regimental officers were falsifying expenses claims. They were also cheating the ordinary soldiers out of a quarter of their provisions, including food and firewood, and selling them on. Cobbett did not realise that this was routine throughout the army and that his petition to the king would upset many people in high places. Things got so hot that Cobbett feared he would be the one to end up in gaol. The affair was his first taste of the difficulties of challenging the system. He fled with Nancy to France, where Louis XVI and Marie Antoinette had just been arrested and would, in due course, lose their heads under the guillotine. The Cobbetts beat another hasty retreat and managed to get on a boat sailing for New York, arriving in October 1792. The newly created republican government of an independent America was just three years old. Its president was George Washington.

Over the next eight years, Cobbett laid the foundation of his future career as a political writer, wielding his pen like a sword and in the process becoming one of the most controversial and reviled men in America. He began by teaching English to French émigrés who had fled the violence at home. Surrounded on all sides by anti-British feelings, Cobbett's patriotism flared. He forgot his own resentment against his native country and began to write passionately in defence of England and George III. The floodgates opened; Cobbett had found his *metier*. He plunged into the thick of American politics writing full-time, bitterly attacking the Democrats and denouncing republicanism. He had so much *chutzpah* that he dared to decorate one of his bookshops the day it opened with huge portraits of the King of England, various grinning government ministers and down-with-the-French banners. This was in July 1796 in Philadelphia, the temporary capital of the new republic, strongly Democratic, overwhelmingly anti-British and keenly pro-revolutionary France.

Cobbett wrote under the pseudonym of Peter Porcupine. *Porcupine's Gazette* became the most widely read paper in America. After he revealed his identity, there were threats of violence against him. The press fell over itself to dig up any dirt, true or false, that could be found on Cobbett. In his excitement he penned a public letter and addressed it to his father:

Dear Father, when you used to set me off to work in the morning, dressed in my blue smock-frock and woollen spatter dashes, with my bag of bread and cheese and bottle of small beer ... little did you imagine that I should one day become so great a man as to have my picture stuck in the windows and have four whole books published about me in the course of one week.

Cobbett had the time of his life, hurling insults at the highest and lowest, until he was sued for libel. He lost and was fined $5,000, an unprecedented sum of money for the offence. Although sympathisers in New Brunswick paid the fine, his property in Philadelphia was sold up leaving Cobbett in financial straits. He tried to set up business in New York but had become so marginalised he decided to return home where he felt he had a better chance of making a career as a political writer. In July 1800, he was given the red-carpet treatment and a hero's welcome on his arrival back in England, where his anti-republican conservative pamphlets had been regularly reprinted.

The Tories, led by William Pitt the Younger, fell on what they thought was their man with open arms. They offered him a job, money, favours, anything to carry on the good work. Cobbett refused it all. Unlike the vast majority of journalists and newspapers, the powers of Cobbett's pen could not be bought. He needed no paymaster nor wanted any hidden agenda. He would never ever become a party man. Cobbett's strength was always to be his ability to tell things exactly as they were, without fear or favour. Rolling up his sleeves, he got down to his writing. This gradually evolved into an all out assault on the establishment and all its works, 'the Thing' as he so marvellously named it. From being a radical conservative, Cobbett the weathercock (as his critics derisively called him for the rest of his life) swung round to become a conservative radical and never blew off course again.

Such was the man Henry Hunt was so eagerly looking forward to meeting as he hurried through the London streets that hot July day in 1805. Hunt was ten years younger than Cobbett. He was born on 6 November 1773 at Widdington Farm, a lone house built in a convenient hollow on the windy Salisbury Plain in Wiltshire. The handsome, redbrick farmhouse is still there, looking much as it would have done then. The nearest village is Upavon where Hunt was baptised in St Mary's Church. It is one of a number of pretty villages stringing along a valley of the River Avon. Years later, when Cobbett was on one of his famous rural rides, he admired this 'fine and beautiful and interesting valley', and observed with pleasure the orchards and stack-yards filled with ricks of wheat, barley and hay, the lofty elm trees, ancient churches and meadows grazed by fat sheep. 'It seems impossible to find a more beautiful and pleasant country than this', he wrote.

Hunt's father was a successful gentleman farmer who could trace his ancestry back to a colonel in the army of William the Conqueror. His wife was a farmer's daughter, half his age. Hunt adored his mother. She died when he was sixteen. He never got over her death. He loved and respected his father, despite their arguments over Hunt's wilful behaviour. Some of his most pleasant memories were of his father reciting the poems of Alexander Pope and speeches from Homer's *Iliad* 'in the most fervent and impassioned manner'. When his father died in 1797, Hunt, the eldest of six children, was left owning or renting 3,000 acres of farmland. He described his background and family in his *Memoirs*, which were written after the Peterloo Massacre while he was shut up between 1820 and 1822 in Ilchester gaol on the sodden banks of the River Yeo in Somerset.

Unlike Cobbett, Hunt had formal schooling from the age of five until he was sixteen. His father then wanted to send his son to Oxford to prepare him to enter the Church. Hunt refused. (He had a poor opinion of churchmen, an aversion he was to share with Cobbett. The pair were to laugh heartily together over the men they called 'the black cormorants'.) Hunt had set his heart on following in the footsteps of his father and becoming a farmer. He got his way and started from the beginning, not daring to complain about his 'sore feet or galled heels' when he realised that he was struggling to do the same work that small plough boys less than half his age were carrying out for sixpence a day. His determination and hard work enabled him to become an excellent farmer. Cobbett, himself a farmer, was to acknowledge and use Hunt's skills.

By the early 1790s, while Cobbett was busy supporting George III and England in a democratic republican America, Hunt's interests in politics were being stirred by talk of the bloody French revolution, the Jacobins behind it and the possibility of an invasion of England. Like Cobbett, Hunt despised Jacobins as revolutionary traitors, atheists and republicans.

The government of William Pitt the Younger was petrified by what was going on over the Channel. It was also alarmed by the early stirrings of trade unionism at home, which had been fuelled by Tom Paine's banned but enormously popular *Rights of Man*. It mobilised for war with France and suspended the Habeas Corpus Act between 1794 and 1801. This suspension by the Pitt government was momentous. The Act is one of the most important pieces of human rights legislation. It began in the thirteenth century as a writ requiring anybody detaining a person to produce him or her in court within a specified period and give reasons for their detention. The Act was suspended during the Jacobite rebellions of 1715 and 1745. Its suspension in 1794 gave the Pitt government *carte blanche* to throw people into prison for an indefinite period and keep them ignorant of all possible charges against them. It was a practice future governments were to imitate.

In keeping with the patriotic fervour sweeping the country, Hunt joined the sons of the local farmers, doctors and wealthy tradesmen and signed up as a volunteer with the Wiltshire Regiment of Yeomanry. He soon became disillusioned by what he perceived to be its amateurish incompetence, and turned his attention to Miss Ann Halcomb, daughter of William, the well-known innkeeper of the Bear Hotel in Devizes market square, which was within reasonable galloping distance of the Hunt family home. Against the wishes of his father, Hunt married Miss Halcomb and had three children, two sons and a daughter. He lived the comfortable life of a gentleman farmer with all its sporting pleasures before he sensationally eloped, in 1802, with the unhappily married wife of one of his friends, Henry Chivers Vince. It was the year Cobbett was busy launching his *Weekly Political Register*.

The new woman in Hunt's life was always referred to, at least publicly, as Mrs Vince. She was to be the great love, the rock and mainstay of Hunt throughout his stormy life until his death in 1835. The press was to use her as a weapon with which to undermine and smear Hunt. Cobbett regarded Mrs Vince as a whore until he knew better. His own wife, Nancy, wanted nothing to do with her. Mrs Vince and Nancy Cobbett were to play a pivotal role in the political partnership and personal relationship of their men.

Hunt revealed in his *Memoirs* that he met Mrs Vince in 1800. This was a significant year for him for another reason. It was the year that he had his first taste of life in prison. It came about as a result of a quarrel with his regimental colonel, Lord Bruce, who dismissed him from the Marlborough Yeomanry Cavalry (Hunt was a patriot and had given the yeomanry another try.) Hunt foolishly challenged him to a duel. Duels were illegal. Hunt was found guilty and had to go for sentencing to the imposing Court of King's Bench in London. The court sat in the south east corner of Westminster Hall, dwarfed by the Hall's huge, stunning, timbered splendour.

One of the attorneys Lord Bruce had hired to argue for a heavy judgement against the impetuous Hunt was Sir Vicary Gibbs. 'Vinegar' Gibbs (as he was popularly called) was to prove in later years the bane of both William Cobbett and Henry Hunt. In his *Memoirs* penned in Ilchester gaol from 1820, Hunt remembered how 'the little, waspish, black-hearted viper, Gibbs, whose malignant, vicious and ill-looking countenance was always the index of his little mind, made a most virulent, vindictive and cowardly attack upon me'. If his own attorneys had not restrained him, wrote Hunt, he would have taken great pleasure in 'dashing back his lies, together with his teeth, down his throat.' Thanks to Sir Vicary, Hunt was fined £100 and was sentenced to spend six weeks in the King's Bench Prison south of the River Thames over Blackfriars Bridge in Southwark, then in the county of Surrey. (Find Belvedere Place today and you will be standing on the spot of the south west corner of the prison.) Ten years later, Hunt and Cobbett were to find themselves briefly together in the King's Bench Prison.

Hunt served his sentence over 1800-1801. His first son, Henry, was just a few months old. Hunt was relatively comfortable during this spell of imprisonment. He hired a spacious private room in the prison marshal's lodge and, on a bond of £5,000 to be paid if he escaped, he was given 'the run of the key'. This meant he could wander freely inside the prison yard and go out as he pleased during the day so long as he returned at night.

During his six weeks in gaol, Hunt's political awareness took a sharp upward curve thanks to the liberal barrister and pamphleteer, Henry Clifford, who also happened to be a friend of Cobbett. Clifford's work regularly took him into the prisons. Hunt learned from Clifford that the radical politician, John Horne Tooke, had previously occupied his room. Tooke was among the early campaigners for an expanded franchise and shorter parliaments. Hunt also learned about the treatment of people who had been confined in dungeons for political reasons under the suspension of the Habeas Corpus Act. Clifford took Hunt to meet one famous case, Colonel Edward Despard, who had been languishing in the Tower of London for several years after falling out with the government, losing his job and daring to claim compensation. Despard was later charged with plotting against the government and found guilty of high treason. He was hanged in 1803. His head was cut off and displayed to the crowd. Such was Hunt's introduction to the uglier side of politics.

From Hunt's *Memoirs,* which were written between 1820 and 1822 after a deep rift had opened up between himself and Cobbett, we know that he was an avid reader of Cobbett's work from the moment he arrived back in England from America. When Cobbett launched the *Political Register,* Hunt rushed to order his copy and became one of his constant readers and admirers. Although he did not agree with all Cobbett's opinions, Hunt admired his style and laughed heartily over his mockery of the fear, whipped up in the country, that Napoleon Bonaparte was about to invade. Cobbett described the anxiety as a state malady appearing by fits and starts. Hunt liked Cobbett's description so much, he quoted an extract:

At last, however, it seems to have settled into a sort of haemorrhage, the patients in Downing-street expectorating pale or red, according to the state of their disease. For some weeks past it has been remarkably vivid. Whether proceeding from the heat of the dog-days or from the quarrellings and fightings and riotings amongst their volunteers, it would be hard to say but certain it is that the symptoms have been of a very alarming complexion for nearly a month.

Hunt's desire to meet Cobbett was fuelled. 'I did not know Mr Cobbett at that time, but I own that I longed to become acquainted with so celebrated a public writer, who had afforded me so much pleasure in the perusal of his literary works', he wrote. His longing increased when, in 1805, Cobbett took up the scandal enveloping Lord Melville (Henry Dundas), one of the closest friends of the prime minister, William Pitt. Melville was treasurer of the navy and used his position to transfer eight million pounds of public money from the Bank of England into his own bank account. Public meetings were held all over the country and petitions flooded in to parliament calling for an inquiry. A county meeting was called in Devizes, Hunt's home territory. He decided to attend. Henry Hunt's big moment had come. It was to be his first public entry into political life.

The Whigs were out in force trying to prevent any petition being sent from Wiltshire on the grounds that it would prejudge the question of Melville's hearing before parliament. Hunt sat down and quickly scribbled out some resolutions of his own in which he condemned Lord Melville's behaviour and corruption and cheats everywhere, whether they were Whigs or Tories. He stood up and gave his maiden speech. Hunt had learned the art of speechifying well from his father and was already a natural actor. He tasted the applause of the crowd, and felt the power of the political orator. Intoxicating stuff. The more experienced MPs, however, persuaded him to drop his resolutions. 'By compliments and by flattery they wheedled me out of the main jet of my resolutions', he remembered as he wrote his *Memoirs*. It gave Hunt his first experience of party political tricks of war. Next time, he decided, he would not be so easily persuaded.

He sent off some notes about the meeting to Cobbett and decided that he simply had to meet him, the man who had 'contributed more than any other individual to bring this nefarious affair fully before the public eye.' Hunt decided to call in on Cobbett the very next time he was in London. From the events that were happening around this time, it is likely that their meeting at Cobbett's rented house at 15 Duke Street, Westminster, took place in July 1805.

There was no bang but plenty of whimpering, at least on Hunt's part. Whatever Hunt expected to happen – Cobbett flinging himself into his arms with joy as he recognised a kindred spirit or giving him a freelance contract to write for the *Political Register* – it did not happen. Picture the scene. Hunt was a mere thirty-one years old. Cobbett was forty-two. Hunt was inexperienced in politics. Cobbett was a wily, shrewd, seasoned operator. He had numerous visitors every day. Hunt was admitted after sending in his card displaying his name and was shown into an unfurnished room without even a chair. This must have been a deliberate tactic by Cobbett, reserved for unknown and unwanted callers. To add insult to injury, Hunt was then kept waiting. Finally, Cobbett appeared.

The two men, proud, confident, passionate and strong-minded, quick to anger and quick to laugh, stood facing each other. Cobbett, the ploughboy turned famous political writer, regarded Hunt, the gentleman farmer turned would-be politician. Hunt saw a tall robust man with a florid face whose hair was cut unfashionably short, quite close to his head. Hunt, ever the snappy dresser with his smart boots and tight breeches over his shapely legs, took in Cobbett's rather old-fashioned blue coat and scarlet cloth waistcoat. 'As it was then very hot weather, in the middle of the summer, his apparel had to me a very singular appearance', Hunt wrote later in his *Memoirs*. Cobbett must have stared back with his best steely gaze at a man ten years his junior, tall, virile and good-looking. He would have noted the excellent manners of a gentleman, a man born into a different class from his own. Cobbett would also have noted Hunt's strong West Country accent that he would mock so cleverly and cruelly in later years. Cobbett, ever the mild persuasive speaker, would have observed and disapproved too of Hunt's excitable passionate way of speaking. Cobbett was restrained and calculating, already an old hand at the game. Hunt was the novice, champing at the bit, ready to leap into the political maelstrom. Such were the two men who faced each other for the first time in 1805 in Cobbett's rented house in London.

Hunt introduced himself as a gentleman from Wiltshire who had taken a lead at the county meeting at Devizes. He told Cobbett that he had sent him the particulars. (Hunt obviously hoped Cobbett would congratulate him on his fine performance.) He recorded in his *Memoirs* how Cobbett replied: 'He addressed me very briefly, and very bluntly, saying that "we must persevere, and we should bring all the scoundrels to justice."' (It was obviously Cobbett's pep talk for relatively uninteresting but enthusiastic

William Cobbett, 1801.
The Museum of Farnham

Henry Hunt. Cruikshank.
Bristol Library

visitors.) 'He never asked me to sit down; but that might have arisen from there being no other seat in the room except the floor', Hunt remembered pettishly. He left, bitterly disappointed by Cobbett's appearance and manners and mortified at the cool reception he had been given. As Hunt wrote in his *Memoirs*, it appeared to him that they were both 'mutually disgusted with each other'. Hunt walked away from the house back up Parliament Street musing upon 'the sort of being' he had just left. He determined never to seek a second interview with Cobbett: 'I thought that of all the men I ever saw, he was the least likely for me to become enamoured of his society.'

Writing in his cold, dark, solitary cell in Ilchester gaol more than fifteen years later, chewing over why his long and close friendship with Cobbett had foundered, and eaten up with bitterness, Hunt recalled how he could not have imagined that the pair could ever have become friends after that disastrous first meeting. 'I own that my calculations did not in the slightest degree lead me to suppose that we should ever be upon such friendly terms and indeed upon such an intimate footing, as we actually were for a number of years afterwards', he wrote. And as his pen scratched and squeaked on, his love and affection for his old hero and friend came flooding back:

We lived and acted together for many years with the most perfect cordiality; and I believe that two men never lived that more sincerely, honestly and zealously advocated public liberty than we did, hand in hand, for eight or ten years ... There never were two men who went on so well together and with such trifling difference of opinion, as occurred between Mr Cobbett and myself.

But in that hot summer of 1805, as Hunt walked up Parliament Street after their initial meeting musing upon the sort of being he had just left, he suspected that Cobbett had taken a dislike to him as much as he himself had disliked Cobbett. Hunt was quite right. Three years later, on 10 April 1808, Cobbett wrote a letter in confidence to his publishing assistant, John Wright, warning him that they must steer clear of mixing with men of bad character, men such as Henry Hunt: 'There is one <u>Hunt</u>, the Bristol man. Beware of him! He rides about the country with a whore, the wife of another man, having deserted his own. A sad fellow! Nothing to do with him.'

The 'whore' was, of course, Hunt's beloved Mrs Vince. The letter, like a ticking time-bomb, was to be dug up and used against Hunt with disastrous effect a decade later in 1818 when he was to stand unsuccessfully as MP for Westminster – with Cobbett's full public support and backing.

Despite Hunt's disappointment about that first meeting, it did not stop him reading the *Political Register*. He was addicted to it. He began to look out for it 'with as much anxiety as I had heretofore looked to the day and hour that the fox-hounds were to meet'. If a copy of the *Register* did not arrive bang on time every week with the post, remembered Hunt in his *Memoirs*, he was as disappointed as if he had been deprived of a good fox-chase. And, despite Cobbett's coolness at their meeting and his doubts about Hunt's character, he accepted for publication in the *Political Register* an address Hunt wrote to the freeholders of Wiltshire during the general election of November 1806.

Freeholders were men who owned their own property valued at forty shillings or £2 a year. This was a right that dated back to 1430. The system of voting throughout the country was arbitrary and incoherent, largely depending upon arrangements made in medieval times. As well as freeholders, there were the householders colloquially called 'potwallopers' or those who 'had a family and boiled a pot'. They could generally vote if they had been living in their house for six months and were not paupers or receiving alms. There were also the 'scot and lot' voters. This phrase dated back to the Saxons and embraced men who paid their local taxes and had gone through the lottery of the local ballot to join the army. Some men had the right to vote because they rented property in towns or cities owned by lords and designated as 'burgage'.

In many towns including, for example, Devizes, Truro, Salisbury, Christchurch and Bath, only members of the corporation or local town hall had the vote. They themselves were unelected. This was the age of the so-called rotten and pocket boroughs. Infamous examples of these included the green mound of Old Sarum near Salisbury in Wiltshire (Cobbett's 'Accursed Hill') and the former gentleman's park at Gatton near Reigate in Surrey, now close to the M25. Both were represented in the House of Commons by two MPs who were chosen by a handful of voters, in Old Sarum's case by people who lived *outside* its boundaries. Landowners were able to nominate candidates or sell the seats to the highest bidder. Gatton was auctioned off by James Christie in 1801 for £90,000, the equivalent of millions of pounds today. Don't worry, said the advertisement of the sale, you won't have to kiss any babies or bribe anybody: 'No tormenting claims of insolent electors to evade, no tinkers' wives to kiss, no impossible promises to make ... with this elegant contingency in his pocket, the honours of the state will await his plucking and with its emoluments his purse will overflow.'

Voters were routinely bribed with hard cash. Their expenses were paid to go to the hustings where they were regaled with copious quantities of food and drink. They could also be coerced by threats of losing their jobs or rented homes. There were no secret ballots either. You went along to the hustings with the rest of the crowds and put your hand up. The bully boys were there to see that you did. If contested, elections could go on for as long as fifteen days in an open rough tough free-for-all. Both Cobbett and Hunt were to take great delight in making the elections last as long as they could to sting the candidates as much as possible. It was a rich man's game. In 1807 three Yorkshire candidates spent a total of a quarter of a million pounds to win their seats. Charles Dickens' comic description of an election in the aptly named town of 'Eatanswill' in *Pickwick Papers* was, in fact, a marvellously accurate representation of just how the thing was. This was the system that many people believed was in need of urgent reform.

Hunt directed his 1806 address at the freeholders of Wiltshire who owned their own properties and did not have to worry about eviction if they voted for the man of their own choice. He urged them to think and act for themselves. They should not submit to having a man thrust down their throats by 'the Beckhampton or the Deptford Club,' he wrote. They should not worry about offending 'Mr Long or Mr Short'. (Members of the Long family had controlled one of the seats in Wiltshire for years. Hunt had been reading the *Political Register* for so long, he had begun to pick up Cobbett's style.) Nor should they vote for somebody who only had his 'uncle's long purse' to recommend him. If they did, they may as well be represented by the uncle's 'old three corner'd hat.' What the voters should demand were honourable and independent men to represent them in the House of Commons. Hunt added a postscript; PS, he wrote, he was addressing them via a handbill because the *Salisbury Journal* was too intimately connected with the 'gagging party' (here, the Whigs) to include it in its newspaper.

Cobbett printed Hunt's address together with his postscript in the *Register* of 15 November 1806. Hunt's feelings can be imagined as he saw his work in print in the most widely-read political paper of the day, alongside letters from famous leading radicals such as the old reform warhorse, Major John Cartwright, veteran of the struggle for universal suffrage, and the young, non-partisan, extremely wealthy aristocrat, Sir Francis Burdett.

The following year, 1807, the name of Henry Hunt popped up again in the *Register* celebrating the triumphant election wins in Westminster by Burdett and the naval officer, Lord Cochrane, whom Napoleon called the Sea Wolf and who was the model for the fictional Mr Midshipman Hornblower. The Westminster wins of 23 May 1807 were a major victory. Both men stood as independents. They beat the system and did it on a minimal budget. There was no bribery, despite Burdett's huge family wealth. Cobbett saw it as the beginning of a new era in the history of parliamentary representation.

Hunt, who was living in the Clifton area of Bristol and getting involved with local politics, decided to celebrate too. He did it in his usual style, hoping he might get into Cobbett's *Political Register* again. He arranged an expensive dinner for 100 people on 2 June 1807 in the Trout Tavern in Cherry Lane off Stokes Croft which was then on the edge of Bristol. The authorities got wind of it and plastered the city with placards with this dire warning: 'DANGER to be apprehended from the proposed dinner to be held this day at the Trout Tavern'. The word DANGER was printed in letters six inches high. Hunt related in his *Memoirs* how 'the time-serving despicable editors of the Bristol Newspapers joined in the cry' and claimed that the dinner was the 'forerunner of a revolution'. Unsurprisingly, it all sounded so exciting that half Bristol turned up outside the Trout Tavern that evening. Hunt told them to go home. It was lucky they did because the city authorities had called out the military with orders to disperse any crowds at the point of the bayonet. (Hunt became adept at controlling the crowds, something Cobbett was to envy him for.)

Hunt got his reward. A victory parade to celebrate Sir Francis Burdett's sensational and uncontaminated 'PURITY OF ELECTION' win took place through the streets of Westminster later that month. (Although Cochrane had also won, Burdett and his followers cut him out of the celebrations.) At least half a million people turned out to watch. It was spectacular indeed, a cavalcade of coaches, carriages and horses, bands, banners, waving handkerchiefs, flowers, laurels, flags, trumpets, music, buglers and pickpockets. The works. It was estimated that 100,000 people alone crammed into Covent Garden. If there was no space for them to stand, they clambered onto the roofs and ridges of every single building in and around the piazza. The procession ended up at the Crown and Anchor in the Strand where there was a dinner for 2,000 people laid on in the Great Room. The toasts at dinner included one to the electors of Bristol who had assembled with 'Mr H Hunt' at their head to celebrate the triumphant election of Sir Francis Burdett. Cobbett described everything in detail in the *Political Register* of 4 July 1807, the procession, the dinner – and the toasts.

Hunt was thrilled. He was the only man in England to have his name honoured in a public toast at what was the largest dinner meeting ever assembled in England, he remembered in his *Memoirs*. At that moment, his dark cell in Ilchester gaol was filled with a radiant light. Hunt's name had been mentioned even though he was unknown to any of the committee, and even to Sir Francis Burdett. But Hunt was upset that Cobbett had not also reported his 'dangerous dinner' at the Trout Tavern and the upheaval it had caused in Bristol. Hunt considered that the discomfort and alarm of the local magistrates meant that the occasion had been a huge success. 'I was set down as a most dangerous fellow and an enemy to the Government', he wrote triumphantly. 'I might now, in fact, be considered to have fairly entered the field of politics'.

Looking at the dinner from Cobbett's point of view, it may well have confirmed Cobbett's doubts about Hunt's character. Nevertheless, Hunt was back in the *Political Register* the following month, chairing a meeting in Bristol to discuss the whole ghastly mess of the electoral system. Cobbett gave it wide coverage and published the entire list of Hunt's resolutions. They included calls for free elections and the sacking of all placemen in the House of Commons. Placemen were MPs who were bribed with lucrative jobs, pensions and sinecures to keep them on side with the government. (Cobbett regularly referred to parliament as the 'Collective'.) Hunt had found his path and, as far as he was concerned, he was on his way to the top. His ultimate goal was already a parliamentary seat. In his ambition, he was going too fast and was too aggressive. He was quarrelling with those who disagreed with him over tactics, and making enemies. 'Where I failed in argument, I of course made up for it in abuse', he admitted ruefully in his *Memoirs*.

The waves continued over the following months. Hunt's political biographer, John Belchem, says Hunt was being seen as nothing less than an arch-revolutionary. This would have all contributed to Cobbett's alarm about the kind of a man Hunt was, causing him to write his 'whore on horseback' letter the following year in 1808. In it, Cobbett confidentially warned his publisher, John Wright, that they had to tread carefully. 'It is impossible for both factions united to calumniate our motives, if we proceed as we ought and do not mix with men of bad character', he wrote.

Hunt was blissfully unaware of Cobbett's letter. He had long got over the disappointment of his first meeting with Cobbett and was enjoying his appearances in the *Political Register*. In April 1809, Cobbett was due to speak at a meeting in Winchester. Hunt was living nearby at a hunting cottage he had built on his farm at Littlecot in Wiltshire. Littlecot was just thirty miles from Winchester. Hunt decided to ride over to the meeting and contrive a second encounter with Cobbett. 'I was anxious to become better acquainted with the celebrated Mr Cobbett, who I expected would be the hero of the day', he remembered in his *Memoirs*.

The meeting's theme was to be systemic corruption and that was to include the very latest juicy scandal, a royal one at that. Mrs Mary Anne Clarke, mistress of the Duke of York, had been using his name to sell army commissions, making thousands of pounds in the process. The duke had resigned from his office of Commander in Chief. (He was later to be reinstated.) Cobbett previewed his meeting in several issues of the *Political*

Register. 'It must be manifest to every man in his senses that unless a stop
be speedily put to the workings of corruption, one of two things will
happen: the complete slavery of us all or the overthrow of the
government', he wrote. (Sharp intake of breath from government
ministers as they eagerly read their copy of the *Political Register.*) 'To make
men liable to punishment for opinions is, at once, to say "slave!" You shall
not utter your thoughts', Cobbett continued. Hunt believed it was around
this time that 'Vinegar' Gibbs, now the attorney general, was instructed
to keep a sharp eye on Cobbett, of whom the government had had enough.
'Ministers had marked him for the victim of their vengeance', Hunt wrote
in his *Memoirs.*

The number of people who turned up to the meeting in Winchester on
25 April 1809 was so large it was adjourned to the Great Hall of
Winchester Castle and then to the Grand Jury Chamber, from where the
speakers could address the throng in the courtyard below. Hunt got a good
spot beneath the windows where he could see and hear Cobbett clearly,
and listened in raptures. 'Three parson prigs' dared to heckle him. Hunt
elbowed his way through the crowds to sort them out. He selected one, 'a
little short squat fellow, in boots and leather breeches'. Hunt got close
enough to dig his elbows in the little reverend's side. Whenever he opened
his mouth to shout, Hunt crushed his ribs. When people were asked to
wave their hats in the air in favour of Cobbett, Hunt whipped off the man's
hat and held it up so high 'the little chattering hero' jumped up and down
to get it back. There was much laughter and excitement, as Hunt fondly
detailed in his *Memoirs.*

A dinner was laid on for Mr Cobbett's friends at the George Inn. To
Hunt's immense pleasure he was invited and, as hoped, managed to have
a word with his hero. He invited Cobbett along to a meeting he himself
planned to organise in Wiltshire. To enable Cobbett to participate fully,
Hunt said he would make him a present of a freehold property he owned
in the county, thus giving Cobbett all rights as a freeholder to take part in
public meetings. Cobbett accepted and promised to cover the event in the
Political Register.

The meeting took place in Salisbury on 17 May 1809. The hall was
packed. Everybody agreed there should be no placemen in the House of

Commons, as had been laid down by William III's Act of Settlement of 1701. The Act gave the crown to the Hanoverians and also banned anybody who accepted a job, position, pension or place of profit from becoming a member of parliament. This latter part of the Act had been watered down over the following decades to become meaningless. The reformers used the Act of Settlement in its original form as their mantra in their arguments for parliamentary reform.

There was a dinner later that evening at the Three Swans Inn. Cobbett and Hunt, who enjoyed so many things in common including an excellent sense of humour, got on like a house on fire. Hunt dated the beginning of his 'political intimacy' with Cobbett from this time. Cobbett had probably forgotten all about his private warning letter to his publisher concerning Hunt the previous year, and his distaste about that 'whore on horseback'. If he did remember, he shoved it as far to the back of his mind as he could. Cobbett had other things to worry about.

2
Shades of the Prison House

The truth is always subversive.
Martha Gellhorn

'My dear Sir,' wrote William Cobbett to Henry Hunt on 28 August 1809 from his country house in Botley in Hampshire, 'never mind about the ewes. I will, for the purpose of uniting the work of crossing with the work of raising stock, get some South Downs'. This is the earliest extant letter between the pair. By the tone of the letter written just over three months after the Salisbury meeting, the men were on close terms and meeting and writing to each other regularly. Cobbett generally addressed his letters to his friends with the relatively formal phrase 'my dear Sir'. He would treat Hunt very differently. Soon he would be paying Hunt the greatest compliment of all and addressing letters to him as 'My dear Hunt'.

Over the years, the correspondence between William Cobbett and Henry Hunt was regular and frequent. Without the modern marvels of telephones, mobile phones and e-mails, people relied on the postal service, often writing many letters a day. The post was speedy and reliable – unless the Office of the Postmaster General happened to be secretly intercepting letters at the request of the government. Thirty-six letters from Cobbett to Hunt survived. There are only two known letters in existence written from Hunt to Cobbett. The latter did not keep much of his own private correspondence and, in any case, his family would have taken great pleasure in burning any letters to him from Henry Hunt. The two extant letters from Hunt are buried in the archives of the Nuffield College Library in Oxford. They survived only because they were in a pile of papers Cobbett handed over to his solicitors Edward and George Faithfull. They were to be used in evidence in a sensational court case in 1829. It is likely they were the last two letters Hunt wrote to Cobbett.

Cobbett's letter to Hunt at the end of August 1809 was a lengthy one covering three sides of paper, written in Cobbett's small and rapid but readable handwriting. The subjects ranged from breeding sheep to the

health of his wife, who had just been delivered of a dead child and had
narrowly escaped with her life. 'I was most cursedly alarmed. I thought
for three hours about nothing for really I was deprived of the power of
thought. If she had died, the better half of me would have been gone',
wrote Cobbett. (Poor Nancy. It was tough being a woman in those days.
Cobbett was genuinely distressed, but stillbirths and early child deaths
were fairly regular occurrences.)

Cobbett's letter also poured scorn on the British campaign against
the French in Spain. The war against Bonaparte was not going well. Sir
Arthur Wellesley, later the Duke of Wellington, had advanced from
Portugal into Spain. His dispatches back home trumpeted his defeat of
the French at the Battle of Talavera at the end of July 1809. Yet within
a matter of days he was in full retreat back towards the Portuguese
border leaving behind 1,500 sick and wounded English soldiers. Hunt
must have mentioned his worries over newspaper reports that Wellesley
had been shot and injured. Cobbett urged him not to become
despondent. '"The gallant Sir Arthur" may yet get off with "the bullets
through his clothes"', he wrote. It was, Cobbett believed, 'A very tame
imitation of Falstaff's pricking his nose with spear grass and hacking
his sabre.' (Hunt must have been overjoyed when he read almost exactly
those words in the *Political Register* just a few days later because Cobbett
had written them to him FIRST.) Cobbett also mentioned his brother-
in-law who was in the army and of whom Cobbett was very fond.
'Damn the rascal who shall sacrifice him for no benefit to his country',
he wrote.

Cobbett ended his letter by telling Hunt that he had sent away two
dogs to be trained. One was for Hunt, so long as he promised to let
Cobbett have it back whenever he wanted to mate it with his bitch. The
letter reveals the bond that had been so quickly forged between the two
men. They were politically in tune and they were also enjoying their
mutual interests of farming and hunting. They were so close, Cobbett
was even telling Hunt about intimate family matters.

Cobbett did not reserve his opinions about the war against France
for his private correspondence. He was writing extensively, boldly and
critically about it in the *Political Register*.

How vain have been all our attempts to stem the torrent of revolution, in every part of Europe! Victories we have sometimes gained; immense armies we have brought, by our money, into the field; we have formed leagues and covenants in abundance … nor have we been wanting in bribing to our aid any passion or any folly of which the human heart is susceptible. But still the fire of revolution goes on; and, instead of damping, we really seem to feed the flame.

Despite the establishment shivers, Cobbett was resolved that nothing would stop him giving his opinions on anything that happened in the war. The Battle of Talavera, he wrote, was no victory and would have disastrous consequences. He shot down in flames Wellesley's defence about what had happened. When the people sorted out the confused mass of insignificant detail, they would find the real truth. Cobbett's criticism was perceptive and to the point:

How many and how many times have we been disappointed in our hopes! How many times has Napoleon been upon the brink of destruction, bodily or political? Still he lives and at the close of every succeeding year, he seems twice as great as he was at the close of the preceding one.

There was nobody else writing like Cobbett and his blunt comment pieces were earning him enemies. The government watched with fury as week after week in the *Political Register*, Cobbett exposed the disastrous campaigns on the continent, cases of corrupt practice and the lucrative system of jobs for the boys at home and abroad. His writing hit the mark every time. The resolutions from Cobbett's Winchester meeting about the scandalous sale of commissions by the Duke of York's mistress had inspired similar resolutions from all over England. They were appearing in the London press and in local newspapers up and down the country. Cobbett published about fifty of them in the *Political Register*. It was unprecedented. People were taking notice; they were getting involved and making their voices heard. Cobbett was leading the way, fearlessly and persistently challenging the system through the *Register*.

It is an observation that can have escaped no man, that despotic governments have never tolerated free discussions on political matters. The reason is plain; that their deeds will not bear the display of reason and the light of truth.

The government decided that Cobbett had to be stopped. It was looking for something it could use to terrorise him into submission. It found an excuse when Cobbett turned his pen from the war against France to condemn the flogging of a group of volunteer militiamen stationed in Ely. The soldiers had dared to stage a protest after a bonus guinea they had been promised was meanly withheld to pay for their army knapsacks. They were sentenced to five hundred lashes each. Part of the sentence was remitted but what remained was horrifically severe. German mercenaries stationed in nearby Bury St Edmunds were rushed to Ely to help suppress any protests and supervise the flogging. Much to the resentment of the people, these mercenaries were widely employed in the country owing to the Hanoverian ties of the kings of England. Cobbett strongly opposed the practice. He was also opposed to the use of flogging in the services. On 1 July 1809, he wrote these powerfully ironic lines in the *Political Register*, the tone and the pace echoing the crack and thud of the whip:

Five hundred lashes each! Aye, that is right! Flog them! Flog them! Flog them! They deserve a flogging at every meal-time. 'Lash them daily! Lash them daily!' What! Shall the rascals dare to *mutiny*? And that, too, when the German Legion is so near at hand? Lash them! Lash them! Lash them! They deserve it. Oh, yes! They merit a double-tailed cat! Base dogs! What! Mutiny for the *price of a knapsack*? Lash them! Flog them! Base rascals! Mutiny for the price of a goat's skin; and then, upon the appearance of the German soldiers, they take a flogging as quietly as so many trunks of trees! – I do not know what sort of place Ely is; but I really should like to know how the inhabitants looked one another in the face, while this scene was exhibiting in their town.

As soon as the attorney general, Sir Vicary Gibbs, who was also a member of parliament for Cambridge University, read Cobbett's article, he filed a so-called '*ex officio* information' against Cobbett, his printer and publishers. Criminal informations had always been used by the Crown's revenue officers to enable them to take action against people who were believed to be withholding taxes. When Gibbs became attorney general, he used his powers as an MP to slip a bill through parliament to extend the rules so that they covered anything he might choose to call an offence. It enabled him to fire off at any time a warning to a newspaper editor that he was under threat of prosecution. The indefinite threat of a charge and a trial hanging over an editor's head was often enough to make him toe the government line and curb his pen. Even if no trial followed, the mere filing of an *ex officio* information against an individual cost him a lot of money, sometimes as much as £200. That money went straight into the pocket of the attorney general.

Gibbs went down in history as the man who used his *ex officio* powers more than any other attorney general. At one point, half the fifty-two newspapers published in London were threatened with a criminal information. It is little surprise that Gibbs was considered to be unpopular, even by his contemporaries. A recorder from Macclesfield described him as 'bad-tempered with a hard, ungracious and repulsive manner'. The life of Gibbs, he wrote, had been 'one long disease.'

Old Vinegar used Cobbett's compelling criticism of the flogging of the soldiers in Ely to hang the threat of an action for seditious libel over his head. Seditious libel was serious business and was a common charge. It was used to accuse someone of undermining the authority of the government, thus bringing it into disrepute with the people who might therefore be encouraged to revolt. It was a nasty catch-all charge and aimed at inhibiting any critical comment of the government and its actions.

Cobbett was very keen to keep the matter quiet, but it is likely that he told Hunt about the sword of Damocles hanging over his head. In his *Memoirs*, Hunt remembered how much he had admired Cobbett's 'spirited article' against the Ely floggings, in which 'he indignantly expressed the natural feeling of an Englishman', and how avidly Gibbs had pounced on it.

The next letter that survived from Cobbett to Hunt was dated 21 March 1810. It was a short note written in haste. Cobbett had decided to replace his South Down sheep with Ryeland ewes. He wanted Hunt to find him about eighty Ryelands and give him some advice on how to go about the swap. By the way, said Cobbett, he owed Hunt for some stockings. There was no mention of Cobbett's problem with the attorney general in this relaxed little note, nor was there any hint that Hunt was himself in trouble with the law as well.

Just over three months later, the pair found themselves together in the King's Bench Prison. Hunt was there for three months. Cobbett was passing through on his way to Newgate Prison where he was to remain locked up for two years. Despite Cobbett's seniority and heavier sentence,

I shall start with how Hunt came to be in the King's Bench for the second time.

Hunt's reputation for independence as a young man and his involvement in non-party, grassroots politics had upset many powerful people in Wiltshire and Somerset. They were out to get him, just as the government was out to get Cobbett. Hunt fought and largely won a series of petty charges of trespass brought against him, defending some of the cases himself, although he still spent a lot of money in the process. Going to court was just as unpredictable and expensive as it is today. One confrontation was with the lord chief justice Ellenborough. Hunt vividly described the encounter in his *Memoirs*:

Ellenborough jumped up once more and, with the most furious language and gestures, began to browbeat me, actually foaming with rage, some of his spittle literally falling on Masters Lushington and another, who sat under him. I own that I could scarcely forbear laughing in his face.

In retrospect, Hunt admitted he had been far too confident and should have been on his guard. He was caught out by a trap laid by John Benett, a wealthy Wiltshire landowner who loathed Hunt as a Jacobin. When Hunt rode by one morning, Benett's bruiser gamekeeper was ready and waiting. He seized Hunt's shooting jacket and pulled it so hard that Hunt nearly fell off his horse. He then stood grinning at Hunt with his double-barrelled gun cocked. Hunt jumped down and unwisely landed a series of blows on the man. Benett then ordered his gamekeeper to sue Hunt for assault. The case dragged on until the end of May 1810 when Hunt was called up to the Court of King's Bench for judgement. He was committed to the King's Bench Prison for three months. Although Lord Ellenborough did not pass sentence, he was sitting in court at the time and was unable to disguise his glee.

Hunt had already experienced six weeks in the King's Bench at the end of 1800 so he knew the ropes. This time he decided to save some money. Instead of hiring the marshal's expensive lodge just outside the prison, he took a comfortable cheaper bed and sitting room over the coffee house inside and still had the run of the key. Hunt settled down to serve his sentence. Just over a month later, on 5 July 1810, who should turn up unexpectedly at the King's Bench, but Cobbett. Sir Vicary Gibbs had followed up his *ex officio* information. Cobbett had been taken to court, tried and found guilty of seditious libel. A formal judgement had been made that day and he had been remanded to the King's Bench to be brought up again on 9 July for sentencing.

At the time of Cobbett's arrival, Hunt was busy writing a letter. Somebody must have rushed up to his rooms to tell him the news that his friend had arrived from the Court of King's Bench and was with the Marshal trying to organise somewhere reasonable to stay other than in the ordinary squalid prison cells. Hunt recorded in his *Memoirs* how he leapt to his feet and hurried to his friend's aid. He offered Cobbett his apartment over the coffee shop, even though this meant that Hunt had to spend four nights in a small dirty cell until Cobbett was moved into Newgate Prison and Hunt could reclaim his rooms.

In a letter written the following day to his eldest daughter, Anne, Cobbett skimmed over Hunt's generosity: 'I am very comfortable here ... I have received and am receiving all sorts of civilities and acts of kindness and want *nothing* but my *family!* Cobbett also forgot to thank Hunt himself. At the time, Hunt was thrilled to be of service to his hero, but in retrospect, he was upset Cobbett had not thanked him personally. In his *Memoirs*, Hunt was sarcastic and bitter about the incident and he laboured the point about how Cobbett had reacted to his offer of his private rooms:

This he accepted without ceremony, and what was very satisfactory to me was that he made no annoying apology for the inconvenience which, in the mean time, I might be put to in finding a situation for myself ... I must give Mr Cobbett the credit for being totally free from any squeamish fears or apprehensions of this sort ... Some persons may be ill-natured enough to miscall this selfishness, and I know those that have been illiberal enough to do so; but, as for myself, I could never be induced to view it in that light ... I was perfectly satisfied to put up with a very small bed-room, in which I could scarcely stand upright, for the four days that he remained there.

Hunt was unfair. It must be remembered, however, that he wrote those petty remarks in his *Memoirs* while enduring the very vile conditions of Ilchester gaol and after Cobbett had abandoned him. Cobbett may also be forgiven for his lack of graciousness in 1810. He arrived at the King's Bench Prison, his brain reeling with the magnitude of what was happening to him. The trial itself on 15 June 1810 had been a disaster. The judge was Hunt's persecutor and Cobbett's own old enemy, Lord Ellenborough, who had successfully prosecuted Cobbett for libel a few years previously. The jury was a 'special' one, packed with wealthy businessmen who were considered to have more brains than the usual *hoi polloi*. If a defendant wanted a special jury because he hoped they would be more competent in their decision-making, he had to pay for the privilege. If the establishment chose to use a special jury, it was because they could be relied upon to deliver the sort of judgement the judge wanted. On this occasion Cobbett faced a special jury chosen by the prosecution, which was led by the attorney general, Sir Vicary Gibbs himself.

As Cobbett's biographer, George Spater, so eloquently put it: 'The efficient government libel machine rolled over Cobbett like the Juggernaut'. Gibbs dismissed Cobbett's accusations that the flogging of the Ely soldiers had been both cruel and unjust, arguing that the soldiers had mutinied and therefore deserved to be punished. Cobbett, who had rashly chosen to represent himself, was not given the chance to point out that in the week before his comments appeared in the *Political Register*, *The Times* had made similar observations about the flogging and called for an inquiry. Cobbett also failed to produce a bundle of letters written to him by leading politicians describing him as a 'loyal subject'. The master tailor and radical campaigner, Francis Place, observed that Cobbett's attempts at self-advocacy even made the court laugh. All in all, Cobbett made a hash of it.

It meant that when Cobbett arrived at the King's Bench Prison wondering what kind of sentence he was going to get, he was in a state of shock. The preceding three weeks had been among the worst of his life. He knew he faced a vindictively heavy sentence which, he feared, would ruin him. He had seriously considered giving up the cause and abandoning his publishing career altogether. The possibility had arisen of a deal being struck with the government. A go-between told Cobbett that if he pledged to end his attacks on the Tory government, he might – but only might – escape a prison sentence. Cobbett agonised at home in Botley over his answer. Faced with a large family, six children, a distraught wife who was pregnant again, and the likelihood of bankruptcy, he decided to accept the deal and quit journalism. He drafted a letter to his lawyer, authorising him to negotiate a deal with the government, and scripted a farewell article for publication in the *Political Register*. The letter was sent off and the article dispatched to Cobbett's publisher. Just hours afterwards, Cobbett changed his mind. He retracted the letter and pulled the article.

At the time, very few people knew what had been going on behind the scenes. Cobbett did not even confide in Hunt. But it was a story that was not going to go away. The press got hold of it and published it the day Cobbett was released from Newgate Prison in 1812. Cobbett denied everything and Hunt, believing his friend's denials, leaped to his defence: 'No man felt more indignant at this attack upon my friend than I did', he wrote in his *Memoirs*, 'I was made to believe that there was not the slightest foundation for the calumny ... and so far was my friend from checking my imprudent zeal, that he encouraged it'. Hunt lost no opportunity to condemn the media stories and, on Cobbett's behalf, he attacked both *The Times* and the *Examiner*, which was owned by the poet and publisher James Henry Leigh Hunt (no relation). As a result, Hunt wrote, they became 'my most implacable enemies' pouring forth 'the most bitter sarcasms, and the most unjust and wanton attacks upon my character, both private and public'. (Leigh Hunt already disliked Hunt at that stage in any case, considering him to be a most dangerous man.)

In 1817, Cobbett confessed in the *Political Register* that there had been a question of a deal, and he tried to justify it. 'I was in the state of a soldier surrounded by an irresistible enemy and has a soldier so situated ever been ashamed to ask his life and to accept it upon condition of *not serving again during the war?*' he wrote.

Two years later, the unpublished farewell article was used in evidence against Cobbett in a court case. The world was able to read in full what Cobbett had so bitterly penned in those three fraught weeks following his guilty verdict. Not only had there been the question of a government deal, but Cobbett had, albeit briefly, accepted it. His enemies poured gloatingly over the words which Cobbett had so painfully penned at the time, that he could no longer continue in publishing, that even if he did, it was obvious his beloved *Register* could never be the same, and that he knew many people would accuse him of deserting the cause.

When he wrote those words, Cobbett probably guessed that Hunt would be among them, which is why he never told Hunt about any part of the episode. It all added to Hunt's bitterness against Cobbett as he sat in the gloom of Ilchester gaol mulling over the events of the past.

This is leaping ahead. From what Cobbett later wrote, it is clear that when he arrived at the King's Bench Prison on 5 July 1810 to await sentencing, he was in a state bordering on collapse. A thousand issues and questions were spinning through his mind. He had very nearly agreed to give up his publishing career. Had he been right to refuse and could he keep his business going if he was jailed? Who would look after his farm in Botley while he was in prison and how would his family manage without him? He must have jumped with relief at Hunt's offer of his rooms over the coffee house. In the circumstances it is no wonder that Cobbett failed to thank his friend as profusely as Hunt would have liked, and little surprise he did not pay Hunt the attention he thought he deserved.

Cobbett was sentenced to two years in Newgate Prison and fined £1,000. On his release he would be bound over to keep the peace for seven years under a bond of £3,000 and he would have to find two people to come up with a further £1,000 each as sureties. It was a crushingly heavy sentence and one the government obviously hoped would blunt Cobbett's powerful pen.

Cobbett moved in to Newgate on 9 July 1810. The prison loomed stony-faced next door to the Old Bailey criminal court. (The entire site is now occupied by the Central Criminal Courts and is still known as the Old Bailey.) Unlike Hunt's experiences a decade later in Ilchester Prison, the conditions under which Cobbett lived in Newgate were comparatively reasonable – as Hunt would complain so bitterly in his *Memoirs*. Thanks to his friends and their money, Cobbett was able to avoid the stinking, cold, gloomy dungeons filled by the ordinary prisoners. On the first day of his imprisonment, he hired an unfurnished room in the prison for five guineas a week. His friends hurried off to bring back a bed, chairs, table and everything needed to make Cobbett comfortable. Nancy Cobbett arrived within half an hour of her husband moving in. The prison keeper made a sitting room available in his house in the Old Bailey next door so

Cobbett in his lodgings in Newgate. The portrait on the wall behind is of
John Hampden.
The Museum of Farnham

that she and the many friends who came to visit that day had somewhere to sit.

Cobbett was gradually able to move out of Newgate altogether into accommodation in the prison keeper's house and ended up with a sitting room and two bedrooms on the top floor for which he had to pay twelve guineas a week rent and another eight in fees. It was a colossal sum of money. Faced with such large bills, Cobbett borrowed money from his friends and also sold *Parliamentary Debates* and *Parliamentary History*, two successful publications that he had begun a few years earlier. He sold them to his publisher, Thomas Hansard, and *Hansard's Parliamentary Reports*, founded by Cobbett, continue to this day.

The cosiness of Cobbett's lodgings was spoiled somewhat by the noisy and frequent public hangings that were carried out right underneath his window. In later life, his eldest daughter, Anne, who was fifteen at the time of her father's imprisonment, described how distressing the executions were. 'Blinds were drawn down, but we heard what was going on. It was very sad and so often occurred then', she wrote in her *Account of the Family*. Anne also left a vivid picture of Cobbett's daily workout at six o'clock in the morning, earlier in the summer, on the roof of the prison from where he would have had a magnificent view of St Paul's Cathedral. Using a pair of dumb bells, he went through a routine of military-style exercises and the movements a farmer would make, digging, raking and so on. Hot and perspiring, Cobbett would then return to his rooms to rest, wash and shave with cold water and put on clean linen '*always*', Anne stressed, to be ready for his breakfast at eight o'clock of tea and a penny roll.

Cobbett's children were devastated by what had happened to their father. Cobbett described their reaction years later in his book *Advice to Young Men* and how James, at the time his youngest son aged seven, could not be made to understand by his eldest brother, William, what a prison was: 'When he did, he, all in a tremor, exclaimed: "Now I'm sure, William, that Papa is not in a place *like that!*"'

Over the two years the elder children took it in turns to stay with their father. Cobbett taught them French, proudly writing home in a letter to his wife that Anne would become 'a capital French scholar'. (Indeed, all Cobbett's children ended up speaking the language fluently.) His sons took lessons with a teacher who lived around the corner from Newgate. They also took dancing lessons inside Cobbett's rooms, an activity of which, their father wrote with amusement, 'they were outrageously fond'. In one letter to Nancy, Cobbett charmingly described how they entertained him one day when he only had a few visitors: 'They put on their pumps and danced the best part of the day and laughed till their jaws ached and so did I. John has got all the steps and capers and he skips and twists himself about like a grasshopper.'

While Cobbett was in prison in London, the rest of his family managed the farming business at Botley as best they could. Cobbett wrote long letters filled with minute instructions, some with detailed drawings of what he wanted done, in an effort to keep afloat what had grown into an extensive enterprise. Nancy was illiterate. One of the children had to read letters to their mother and pen her replies. It was a tough time for her, worrying about her beloved Billy far away in London. She had also had yet another miscarriage, His wife's anxiety nearly drove him mad. Cobbett wrote the following anguished words in answer to a letter from Nancy in October 1811:

The letter which I have just received from Botley has sunk my heart within me. All is unhappiness! All is worry! All is misery! ... I beg of you not to set your mind to work thus to make misery for yourself ... The last Botley letter is really a complete maddener. It is enough to drive me crazy; and, the torment is so much the greater because of the delay in getting the answer to you. Do not inflict such deep and so often repeated wounds upon my heart. I know well that you do not intend it. I know how dear I am to you and that all you say proceeds from your love for me and your anxiety about me. But, I beg you to consider that I cannot hear of your unhappiness and be happy myself.

It was a terrible time for the Cobbett family beset by troubles and difficulties. The debts piled up and Cobbett was indeed to go bankrupt eight years later. Unsurprisingly, Nancy could not stop worrying about their situation, nor did she stop telling Cobbett exactly how she felt. She also continued visiting the doctor to get drugs to help her cope, despite Cobbett's fierce scorn at her need of 'physic'. Cobbett poured out the depth of his torment and frustration in a letter:

My soul was never so sunk as it is at this moment. Do not thus harass my mind, I beseech you ... I have no human being to speak comfort to me ... Do not tear my heart in pieces ...

Now, will you spare me? Will you have compassion upon me? I could cry like a child at the receipt of these letters. They kill me by inches.

Despite the family troubles, Cobbett forged on in prison. He read many of the daily newspapers and weekly magazines, entertained his numerous visitors, who included Henry Hunt, and poured out articles for his beloved *Political Register* to which he defiantly added the phrase, 'State Prison, Newgate,' lest anybody forgot where he was and what was happening to him. He survived his two years inside triumphantly, although he never forgave the establishment for what it had done to him. Years later, he was still writing letters to the king asking for the return of his £1,000 fine. His problems were compounded by anxiety over his complicated finances and quarrels with his printers, booksellers and publishers. Cobbett suspected them all of cheating him and sued one of them, his partner and publisher John Wright. His daughter Anne noticed the difference in her father:

Papa's health did not suffer in Newgate, but his temper did. He left it an altered man in many respects. Miss [Mary Russell] Mitford says truly that he never talked politics in society, never broached them at least. After Newgate he talked of little else. He was so angry at being so ill used ... It all wounded him very deeply.

Cobbett emerged from his spell in prison a bitter and angry man. The impact of his experiences fuelled the darker side of his character and sharpened what was already a strong egoism and fierce determination to succeed. It explains much of Cobbett's later manic and violent jealousy against anybody who he thought threatened his hard-won position as the man who had done the most to enlighten the people of Britain – and in particular, therefore, it explains much of his later jealousy against Henry Hunt.

In 1810, however, the friendship between the two men strengthened and flourished. While Hunt remained in the King's Bench Prison, he used the privilege of 'the run of the key' to visit Cobbett regularly, crossing the River Thames over old London Bridge and heading straight up into the city, over Ludgate Hill to Newgate and the Old Bailey. By mid-August, Hunt was out of prison and back home in his hunting cottage in Littlecot in Wiltshire. He continued writing to and visiting Cobbett in London. By now, Hunt was as important to Cobbett as Cobbett was to Hunt. In a letter sent to Hunt from Newgate on 9 January 1811, six months in to his sentence, Cobbett was deeply anxious about Hunt who was ill. This is the first extant letter in which Cobbett addressed him as 'my dear Hunt'. In it, Cobbett begged Hunt not to attribute a delay in replying to his letter to any want of feeling on his part. In fact, he wrote, Hunt's letter had quite alarmed him:

For, I sincerely declare that there are not above ten people in the whole world (of which my wife and children make seven) by whose dangers of health I should be so much afflicted in mind. If you were to die I should think the world a great deal less worth living in; but I anxiously hope that this will find you better. What you wish from me you shall have by next Tuesday's post ... God bless you, my dear Hunt, and restore you to health. Twenty such men as you are wanted and I am afraid there is but two or three.

In March 1811, Hunt moved from Wiltshire to Rowfant, near Worth in Sussex, where he had taken the lease on a large estate. He had put on two stone during his spell in prison and was too heavy to go hunting. In any case, he missed farming. The move to Sussex also meant he was nearer London, so he could continue his visits to Newgate, where he not only saw Cobbett but also met up with many of the other reformers who visited, including Sir Francis Burdett and Major John Cartwright.

Burdett had experienced his own taste of prison the year before. The case had been a sensational one. Burdett had attacked the government for excluding journalists from the gallery of the House of Commons during a debate on the fiasco on the Dutch island of Walcheren when the British expeditionary force had had to return to England after the loss of thousands of men to malaria. Cobbett published a stinging letter, apparently from Burdett, on the issue in the *Political Register*. (Cobbett later revealed that he himself had written it.) As a result, the House of Commons voted to commit Burdett to the Tower of London for contempt of parliament. This caused an outraged mob to run wild in London for three days. On the day Burdett was arrested and removed to the Tower, the government made sure there were no demonstrations by deploying 50,000 troops onto the streets. Cobbett observed in the *Register* that the War Office had ordered in soldiers from every regiment within a hundred miles of London.

Burdett spent two months in the Tower. Hunt went over from the King's Bench Prison to visit him. When Burdett was due to be released, people poured into London from all over the country. (It is incredible to think of the journeys they had to make to get there and the costs they incurred.) The streets were jam-packed. Nobody went to work. All gathered to greet their hero who was to head a triumphal procession from the Tower to Piccadilly. In the event, Burdett disappointed everybody. He lost his nerve and slipped out of the Tower by boat, earning himself the nickname, 'Sir Francis Sly-Go'. Both Cobbett and Hunt were furious that Burdett had ducked out of such a wonderful opportunity to promote the cause of freedom and free speech, and they never let Burdett forget how he had let down the cause of reform.

The conversations between the reformers in Cobbett's rooms in Newgate crackled with debates about parliamentary reform and how it was to be achieved. George III was by then so ill with porphyria, the genetic illness now thought to have made him insane, that his eldest son took over as Prince Regent. Hunt decided to hold a county meeting in Somerset, drum up some support for reform and get some resolutions and a petition together for the prince to give him a taste of what was to come. Cobbett would have thoroughly approved of Hunt's plans. As soon as George had become Prince Regent, Cobbett addressed a public letter to him in the *Political Register*. It was to be one of many. (Oh the impudence!) The Prince Regent, wrote Cobbett, should never forget that governments could only last if they had 'the arms and the hearts of *the people*'; he could not be unaware that the people of the kingdom most anxiously desired a reform of the system for their freedom and happiness. Cobbett signed off the article with his usual 'State Prison, Newgate'.

Hunt's meeting took place at Wells on 6 March 1811. He described it in his *Memoirs*. About 5,000 people turned up. Some of them had been hired by both the Whigs and the Tories to hiss, hoot and make a noise whenever he spoke. Sir John Cox Hippisley, an elderly Whig MP, employed a steward of Lady Waldegrave to organise cartloads of farmers, who were primed to hold up their hands against 'HUNT'. They were a gang of slaves collected off the Mendip Hills, observed Hunt, 'a set of fellows as ignorant of all political matters as they were illiterate and besotted'. The parsons or 'black cormorants', as he called them, were also out in force to join in the howling. Hunt, however, had a powerful voice and, 'inspite of the beastly howling of these mongrel curs', he simply raised it a few decibels and shouted over the top. (This was the technique which would help Hunt become the leading public speaker in the country and one he would use to the full when he finally got into parliament.) Hunt told the farmers they could only escape ruin if the landlords lowered their rents, if the parsons reduced their tithes, and if they joined the people to demand a reform of the House of Commons.

Although he lost the vote for his resolutions that day, Hunt wrote a public letter in which he thanked the people who attended. Cobbett used the letter in the following issue of the *Political Register* on 9 March 1811 and prefaced it with an introduction. A great deal was done, Cobbett wrote. Many people were assembled; '*Discussions*' took place and '*Truths*' were uttered to them. The resolutions were lost, but both the 'INS' and the 'OUTS' (Cobbett and Hunt-speak for the Tories and the Whigs) had had to work very hard to make sure that had happened. Hunt was ploughing new and untilled ground, and, Cobbett went on, 'it is now broken up and the seeds of Reform are safely deposited in its bosom. The *yeomanry* and *tradesmen* have now seen that they are something'.

Letters of criticism poured in complaining that Cobbett had down-played the fact that Hunt lost the vote and that the whole meeting had been nothing more than a rebuke to the Jacobins. Defiantly, Cobbett returned to the subject the following week. Support for Hunt flowed from his pen. Cobbett bashed Hunt's bullies in marvellous prose. On this occasion (as on many others), there was a Shakespearian ring to it. The critics, snorted Cobbett, were 'poor stammering, boggling shiftless things, that shrink into air when pitted against men of mind and of independent views'. Hunt had given an excellent address, he wrote, and it had all been a complete victory for him. Hunt was thrilled – noting that Cobbett devoted eight pages to the subject. In his defence of Hunt, however, Cobbett made an interesting observation. Years later, his words would ring in the ears of both men. Reform, wrote Cobbett, was not something that could be hurried:

We who are for a reform have no need to be in a *hurry*. Our part is to keep steadily on in the track that we are pursuing: act where we can and where we cannot, let the thing work its own way, perfectly satisfied that reform *must come* and hoping that it will come in due time.

Cobbett was a shrewd and experienced operator. There was an implicit message for the impulsive, impatient and ambitious Hunt in those words. They laid down a marker for the way Cobbett wanted to do things and how he intended to act, no matter what Hunt thought or did. In these early years, Cobbett was full of advice and warnings for the younger man. He gave it politely and diplomatically, in public and in private. In a letter to Hunt written on 10 February 1812, Cobbett said that he had decided not to use one of Hunt's Addresses in the *Political Register*. It had been a good speech and even the worthy old veteran, Major John Cartwright, had highly approved of it. Cobbett was sure, however, that Hunt would find his reasons for not publishing it very convincing when Cobbett would have the pleasure of telling him in person. In the meantime, this was his advice to Hunt:

I would recommend to you <u>not to write anything</u>, which, by possibility, can expose you to the fangs of the villains; for, you may be assured, that they would think much less of shedding your blood than the blood of one of their lean pigs or sheep or even one of their cats ... If anything should appear <u>in print</u> relating to you let me have it as quickly as possible.

The tone is loving, almost fatherly. Apart from the affectionate letters Cobbett wrote to his family, he did not write to anybody else as he wrote to Hunt. There was a ten-year age gap and Cobbett treated Hunt protectively, as if he were his own son, but one that was also adult enough so that they could enjoy together all the delights of a mature friendship and companionship. He also looked upon Hunt as his disciple whom he, Cobbett, could teach and guide. For Hunt's part, Cobbett filled a gap in his life. Hunt confided in his *Memoirs* that the death of his beloved father when he (Hunt) was twenty-three had been a 'great misfortune'. Cobbett patently became the father figure Hunt so missed. Cobbett was also a great man and the greatest political writer of all times. Hunt, who did and thought everything in superlatives, would have also found that very important.

After Cobbett's death, his third son, James, made some notes for a biography of his father. This never materialised but the notes survived. In them, James observed that his father 'had but little individual attachment'. He 'liked people's company; & they liked his (when he was agreeable). But he formed very little of *friendship*. And wd. break off with any one, however old an acquaintance, on any affront, or being crossed in his will ... He might be sd. to *use* others, rather than to act with them'. In fact, there were many people who were devoted to Cobbett, but James' retrospective words fitted in many ways. Cobbett retained an aloofness and apartness from people. This clearly emerged in his writings. He did indeed 'use' people and he knew it too. He even boasted about it. In the issue of the *Register* on 26 January 1828, Cobbett wrote: 'It is, in short, the caring nothing for any body, that has enabled me to obtain something like justice for myself'.

Cobbett's friendship with his 'dear Hunt', however, was arguably the exception in his life. Cobbett would break off with Hunt, as Hunt would break off with Cobbett. Yet right to the bitter end, their relationship was a special one. In these early years, the friendship between the men blossomed. It was vigorous, warm and enjoyable. Hunt continued to gallop backwards and forward to London to see Cobbett in Newgate, and the pair maintained a cordial correspondence. In that letter to Hunt of 10 February 1812, Cobbett commented that it was likely there would be a change in the government. This, he said, would bring about a general election and he made mention of a seat in Bristol.

Two months later, Cobbett was backing Hunt from Newgate with all the power of his pen, as a parliamentary candidate for one of the two Bristol seats.

3
The Bristol Election

Hypocrisy is the most difficult and nerve-racking vice that any man can pursue; it needs an unceasing vigilance and a rare detachment of spirit. It cannot, like adultery or gluttony, be practised at spare moments; it is a whole-time job.

W Somerset Maugham

The Bristol election of 1812 marked a high point in the political collaboration and friendship of William Cobbett and Henry Hunt. This was the moment when Hunt stepped into the full glare of the political spotlight in what was then England's third biggest city when the press, or 'reptiles' as Cobbett called them, were to pounce triumphantly on the skeleton in Hunt's cupboard, Mrs Vince. Oh how the press thrill at the scent of a sex scandal. Cobbett supported him from his prison lodgings in Newgate with all the power and force that only his pen could wield. It was no handicap for Cobbett to be in prison. His pen was the only weapon he needed.

Since the triumphant victory at Westminster in 1807 of Sir Francis Burdett and Lord Cochrane, when Hunt tasted the power, glory and excitement of an election and held his 'dangerous dinner' at the Trout Tavern, he had regularly promised the electors of Bristol that he would one day stand in their city as an independent candidate in a 'pure' campaign (no dirty tricks, no bribes). The Whigs and the Tories, or 'the two corrupt factions' as Hunt called them, had sewn up Bristol between them to save time and money. There were two seats for the city and it was quite simple: the Whigs held one, the Tories the other. It had reduced a great city to a level with the rottenest of rotten boroughs, said Hunt. He promised that when he offered himself as a candidate, there would be no bribery or corruption from him. He would not spend one shilling to win the seat, nor would he accept, if he were elected, a place of profit or a pension either for himself or for any members of his family. No fat cat jobs or sinecures for him or anybody connected with him.

Hunt felt his time had arrived. A general election was on the horizon and the Whig MP for Bristol was due to stand down. The liberal Whigs, fearing the sort of contest Hunt was likely to run, adopted the lawyer Sir Samuel Romilly as their candidate. Romilly was already one of the two members of parliament for the Duke of Norfolk's rotten borough of Arundel in Sussex and therefore unused to pressing the flesh. He was not accustomed to having to sell himself to constituents, and felt uncomfortable about having to speak at public meetings. He allowed himself, however, to be persuaded to make a public entry into Bristol to show himself to the electorate. The day appointed was 2 April 1812.

Hunt was ready and waiting. He mingled with the crowd outside the Bush Tavern (Lloyds Bank at the time of writing) opposite the Exchange in Corn Street to see what kind of reception Romilly would get. The party arrived and set up at the Bush from where Romilly was to speak to the crowds through a window. To Hunt's unspeakable delight, Sir Samuel was greeted with boos, howls and cries of: 'No bloody bridge! No murderers'. Sir Samuel had been foolish enough to choose among his companions an alderman of Bristol who, some years previously, had ordered the military to fire upon the people during a riot over the high tolls of Bristol Bridge. A number had been killed. Hence the angry reaction of the people to the arrival of Romilly's party. Sir Samuel was so disconcerted by his reception, he retreated inside the tavern, doubtless to fortify himself with a stiff drink.

There was a lull in proceedings. Up stepped Hunt. He climbed on to one of the four ancient brass and copper flat-topped pedestals in the street, which still stand in a line in front of the Exchange. He was gratified to be hailed with shouts by many who already knew him. Hunt stood in the pouring rain for more than one and a half hours and spoke of the pressing need for a radical reform of the whole parliamentary system. A man held an umbrella over him while he spoke.

There were many weavers among Hunt's listeners whose trade had been badly hit by the introduction of new equipment and working practices. They wore cards in their hats bearing Romilly's name. The cards had been handed out by the Whig party earlier in the day as part of its electioneering tactics. Nevertheless, the weavers, along with everybody else, listened in profound silence to Hunt, and his speech was only interrupted by applause. When Hunt reminded the crowd how rotten and corrupt former Whig governments had been, the windows of the room in the Bush Tavern in which Romilly and his friends were sheltering were suddenly shut. The crowd ordered the windows to be re-opened (they would have smashed them otherwise) so the unfortunate party was compelled to listen to Hunt whether it liked it or not. Hunt continued for another hour while Sir Samuel's public dinner laid on in the nearby Assembly Rooms in King Street got cold. The streets were so densely packed with people, neither Romilly nor his party dared to attempt to force a way through the crowds to get there.

The newspapers reported the event as if it had been a great triumph for Romilly. The Whig newspaper, the *Morning Chronicle*, edited by James Perry, was among the London newspapers to claim that Romilly was hailed with enthusiasm and applause in Bristol. The paper made no mention of Hunt's speech. *Felix Farley's Bristol Journal* (Tory) managed to avoid any mention of Hunt at all. The *Bristol Gazette* (Whig) explained that the windows at the Bush Tavern were shut because the party inside had some business to conclude. Cobbett, sitting in his rooms in the prison keeper's house in Newgate, faithfully reported in the *Political Register* everything that had really happened. Hunt, he wrote, had exposed the conduct of the Whigs who had been in power when George III came to the throne, reminding his listeners how they had handed out sinecures, places and pensions in abundance and how they had cheated the ordinary people by pocketing the public money. Sir Samuel Romilly and his entourage had indeed been compelled by the crowds to open the windows and listen, chortled Cobbett, and thousands of people had indeed applauded Hunt's speech even though there had been no mention of this in the local newspapers. The crowds dispersed peacefully after accompanying Hunt to his place for dinner. After that, Cobbett went on, Sir Samuel and his party were at last able to go to theirs, 'having first been cheered by beholding the card with his name in it pulled out of hundreds of hats by the weavers themselves and torn to pieces'.

Years later in Ilchester gaol, Hunt was grateful all over again for Cobbett's heroic support. The newspapers' coverage, he wrote, was so:

... glaringly unfair and partial, that Mr Cobbett wrote a very long and able paper upon the subject exposing and chastising the Whigs for their duplicity and deception, and, at the same time, he did not fail to represent the conduct of Mr Perry in its true colours.

Hunt expected the election to take place after the dissolution of parliament later in the year, but the Tory MP for Bristol unexpectedly resigned his seat and on Tuesday, 23 June 1812, a snap by-election in Bristol was announced. Hunt only learned the news when his newspaper was delivered two days later as he was sitting down to dinner at home in Rowfant in Sussex. The election was to be held the following Monday in Bristol. This meant he had just three days to get there to be in time to announce his candidature at the hustings. Hunt galloped off the next day to London from where he took the mail coach to Bath, arriving at 10 o'clock on the Saturday morning. He spent the journey studying *Disney's Abridgement of Election Law*, a popular book on election procedure he managed to buy before leaving London.

From Bath, Hunt took a post-chaise and arrived in Bristol that evening. He galloped to the entrance of the city at Temple Gate in Totterdown in style. A long pole had been attached to his carriage. The pole was topped by a giant loaf of bread bearing the motto 'Hunt and Peace'. Hunt's arrival in the city was greeted by cheering crowds, an 'immense multitude', as he phrased it in his *Memoirs*. *The Times* sneered that 'his appearance was grotesque in the extreme'. The newspaper did admit that a 'multitude' turned out to greet Hunt but sniffily said it was composed of 'chiefly the working classes'.

Hunt got a good reception. The people took his horses out of the traces and they themselves pulled the carriage carrying Hunt into the city. He made his way straight to his pedestal outside the Exchange and prepared to address a crowd of around 20,000 people. 'I never had seen such enthusiasm in my life', wrote Hunt in his *Memoirs*. The deafening roars of approval from the crowd must have been intoxicating, fire in the ears, wine in the blood. Cobbett took great pleasure in reporting that the Tory election circus was caught out by Hunt's arrival. How great was the consternation of the party who had sewn up the election between them, he gloated in the *Political Register* of 4 July 1812.

Sir Samuel Romilly had decided not to stand because the vacant seat belonged to the 'Blue Interest' and it was assumed that the Tory candidate, the local banker, Richard Hart Davis, would be returned unopposed. Hunt's arrival, however, put the cat among the pigeons. His speed-reading of *Disney's Abridgement* had informed him how to make sure the polls were kept open for the entire fifteen days of the election instead of being closed after just a few hours. This was going to cost the Tories a lot of money and, heaven forbid, they might even lose the seat. And so the dirty tricks campaign against Hunt began.

The Tories paid four hundred men, including miners from Kingswood coal mine, (Hunt called them the 'greatest ruffians' in Bristol) to become so-called special constables, a sort of freelance police force hired for the occasion. They were armed with heavy ash sticks two feet long and painted sky blue, the party colour. Hunt had to force his way into the hustings at the Guildhall in Broad Street – one of the narrowest streets in Bristol – while his supporters were bludgeoned by the hired ruffians. It was reported that one man was killed, a child was trodden to death and a number of people were badly injured. In the evening there was heavy fighting through the streets. The Tories had by then doubled the numbers of their freelance specials to eight hundred. They were out in strength, wielding their heavy sticks. The people fought back furiously, smashing up Tory headquarters at the White Lion Inn. They roamed around the town, breaking the windows of the Council House and of the elegant British Coffee-Room (now a pub/restaurant). Several houses were also attacked, their windows broken and gardens torn up. Some of the rioters marched to the Clifton home of the Tory candidate, Richard Hart Davis, where 'that gentleman was quietly reposing after the fatigues of the day in the bosom of his amiable family', as one of the local newspapers so elegantly put it. The rioters smashed in his windows, tore down the gates and pulled up all the shrubs and iron railings in the front garden, 'presenting a scene of ruin and devastation'. The newspaper was, however, happy to report that the news of an attack against the house of 'Mr Davis's venerable mother at Whitehall' was unfounded.

Felix Farley's Bristol Journal pinned all the blame on the crowd which it described as 'a noisy and blood thirsty mob'. The *Bristol Gazette* delicately reported that the prevailing opinion appeared to have been that 'the Blue Party had acted wrong in arming so many pretended constables with bludgeons'. In fact, the city magistrate blamed Richard Hart Davis and his Tory backers for having appointed and armed so many men, and ordered that they should be disbanded forthwith. Instead, the local authorities ordered the military into the city to control the crowds. This was contrary to normal procedure at elections when all soldiers were routinely ordered to withdraw from towns. At the Bristol by-election, however, the military was deployed in force.

In a private letter to Hunt on 4 July 1812, Cobbett said the move to bring in the soldiers was abominable. 'It seems to me impossible that the election can stand, if troops have really been marched into the town,' he wrote, and urged Hunt to keep detailed notes so that a formal appeal could be lodged. (In the event, Hunt's petition complaining about the presence of the military, the deployment of armed thugs by the Tories and the closure of the polls a day early was lost with the dissolution of parliament.)

In his *Memoirs*, Hunt painted a vivid picture of the military presence as he arrived at the top of Broad Street on his way to the hustings:

I found, to my surprise, that I had to pass the whole of the way down that street to the Guildhall between double lines of the military drawn up on each side of the street with arms supported and bayonets fixed. This was not only a novel scene, it was such a one as had never before been exhibited at an election in England.

Hunt dealt with this on the spot by removing his hat and calling for three cheers for 'our friends, the soldiers'. The crowd complied and the soldiers joined in, even shouting 'Hunt for ever'. (This was a frequent tactic of Hunt. He was to try it at Peterloo in Manchester in 1819, although that was one time it failed to work.) During the Bristol election there were several confrontations between the crowds and the militia. Cobbett described one such encounter when Hunt bravely urged the soldiers to love freedom and act as brother to brother. He said if the soldiers had to shoot, they should shoot him first, and dramatically ripped his shirt undone, baring his chest. It was stirring but frightening stuff.

The provincial and London newspapers gave Hunt a hard time. The poet Leigh Hunt, who edited the liberal and reform-minded *Examiner* with his brother John, lamented the misfortune that the family name happened to be 'Hunt' and disclaimed any connection with Henry Hunt. The Hunt brothers were in the middle of a campaign against their namesake. The previous year, in 1811, they had reported Hunt's ill-advised comments at a public dinner that the attorney general, old Vinegar Gibbs, would 'admirably grace a lamp-post', or in other words, Gibbs should be strung up and hanged.

Among the worst of the newspapers to undermine Hunt during the Bristol election was *Felix Farley's Bristol Journal*. It published several anonymous letters viciously attacking Hunt, the Jacobin, and dredging through past scandals. The writers posed a series of questions. Was Hunt a man fit to enact laws when he had spent the whole of his life breaking them? Had he not been confined in prison for breaking the country's laws? Did he not say that the attorney general should be strung up on a lamp-post? Had not Sir Francis Burdett himself said Hunt was too desperate and too dangerous a man even for his party to support him? Was Hunt not connected with a group of seditious men who wanted to overthrow their glorious Constitution? Did he not live in open adultery with another man's wife? The *Journal* was altogether outraged. How dare such a man stand as a candidate for parliament and how dare anybody consider voting for him, it thundered:

To retail the ribaldry, the coarseness, the rudeness of this reported adulterer's conduct during the last five days would out-do the pages of the grossest jest book. Deluded fellow-citizens, before the last day of the poll arrives, depend upon it, your eyes will be opened. Ye parents, ye mothers, is it the fornicator, the seducer of the wife of his most intimate friend, is it the man who has abandoned an amiable wife and three young children, that you would support in competition with a native of your own city, full of charity and good works?

Hunt said that his hair turned grey during those fraught weeks of 1812. His family thought he aged seven years. He recalled bitterly that, apart from Cobbett, every newspaper in the land was against him, and that they were joined by supporters of both factions, the Tories and the Whigs, who fabricated 'every species of calumny' against him. 'There was no falsehood too gross to serve their turn', he wrote in his *Memoirs*. There had been no law, no protection for either himself or his supporters. He had received at least ten anonymous letters containing death threats. One person had even written a letter addressed to Mrs Vince in Sussex claiming that Hunt had been lynched and killed by the mob and asking for instructions on where he was to be buried. The letter purported to be from the chairman of Hunt's election committee. Fortunately, the letter just missed Mrs Vince, who had become so anxious about what was going on, she had set off for Bristol the day before the letter was delivered. She and Hunt found it waiting for them when they returned home together after the election was over.

It is not surprising that both Cobbett and Hunt became paranoid. They received constant death threats and lived for years under a barrage of lies and insults from the mainstream press and the establishment, Cobbett's 'Thing'. It is worth noting that during the Bristol by-election, the Tories also took revenge on the people who did have the guts to stick their hands up and vote for Hunt. They posted up a public notice immediately afterwards on which was written the names, addresses and trades of the 235 men who had voted for him. It meant their businesses were likely to be boycotted and served as a warning of what could happen to anybody who did not toe the line in the future. Hunt published in his *Memoirs* the full list of the men who had supported him, not only to give them credit for their bravery but also, he wrote, to give posterity an idea of what went on in the nineteenth century.

When Hunt looked back at the Bristol by-election from his Ilchester cell and remembered how he had been attacked and tormented, his pen acquired a Cobbettian tone. He had pored over Cobbett's colourful prose for so long, his pen almost outdid the master's. He had faced, he wrote:

> ... the hireling legion, consisting of a swarm of more foul and noxious vermin than Moses inflicted upon the land of Egypt. It was made up of all the attorneys and pettifoggers with their clerks, scamps and runners; every man or rather every reptile of them being profusely fed to bark, to snarl, to cavil and to bully and all of them more ravenous and ferocious than sharks or wolves.

Hunt singled out one of the attorneys in particular, appropriately called Leech, who had told Hunt in public that he would like 'to suck his blood'. The attorney's words, Hunt observed wryly, were received by his friends with great applause. Hunt got his own back in his *Memoirs* with this graphic description of Mr Leech:

Such a looking creature I had scarcely ever seen in human form. He had coal-black, straight hair, hanging down a sallow-looking face that had met with very rough usage from the ravages of the small-pox. In fact, his face resembled a piece of cold, dirty, honey combed tripe and had very little more expression in it and the whole was completed by two heavy, dark eyes, which looked like leaden bullets stuck in clay.

Hunt's consolation was that he had Cobbett's support and backing throughout. Cobbett was coming to the end of his two-year sentence in Newgate, eagerly following the news and maintaining Hunt's morale and spirits in private letters and through articles in his defence in the *Political Register*. Even as Hunt galloped towards Bristol to reach the hustings in time to declare his candidacy, Cobbett dashed off a letter of reassurance. Older and far more experienced, Cobbett knew exactly what was in store for Hunt and knew that Hunt had no real chance of being elected. Cobbett's letter of 27 June 1812 was generously kind and carefully diplomatic:

I hardly know what advice to give you. Indeed your activity and courage supply the place of all other things. But if you make but weak fight now, never mind that. You will make better fight next time and, I am of opinion, that you will finally carry your point ... I hope to hear from you as soon as possible and I am sincerely yours, Wm Cobbett

Cobbett also drafted a letter to 'the Independent Electors of Bristol' for publication in the *Political Register*. The draft still survives. The important bits to be put into capital letters or underlined were carefully marked out for the printer. Cobbett wrote easily and fluently. There was relatively very little scratched out or altered. The article appeared in the *Register* on 4 July 1812, the last issue of the *Register* to be published before Cobbett left prison five days later. It was a superb summary of the political situation. Bristol, he wrote, had for a long time been the sport of the two artful factions (Whigs and Tories) who had divided between them the profits arising from their election wins. They had tried to keep Hunt out by the speed with which the 'little snug, rotten-borough-like election' had been organised, but they had failed. As the Bristol voters had seen for themselves, the conduct of Mr Hunt was in stark contrast. He was not a man 'to be intimidated by the frowns or the threats of wealth or rank'. He was not to be made to abandon his duty towards them from any consideration of danger to himself. He was not to be 'brow-beaten into silence', nor did he content himself with talking about defending their liberties:

He acts as well as talks. He hears that the enemy is at your camp and he flies to rescue you from his grasp. He does not waste his time in a tavern in London, drawing up flourishing resolutions about 'public spirit.' He hastens among you. He looks your and his adversary in the face. He shows you that you may depend upon him in the hour of trial. These, Gentlemen, are marks of such a character in a representative as the times demand.

Cobbett's letter continued thrillingly. He knew, he wrote, that all the advantages were on the side of Richard Hart Davis, the people's 'adversary'. Perhaps on this occasion the voters would be unable to defeat him and they would be handed over to Hart Davis as if they were 'a cargo of tallow or of corn'. At the very least, however, the independent electors of Bristol would have a chance, an opportunity, to try to vote for the candidate of their choice. They would have an election and they would not have had one had it not been for Mr Hunt. At the very least, they would have some days of liberty to speak their minds, to declare aloud their grievances and their indignation. For that liberty, they would be indebted to Mr Hunt and solely to Mr Hunt. He was coming to them in their moment of real need, to harass their enemy, Hart Davis, to make his victory cost him dear and, by exposing the sources and means of his success, to lay the foundation of his future defeat and disgrace. Cobbett signed off: 'I am, your friend, Wm Cobbett. State Prison, Newgate'.

It was a marvellous piece of writing on the part of Cobbett, a public tribute to his friend. Cobbett knew that Hunt would lose. It was impossible that he could beat the unfair and corrupt system – and of course Hunt did lose by a large majority. If there had been a secret ballot, he would have easily taken the seat. Hunt had the satisfaction, at least, of knowing that the long fortnight cost the Tories nearly £30,000. By contrast, Hunt's own bill totalled about £30.

Cobbett stayed with the subject of the Bristol by-election in the *Political Register* for the next few weeks. He chortled over the volleys of mud, stones and dead cats that were hurled at both the Whigs and the Tories by the people, and faithfully reported all the dramatic events, including the violence of the special constables and the fixed bayonets of the soldiers. Hunt, wrote Cobbett, was 'a man of principle and courage.'

He had 'stood the poll' for the entire two weeks in the face of horse and foot soldiers and without the aid of advocate or attorney. 'Gentlemen, this is, as I verily believe, what no other man in England, whom I know, would have done.' And Cobbett repeated yet again, hammering the point home, that without Hunt, the electors would not even have had the chance to vote:

Without such a man the stand could not have been made; without such a man you could not have had an opportunity of giving utterance to the hatred which you so justly feel against the supporters of that corruption, the consequences of which you so sorely feel.

It was in this issue of the *Register* on 1 August 1812 that Cobbett confronted the thorny subject of Hunt's separation from his wife to live with another man's. He did it in his second public letter to the Bristol electors. Cobbett had a rare style of writing. Unlike the tortured, pompous English used by the newspapers and journals of the day, he wrote clearly and simply. Even the least educated could understand what he was saying or alluding to. He often repeated himself to get his message across and make sure it was remembered. Cobbett had the knack of making his readers feel as if they were being spoken to by an old friend who knew them well.

This second letter to the voters of Bristol was sensational. Had the newspapers been right to raise the subject of Hunt's private life, Cobbett asked rhetorically. Absolutely not. He condemned the taunts and jeers Hunt had endured. One Bristol attorney had published a pamphlet against Hunt in which he argued that if a man broke his promise to his wife, he would be sure to break his promises again, for example to the people of Bristol. Such rubbish, Cobbett snorted. What hypocrisy. Would these critics ask '*peers and princes*' to follow the same rules? (A reference to the Prince Regent, who continued to scandalise society with his own love life and ill-treatment of his wife, Caroline, and to much of England's aristocracy. It was a clever child who knew who his or her real father was.) He himself did not think lightly of such matters, Cobbett went on. The breakdown of a marriage was always to be lamented, but nobody could know what was the real cause of the separation:

It is impossible for the public to know the facts of such a case. They cannot enter into a man's family affairs. The tempers and humours of wives and of husbands nobody but those wives and husbands know. They are, in many cases, unknown even to domestic servants and to children; and, is it not then the height of presumption for the public to pretend to any knowledge of the matter?

Given Cobbett's conservative attitude to marriage and adultery, this was an extraordinary piece of writing. Cobbett was publicly supporting a notorious adulterer. It shows just how highly he regarded Hunt. In this public letter to the Bristol electors, Cobbett soothed Hunt's hurt pride and dignity and warned his readers not to be fooled and diverted by the revelations about Hunt's private life. Every man who attacked corruption, who made war upon the 'vile herd' that lived upon the people's labour, wrote Cobbett, should expect to be himself attacked. He must expect to be ever the object of the bitterest and most persevering malice. Unless he had made up his mind to endure 'calumny', he should at once quit the field. Calumny was a weapon that would be used against him all the time, and, to make his point, Cobbett brilliantly transformed the word into the shape of an insidious woman:

No sooner does a man become in any degree formidable to her, than she sets to work against him in all the relationships of life. In his profession, his trade, his family; amongst his friends, the companions of his sports, his neighbours and his servants. She eyes him all round, she feels him all over and if he has a vulnerable point, if he has a speck, however, small, she is ready with her stab. How many hundreds of men have been ruined by her without being hardly able to perceive, much less name, the cause; and how many thousands, seeing the fate of these hundreds, have withdrawn from the struggle or have been deterred from taking part in it! Mr Hunt's *separation from his wife* presented too fair a mark to be for a moment overlooked.

Nobody, wrote Cobbett, including himself, had anything to do with Mr Hunt's family affairs any more than he had with theirs. Everybody should simply observe his conduct as a public man. If he served them well in that capacity, then he was entitled to their gratitude.

For good measure, Cobbett returned to the subject a fortnight later in the issue of the *Register* of 15 August 1812, when he expanded on the reasons why such quantities of dirt had been thrown at Hunt and why his adultery had been so exploited by all sides. It was simply because Hunt supported a reform of parliament, the end of corruption and the abolition of pensions and sinecures. Hunt had himself made a solemn promise that he never would, as long as he lived, either directly or indirectly, pocket a single farthing of public money. This was the true reason for the fury against him; this was the real cause of the hatred, the rancour, the poisonous malice of both factions against Mr Hunt. It was all because of his war upon the tax-eaters who pocketed the people's money. This was why they condemned his separation from his wife:

They well know that the success of Mr Hunt would defeat their scheme and therefore they hate him. They do not dislike him for his separation from his wife. They would not give his wife a bit of bread to save her life if she was a beggar instead of being, as she is, well and liberally provided for. They would see her drop from their door dead in the street, rather than tender her a helping hand ... To speak of the separation suits the turn of the hypocrites ... By having recourse to it, they can cast calumny on their foe without letting their real motive appear ... The whole mystery lies here. Whoever or whatever will give them the best chance of getting at the public money is the man or the thing for them.

There are many people today who would appreciate Cobbett's words. Many politicians and people in the public glare would be only too grateful for a Cobbett to support them. The irony was that when the 'whore on horseback' letter came to light a few years later, to the mortification and horror of both Cobbett and Hunt, it was to be the perfect 'stab' by their enemies against them both. As Cobbett penned his articles in 1812 for the *Political Register*, he had probably forgotten all about those private words he wrote in 1808 warning his publisher that Hunt was a dangerous man who lived with a 'whore'. Cobbett had also maybe forgotten – or conveniently overlooked – what he had written at the end of the eighteenth century while in America, about the radical English scientist, Joseph Priestley, who had been hounded out of England and forced into exile there. Priestley had become a target for Cobbett because of his support for the French revolution and his criticism of the British establishment. Cobbett's pen had been merciless against him. No man had a right to pry into his neighbour's private concerns, he wrote. People's opinions were their own – but only until they decided to put them before the public:

... when he makes those opinions public, when he once attempts to make converts, whether

Hunt, Dr Watson and Cobbett are outside a brothel called 'Adultery Place'.
Hunt is wearing a cap of liberty in the form of a fool's cap and holding a bag
inscribed 'Penny Subscription'. Cobbett writes at a low table on the Evening
Post. He has two heads. From one mouth issues, 'Hunt the Virtuous...' and
from the other, 'Hunt a Whoremonger...' 1820.
© *The Trustees of the British Museum*

it be in religion, politics or anything else, when he once comes forward as a candidate for public admiration, esteem or compassion, his opinions, his principles, his motives, every action of his life, public or private, becomes the fair subject of public discussion.

Strong words and opinions which still arouse so much controversy today. Cobbett wrote them in 1794. By 1812 and the Bristol election, Cobbett had conveniently forgotten what he had written in 1808 and in America. Hunt had become Cobbett's most faithful and loyal partner, and Cobbett was faithful and loyal to Hunt. In Cobbett's eyes, Hunt was a man of principle and courage. He had many against him. He had acted in Bristol as no other man in England would have done. Although Cobbett detested adultery in any shape or form, he mounted a magnificent defence of Hunt, his separation from his wife and his relationship with Mrs Vince. Privately, Cobbett thought of adultery as a kind of cancer. In 1829, he was to make his views perfectly clear in his book, *Advice to Young Men*. Yet when it came to his dear friend Hunt, Cobbett remained tolerant, despite the upset and fury this caused his own conservative-minded wife, Nancy.

At the time, Hunt must have read and re-read Cobbett's words with tears of gratitude in his eyes, and, years later, as he looked back at the glory days of his friendship with Cobbett from his lonely cell in Ilchester Prison, he took comfort all over again from the support Cobbett had given him. He reprinted in his *Memoirs* much of what Cobbett wrote during the Bristol election of 1812 and, despite his bitterness at how Cobbett had subsequently abandoned him, Hunt paid grateful tribute to him. 'No man had ever been so grossly attacked and belied as I was, by the whole of the public press; with the exception of Mr Cobbett, who stood manfully by me', he wrote.

Cobbett's support for Hunt during the Bristol election was noted and remarked on by the establishment. The two men were repeatedly linked together in the newspapers. The *Bristol Gazette* devoted lengthy paragraphs to Cobbett's loyalty to Hunt in the pages of the *Political Register*. The *Gazette* considered Hunt to be nothing less than a revolutionary. His speeches, it said, were inflammatory and seditious. Hunt's supporters were nothing more than 'deluded victims'. How could Cobbett criticise the political parties for acting together against Hunt when they were only trying '*to prevent murder?*' How could Cobbett quibble over words when he condemned the use of violence so strongly himself in his own writings:

Be assured, Mr Cobbett, that these men whom you seem to have taken under your wing are the veriest rabble and scum of the town – men who have escaped transportation or the gallows, perhaps every week of their lives since they were fourteen years of age, whose minds are barren of all good and whose hearts have been still more corroded by the revolutionary harangues of your friend Mr Hunt.

Felix Farley's Bristol Journal also reported on what it called the 'calumnies and misrepresentations' of Cobbett's *Register*. *The Edinburgh Review* dismissed whatever Cobbett had written. He had changed his mind so often, sneered the journal, it was of little interest what opinions he held.

The propaganda against both men came in inventive shapes and forms. A mock theatre bill was widely circulated in Bristol. It was published by J M Gutch, owner of the Tory newspaper, *Felix Farley's Bristol Journal*. Its comic tone was belied by its sinister message. The bill advertised 'a new Low Comedy' called *The Banditti*. This was to be accompanied with the usual Georgian theatrical delights of 'appropriate Machinery, Dresses and Decorations'. It was to be presented by the 'Theatre Republique' on Thursday, 9 July 1812 (the day of Cobbett's release from Newgate), and every evening during the election at the Talbot Tavern (where Hunt was staying). Hunt was to play the starring role as the Banditti leader, Hal Halter. Citizen Cobbett was billed to play Furioso Firebrando, 'Being his first appearance in Public for these 2 years'.

The poster also made offensive mention of Mrs Vince who, it said, had offered to play Mother Midnight although Dr Hornbrook deemed it 'highly imprudent in her present state of salvation to appear in publick'. (Hornbrook was among Hunt's supporters in Bristol.) Black Sal of Tower Lane had kindly undertaken to read Mrs Vince's part at short notice. The Grand March of 'Ça Ira' (the revolutionary Jacobin march) was to be played, and 'Citizen Hunt' would recite an ode to the memory of Thomas Paine composed for the occasion with an 'Elegiac Effusion on the Loss of his Cap of Liberty Which was unfortunately stifled in a Dung-heap at the White Lion Stables' (Tory party HQ).

The poster concluded with the deadly information that after the play,

Citizen Hunt would then star as Harlequin in a new pantomime called 'All's UP Or D.I.O' (Deus in Omnia – God in everything). He would take 'a surprising leap from a cart, being positively his last Appearance in any Character'. The final mocking words on the poster were: 'Vive la Republique'.

No wonder Hunt's hair turned grey during the Bristol election.

4
The Whore on Horseback

Who can find a virtuous woman? For her price is far above rubies.

Proverbs

As soon as the election was over, Hunt headed back to his home in Sussex. He went via Botley in Hampshire to visit Cobbett to congratulate him on his recent release from Newgate and to chew over what had happened in Bristol. Hunt recorded in his *Memoirs* written years later in Ilchester Prison that Cobbett welcomed him with open arms, but Hunt was surprised to find that the reception from the other family members was 'most rude, unhandsome and disgusting'. Now, why was that?

Hunt thought Mrs Cobbett disliked him because of an incident which had occurred in Newgate Prison. One evening there was a large gathering of people in Cobbett's rooms. As ever when he chose to be, Hunt recalled, Cobbett was the life and soul of the party, keeping everybody roaring with laughter at his jokes and quick wit. Suddenly he stopped and asked Hunt if he would promise to do him a favour. Mrs Cobbett looked as if she were in on this particular joke. Hunt agreed, and described what followed: '"Well," said he, "promise me then that you will never wear white breeches again!"' There was a deathly silence. Hunt was devastated. He was wearing a clean pair of white cord breeches and a neat pair of top boots. They were the height of fashion and Hunt's favourite clothes at the time. Like lightening Hunt responded. He would promise, he said, but only if Cobbett promised that he would never wear dirty breeches again. Hunt had already spotted that Cobbett was wearing a not very clean pair of old drab woollen breeches. He immediately regretted his words. He described the scene in his *Memoirs*:

The laugh was now turned against my friend and I instantly felt sorry for the repartee. I saw that my friend was hurt. He thought it unkind and dropped his under lip. Mrs Cobbett's eyes flashed the fire of indignation and she was never civil to one afterwards.

At the time, Hunt realised that Cobbett was hurt and that Nancy

Cobbett, who prided herself on being a good housewife, was looking daggers at him. From that moment, Hunt said, Nancy Cobbett treated him like an enemy. From then on, Hunt was always afraid that those who hated him slandered him to Nancy and 'endeavoured to injure me in the estimation of my friend, by poisoning the ear of his wife.'

However, Hunt was missing the point or he was searching for a way to explain Mrs Cobbett's dislike of him to his reading public without having to write something like: 'Look, the reason she loathed me so much was because of the fact that I had left my wife and was living with somebody else's.' The incident over the dirty breeches in Newgate Prison was a symptom, not a cause. Nancy Cobbett was a traditional, conservative-minded woman. Like most, she disapproved of the fact that Hunt had left his wife to live with Mrs Vince, and would have avoided associating with her. She was appalled that her husband, who she knew condemned adultery, overlooked Hunt's transgressions. Nancy Cobbett did not or could not, however, prevent Cobbett taking their sons to visit Hunt and Mrs Vince. There are many references in letters to the friendship between the Cobbett boys and Hunt's two sons, and good wishes were regularly sent, but there was never a personal word in any of Cobbett's letters for Hunt from Mrs Cobbett, and Cobbett refrained from mentioning his wife, at least directly.

So, when Hunt stopped off in Botley from Bristol on his way home, Mrs Vince was not with him because Nancy would never have allowed her into the house. The couple had been together when they left Bristol to return to their home in Sussex; Mrs Vince must have gone elsewhere. Knowing that she could not visit Botley because of Mrs Cobbett's prejudices, she may have taken the opportunity to visit her own family who lived in the south of Sussex. When Hunt knocked at the Cobbetts' front door, he was only accompanied by a close friend.

The reason why Nancy Cobbett was so rude and unpleasant to Hunt during the visit was blindingly obvious. The whole scandal of Hunt's adultery had been exposed in Bristol by the newspapers during the election. It was no longer a private relationship behind closed doors. It was out there in the public domain and was obviously a scandal that was never going to go away. Hunt was the best friend of her 'Billy'. Cobbett was involved by association – and supporting Hunt! Nancy Cobbett must have been disgusted and startled that her husband was acting in a manner against his own usual principles. What she must have said when her husband penned his superb defence of Hunt in the *Political Register* a couple of weeks later does not bear thinking about. The whole affair must have been a source of embarrassment for Cobbett the traditionalist as well, although he managed to get round his conservative scruples about such matters to defend Hunt so brilliantly.

It is safe to say that Cobbett ignored or tried to ignore his wife's dislike of Hunt, although she gave her husband a very hard time with her sharp tongue about which he was to complain so bitterly years later. Nancy tried many times to end her husband's relationship with Hunt, something the latter himself discussed with Cobbett. This is revealed in a letter Cobbett wrote to Hunt on 5 February 1814: 'No. You are, in no manner, forbidden to go to Botley, and will never be to any dwelling of mine. These "prejudices", of which you speak have no weight at all on my conduct; if they had, I should hate myself, as a most contemptible fellow.'

Another glimpse behind the scenes comes in a three-page letter written from Botley the following year, on 24 October 1815, after Hunt was ill, probably with his first minor stroke. Although there are water damage marks, the crucial words can just be deciphered. Cobbett said that his boys begged him to tell Hunt how grateful they were for his and Mrs Vince's kindness to them, and that he, Cobbett, felt the same. Everybody at Botley was also very pleased to find that Hunt was better, Cobbett went on, ' ... for inspite of all damnation settings-on and perverse prejudices, there is here a great deal of kindness of heart.' There was no mention of Mrs Cobbett's name but the letter clearly reveals just what pressure she continued to put on her husband to make him give up Hunt. Her most desperate attempt to end their friendship was to be a threat of suicide if Cobbett refused.

In the extant letters to Hunt from January 1814 onwards, Cobbett rarely failed to pass on his respects to Mrs Vince, desiring to be kindly remembered to her or hoping she was well. It is a tribute to Cobbett, his love for his friend and the qualities of Mrs Vince herself that he behaved so well towards her. Cobbett felt just as his wife Nancy did about adultery.

He was literally repelled by it. Cobbett's 'whore on horseback letter' of 1808 had been written from the heart, although he was so very ashamed of it when it became public knowledge. He was to write extensively about the subject in 1829 in his semi-autobiographical, moralistic and eminently readable series of letters published in the *Political Register*, which became the book, *Advice to Young Men*. In the section 'To a Husband', Cobbett wrote that as bad as infidelity was in a husband, it was far worse in a woman. The man was not cut off from society as a result; women certainly were:

Why is the disgrace *deeper*? Because here is a total want of *delicacy;* here is, in fact, *prostitution;* here is grossness and filthiness of mind; here is everything that argues baseness of character ... No woman, married or single, of *fair reputation*, will risk that reputation by being ever seen, if she can avoid it, with a woman who has ever, at any time, committed this offence ... She is branded with infamy to her latest breath.

Cobbett also criticised men who wooed, won and married their girl only to leave her, regardless of the consequences – just as Hunt had his wife, Ann:

Is a promise solemnly made before God, and in the face of the world, nothing? Is a violation of a contract, and that, too, with a feebler party, nothing of which a man ought to be ashamed? But, besides all these, there is the *cruelty*. First, you win, by great pains, perhaps, a woman's affections. Then, in order to get possession of her person, you marry her. Then, after enjoyment, you break your vow, you bring upon her the mixed pity and jeers of the world and thus you leave her to weep out her life. Murder is more horrible than this, to be sure, and the criminal law, which punishes divers other crimes, does not reach this. But in the eye of reason and of moral justice, it is surpassed by very few of those crimes.

Both Hunt and Mrs Vince may have squirmed a little when they read those passages. Nancy Cobbett herself may have done some squirming too. Also in the section 'To a Husband', Cobbett made it clear he believed that the man and the man alone should choose who his friends were: '... whom he is to have for coadjutors or friends; all these must be left solely to the husband. In all these he must have his will or there never can be any harmony in the family.'

In a letter to his 'dear Hunt' written from his farm at Barn Elm in Surry on 9 January 1829, Cobbett made an unusual reference to Mrs Vince, who by then had been living happily with Hunt for twenty-seven years. It came at the end of a reassuring letter to Hunt, who had just had a very bad council meeting at the City of London, during which the whole scandal had once again been mentioned and Mrs Vince's name insulted in the council chamber. In his letter, Cobbett sent his best respects to Mrs Vince, who had, he hoped, 'too much sense to <u>feel</u> that which <u>all</u> people despise.' It was a curiously clumsy phrase. Maybe Cobbett, who was mapping out his *Advice to Young Men*, realised there would be implications with what he intended to write. When he did write it, Cobbett allowed himself a small get-out clause. If, among other things, the husband had been 'cold and neglectful' to his wife, he wrote, (as Henry Chivers Vince had been to Mrs Vince) then it was all his own fault. Moreover, it seemed to Cobbett that in nineteen out of twenty cases, the infidelity of wives was '*fairly ascribable to the husbands*'. His apparent reasonableness, however, was slightly upset when he added that the woman's family, children and the world would still be right to abhor her.

The year of 1829 would turn out altogether to be a momentous year for both men. Cobbett would face an alleged homosexual scandal, putting more pressure on his already strained family life, and Hunt would terminate their friendship, forbidding Cobbett to write to him or appear at his door ever again – much to Cobbett's dismay and Nancy's delight. There are several extant letters from Cobbett to Hunt through 1829. The last one was dated 21 July 1829 and was almost certainly among the last he wrote to Hunt. In his closing words, Cobbett sent his compliments 'to the ladies.' The 'ladies', of course, included Mrs Vince.

So who was this Mrs Vince, a woman so well known that she was a talking point in society drawing rooms? How did everybody know who she was, although few people in modern times have the least idea about her identity and background? Who was Hunt's beloved, the mysterious woman whom Cobbett referred to so indelicately in the fateful letter to his publisher in 1808 and whom even he came to respect and admire? And how did she compare with Nancy Cobbett who refused to associate with her?

Hunt's lifelong love story was laid before the public in the second volume of his *Memoirs*, which were written in the depth of his misery in Ilchester Prison, or 'Bastile' as he called it. It is a rare piece of early nineteenth century writing. There is little else like it. It was a bold man who could write for public consumption so frankly and in such detail about how he left a wife to set up with another woman.

It may be remembered that Hunt fell impetuously in love with the daughter of the publican of the Bear Inn in Devizes, still a landmark on the town's market square. After a whirlwind romance and despite the discomfort of his father, who thought his eldest son could have done better, Hunt, aged twenty-two, married Ann Halcomb in St John's Church in Devizes on 19 January 1796. The pair set up home together in Hunt's birthplace at Widdington Farm. A year later, on the death of Hunt's father, the young couple moved into Chisenbury House close by, another of the family's leased properties that Hunt inherited. He was later to live there with Mrs Vince. The house, now called Chisenbury Priory, is on the east bank of the River Avon, an elegant mansion with a fine eighteenth century red brick facade. Here Hunt and Ann lived in a busy social whirl, mixing in 'a more fashionable, more accomplished society', as Hunt described it, than Ann was used to, and she may well have found herself out of her depths. Certainly by the turn of the century, Henry was becoming rather bored with poor Ann. He confessed he began to find polished manners rather attractive. Enter Mrs Vince. From Hunt's description, she was physically similar to his late mother, whom he had adored and who, to his lasting grief, died when he was fifteen. His mother had been a tall, slender woman, elegant and 'very fair'. Mrs Vince was physically similar. She was also at least four years older than Hunt. He fell passionately in love. Locked up in his lonely cell in Ilchester gaol, Hunt relived it all in his *Memoirs*:

I frequently met a lady, who had been bred up and educated in the highest and most fashionable circles. She was tall, fair and graceful and, as far as my judgement, went, every charm and accomplishment, both corporeal and mental, that could adorn an elegant and beautiful female, appeared to be centered in her. At first sight I was struck with her superior air and graceful form, but I soon began to admire the beauties of her mind more than I had at first sight been captivated by her person.

Mr and Mrs Vince lived just ten miles away in West Lavington. They had three children, a girl and two boys. Henry Chivers Vince, who came from a well-known Wiltshire family, was one of Hunt's best friends. The couple were part of the social scene. Hunt said that Vince was careless and inattentive of his wife and paid no attention to the fact that she preferred Hunt's company to that of her husband. Hunt and Mrs Vince sought each other out at parties and social occasions. People noticed they were an item, although Hunt stressed the relationship remained platonic despite all temptation. Hunt was an honest man. There is no reason to disbelieve him. Nevertheless, Ann Hunt became increasingly anxious as she could see her husband falling in love with another woman. The situation carried on for two years until 1802 when there was a period of six weeks during which Hunt was unable to see his beloved. He described in his *Memoirs* how he became feverish. (This was the period before Englishmen got a stiff upper lip. In these times, men wept and displayed all their emotions at the drop of a hat.) In his fits of delirium, Hunt raved for Mrs Vince. Ann, who must have been a very generous woman, suggested that Mrs Vince should be sent for.

Hunt recovered his senses but life, he wrote, had become a blank: 'My very soul was absorbed in thinking and longing for the society of one dear object ... I struggled to break the spell, but I found it impossible; every effort that I made, only served to wind it more closely round my heart.' (It can be imagined how well Hunt's *Memoirs* began to sell at this point. This was better than any of the contemporary cheap fictional romances.) Hunt told Ann their marriage was over. The die was cast. He went to Brighton race-week. He knew the Vinces were there. He ordered a curricle, picked Mrs Vince up from where she was staying, and the pair, trembling at the enormity of what they were doing, sped off to London.

Hunt formally separated from his wife. It was agreed that their daughter would stay with Ann, that the two sons should live with Hunt and that both parents would have free access to their children whenever they pleased. His elder son, Henry, born in August 1800, was around two years old by then. His second son, Tom, was born in May 1802 and he remained with Ann until he was five before joining his brother and father. Poor Tom. Despite the amicable settlement, he ended up a very disturbed young man with a major drink problem, running away to live rough in London. Nothing changes.

Hunt gave his wife a liberal settlement of £250 a year and allowed her to take whatever furniture and possessions she chose. The newspapers reported endlessly that he had thrown her out of his house with nothing to her name. 'How incessantly was this falsehood bawled out ... How often was this lie vomited forth upon the hustings', Hunt wrote in his *Memoirs*. Ann herself remained loyal to Hunt. In 1829, she told her son Tom that if he set up business in opposition to his father, she would not advance one penny to help him.

The news of the elopement of Hunt and Mrs Vince was splashed all over the newspapers. It was a big society scandal. Everybody who was anybody knew exactly who Mrs Vince was. She was Catherine Bisshopp, cousin of Sir Cecil Bisshopp, the eighth baronet, whose family seat was the magnificent Elizabethan pile at Parham in Sussex. She was named after her aunt Catherine, who went on to become the second wife of Charles Jenkinson, first Earl of Liverpool, thus becoming stepmother to his eldest son, Robert. The latter was prime minister between 1812 and 1827, and it was Robert Jenkinson's Tory government with its cast of characters, including the foreign secretary, Viscount Castlereagh, and the home secretary, Lord Sidmouth, who would turn the country into a state of fear and oppression and seek to bring about the hanging of Henry Hunt.

To complicate matters, Catherine was illegitimate. She was born around 1769. Her father was Harry Bisshopp, son of the sixth baronet and Colonel of the Cheshire Fencibles. Catherine and her sister, Harriet, were born in Ireland where her father was serving in the army. Colonel Bisshopp returned home shortly afterwards to live in the village of Storrington close to Parham, happily having two more illegitimate children before he made their mother an honest woman and went on to produce a host of legitimate ones.

Illegitimacy was not a big issue in Georgian and Regency England. The Prince Regent and his royal brothers openly flaunted their mistresses and produced plenty of illegitimate children. Many aristocrats lived similar lives. Hence Cobbett's sneering remarks during the Bristol by-election about princes and peers. Parentage was often hazy. Even William Lamb, second Viscount Lord Melbourne, who was Queen Victoria's favourite prime minister and whom Cobbett knew well, never really knew who his father was. Melbourne enjoyed discussing the subject with several of his

Whig peers who were in a similar situation. In his biography of Lord
Melbourne, David Cecil elegantly commented: 'The historian grows
quite giddy as he tries to disentangle the complications of heredity
consequent on the free and easy habits of the English aristocracy.'

At least Catherine Bisshopp/Vince knew exactly who her mother and
father were. The larger Bisshopp family, nevertheless, strongly
disapproved of the fact that Harry's elder children were born out of
wedlock and a cloud hung over his head forever. There was no mention of
Harry's wife in the Bisshopp family's own official records and Harry's
entry was confined to a laconic phrase: 'Born 1745. Died 1821. Colonel
in Cheshire Fencibles.' When Catherine and her sister, Harriet, both got
married in Storrington parish church near Parham during one week in
September 1791, however, their formidable aunt Frances, who was a maid
of honour to Queen Charlotte, was a guest at both weddings. She took the
opportunity to get hold of the parish register to rip out the baptismal
entries of Harry's two other illegitimate children, who were born in Sussex
before their parents got married. No doubt the family shook a collective
head and said – told you so – when Harriet, whose husband unluckily
suffered a massive stroke two years after their marriage, eloped with the
eldest son of the Earl of Portmore in 1801. The story occupied several
columns in *The Times*. When Catherine eloped with Henry Hunt the
following year, there must have been even more rolling of the Bisshopp
eyes.

Such was Catherine's family, rich, well connected and with the usual
skeletons in the aristocratic cupboard. No wonder Nancy Cobbett turned
up her nose at meeting Catherine Vince and detested Henry Hunt as
immoral, dangerous and the man who led her beloved Billy astray. But
could there have been a double edge to her dislike. Could Nancy have
been, well, jealous?

Nancy Cobbett was born Ann Reid on 28 March 1774 in Chatham
Barracks. Her father, Thomas, was a sergeant of the Royal Artillery.
Cobbett first met her in 1787 when he was serving as a regimental sergeant
major in St John in New Brunswick in Canada. He told the story of their
romance in *Advice to Young Men*. Their first meeting was in company. Ann

was just thirteen years old. Cobbett was twenty-four. He thought she was beautiful, but more importantly, he saw that she appeared to have 'that sobriety of *conduct*' of which he so approved. (She did not giggle and flirt.) Three days later he saw Ann Reid again. The setting was the dead of winter and the snow was several feet deep on the ground. Cobbett was taking his usual morning walk when he noticed her in the snow scrubbing out a washing-tub. (Nancy later said it was a tea pot, but she helped her mother wash soldiers' clothes to supplement the family income, so Cobbett was probably right.) Like Hunt, Cobbett fell in love, although his description of what happened years later in *Advice to Young Men* was more prosaic than Hunt's narration of his passion:

Our road lay by the house of her father and mother. It was hardly light, but she was out on the snow, scrubbing out a washing-tub. 'That's the girl for me,' said I ... From the day that I first spoke to her, I never had a thought of her ever being the wife of any other man, more than I had a thought of her being transformed into a chest of drawers. I formed my resolution at once, to marry her as soon as we could get permission, and to get out of the army as soon as I could. So that this matter was, at once, settled as firmly as if written in the book of fate.

The Reids were going to return to England long before Cobbett. Arrangements were made and Cobbett gave Ann a hundred and fifty guineas to use as she chose when she got home. It was around five years before Cobbett got back to England. He rushed off to find his fiancée and marry her. Ann calmly handed him back all the guineas. The enterprising young lady had found a job and lovingly guarded Cobbett's guineas for his return. The couple were married in Woolwich on 5 February 1792. Ann Cobbett signed her name with a cross.

Cobbett loved his pretty, plump wife with her curly dark hair. She was just five feet two inches tall. He called her his 'Nancy' and his 'little girl'. Nancy Cobbett experienced many miscarriages and post-birth deaths, but succeeded in bearing her husband four boys and three girls. Cobbett described his marriage with lyrical happiness in his writings. 'Give me for a beautiful sight, a neat and smart woman, heating her oven and setting her bread!' he wrote in *Cottage Economy*, which was published in 1822 (just when Hunt was criticising Nancy Cobbett in his *Memoirs*). 'If the bustle does make the sign of labour glisten on her brow, where is the man that would not kiss that off, rather than lick the plaster from the cheek of a duchess?' Parts of *Advice to Young Lovers* are an extensive love letter written by Cobbett to his wife, his benchmark for all women, even though Cobbett penned it when he and his wife were going through a major crisis in their lives (partly involving Hunt).

Cobbett did not want or feel the need for the kind of companion Hunt looked for and found in Mrs Vince. Catherine was a highly educated woman with an interest in politics and an astute judgement. Cobbett himself commented on this in a letter to Hunt from America in 1818. Mrs Vince, he wrote, had been quite right in her observations when she observed that Sir Francis Burdett lacked principles and courage. Mrs Vince was with Hunt at a meeting in Barnet in 1819 of a group of reformers when they wisely advised Hunt to cut relations with the dangerous Spencean radical, Arthur Thistlewood. Her presence was mentioned in an angry letter Thistlewood subsequently wrote to Hunt, which was leaked to and published in *The Times*.

By contrast, Nancy Cobbett could not read or write and never learned to do so, despite the literacy of her husband and her children. Cobbett valued her as an excellent mother to his children and for her skills in the home, his farms and the kitchen. It is unlikely that Catherine Vince was able to produce pies and puddings to equal those of Nancy Cobbett, and certainly could not have made the delicious beer that Nancy produced. It is also unlikely that Mrs Vince ever went near a wash-tub. Her servants would have dealt with all that – hence the significance of the unfortunate comment Hunt made to the Cobbetts during his fateful visit in Newgate Prison concerning the filthiness of his friend's breeches, and the comparison with Hunt's own gleaming white cord trousers. Hence too the fury of the Cobbett family when Hunt, from his cell in Ilchester Prison, dared to criticise Mrs Cobbett's inability to retain her servants. Unlike Catherine, Nancy Cobbett had not been brought up to have servants and no doubt thought she could do everything better herself – which indeed she probably could. This would, inevitably, have put their backs up and might well explain why they did not last long in the Cobbett household. 'Mrs Cobbett was, what was called amongst the gossips, very unfortunate in getting maid servants; they seldom suited long together', Hunt wrote bitingly. He could not ever remember going to Mr Cobbett's house and seeing the same maid servants. (There were screams of rage from the Cobbett household when they read that bit in Hunt's *Memoirs*.)

Despite the scandal surrounding Catherine Vince, she had been born and bred a lady and knew exactly how to behave in all circumstances. She was elegant, beautiful and always fashionably-dressed. She came from a handsome family. The portraits of the women at Parham reveal them to have been strikingly good-looking. The eighteenth century writer Horace Walpole commented on their beauty. There was simply no comparison between Catherine Vince and the homely Nancy Cobbett. Although in Cobbett's eyes, his wife was beautiful, she was short, dark and plump, the exact opposite of the fair, willowy Catherine. What was more, Nancy wore very unflattering clothes, including rough flannel underclothes and (gulp) breeches. Cobbett pleaded with her to change her dressing habits in a letter written from Newgate Prison 19 August 1811:

And now, my dearest Nancy, I do hope that you will make yourself easy for a little while longer. I must repeat to you my advice about wearing <u>less flannel.</u> Pray do leave off some of it. It <u>rubs</u> you and <u>scrubs</u> you, all to pieces. I am sure it does you harm; and I hope you will tell William to tell me that you have left off the <u>Breeches</u>, at any rate. I do not like to see you with <u>waistcoats</u> and <u>breastplates</u>, but the <u>Breeches</u> is the worst of all. Now, pray mind what I say about these nasty <u>Breeches.</u>

Not that any of this put Cobbett off. Although he was irritated and infuriated by his wife's depression and anxiety over the future, and wrote to her, sometimes in agony, beseeching Nancy to spare him her laments, Cobbett's letters to his wife from Newgate were in the main fond and affectionate, romantic even. In one, for example, he thanked her for some apricots. They were 'the most delicious things I ever tasted, except your lips, you know', he wrote lovingly. In another, Cobbett told Nancy to 'take a thousand kisses in imagination'. Another time, Nancy was urged to 'kiss all the dear children for me and take, in imagination, a million million of the sweetest kisses for your dearest self'. And oh how often he thought of her dear face and sweet voice.

What Nancy Cobbett and Catherine Vince did have in common was that they both had much to put up with. They were the partners of two of the leading radical reformers of the day and paid the penalty for it. They lived with fear – fear of plots, assassination attempts, violence, exile, prison sentences, financial uncertainty and ruin. Cobbett wrote to his publisher, John Wright, in the autumn of 1805 begging him never to speak or hint in the presence of Mrs Cobbett 'anything relative to my pecuniary concerns or concerns in trade of any sort or kind ... I cannot blame her anxiety; but, as I cannot remove it, it is better not to awaken it.'

Mrs Vince stayed the course. She had her own private money to help bail Hunt out. She was there, loving and supportive, right up to the end. The writer and reformer Samuel Bamford, who was gaoled with Hunt after Peterloo, left a rare glimpse of Mrs Vince and Hunt together in his book *Passages in the Life of a Radical*. Bamford described how he went to London and dropped in uninvited on the couple at their rented house in Wych Street off the Strand (since lost under the Aldwych) in the run up to the trial. They generally only allowed close friends and relatives into their home. Bamford wanted to see Mrs Vince, 'a certain tall and personally fine-looking lady, whose history had excited much of my curiosity'. What he saw made a deep impression. They were a handsome couple in the autumn of their lives, who undoubtedly shared a 'true tender love', he wrote:

Hunt and Mrs V. had, in their early days, evidently been two of the finest of their species; they were as yet neither feeble nor bent, though somewhat marked by years. I compared them to a storm-beaten column and a stately tree, from which the sun was already departing.

Unlike Hunt and Catherine Vince, the Cobbetts did not last the course. Cracks began to appear in Cobbett's family life in 1827 and the situation only got worse after that. Sadly, when Cobbett and Hunt wrote publicly and acrimoniously about each other a few years later, Hunt declared that everything Cobbett ever said or wrote about his family life was a complete and utter lie. There is something heartbreakingly sad that the man who created such a glorious image of family life in his books and who said that happiness should be the object of everyone, spent the last few years of his life bitterly separated from his own family and died determinedly unreconciled with his 'dear little girl' and all his sons and daughters.

Perhaps if Nancy Cobbett had realised that despite her unorthodox lifestyle, Mrs Vince was indeed a virtuous woman, and if she had accepted Catherine's position and befriended her, life might have been a little easier for the two couples. They could have stood together. As it was, Cobbett's family and his friendship with Henry Hunt would eventually fall apart.

5
Pistols and Lamp-Posts

The only lesson we learn from history is that we do not learn from history.
Robert Fisk

Despite the prejudices of Nancy Cobbett, William Cobbett and Henry Hunt embarked on a halcyon period together. It was the calm before the storm. The war against France rumbled on in spite of Napoleon's crushing defeat in Russia in the winter of 1812 when he lost an army of half a million men. At home, the fire of the Luddite movement was spreading to the north of England. It had first begun in the Midlands where highly skilled stocking workers took to smashing the inadequate wide frames they were forced to use to produce cheap and shoddy goods. They got their name, Luddites, because they issued proclamations and notices in the name of the mythical King or Ned Ludd who was linked with the legends of Robin Hood. Now textile workers in Lancashire and Yorkshire were earning the same name for attacking the mills there and trying to destroy the new power-looms and shearing-machines which were throwing them out of work. There were also food riots. Petrified of a Jacobin-style revolution in the country, the government set about suppressing the violence by hangings, transportation and imprisonment.

Cobbett continued with the *Political Register*, although he had to keep a wary eye out. He had completed his prison sentence but was still bound over to keep the peace. If he upset the government during the following seven years, he faced a large fine of £3,000. Mentally bruised and battered from his imprisonment in Newgate, Cobbett soothed his soul by immersing himself in farming and the friendship of Hunt.

Cobbett had moved his family out of Botley House to try to save money. He hoped to rent it out, although he never did. He took out a lease on a smaller house next to the mill opposite just over the River Hamble. The elegant Georgian house, now called Sherecroft, is still there. He also leased 106 acres of land which he began to farm along with some of the neighbouring land he still owned. By 1813, Hunt was living relatively close by. He had moved out of Sussex into Hampshire and was renting a cottage in Middleton, along with the manor of Longparish, near Andover on the then main London road. It was just twenty-five miles away from Botley and was fine sporting country, extending over nearly 10,000 acres and teeming with partridges and pheasants. Cobbett must have rubbed his hands with glee when he heard. Then, in 1814, Hunt took the opportunity to buy the lease at Cold Hanly Farm near Whitchurch (Cole Henley today) when it was put up for auction. The two men were able to indulge in and share their mutual passions for hunting and farming.

Hunt partly decided to rent Cold Hanly Farm because, much as he enjoyed field sports, he missed farming. He was also inspired to do so by Cobbett. The latter badly needed to make some money. He planned to do it by growing wheat, a lucrative crop during the war with France. He was encouraged to do this by Hunt, although both men missed the market. The fine harvest of 1813 produced a surplus and brought the price of corn down. Despite the introduction of a Corn Law in 1815, it would never again rise to war-time prices. Cobbett was to spend his life experimenting on his farms, looking for crops, seeds and methods that would not only bring in some much-needed income but could also be used by people to improve their standard of living. At this point in his career as an innovator, Cobbett was busy reading the books written by the early eighteenth century experimental farmer, Jethro Tull. The latter invented a machine drill and pioneered the system of sowing seeds in furrowed rows or 'drills', as they were called, as opposed to the common practice of 'broadcasting' seed or scattering it on the land by hand. The drills were wide enough to allow farmers to plough, hoe and even grow other crops between them throughout the whole of the growing season.

As soon as Cobbett came out of Newgate in the summer of 1812, he transplanted a crop of Swedish turnips, his famous 'Ruta Baga' (swedes) into newly-ploughed ground, as Tull described. They became, Cobbett said, the largest and finest of all. (Cobbett always said his farming practices resulted in the biggest and the best, while Nancy sighed in the background.) He published in the *Political Register* a letter from one of his fans, who had followed Cobbett's Tullian instructions, grown a wonderful crop of swedes and won a prize of five guineas from the Wharfedale Agricultural Society.

So it was Cobbett's enthusiasm for Tull's methods that inspired Hunt to take the lease on Cold Hanly Farm. He wanted to try them out for himself, as he described in his *Memoirs* years later:

My principal inducement to take this farm, which contained about four hundred acres of land, was my wish to try the experiment of raising large crops of corn in the manner recommended in Tull's Husbandry; which work I had been reading with great pleasure, on the recommendation of Mr Cobbett ... Unfortunately, both Mr Cobbett and myself placed too great reliance on the opinions and assertions of Mr Tull. We both suffered severely in pocket.

Hunt was in a bitter mood when he wrote down his recollections of this period. The collapse of their friendship had soured his memories and he only remembered the bad bits, his financial losses from the farm near Whitchurch (largely his own fault) and the difficulties caused by bad weather. From the tone of the extant letters between Cobbett and Hunt, however, these years in Hampshire together were a high point in their friendship.

Cobbett filled his letters to Hunt with news and enthusiastic reports of his latest agricultural trials, together with comments on Hunt's own experiments. Towards the end of November 1813, Cobbett wrote to Hunt about his newest purchase, one of the new-fangled threshing machines. The farm labourers hated these machines because they put so many of them out of work. Between 1830 and 1831, during the so-called 'Last Labourers' Revolt' or the 'Captain Swing' riots, hayricks would be burned and threshing machines smashed up all over the country as starving men rioted in protest over the lack of work and their desperate poverty. Cobbett supported the down-trodden labourers, his beloved 'chopsticks' as he called them. (He would be so surprised today to find that the word would be considered patronising.) He wrote graphically in the *Political Register* about the greed of the farmers, who kept wages to the bare minimum, and the grinding conditions of the labourers. Nevertheless, faced with ever mounting debts, he was not averse to trying out the new inventions to try to boost his own income.

The letter to his 'dear Hunt' on 22 November 1813 reveals that Cobbett was pleased with his new thresher. It went excellently well with just one horse, he reported. It would certainly thresh a load a day. 'I should have answered your letter sooner, but it was not until this day that the machine was tried', wrote Cobbett. He commiserated with Hunt over one of his experiments with his wheat: 'I am sorry for the result of your steeping adventure. But, it is no more than you had reason to expect. Nature never called for, nor tolerated such violences against her.'

Hunt's 'violences' had become a joke between the pair over the years. As part of the fall-out from the Bristol election, Hunt was sued by a man who claimed Hunt owed him money for his services during the election. In fact, the man had not only volunteered to help Hunt, he had also sold gossip and information about him to his political opponents. Hunt represented himself in court and was complimented by the judge for his 'moderation'. The judge was none other than Cobbett and Hunt's old adversary, the former attorney general, Sir Vicary Gibbs, who, Hunt had unwisely said at a public dinner in 1811, would 'admirably grace a lamp-post'. In the *Political Register* of 11 September 1813, Cobbett reported Gibbs' compliment to Hunt, and re-capped on the history between the pair. Perhaps rather undiplomatically, Cobbett reminded his readers of Hunt's remarks about Gibbs at the dinner in 1811, how they were taken to be an indication of Hunt's 'savage and blood-thirsty mind', and how 'envious miscreants in London' (the poet and publisher Leigh Hunt and his brother) had offered themselves as witnesses if Gibbs decided to prosecute. What must everybody be feeling when the very person who Hunt implied should be dangled by his neck until he was dead was now complimenting Hunt on his moderation, Cobbett crowed. That was one in the eye for all their enemies including the reptile press.

Hence the allusion in Cobbett's letter to Hunt in November 1813 about his 'violences'. Hunt may have laughed wryly as he read the lines.

The friendship continued to flourish. At the beginning of 1814, Cobbett was in London, where he regularly stayed to keep a toe-hold in the great wen, catch up with the capital's gossip and run his publishing business. His thoughts were with his 'dear Hunt', and he sat down to write his friend a long letter. If the bad January weather were to improve, wrote Cobbett, he would drop in on his way back to Botley and take a look at Hunt's wheat. His own had been such a success that he was now planning to sow even more. He hoped to raise enough seed both for himself and

Hunt to use in two years' time. He had also thought long and hard about Hunt's idea to plant more wheat rather than root crops and considered it to be a good one. Even though all his own root-crop plants were prepared and the ground richly manured in readiness, he would take Hunt's advice and plant wheat instead, and Cobbett continued: 'I must <u>see</u> you before I can say half what I have to say to you upon this matter; but I could not refrain from saying this much, lest you should go to plague yourself with any of these bulky matters.'

Thus wrote the older man in fatherly tones to the younger. He knew Hunt would otherwise agonise over what he had said to Cobbett regarding planting wheat instead of swedes, and what Cobbett was going to do about it.

Hunt was a supremely confident man but he worried about his friendship with Cobbett. He had good reason to do so. Nancy Cobbett was, as usual, upsetting Cobbett with her complaints about his acquaintance with that 'bad man', as she called Hunt, and the 'whore' he lived with. Hunt recorded in his *Memoirs* that he was constantly fearful that Nancy would poison Cobbett's mind against him and succeed in wrecking their friendship. He knew she complained about him to Cobbett's friends and acquaintances, hoping that they would report back to Cobbett and increase the pressure on him to abandon Hunt. It may be inferred that around this time, something happened which made Hunt believe that he was banned from visiting Botley altogether, and that he had written to Cobbett asking him whether it was true. In a reply written from London on 5 February 1814, Cobbett vehemently denied that Hunt was forbidden to visit Botley:

The former part of your letter requires no answer; but the latter part does. No, you are, in <u>no manner</u>, forbidden to go to Botley and will never be to <u>any dwelling of mine</u>. These 'prejudices' of which you speak have no weight at all on my conduct. If they had, I should hate myself, as a most contemptible fellow. I have been detained here much longer than I expected; and I must return by Alton and Twyford, or I shall go round and see you, though this is, really, no time for looking at land.

There was another reassurance for Hunt from Cobbett in the second part of his letter. It may be guessed from what he wrote that Hunt was trying to tie Cobbett even closer to him, suggesting that they should start up a Tullian Society together. Hunt, who wore his emotions on his sleeve, had even told Cobbett of his reason. The suggestion made Cobbett laugh. Nothing, he wrote, could break their friendship – unless Hunt chose to do so himself: 'As to the Tullian Society, there is nobody but you and I, who, at present would meet. However, as to your chief reason for the proposition, it is good for nothing, for you may be assured, that if our intercourse cease, it will be your own choosing.' This assurance would haunt both of them fifteen years later.

The harvest of 1814 was an excellent one. Once again it meant that prices would be kept down by a surplus of grain. Nevertheless, Cobbett was happy with his wheat crops. By June, he was writing to Hunt that, with the exception of one field, his drilled winter wheat was so good, he was going to harvest far more than his neighbour. He was very grateful to Hunt for sending him the mouse-poison which appeared to have been very efficient, 'I had great need of it for the damned vermin were doing great mischief', wrote Cobbett.

By July, there was jubilation in an excited note Cobbett dashed off to Hunt:

I have only just now received your 2 letters. I set out on Wednesday morning and I must be at Winchester on Thursday morning at 9 o'clock. I cannot, therefore, go to your home this time. Almost the whole of the heavy hand-cast wheat is down in my neighbourhood. Mine stands like a post.

By 23 August 1814, Cobbett needed more of the poison that Hunt had promised to send. He had examined all the fields of wheat in the neighbourhood and it looked as if his own winter wheat was very little blighted, if at all, by comparison. Meanwhile, his spring wheat was beautiful, the straw bright as silver and the grain plump and thin-skinned.

It looks as if Cobbett got one or several of his children to write that August letter, something he did regularly to improve their writing skills. A star was carefully inserted next to the word 'poison'. It referred to a note at the top of the page, which informed the reader that the poison was, 'For mice, eating newly-sewn peas'. The words were written in a young child's careful, rounded hand. As the letter went on, the handwriting altered, the words became larger and larger and there was a mistake in the last line. It said that a neighbour was 'staggered' (by Cobbett's results) and would 'sow his wheat broadcast next season.' The child must have missed out the word 'not' before the word 'sow', which was slightly fluffed. Did the writer's attention wander? In 1808, Anne Cobbett, then aged thirteen, confided in her diary that her father made her copy all the letters he wrote to teach her how to write: 'Not amusing letters to me, at all. Politics, coursing, field sports, planting, etc. etc. etc.' (All Cobbett's children probably thought the same. The scene can be imagined. 'Oh no, Pa wants to write yet another boring old letter to Hunt and it's my turn to do it.' Snore.)

By 1815, the tone of the letters between the two men had changed. Farming interests were left to one side and politics took over. The pair were busy working together, planning strategies, attending county meetings and writing out their radical resolutions and petitions. The political landscape had changed. Napoleon Bonaparte had surrendered in April 1814 and had been dispatched to the island of Elba, off the Italian mainland. At last, England faced peace.

The farmers and landowners had done well out of the war, selling their grain to the government to feed its armies. The markets had been keen and the prices buoyant, helped by poor harvests and the interruption of trade, and that was how the corn growers wanted them to stay. They were worried that cheap corn would now come flooding in from France and began to panic about how they could maintain their standard of living. The government, they said, could solve the problem by updating the Corn Laws and increasing the level of the home price at which cheaper foreign corn could be imported. The farmers ignored or overlooked the fact that a new Corn Law would not stop prices falling during good harvests or guarantee high prices at other times. They also shrugged off the fact that a loaf of bread would remain expensive to buy.

The government set up special parliamentary committees. Petitions flooded in from all over the country, urging parliament to oppose any decision to pass a new Corn Law. The petitions piled up, largely unread. It was fairly obvious what the decision of the committees would be. Many members of parliament and peers were farmers and landowners with a vested interest in high corn prices. They, too, did not care about the cost of a loaf of bread. What they did care about were the riots in London whenever the subject was discussed in parliament. They viewed the protests as unnecessary violence carried out by potential revolutionaries who had to be suppressed.

As well as the Corn Bill controversy, there was also the thorny question of the war income tax. This fell on those who owned property and land and had an income. The tax had been introduced in 1799 with a government promise that it would be lifted as soon as the war ended. It was repealed in 1802 after the Peace of Amiens, but reintroduced as the 'property tax' in May 1803 after the resumption of the war. Nobody was fooled by the new name. It was still a tax on all forms of income and trade, commercial and professional. Now the wealthy were clamouring for the tax to be abolished. The radicals said that it could only be abandoned if the government cut spending, reduced sinecures, places and pensions and disbanded the army, otherwise, they argued, it was obvious that taxation on goods and services would have to be increased to make up the difference. In other words, the indirect taxes paid by the poor would cushion the lifestyles of the rich.

Cobbett wrote extensively about taxation in the *Political Register*. There were taxes, for example, on tea, coffee, soap, salt, leather, sugar, tea, candles, tobacco and malt, all the necessities of life. All these indirect taxes, Cobbett wrote, were 'grievously oppressive and have produced distress, misery and degradation throughout the whole of the middle and lower classes of the people'. Cobbett had a foot in both camps. As he was himself a farmer, landowner and house owner, he also had to pay direct taxes. These included the property, window and corn taxes, as well as the poor rate, church tithes, taxes on the men he employed and on the horses and dogs he owned. In short, he wrote, life was made thoroughly miserable by the demands of the government which squandered so much of the money on jobs and pensions for the boys.

Although Cobbett worried about the price of a loaf of bread and the plight of the poor, he could also see the situation from the farmers' point of view. He realised that if the government did not cut spending or reduce taxation, a Corn Bill would be necessary to shore up the farmers who would otherwise go bust. He understood the farmers' demand for tighter Corn Laws and excused them for it:

If it be resolved that the taxes *shall not be reduced*, a Corn Bill *must* be made, for, without it the taxes cannot be collected ... It is the *taxes*, the *taxes*, the *taxes*, the *taxes*, the *taxes*. They *do not* keep pace with the price of corn. They fall upon cheap corn with the same weight as upon dear corn ... It is not the *farmer* who wants a Corn Bill: it is *the Government*, that it may be able to get taxes.

This was where Cobbett and Hunt disagreed. Although Hunt was himself a farmer, he was consistent in his opposition to the Corn Laws. He described in his *Memoirs* how he read what Cobbett was writing in the *Political Register* and detected a leaning towards a Corn Bill. As soon as the evidence given before the special parliamentary committees was published, Hunt rode over to Botley to urge Cobbett to take a more decided stand against any move to introduce a bill. His arguments were successful:

I argued the injustice of making the mechanic and the labourer pay a war price for his bread in time of peace and I maintained that it was the duty of the farmer and the landholder to petition for a reduction of taxation, so as to enable him to compete with the foreign farmer, instead of petitioning for a monopoly by his exclusion. In five minutes my friend Cobbett was either convinced of the propriety and justice of my remarks, or at any rate he professed to be so ... from this time forward Mr Cobbett took the most decisive part in opposition to every movement of the Corn Bill gentry.

While Cobbett wrote, Hunt was busy speaking. His old enemy, John Benett, the wealthy landowner from Wiltshire, whose gamekeeper provoked Hunt into the assault which landed him in gaol, had volunteered to give evidence in favour of the Corn Bill to the parliamentary committees. Benett was also drumming up support for the bill at private meetings of farmers, urging them to petition parliament for a new Corn Law. A meeting had been organised at the Lord's Arms Inn in Warminster in Wiltshire at 12 noon on 6 January 1815. Hunt got wind of what Benett was up to. Smelling revenge, he leaped into his gig and whirled off to Warminster.

Taking up position in the Lord's Arms, Hunt ordered a late breakfast. As he ate it, he watched as John Benett and a large group of Wiltshire landowners turned up at the inn. They moved off to the Town Hall nearby, 'as pretty a little snug cabal as ever was mustered upon any occasion. They passed my window and went smirking along, little dreaming that they should meet with the slightest interruption or opposition to their measures', wrote Hunt, enjoying the moment all over again in his *Memoirs*. He followed them in and found that news of his arrival in Warminster had spread around the town like wildfire. The Town Hall was packed with excited shopkeepers and townsfolk and there was standing room only.

Hunt listened patiently while Benett told the assembled farmers that none of the evidence in favour of a Corn Bill given before the parliamentary Corn Committees had been contradicted. The farmers would be ruined if restrictions on cheaper foreign corn were not tightened up. Even the tradesmen and the labourers, Benett claimed, were in favour of a Corn Bill. Finally, Hunt got to his feet. It was an exclusive meeting, he said. It was nothing more than a 'Conclave of Cardinals with closed doors'. They should call a proper public meeting, allow the public to have a vote, not just the farmers and landowners, and then they would hear the real story. The Corn Bill would only benefit the landowners who wanted to keep raking in their high war-time rents. Even the farmers were of secondary importance. More than half the labourers in his home parish of Enford in Wiltshire were already paupers and starving. Over the past thirty years the cost of bread had gone up three times more than wages, while the value of land, owned by landowners such as Benett, had gone up more than six times.

It was all reported in the *Bath Journal*. The meeting ended in tumult and confusion. Most people declined to vote in favour of a petition, and Benett and his cronies were forced to scuttle off to the Lord's Arms to take refuge in a private room (and fortify their spirits). The town crier relayed what had happened at the meeting to the inhabitants of the town, who cheered at the news. To Hunt's delight, the report in the *Bath Journal* was re-produced in several other newspapers including *The Times*.

Just three days after Warminster, Hunt headed off to hijack another rich men's meeting in Wells in Somerset, this time over the abolition of the property tax. He knew that another of his old political enemies, Sir John Cox Hippisley, would be there. (In the past, Hippisley had paid bands of people to shout Hunt down at public meetings.)

Hunt arrived in town and drove through the streets in his tandem. The people rushed out to hail him 'like a hero', he recorded triumphantly in his *Memoirs*. His arguments won an amendment of the resolutions to include a call for the abolition of all wartime taxation, not just the property tax. Mischievously, Hunt also called for a vote of thanks to the government for having recently signed a peace treaty with the Americans, who were, he said, 'the only free remaining people in the world'. His comment infuriated Sir John Cox Hippisley who, Hunt crowed, 'palavered and whined and begged and prayed' him to withdraw the motion. For Hippisley, it was the equivalent of toasting the Jacobins. The Americans were a set of slaves to the French government and he hated them all, Hippisley spluttered to the jeers of the audience.

It was another triumph for Hunt and he wrote to Cobbett telling him all about it, because the latter sat down shortly afterwards on 19 January 1815, and began to pen an article for the *Political Register* about Hunt's achievements. As Cobbett scribbled away at home in Botley, he paused and chuckled at the mental picture that flashed across his mind of Hunt, first in Warminster outwitting Benett, and then just days later baiting Cox Hippisley in Wells. He pushed aside his article for the *Register*, and, taking a clean sheet of paper, he wrote Hunt a quick jubilant note:

My dear Hunt,
I shall be at Winchester early in the morning of the Meeting, at the George. You did B. famously. I know all about the <u>Malt Tax</u>, the date of the law, the amount of the Tax, etc etc etc. When it is to expire and all the rest of it.
I am about Cox H now. That was a good hit.
    Yours faithfully,
    Wm Cobbett

Cobbett's article on the Wells' meeting appeared in the *Political Register* two days later, on 21 January 1815. He was obviously thrilled that Hunt had managed to rattle Hippisley's cage in public, and he taunted Hippisley about his professed hatred of the Americans. Why, Sir John, Cobbett sneered, 'You surely cannot hate them because they keep no sinecure placemen and no pensioners ... You surely cannot hate them because in their country the press is *really* free and *truth* cannot be a libel'. What's more, Cobbett pointed out triumphantly, the meeting had hissed him for saying what he did.

Cobbett was delighted with Hunt's activities and wanted to be in on the action as well. He fully intended to be so in a few days' time in Winchester where the pair planned to take over a meeting organised to campaign for the removal of the property tax. As Cobbett said in his note to Hunt, he would he at the George Inn beforehand and was already mugging up on the tax on malt so that he would have all the facts at his fingertips. (The tax had increased by more than two hundred per cent since 1802 making beer, a staple drink for the poor, expensive both to produce and buy.)

It can only be assumed that Hunt did meet Cobbett at the George before they went together to the meeting. In the *Political Register* of 4 February 1815, Cobbett merely wrote that 'some gentlemen' joined him at the inn at 11 o'clock that morning. In describing the scene, Cobbett only referred to himself. *He* (my italics) got a table close to the fire, at which *he* wrote an alternative petition ready for the meeting. *He* was in such a hurry that *he* had to flap the paper before the fire to dry the ink. When word was brought that the meeting had begun, *he* crammed the paper into his pocket without reading it even once over and rushed off to Winchester Castle, interrupting a speaker in full flow.

Cobbett reported his own speech at length and also re-published a lengthy article from the *Courier*. It can be seen that Hunt addressed the meeting and seconded Cobbett's petition calling for the abolition of all the war taxes, including the malt tax. Cobbett did mention that Hunt was howled down and constantly interrupted, although, he wrote, Hunt managed to make the Whigs feel 'sore'. His report of Hunt's speech is unusually confused and rambling. Putting the pieces of the jigsaw together – Hunt's triumphs in Warminster and Wells and the way Cobbett reported the Winchester meeting – it looks very much as if Cobbett needed to feel that he was in the driving seat, not Hunt.

Events were moving quickly and confusingly. The government caved in to monied pressure and abolished the property tax. It was obvious it was also going to pass a new Corn Bill. While all this was going on, Bonaparte set sail from Elba on 26 February 1815, re-entered France and, to the delight of the reformers, was given a hero's welcome on 20 March in Paris. Cobbett criticised Bonaparte for the 'paltry and nauseous vanity' in which he declared himself emperor, tartly observing that 'talents and courage are not hereditary'. Nevertheless, he considered Bonaparte to be 'a great soldier ... the most skilful and brave captain that ever lived'. Cobbett also admired the Frenchman for his integrity and reforming skills and for the way he had swept away the tyranny of France's Bourbon kings, overturned the other corrupt and despotic European monarchs and abolished the Spanish Inquisition. (This was re-introduced after the restoration of the Spanish king.)

Hunt was impressed with the reception Bonaparte got in Paris. 'If ever there was a legitimate monarchy, Napoleon was now that man; for he was voluntarily elected and placed upon the throne by the united voice of the whole people', he wrote later in his *Memoirs*. The renewal of hostilities against Bonaparte infuriated Hunt. He was outraged that Britain should try to force upon France a government which the people patently did not want. He called on the Westminster reformers (Sir Francis 'Sly-Go' Burdett etc) to arrange a meeting in protest. Much to Hunt's disgust, they dithered and delayed. In wry amusement, Cobbett wrote to Hunt on 5 May 1815 explaining why they were reluctant. They probably felt pretty alarmed at the revolutionary movement Hunt appeared to be setting up, he suggested, with a glint of laughter in his pen:

I should not at all wonder if they move to give up the idea of a Meeting to avoid so dangerous a man as you, whose very name seems to signify pistols and lamp-posts ... The petty aristocrats of the Strand will feel uncommon alarm at the revolutionary movement you are making. I question if the Congress felt greater alarm at the return of Napoleon ... If you were about 4 and a half feet high and built in proportion, the question would be very soon decided. One of the Committee would be appointed to pull you down. But, under existing circumstances, though such a measure may be thought perfectly just, it will not, I am convinced, be deemed expedient.

They would probably discuss the matter in cabinet, Cobbett continued solemnly; they might attempt a coalition against Hunt or they might try negotiation. If they asked his (Cobbett's) advice, he would beg leave humbly to tell them to resolve at once to enlist under Hunt's banners or quit the field forever.

The pair must have laughed at these words but Cobbett's real message to Hunt was contained in a message in the heart of the letter: 'Bodies such as I am speaking of move slowly. The gravity and dignity of their character forbid any thing like precipitation, especially when the matter to be discussed is of so much importance.' The older man was warning the younger to move more slowly, not for the first or last time.

England, meanwhile, was in uproar over the Corn Bill. There were riots in London every night during the week leading up to the passing of the Bill in the House of Commons on 10 March 1815. Vast crowds besieged parliament shouting, 'No starvation! No Corn Bill!' They stopped the carriages of the MPs as they approached Westminster, forcing the quaking men to get out and walk through the crowds to be hooted, hissed and hustled. The attorney general was surrounded. A halter was waved threateningly at him – shades of Hunt's 'lamp-post' threat against the previous attorney general, Sir Vicary Gibbs, four years before. The houses of the hardline barrister Lord Eldon, and the hated foreign secretary, Lord Castlereagh, were among those attacked. Their windows and furniture were smashed. The military was deployed in force and one rioter was shot dead.

During this stormy week, Cobbett forgot all about gravity and dignity when he and Hunt were to be found shoving their way into the council chamber in Salisbury in Wiltshire, pushing the officials back 'step by step and inch by inch, till the worthy Sheriff once more took the chair, amidst the deafening shouts of the largest county meeting that I ever witnessed', wrote Hunt joyfully in his *Memoirs*. He had organised this last-ditch meeting against the Corn Bill with Cobbett's support. They decided on the day to give up the idea of petitioning the House of Commons and direct it instead to the Lords. While they were busy scribbling down a new set of resolutions, the Sheriff took advantage of their absence to open the meeting – and close it immediately. Cobbett and Hunt charged off to the Town Hall, catching the Sheriff and his men still inside. Forcing their way into the building, they slowly advanced up the passageway side by side, their supporters surging in behind them. Hunt recorded the rough, picturesque stuff in his *Memoirs*. Cobbett selected the respectable details to relate in the *Political Register*.

It was a spectacular affair. Two loaves of bread, one large, one small, were carried into the council chamber stuck on two long poles. The large loaf was decorated with ribbons, while the small loaf was draped in mourning crape. This was almost certainly Hunt's idea. It was reminiscent of his arrival into Bristol during the 1812 by-election. Cobbett might have been privately amused, but he clearly wanted to disassociate both himself and Hunt from any accusations that they had tried to stir up the people to violence. He reported gravely in the *Political Register* of 11 March 1815 how Mr Hunt asked that the loaves be removed at once in case the sight moved the crowds to riot. There was no attempt, not even the smallest, stressed Cobbett, to inflame or to mislead. Nobody tried to stir up the labourers to cut the throat of his employer or to set fire to his house or barns. The conduct of the people was equally good, wrote Cobbett. There was not a word of violence or folly. He did report that some boys later paraded a 'thing' through the streets, stuffed with straw to represent a supporter of the Corn Bill. This was hanged and beheaded outside Mr Hunt's lodging. Cobbett's only comment on this was that the 'fun' ended there. He was very well aware, he wrote, that the establishment and its dirty tricks brigade were very keen to depict Mr Hunt and, by extension Cobbett himself, as men of violence. ('Told you so,' said Nancy in fury back home.) All in all, Cobbett went on, he was impressed with the way Hunt handled the whole event: 'Mr Hunt gave early proof of his desire to discharge this duty and of the weight which a man may have with the people if he proceed in the right way'.

The rioting continued in London when the Bill went up to the House of Lords a few days later. The streets surrounding parliament were blocked off with double barricades of timber and artillery cannon were placed at strategic intervals. The cavalry was out in force and the infantry ready and waiting with bayonets fixed. The Lords passed the Corn Bill on 20 March 1815.

Shortly afterwards, the government re-introduced the property tax. The tax was not lifted, even after Napoleon was finally beaten by the Duke of Wellington at the Battle of Waterloo on 17 June and safely exiled to the British-held Island of St Helena in the middle of the South Atlantic Ocean. The campaign against the tax was to begin all over again.

Towards the end of July 1815, Hunt paid the penalty for the stress and pressure he was living under, galloping up and down the country, attending meetings, under attack from the 'loathsome' newspapers, as he called them. (Cobbett compared the proprietors to 'insects which fatten in a poisonous atmosphere'.) Hunt was at home in Middleton Cottage near Andover when he woke up with a violent headache. It was like the ringing of a church bell in his ear, he later wrote, and he could hardly see or speak. The 'horrid roar' in his ears became like the singing of a tea kettle and it was several days before he could walk. The doctor ordered him to cut out alcohol, eat little meat, exercise regularly and lose a pound of blood at least once a month for a year. (The attack presaged the heart trouble that would finally kill him.)

It took Hunt months to recover, although he still hoped to go with Cobbett to the Weyhill sheep fair outside Andover in October as they had planned. Cobbett wrote to Hunt from Botley on 2 October 1815 and said that he would only accompany Hunt if the latter felt up to it:

I shall, agreeably to the information and kind invitation contained in your letter, set off either on Thursday about noon or on Friday morning. I must have you with me, if possible, for I am an utter stranger to the business. Nevertheless, being a pretty apt scholar, I will venture alone, much rather than expose you to the chance of a relapse.

There was another letter from Cobbett to Hunt on 24 October 1815. Cobbett was happy to hear that Hunt was getting better, even though progress was slow. He gently teased his friend who, as Cobbett so well knew, never did things by halves:

I need not say that I am very happy to hear that your restoration to health is regularly advancing. The slowness of the progress is of little comparative consequence, though it does not square so well with the impatience of a man who has for so many years exceeded all others in bodily exertion.

It would appear from this letter to Hunt that Cobbett did meet up with him at Weyhill and considered Hunt's observations of the animals. He bought various flocks of ewes and had them herded back to his farm in Botley. Cobbett's letter reported that the sheep were safely in his meadow munching on fine hay and mangle wurzles, and he paid graceful tribute to Hunt for his knowledge and experience. Cobbett's words of praise are fatherly, as if he were congratulating a son. Hunt must have written previously to Cobbett anxiously asking if his observations at Weyhill had hit the mark. In this letter, Cobbett's words were reassuring:

You have very accurately described the opinions and contrasting interests which prevailed at the sheep fair at Weyhill, and, in that description I have sufficient evidence of the undiminished clearness and strength of intellect which mark all your expressions.

Hunt, wrote Cobbett, would be pleased with the 'care and judicious feeding' the sheep were getting. The 'cheap-corn farmers' had almost forgotten their own miseries to rejoice at his folly in buying them. They all agreed that Cobbett would lose his money and the lambs would starve to death. Even the farmers' wives pitied his sheep. 'Their husbands will do well to lay in a good cargo of gin to keep up their spirits under such melancholy reflections', he joked.

The letter ended with the reassurance that everybody at Botley was very pleased to know that Hunt was getting better. 'For in spite of all damnation settings on and perverse prejudices, there is here a great deal of kindness of heart', wrote Cobbett.

In a postscript he told Hunt it was so wet, the coppices were like rivers.

6
Spa Fields

Poor naked wretches, wheresoe'er you are,
That bide the pelting of this pitiless storm,
How shall your houseless heads and unfed sides,
Your loop'd and window'd raggedness, defend you
From seasons such as these? O, I have ta'en
Too little care of this!

King Lear

Nobody walking up Margery Street off the busy Farringdon Road in
London today would have any reason to know that on the morning of 15
November 1816 thousands of people were streaming up what was then a
track close by in the fields, past the Spa Fields Cake House (the Old Pie
Shop) at Coppice Row Gate, heading for the tavern at the top of the hill
called Merlin's Cave. Behind them loomed the awful House of Correction
in Cold Bath Fields (at the time of writing this, Mt Pleasant Sorting
Office).

The first Merlin's Cave tavern was built in the early eighteenth century
near London's major fresh water source, the New River Head, and Sadler's
Wells Theatre. It was a popular refreshment house with extensive public
gardens and a skittle ground, and was situated at the top of the hill in the
fields above Clerkenwell, which were then known as Spa Fields. The track
to the top of the hill followed a diagonal from what is now the corner of
Farringdon Road and Rosebery Avenue to where Margery Street meets
Amwell Street. Some may remember the pub of that name there in the
twentieth century. In the 1970s, the blues jazz singer George Melly,
among others, performed at Merlins' Cave. The pub was finally
demolished in 1999. There is no trace of it left, although one of the streets
nearby remembers it in its name of Merlin Street. Sadly there is no plaque
to the famous tavern nor what took place there on that historic day in
November 1816 and on two more days shortly afterwards.

On that blustery winter's day in November, Merlin's Cave was crammed
to bursting point. Not only had it filled up with excited local customers but

also with spies, journalists, policemen and magistrates. They had been there since the crack of dawn, turning the tavern into an impromptu operational headquarters. They were all waiting for the arrival of one man, Henry Hunt, now the most exciting of all the public speakers, who was due to speak that day at what was to be the first of the three public meetings of Spa Fields. It was at Spa Fields where Hunt, ably supported by Cobbett's pen, established a public platform to campaign for parliamentary reform and one man one vote that would spread across the country.

Much had happened in the twenty months since Cobbett and Hunt shoved their way into Salisbury's Town Hall to protest against the Corn Bill. The Duke of Wellington had smashed Bonaparte's army outside Brussels at the Battle of Waterloo on 18 June 1815, finally ending the long war with France. After the joy of the celebrations had come the reality of peace. The government thoughtfully kept an army to be used against any unrest and potential Jacobin revolutionaries at home. But thousands of soldiers and sailors were demobbed, many of them without being given their pay or their hard-earned bonuses – even those who fought at Waterloo. The roads of England were busy with desperate men, hurrying along, hunting for a job.

Britain's ex-war heroes were in competition with thousands of people in a similar position. The rains that turned the coppiced woods in Botley into rivers, as Cobbett described to Hunt in October 1815, continued to fall in 1816, destroying much of the harvests. What corn there was fetched a high price, but there was not nearly enough. Staring ruin in the face, the farmers laid off their labourers in droves. In the towns and new industrial cities, textile workers continued their Luddite-style protests against reduced wages and the loss of jobs. Life was becoming desperate. The new Corn Law kept cheaper foreign corn off the market. The price of a loaf of bread soared to a new high. Hunger and unrest stalked the land.

Cobbett and Hunt blamed the situation onto what they considered to have been an unjust war against France, the main object of which, they said, had turned out to be the stifling of civil, political and religious freedoms. People, they said, faced heavy taxation as a result. Cobbett analysed the political situation and recorded the scenes across the country in the *Political Register*. In March 1816, three hundred labourers had applied to him for work. He was unable to employ any of them. Their distress was appalling and it was a common sight, he wrote: 'I see scores of young men, framed by nature to be athletic, rosy-cheeked and bold ... I see them thin as herrings, dragging their feet after them, pale as a ceiling and sneaking about like beggars.'

Later that month there was more from Cobbett's pen in the *Register*:

It is now become a common practice to *discharge* almost the whole of the labourers, send them for relief to the *parish* and then to *hire them of the parish* at sixpence a day; thus reducing them to the lowest possible scale of bodily sustenance and degrading them to nearly the level of beasts.

Was nobody responsible for this terrible misery? Cobbett asked: 'Shall we endure all this misery without *calling to account* those, who have had the management of our affairs?' By April 1816, he was reporting the increasing numbers of farmers who were going bust: 'The sales by distress warrants for rent and taxes have become more and more common. The property at these sales is really *given away* ... Hundreds quit their farms by *night*, steal away their goods and flee the country.'

By June 1816, there were riots in East Anglia. Cobbett quoted reports from a Norwich newspaper of labourers smashing up threshing machines, burning down barns, corn stacks and rich men's houses and attacking mills. Their cry was for cheaper bread. Marches were taking place in the dead of night and people were arming themselves with iron spikes and wooden staves, brickbats and stones, guns and pitchforks. The cavalry, dragoons and yeomanry were being called out against them. There were also disturbances in the north of the country. The newspapers called the rioters insurgents, savages, villains and monsters. Cobbett hit back: 'The fact is, they are people in *want*. They are people who have *nothing to lose*, except their lives'.

People flocked to escape the miseries of Britain. The newspapers reported in one month alone that more than two thousand passports were granted to people wishing to emigrate to continental Europe. Cobbett pointed out that no certificates were needed to go to America, the land of the free, whither thousands of people were heading. The government was so upset by his reports about the opportunities and standard of living in America that it organised the interception of parcels of American newspapers sent to Cobbett in England, and charged him large payments for delivery.

There were riots in Somerset and in Leicestershire. In Nottingham, parts of Belvoir Castle were burned to the ground. In Birmingham, a group of colliers threatened to drag their wagons to London and present the coals and a petition to the Prince Regent in person. People were being hanged, transported and imprisoned. 'The most distressing, the most awful scenes are constantly passing before our eyes', wrote Cobbett. He wanted a dispassionate examination of the causes for the misery and unrest in the country. He knew very well that the government was using its spies and informers as *agents provocateurs* to keep the political temperature boiling in order to justify the severe measures of repression. The mainstream press was helping to whip up alarm and fear of an imminent revolution. Cobbett called for responsible newspaper coverage. His words echo down the centuries: 'Let us have *free* but not *mischievous irritating* discussion; let the public be instructed, but let them not be *inflamed.*'

The government had no intention of tackling the distress in the country. The main concern of ministers was how to cope with the rising national debt left over from the war. Viscount Castlereagh, handsome, cold, narrow-minded and hated by the people, was leader of the House of Commons as well as foreign secretary. He could only see what he described as 'the ignorant impatience of the people to obtain a relaxation of taxation'. The fat, libidinous Prince Regent mouthed platitudes about the distress and difficulties of the people, even after the City of London petitioned him personally over 'the afflicting scenes of privations and suffering that everywhere exist'. The causes were 'unavoidable' and any difficulties were merely 'temporary', he wrote in reply. He too was loathed and despised by the people, having run up debts alone of nearly £400,000 while farm labourers were earning a few shillings a week with half of them eaten up by the taxes on necessities. George did nothing to curb his own extravagant spending. In this eventful year of 1816, he persuaded parliament to promise to pay his daughter Charlotte £60,000 a year when she married Prince Leopold of Saxe-Coburg. This enormous sum continued to be paid to the German prince after Charlotte died shortly after being delivered of a still-born son.

The county meetings calling for a reduction in taxes continued. Cobbett and Hunt went along to a couple together, trying to broaden the issue into calls for reduced government spending, a cut in pensions and sinecures and a reformed parliament. In terms of public speaking, however, 1816 was Hunt's year, the year that culminated in the meetings at Spa Fields and in which Hunt became established in the public mind as 'Orator Hunt'. Hunt's political biographer, John Belchem, traced the nickname to the poet laureate, Robert Southey (a former radical, turned Tory). It was taken up and used as a term of contempt against Hunt by the establishment press. Nevertheless, Orator Hunt became the darling of the people. He did the speaking at those dangerous mass meetings, effortlessly controlling potentially riotous crowds, and Cobbett did the writing, producing the popular journalism which informed the people so well. In the run-up to Spa Fields, he began publication of a cheap version of the *Political Register*. It cost twopence. His enemies called it the '*Twopenny Trash*'. (Cobbett liked the name so much, in later years he published a monthly pamphlet called just that.) Much to the government's fury, sales quickly soared to an unprecedented forty to fifty thousand copies a week and grew to a staggering 200,000. By comparison, *The Times* sold about five thousand copies. 'Let Corruption *rub that out*, if she can', Cobbett wrote triumphantly.

These were the strengths of William Cobbett and Henry Hunt and they used them effectively, complementing each other. This was the year when the pair worked together, side by side, at the height of their political strength as a team. It was the perfect partnership.

Hunt's first public meeting in London in 1816 took place on 23 February in Old Palace Yard, Westminster. In those days, both Old and New Palace Yards were busy public places. Today, the latter is a gated area of garden in front of the grand northern entrance to Westminster Hall. In the early nineteenth century, it was a large open space stretching down to the river, bordered on the Bridge Street side by houses. The independent, pro-reform MP for Westminster, Lord Cochrane, lived in New Palace Yard. He simply emerged from the front door of his house, crossed the Yard and walked into Westminster Hall through the grand entrance to make his way

to the House of Commons in St Stephen's Chapel. Old Palace Yard to the
south is now largely lost beneath roads and car parking. Regular public
meetings were held in both Palace Yards, unthinkable today.

On that wintry day in February 1816, people crowded into Old Palace
Yard for a meeting which had been organised by the Westminster
Committee. It had been called ostensibly to protest against the re-
introduction of the property tax and to call for the disbanding of a
permanent army. The committee, however, had an ulterior motive.
Members had been planning for some time to oust Lord Cochrane, whose
reputation had been blackened by a Stock Exchange hoax for which he
had been imprisoned, and have him replaced by the Scottish lawyer and
rising young Whig politician, Henry Brougham, who would thus
represent Westminster alongside Sir Francis Burdett. The real aim of the
meeting was to promote the Whig party and introduce Brougham to the
Westminster voters as an eligible candidate.

Hunt got wind of what was going on and hurried up to London from
Winchester where he and Cobbett had been causing havoc at a meeting
against the property tax. Both men were outraged that the Westminster
Committee or 'Rump', as they derisively called it, was betraying all its
original radical principles and promoting one of the two mainstream
political parties. Hunt recalled in his *Memoirs* how Brougham stood on
the platform 'smirking, bowing and smiling' as resolutions praising the
Whigs were about to be put to the crowds. Hunt stepped on to the
platform and took control of the meeting. To his great delight all eyes were
upon him. It was a big moment. 'I coolly pulled off my hat, and before I
could say a word, I was greeted with a shout that might have been heard
at the Palace and at Brookes's', he wrote. Hunt shot down the attempts to
congratulate the Whigs for their work in parliament, and prevented
Brougham from even opening his mouth to speak. Brougham and his
Whig entourage made a hasty exit from the rear of the platform and
through the King's Arms Inn.

Cobbett reported the event in the *Political Register* of 2 March 1816,
describing how Hunt reminded the crowds that when the Whigs were in
office between 1806-1807 (the Ministry of All the Talents), they had
increased sinecures and pensions, the allowances of the royal family and

income tax. Lord Grenville had not only been first lord of the treasury, but also auditor of the exchequer, so he was in effect watchdog over his own spending. Similarly, the chief justice, Lord Ellenborough, had also sat in the cabinet. This meant he had not only decided on prosecutions but also judged the cases. The Whigs were just as bad as the Tories, Hunt thundered, and would be so again. He was greeted with cheering and applause; the Whigs were hissed and booed, and Brougham and his cronies had slipped away leaving Hunt victor of the field. Cobbett crowed over Hunt's success, taking a potshot at anybody who dared to suggest that the crowds had only applauded Hunt as a popular demagogue:

It was the *matter* and not the *man* that gained the ear and moved the tongue of the Meeting. It was not the *name* of Hunt, which drew forth the applause of so many thousands of men, but the numerous, the interesting, the apt facts, the home truths and the bold and manly manner of stating them.

Cobbett also defended Hunt from an attack by his old enemy, the poet and publisher Leigh Hunt, who wondered in his *Examiner* whether Hunt had been paid by the Tories to bash the Whigs at the Westminster meeting. (It was an accusation that Cobbett was himself to make in later years against Hunt, equally unfairly.) On this occasion, Cobbett was outraged at the slur against his dear friend. His pen was merciless against Leigh Hunt: 'The smallest of reptiles are said to be the most full of spite ... Horse-whipping is out of the question, when it is a pigmy who is saucy', he wrote. (The joke was that Leigh Hunt was six feet tall.) And Cobbett continued:

Maybe Mr Leigh Hunt, author of the everlasting sonnets and a paid-for paragraph monger, feared he would be mistaken for Mr Hunt, the politician, fox-hunter and pheasant-shooter ... I will venture to say that my friend Mr Hunt produced more *political* EFFECT at the last Westminster meeting than Mr Leigh Hunt will have produced at the end of his life even if he should live to the age of Noah.

How Cobbett and Hunt would have enjoyed reading *Bleak House* by Charles Dickens, published long after their deaths, in which Dickens caricatured Leigh Hunt as the ruthless freeloader, Harold Skimpole. The two men were enjoying their political partnership and having fun together. There are several extant letters from Cobbett to Hunt around this time. The subjects included political matters and farming chat. In a letter written from Botley on 16 April 1816, Cobbett promised to send Hunt a side of lamb the following week and invited him to ride over and stay a week when the weather got warmer. He also praised Hunt for being 'a deeper politician' than people might have thought.

The pair both went to the Westminster Committee's anniversary 'purity of election' dinner on 23 May 1816 and laughed together over the failure of Henry Brougham to show up, so fearful he was of having to face Hunt after the verbal drubbing he had been given at the Westminster meeting earlier in the year. Cobbett laughed to himself all over again two years later in exile in America about the incident, relishing how Brougham and the Westminster Committee had developed a devilish aversion to Hunt. He shared his amusement with his readers back home, describing the scene at that May dinner of 1816 in a public letter to Hunt in the *Political Register*:

When *you* appeared in the passage, Mr Brooks, who sat nearest to me, having caught you in his eye ... said in a sort of whisper: 'by --- here is Hunt *too*!' ... You came and took your seat by me and their grimaces in showing you a seat were like those which the devil is said to practice when he crosses himself with holy water.

In September 1816, Hunt was busy speaking at another Westminster meeting called by the reformers over the distress of the country. Peace with France had been made, but what kind of peace was it? Hunt asked. The Bourbons were back on the throne, against the will of the people. Ferdinand, King of Spain, was also back – along with the Inquisition. In England, even the public plunderers could not deny the widespread public distress. Yet the system's friends dismissed sinecures as mere 'flea bites'. It was true that a flea bite was only a 'nasty, dirty, shabby blotch', but they were all being flea-bitten from 'the crown of the head to the sole of the foot', roared Hunt. The only solution was a reformed House of Commons.

The crowds loved it, and so did Cobbett who reported Hunt's speech at length in the *Register* of 21 September 1816. The crowds, he said, ate out of Hunt's hand. Cobbett got his eldest son, William, then aged seventeen, to write a letter to Hunt congratulating him on his success and for having taken refuge in a shop, at least temporarily, to avoid the enthusiastic crowds. 'My father desires me to tell you he admires your modesty in avoiding the greetings of the people very much but that he is very glad you were obliged to give up to them at last', wrote William junior primly.

The following month, Cobbett stayed with Hunt at his Hampshire home, Middleton Cottage, near Andover. While he was there, he wrote an open letter to Sir Francis Burdett, which appeared in the *Register* of 12 October 1816. Cobbett included Hunt's address, Middleton Cottage, at the top of the article, demonstrating to his readers his close relationship with Hunt. The article explored what a reform of parliament could achieve. Cobbett headed the letter with these words: 'What GOOD would a Reform of Parliament now do? And in WHAT MANNER can it take place without creating confusion? Sir, these are the questions which the sons and daughters of corruption *now* put to us'. Cobbett went on to answer his own questions in detail. There were some, he wrote, who believed that if something were not done, the peace of the country could not be preserved and there would be an open rebellion. Unfortunately, the three reform meetings that took place at Spa Fields in Clerkenwell in north London over the following months convinced the establishment that that was exactly what the country was facing – nothing less than a revolution. The meetings would precipitate Lord Liverpool's already tough government into some of the most repressive steps to be taken against human rights and freedom of speech.

The countdown began when Henry Hunt received two letters in the September. The letters came from the Spenceans, followers of the radical bookseller Thomas Spence, who had died two years earlier. Spence had promoted the revolutionary theory that land and wealth should be taken away from the landowners and aristocrats and handed back to the people. The leading Spenceans included Arthur Thistlewood, Dr James Watson and his son of the same name. (Four years later, Thistlewood would lead a plot to kill the top members of the government and lose his life as a result.) In 1816, the Spenceans' letters to Hunt invited him to speak at a public meeting they were organising for distressed workers and manufacturers throughout London, including the notoriously poor weavers of Spitalfields. A petition could then be drawn up to the Prince Regent outlining their poverty and misery and begging for relief. The place was to be Spa Fields and the date Friday, 15 November 1816.

In fact, their goal was far more ambitious than simply to win relief for the poor. The real goal, which they did not, of course, reveal to Hunt, was to use the occasion to precipitate a revolution. Thistlewood had also sent invitations to Cobbett, Sir Francis Burdett, Major Cartwright and several other radical politicians. The Spenceans needed a famous public speaker to attract the crowds. All declined apart from Hunt. He accepted, despite a warning from the ever-suspicious Cobbett that it would be a 'dangerous experiment'. A few weeks earlier, Cobbett had spotted a newspaper report about some placards posted up in London pubs. The language was inflammatory, inciting people to riot or worse:

BRITONS TO ARMS. The whole country waits the signal from London to fly to Arms. Haste, break open gunsmiths and other likely places to find arms! Run all constables who touch a man of us; no rise of bread; no Regent; no Castlereagh; off with their heads; no placemen, tythes or enclosures; no taxes; no bishops, only useless lumber! Stand true, or be slaves for ever.

Cobbett was suspicious about exactly who had posted up the placards and why, and he warned Hunt to be on his guard against spies and informers. He was certain that if Hunt were not careful, a trap would be laid to destroy him. Nevertheless, Hunt accepted the invitation. He got his first whiff of danger when he asked to read the proposed address and resolutions before the meeting. Thistlewood reluctantly agreed to his request. As Hunt read them, a shiver went down his spine. The contents were undoubtedly treasonable. The demands included Thomas Spence's idea to hand land back to the people. Part of the plan included marching to Carlton House to demand a meeting with the Prince Regent. Hunt recalled in his *Memoirs* how he galloped over to Botley to consult Cobbett, who helped him re-draft the resolutions and draw up a safe address to the Prince Regent.

On the morning of the meeting, Hunt met up with Thistlewood to give him the new water-tight resolutions, which now confined themselves to calling for a reform of parliament, and the re-written petition. As they were sorting out the paperwork, a messenger arrived. He was out of breath and excited. Crowds were gathered in front of Merlin's Cave in Spa Fields and they were impatient for the meeting to begin. Hunt and Thistlewood climbed into a hackney-coach and drove to the spot, arriving with minutes to go before the appointed time of one o'clock. Their arrival was hailed with deafening shouts. It was the biggest crowd Hunt had ever seen. (Both Cobbett and Hunt claimed there were nearly 100,000 people at the meeting.) Banners waved proclaiming the words 'FEED THE HUNGRY, CLOTHE THE NAKED'. (The *Courier* sneered at the flag as 'a standard of rebellion'.) The coach had difficulty getting through the crowds to the top of the hill. No hustings platform had been put up and nothing had been arranged. Hunt clambered on top of the coach and prepared to address the people. He was aware that he had been followed onto the roof by a man whom he did not recognise. Much to Hunt's horror, the stranger proceeded to unfurl a large tricoloured flag in red, white and green, the flag of revolutionary France.

The man was John Castle or 'Castles', as Cobbett called him, one of the most notorious of the spies and *agents provocateurs* of the home secretary, Lord Sidmouth. The uninspiring and humourless son of a doctor, Sidmouth was hated by the people. His spy network was extensive. These men hung around taverns and meeting houses, inflaming people's emotions and tricking them into revolutionary conspiracies. They wormed their way into groups like the Spenceans, urging them on to bigger and better conspiracies. They reported back to Home Office HQ in London and were well paid for their work. Castle tricked Thistlewood at Spa Fields; George Edwards encouraged him and his friends, fatally, in the Cato Street conspiracy in 1820. Cobbett had been quite right in his assessment of the potential snares and pitfalls Hunt would be exposed to at Spa Fields.

On top of the hackney coach and surrounded by thousands of people, Hunt had too much to do to worry about Castle and his revolutionary flag. The crowds were growing and needed attention. The wind was blowing so hard he could hardly keep his balance. He jumped down and took refuge in the front upper room of Merlin's Cave from where he addressed the crowds from a window for about an hour. By now Hunt had developed his technique of question and answer routines and jokes. He made the crowds feel as if he were talking to them as individuals – just as Cobbett did with his pen. He spoke their language with passion, making complex issues simple to understand. Given the vast numbers of people that Hunt addressed and how difficult it must have been for everybody to hear, it is an indication of his speaking abilities that he managed to hold their attention and control any potential violence.

At Spa Fields that day, Hunt spoke of the burden of the civil list and the allowances paid to the royal family. He named and shamed the most well-known recipients of sinecures and public pensions, who were paid vast sums of money out of people's taxes, while the people themselves groaned under the weight of taxation. The butchers and bakers, whose shops were so often attacked by people protesting about the high price of food, were not to blame, he said. They too had to pay heavy taxes. Nothing would change, shouted Hunt, until parliament was reformed. The best way of achieving this was by peaceful means and good order. Violence would wreck everything.

The resolutions and petition to the Prince Regent that Cobbett had largely drafted, were unanimously adopted. To Hunt's discomfort, Thistlewood unexpectedly added a resolution that the meeting should reconvene a fortnight later on Monday, 2 December so that Hunt could report back on how the Prince Regent had replied. Reluctantly, Hunt agreed.

In his *Memoirs*, Hunt described how he returned to his inn for a private dinner. It was gatecrashed by a group of people including Arthur Thistlewood and John Castle. The latter proposed a treasonable toast. 'May the last of Kings be strangled with the guts of the last priest', he said, and pretended to fall into a drunken sleep. Hunt resolved never to have anything to do with Castle again and also to avoid the company of the Spenceans for the time being, at least in private.

The first Spa Fields meeting created uproar throughout the country. The press called Hunt all the revolutionary names it could think of. The *Courier* condemned Hunt's speech for having inflamed the people. The newspaper, which supported the Tory government and was paid handsomely for doing so, published one of the original treasonable resolutions drawn up by the Spenceans and claimed that Hunt had proposed it at the meeting. It was obvious that the inflammatory resolutions and address had been leaked in advance, probably by Castle, to the home secretary, Lord Sidmouth, who had passed them on to the *Courier*.

While Hunt waited for a reply from Sidmouth as to how the Prince Regent would respond to the Spa Fields' request, Cobbett remained suspicious and worried. He was convinced Sidmouth was trying to ensnare Hunt and have him hanged for treason, although he did not dare to reveal this publicly in the *Political Register* until he was safely in exile in America some six months later. He wrote a letter to Hunt on 20 November 1816 from a secret address in London, fearing that Sidmouth had them both under surveillance:

I have your letter. If I remain in town till you come again, you shall know where to find me. If Sidmouth sends you an answer before you come, do not send it to me for fear of being opened. I would send him no answer. Write to me under cover to Mr Margrand No 1 New Broad St. Court London. If you come you will hear of me at his office.

Cobbett's letter went on to say that he would be defending Hunt that week in the *Political Register* against the newspaper attacks, and he had a warning for Hunt on how he should now proceed:

The atrocious villains shall not calumniate you at this rate without my speaking. But, be very cautious what you say and more especially what you write. It will be your own fault if you fall into difficulties or disgrace. For me, though I will never be persuaded by you to do what I do not approve of, nobody shall ever persuade me to keep aloof from you, while you act for the good of the country.

Cobbett fulfilled his promise to defend Hunt. He did so in a masterly article in the *Political Register* of 23 November 1816:

Since my long acquaintance with the press, I do not think that I have ever witnessed so much baseness of conduct. If Mr Hunt had been the most notorious pick-pocket, if he had been a ragamuffin covered with a coat hired for the day; if he had been a fellow who took up his lodgings in the brick-kilns or in the niches on Westminster Bridge; and, if he had actually proposed to the Meeting to go directly and plunder the silversmith's shops and cut the throats of all who opposed them; if he had drunk off a glass of human blood by way of moistening his throat ... if he had been and had done all this, the London press could not have treated him in a worse manner than it has ...

All Mr Hunt did, Cobbett continued, was to speak at a meeting to help distressed people. It broke up quietly with no rioting. Was it Mr Hunt's fault that a mob attacked the shops of some bakers and butchers in the evening? After all, Mr Hunt had spent a quarter of an hour trying to convince the people that such violence was wrong. Was it not rather the fault of 'those pestiferous vehicles of falsehood, the *Courier* and *The Times*', which incessantly inveighed against greedy bakers and butchers? As for the attack on the office of the *Morning Chronicle*, that might possibly have been because of something Mr Hunt might have said at the meeting. Was Mr Hunt to endure the newspaper's lies against him for years and never reply? All three papers, wrote Cobbett, had repeatedly called for Hunt to be either hanged or murdered. Why should he worry about a crowd breaking their windows? And, went on wily Cobbett, leaving Hunt an escape route: 'I have no doubt that many things escaped Mr Hunt during his speech that he himself wished he had uttered in more select phrases. But who is there who is so very choice upon such occasions?'

Hunt must have been pleased with this report, but there was something

'Will of the Whisps – or – Glimmerings of Reform'
Hunt drives the coach on the Road to Reform – 'To Chaos' – with Cobbett behind holding a lantern. At the side, Cochrane holds another. Their confused supporters flounder in the 'Quagmire of Sedition'.
Thought to be George Cruikshank, 1817 or 1818.
© *The Trustees of the British Museum*

else of interest for him in this issue of the *Register*. It was a short article revealing the development of Cobbett's thoughts about who exactly should get the vote. Just a few weeks previously, Cobbett had written an analysis of how the voting procedure could be reformed. The day for voting for an annual parliament should be fixed by law, he said. Notices should be put up on church doors in every parish, and the news announced from the pulpit. On the selected day, churchwardens and overseers should assemble at the church where there would be a box into which the voter (a male tax payer) could put his ballot paper. The voter would have previously written or got somebody else to write down the name or names of the men he wished to represent him in parliament. Cobbett was decades ahead of his time. There were still another fifty-six years to go before secret ballots would be introduced.

Hunt had been impressed by what he called Cobbett's 'masterly detail', but he thought Cobbett was wrong not to back one man one vote. To his great delight, Cobbett changed his mind after the first Spa Fields meeting, writing in the *Register* that he had been considering all the indirect taxes people had to pay. The taxes were just as heavy on them as direct taxes were on the wealthy. Cobbett was now convinced that nothing short of universal suffrage would do. All men deserved to have the vote, he wrote. Cobbett attributed his conversion to the persuasions of Major Cartwright rather than to Hunt – something Hunt was to remember with bitterness.

Despite Cobbett's public endorsement of universal (male) suffrage and his stout defence of Hunt, the press attacks against the latter continued. Hunt was a traitor who wanted to overturn the establishment in a bloody revolution, they said. *The Times* urged his assassination. On 21 November 1816, the newspaper announced Hunt's death, claiming that he had got drunk at a gin shop in Holborn, fallen into building work at Waterloo place and had been found dead. A few days afterwards, *The Times* reported that it had been misinformed. Hunt was, in fact, in a 'melancholy state of insanity' in Bedlam (the Bethlem Royal Hospital for the insane in Lambeth). Mrs Vince also received dozens of anonymous letters announcing the death or serious injury of Hunt. It was a difficult time and, on top of that, the second Spa Fields meeting loomed.

Hunt told the Spenceans that he would not speak with them

beforehand. He was going out of London, he told them, and would see them at Spa Fields on the day of the meeting at 1 o'clock precisely. On the Sunday morning, Hunt left London and drove his tandem to a friend's house at Wanstead in Essex. A tandem was a smart two-wheel carriage drawn by two horses, one harnessed in front of the other. On this occasion, Hunt's favourite horse, Bob, was as usual in the lead. Bob was by now famous and instantly recognisable as Hunt's horse. Hunt stayed the night in Essex. Cobbett also happened to be out of town that Sunday night. It was all part of a pre-arranged plan, a good old-fashioned alibi, organised by the far-sighted Cobbett. He had also made sure that his *Letter to the Luddites*, which unequivocally condemned the use of violence and argued that the only way forward was for people to hold public meetings and petition parliament for reform, took up the entire issue of the *Political Register* that same weekend.

Hunt left Wanstead the morning of Monday, 2 December 1816. As he rattled over the cobbles along Cheapside in the City of London, he spotted a crowd heading in the opposite direction towards the Bank of England and Mansion House, home of the Lord Mayor of London. As he sped past Bow Church, he noticed John Castle who was also heading away from Spa Fields. Castle shouted to Hunt that the Spa Fields meeting had broken up, that Dr Watson's son had taken over the Tower of London and Hunt should join them. 'What a ———— scoundrel,' Hunt said to himself (he recorded it thus in his *Memoirs*) and galloped on to Spa Fields.

The crowds had gathered, even bigger than before, and there was a party atmosphere. The radical publisher and writer William Hone described what he saw: 'The Fields at this time had the appearance of a fair, covered with people and stalls for the sale of fruit, gingerbread etc.' Hunt arrived and found the cheers almost too loud to bear. He made his way straight to Merlin's Cave. The police, the press and the magistrates were already installed. There was no sign of any of the Spenceans. Hunt addressed the crowds, first giving them the news of the donation by the Prince Regent of £4,000 to the Spitalfields Soup Committee. The people, he said, should now petition the House of Commons and demand universal suffrage, annual parliaments and voting by ballot. Anybody who committed any act of violence or caused any breach of the peace was the greatest enemy of reform, he warned.

As the meeting drew to a close, Hunt was not surprised to be told there had been serious riots in the city. As he rode back to his inn, he passed the House of Correction in Cold Bath Fields. It was surrounded by police officers armed with sticks. Hunt was proud that despite the number of people following him, they did not break one pane of glass. He managed to get hold of a second edition of the *Courier*. The banner headline screamed accusingly: 'SPA FIELDS MEETING'. Whatever had happened, Hunt knew he was going to get the blame.

The story got wide coverage. Urged on by John Castle, the Spenceans had turned up bright and early at Spa Fields to find a couple of hundred people gathered. Handbills had already been handed out: 'A pot of beer for a penny and bread for two pence: HUNT REGENT and COBBETT KING: Go it, my Boys!' (Cobbett was convinced they had been issued by one of the city's police offices.) The Spenceans addressed the crowd about their plan to distribute land back to the people, shouted they were off to storm the Tower of London and urged everybody to join them. As part of the plot to incriminate Hunt, Castle had wrapped up a few bullets (musket balls and a canister of gunpowder according to *The Times*) in an old stocking, leaving them clearly visible in a waggon.

About forty people, reinforced by a party of disaffected sailors who had mostly been laid off without pay, followed Dr Watson's son. They looted a gunsmith's shop in Skinner Street and made off towards the Royal Exchange opposite the Mansion House, firing the guns in the air as they passed along Newgate Street and Cheapside. A second group looted another gun shop and, led by Watson, marched off to the Tower. Their courage failed when half a dozen mounted soldiers turned up. Later that evening, Dr Watson and Thistlewood were among those arrested. Their houses were searched and every scrap of paper scrutinised to link Hunt or Cobbett to the events. Nothing was found.

The next day, the London papers were crammed full of various misleading accounts of events. They blamed Hunt and included Cobbett. *The Times* called them both incendiaries who 'cast about their fire-brands and arrows'. The *Morning Post* declared that both men should 'lose their lives'. One newspaper, the *Antigallican,* published a drawing of a hangman's noose.

Cobbett rode to the rescue in the *Political Register* on 14 December 1816 in the shape of a public letter to Hunt, who re-printed it in full a few years later in his *Memoirs.* Cobbett backed Hunt to the hilt but also slipped in a host of subtle warnings and advice for him. The letter began in Cobbett's best lyrical prose:

Sir. The summer before last, when you came over to Botley and found me transplanting Swedish turnips amidst dust and under a sun which scorched the leaves till they resembled fried parsley, you remember how I was fretting and stewing; how many times in an hour I was looking out for a south-western cloud; how I watched the mercury in the glass and rapped the glass with my knuckles to try to move it in my favour. But great as my anxiety then was and ludicrous as were my movements, ten thousand times greater has been that of Corruption's Press for the coming of a PLOT ... They sigh for a PLOT. Oh, how they sigh! They are working and slaving and fretting and stewing; they are sweating all over; they are absolutely pining and dying for a Plot!

The newspapers were claiming, Cobbett continued indignantly, that he and Hunt had met beforehand with Lord Cochrane in the King's Bench Prison and cooked the whole thing up between them. What a lie! In fact, Hunt had been at Wanstead in Essex, while he himself had been at Peckham in Surry. They had witnesses to prove it. (They had, indeed, thanks to Cobbett's foresight.) There were a hundred other falsehoods from the 'sons of Corruption'. *The Times* had even written that Cobbett's own son, William, had been involved and might be charged along with everybody else with a crime against the state. This had greatly alarmed his mother and sisters and was, of course, another lie. (Nancy must have hit the roof. 'Oh Billy, for God's sake! What next!') Cobbett continued gravely, addressing Hunt directly:

You, conscious of your honourable motives, and listening only to your courage, have always been deaf to the entreaties of those who cautioned you against the danger of spies and false witnesses ... Do you think that men so lost to all sense of shame, and so devoted to everything that is corrupt, do you think they would hesitate one moment to bribe villains to swear falsely against you or against me or against any man, whom they thought it their interest to destroy? ... Be you assured that there is nothing of which such men are not capable.

Nevertheless, Cobbett went on, the campaign to put Hunt down had failed. His speeches, the resolutions and the petition, the punctuality and decorum of the proceedings, all entitled him to public applause. If there had been any 'momentary errors and indiscretions' arising from 'an excess of zeal', they would not be remembered. People could see for themselves that when Hunt spoke with violence, he was only attacking a violent thing. Hunt's portraits, by three different artists, were now in the shop windows. His speeches and resolutions for a clean up of parliament were being cried through the streets and sold in separate editions. The talk in the taverns and pubs was all of Hunt. The 'vipers' had made his name famous throughout the land. The newspapers had reported that 'Hunt was SEEN, in his Tandem, going towards his home on Thursday last!' They seemed to think the public was more interested in Hunt than they were in the Prince Regent or the Queen. Hunt's tandem, wrote Cobbett, was now more famous than the royal coach, and his horse, Bob, more famous than the charger of Old Blucher: 'They have made you the only one of your kind; there is now but one Mr Hunt in the world. Your ambition must be a cormorant indeed, if this does not satisfy it.' Then followed Cobbett's thrilling warning to Hunt. As 'the vile men' had added to his power of serving his country, Hunt could now safely moderate his zeal:

Guard against this excess in future. Take in a little sail and add a little to your ballast. Exchange a little of the courage of the lion for a little of the wisdom of the serpent. Give up a little, and only a very little, of the stubborness of the oak, for a little and only a very little, of the pliancy of the reed. Do this and trust to the folly and knavery of these stupid and malignant wretches to make you a great man.

It was a masterpiece of writing, Cobbett's pen at its best, a powerful mixture of praise, love and caution. Never did Cobbett write about anybody as he did about Henry Hunt. The conversations the pair had together may be imagined; Hunt, the younger man, still inexperienced in politics, impatient and ambitious; Cobbett, admiring Hunt's qualities and enjoying his fire and enthusiasm, but ever concerned to warn him about the pitfalls and snares. Cobbett also made Hunt strong promises. This is clear from one short letter Cobbett wrote to Hunt that survived. It is undated and only says 'Monday Evening' at the top. From the letter's tone and content, it is reasonable to guess that it was written around this

time, when Hunt attended a meeting at the City of London's Common
Hall and refused to consider a reconciliation with the moderate reformers
who were critical of the Spa Fields meetings. Hunt must have asked
Cobbett for support. This is how Cobbett replied in the letter:

> I am, my dear Hunt, incapable of doing what we talked of, until I know <u>what</u> has taken
> place at C. H. ... But, I will <u>go to you</u>, if necessary, <u>tomorrow evening</u>. It is, I hope, quite
> unnecessary for me to repeat my assurance that nothing short of sickness or death shall
> ever deprive you of the fulfilment of my solemn promise made this day. But, I beseech you
> be careful to do nothing to expose yourself to the treachery of villains. You have a host of
> enemies now even greater than I have. I beg you, therefore, to be on your guard.

What was Hunt's request? It was a very solemn promise indeed. Only
sickness or death was to prevent Cobbett fulfilling it. Was it to help Hunt
become an MP or was it, more generally, to help him whenever he needed
it? There can be no firm answers. Subsequent events, however, would
suggest that it was a promise Cobbett did not keep.

Hunt was, meanwhile, making preparations for the third Spa Fields
meeting scheduled in the New Year, for Monday, February 1817. In the
middle of it all, he received an invitation from the reformers of
Portsmouth to chair a meeting on Portsdown Hill. Cobbett suggested that
as Hunt was so busy, he would answer for him and arrange the details. The
date Cobbett agreed with the Portsmouth reformers happened to be the
very day when Hunt would be busy at Spa Fields. Cobbett said he would
go to Portsmouth in Hunt's place with Lord Cochrane. In his *Memoirs*,
looking back at events, Hunt was annoyed that 'a good deal of trickery
and management' prevented him from taking up the invitation himself.
'I had no suspicions that my friends were jealous of me', he wrote.

At the time, however, Hunt agreed that Cobbett should go in his place.
The pair made arrangements to raise three cheers at both meetings just
after 2 o'clock. (There were several other meetings held that day around
the country and similar arrangements were made for them.) *The Times*
reported the cheering at both Spa Fields and Portsdown Hill according to
the arrangement. The newspaper also sharply commented that Cobbett
and Lord Cochrane had only gone into Hampshire 'in order to keep clear
of Hunt'. Cobbett described the loud cheers at the Portsmouth meeting
in the *Register* but he did not link them with, or mention, Hunt and Spa

Fields. He practically filled one entire issue of the *Register* with the success of the Portsmouth meeting, reporting that 20,000 people turned up. He made no reference to the third and final Spa Fields meeting which had been going on peacefully and successfully at the same time.

Although the friendship of the two men at this time was a glorious one, the clues reveal whiffs of jealousy on Cobbett's part. Cobbett was to suffer badly from the green-eyed monster. In later years, his jealousy of Hunt was to make him almost mad. That was not the case at this moment in their history, although the signs are visible. While publicly praising Hunt to the skies, Cobbett kept himself firmly in the picture too. Cobbett was Cobbett, the man with the most influential pen in the country, the man who informed the people, the man whom the government would also like to get rid of. It was his boy who had triumphed at Spa Fields, despite the misgivings of the other reformers, just as he, Cobbett, had predicted. In the *Register*, published just two days before the third Spa Fields meeting, Cobbett proudly described Hunt as '*Mr Hunt, Hunt the Great,* for I foretold that the stupid malice of the corrupt would make him a *great man*'. Hunt was a 'great man', but it was Cobbett who had helped to make him one.

It was only in retrospect, after Cobbett had abandoned him, that Hunt detected Cobbett's jealous jostling for position. Hunt was a good-natured man. Even the nineteenth century biographer Robert Huish, who did not like him, wrote of Hunt's 'open, straight forward manliness'. According to Huish, Hunt had 'innate pride, a noble sense of honour about him, which would not let him stoop to a mean or pitiful action'. At that third Spa Fields meeting, Hunt was so proud of his famous friend, he informed the crowds that Mr Cobbett was his 'great teacher in politics ... who had always been his friend and whom he hoped he should continue to call so to the latest period of his existence'. Hunt's remarks were reported in *The Times*. Their friendship was at its height and Hunt had no cogent reason at this point to suspect or question Cobbett's motives.

Cobbett probably did go to the Portsmouth meeting because he wanted a taste of the glory and excitement too. He may have also been concerned at what exactly was going to happen in London, as *The Times* so crudely suggested. Before leaving for Portsmouth, Cobbett warned his children not to leave their house in London on the day of the meeting. He was right to be cautious. Castlereagh gave orders beforehand that the crowds were to be dispersed by military force. There were also plans to shoot Hunt. (This information came from the diarist Captain Rees Howell Gronow. He told Hunt in later years that he had him in his sights and had been prepared to pull the trigger.) As Hunt drove into town, he saw nine pieces of artillery being pulled over Blackfriars Bridge by men from the Woolwich Arsenal.

The third and last Spa Fields meeting passed off without incident. The sinister plot makers had given up for the time being. The government, however, was drawing up the draconian measures it hoped would make life so difficult, not just for Cobbett and Hunt but for all the radical reformers, they would simply have to abandon the cause. The government war on what it saw as 'Terror' was about to begin.

7
Flight

The age-old technique of any authoritarian or repressive government has always been to exaggerate the terrorist threat to justify their actions.
Liberal Democrat, David Heath MP, 2006

The political temperature was rising. The corridors of power were filled with anxious talk of a revolution. Government ministers were holding crisis meetings. Pep talks were being given to their minions. Letters were intercepted and copied. The originals were destroyed or sent on, the recipients unaware of the copies lying on official desks in London. Top secret notes and documents flooded in to the Home Office from across the country, dispatched by spies, informers, anonymous 'gentlemen', Justices of the Peace and police chiefs. They told of illegal meetings, dark plots, seditious conversations, unrest and disturbances. Home Office papers reveal that the notoriously corrupt deputy constable of Manchester, Joseph Nadin, described big angry meetings of the 'lower orders', at which there were calls for a general union to be set up covering the entire country. It went to prove beyond doubt that sedition, conspiracy and a bloody Jacobin-style revolution were close at hand. The floodgates had opened and life as everybody knew it was in imminent danger of being washed away in a sea of blood.

Hunt and Cobbett were firmly in the eye of the storm. In between the Spa Fields meetings, Hunt went to Bristol at the end of December 1816 to encourage the city to raise its own petition for reform. He arrived to find the city like a besieged fortress. The cavalry corps from Trowbridge and Dorchester had been deployed along with the North Somerset Yeomanry. Just to be on the safe side, the Bristol authorities had also signed up 2,000 men as special constables for the day. Despite the show of force, thousands of people flocked to hear 'Spa Fields' Hunt speak. He did so in the pouring rain from his gig parked on Brandon Hill. The city authorities had banned the erection of a hustings platform. 'We want no tumults, no riots, we want only our rights', he shouted to cheers and thunderous applause. There were similar scenes a week later when he went to speak in Bath.

Cobbett accused *The Times* and the *Courier* of eagerly anticipating a blood-bath at Bristol. 'Raven-like, they are now croaking for blood', he wrote. He gave wide coverage to Hunt's meetings at Bristol and Bath in the *Political Register*, even spending Christmas Day of 1816 busily preparing articles for publication. In the issue of 18 January 1817, Cobbett pointed out that many thousands of men had assembled at Bath 'in the most peaceable manner'. He urged trades people to hold meetings but to do so openly, without secrets and without disguises. He also included a vivid description of starving labourers who had no meat to eat and only water to drink:

A short smock frock is the general garment and not only are many of these made of sack-cloth but I have seen many actually made out of old sacks which had become too rotten to hold corn! ... Many of them have no stockings, bits of rag are wrapped round their feet to keep their feet from perishing in their shoes and pieces of old sack or rags of some sort are tied round their legs instead of stockings.

The government ignored or refused to acknowledge the underlying message of what was going on. Its spies and agents worked overtime, spinning plots and tales of conspiracies to keep their London masters happy. Not everybody was convinced. The liberal Whig, Lord Holland, described in his *Memoirs*, which were published decades later, how 'Lord Sidmouth ... listened with inauspicious complacency to every tale which officious magistrates and designing spies brought of conspiracies and impending tumults'. His view was, however, a minority one. The notes and papers 'proving' the plots were gathered up and bundled into the infamous green parliamentary bag of the home secretary, Lord Sidmouth, a sort of nineteenth century dodgy dossier, to be produced as irrefutable evidence when the time came.

There was an awful lot of it. Despite Hunt and Cobbett's best endeavours, the Spa Fields meetings became firmly linked in a frightened public's mind with the Spencean plot to storm the Tower and overthrow the government. Cobbett and Hunt were demonised. The writer of evangelical halfpenny tracts, Hannah More (Cobbett called her 'the Old Bishop in petticoats') penned a nasty little rhyme about them:

What follies what falsehoods were uttered in vain
To disturb our repose by that Jacobin Paine.
Shall Britons that traitor who scorned to obey
Of Cobbett and Hunt now become the vile prey?

That 'England expects you should all do your duty'
Is a phrase, I am sure, that cannot be new t'ye.
But can you your hero so sadly affront
To confound the great Nelson with Cobbett and Hunt?

The Times linked their names together repeatedly. 'Cobbett and Hunt' became a catchphrase in its columns, a shorthand phrase for all things revolutionary and uncontrolled. On 25 January 1817, for example, *The Times* informed its readers that 'Messrs Hunt and Cobbett' went to court together to argue the cause of a young boy, Thomas Dugood, who was

'Advocates for Reform shewing the White Feather!! or a new way to Hunt out a troublesome customer!!'
Following the fracas at the British Coffee House and Cobbett and Hunt's visit to Jackson's Boxing Club in Bond Street. Hunt and Cobbett, white feathers in their hat, run for the door. Cruikshank, 1817.
© *The Trustees of the British Museum*

imprisoned for tearing down a poster defaming Hunt. Three days later: 'If Cobbett and Hunt were honest men, and really wished well to the cause of reform, they would abstain from meddling with it', thundered the newspaper. One story included the phrase, 'Mr Cobbett, with his associate, Hunt'. On 8 February, *The Times* referred to 'HUNT and COBBETT's mob'. On 24 February, the newspaper scoffed at Hunt when he attended a meeting alone, asking him where his 'master' was. 'Why was not Cobbett the father present?' it sneered. On the same day, it published a letter from an indignant reader: 'In vain might Mr Cobbett write and Mr Hunt and other mob-orators declaim, if the public-house did not afford the means of collecting circles in which seditious publications and inflammatory speeches may be read'.

The newspaper also took great delight in reporting a visit on Friday, 14 February by the two men to the well-known boxing club 'Jackson's Pugilistic Rooms' in Bond Street. The visit followed an altercation on the morning of the day of the third Spa Fields meeting at Hunt's inn, the British Coffee-house in Cockspur Street off Pall Mall, when the landlord tried to throw him out. Hunt challenged the man to a fight. Cobbett went with Hunt to Jackson's as his 'second' and managed to prevent any fight taking place. Hunt recalled the incident in his *Memoirs* and described Cobbett, fondly and humorously, as 'perhaps the worst second in the world'. It is incredible that the pair could have got involved in such an incident at such a time. The newspapers and caricaturists had a field day jeering at and lampooning the pair. In fact, Cobbett often prevented or dissuaded Hunt from challenging people, including Sir Francis Burdett, to duels of some kind or another.

As well as the constant hatchet jobs on Cobbett and Hunt, the newspapers devoted pages to the court cases of the people who were arrested in the Spencean riots. In January 1817, five people were tried at the Old Bailey for rioting in the City of London on the day of the second Spa Fields meeting. The most prominent of these cases was that of the seaman John Cashman. Wounded nine times in the service, he had arrived in London to try to get the pay he was owed, plus the good service award he had been promised. Like so many others, he was unsuccessful. Disaffected and embittered, Cashman became caught up in the rioting.

He was found guilty and hanged in front of Mr Beckwith's looted gun shop in Skinner Street before a shocked public. Cashman was the only casualty. Although all the Spencean leaders were arrested and charged with high treason, not one was successfully prosecuted. Hunt's revelations about Castle convinced the jury to acquit Dr Watson at his trial, and the attorney general dropped charges against the others.

Fuelled by Hunt's speeches and Cobbett's pen, meetings to petition for the reform of parliament continued to be held across the country. Their message was clear and consistent. The ball was firmly in the government's court, as Cobbett wrote in the *Register*:

When meetings are held and the people's attention drawn towards the *real causes of their misery*, they at once see that the remedy is not a riotous attack upon the property of their neighbours and they wait with patience and fortitude to hear what answer the parliament will give to their petitions.

Delegates from scores of towns and cities, armed with their petitions, along with members of the Hampden Clubs (named after the parliamentarian, John Hampden, who fought against Charles I) were invited to a major conference in London on January 1817 at the Crown and Anchor inn on the east side of Arundel Street off the Strand. The well-known watering hole had a large meeting room which could accommodate up to 2,000 people. The meeting had been called by the club chairman, Sir Francis Burdett, although in the event he was too scared to attend, much to the fury of the reformers including both Cobbett and Hunt. The plan was to draw up a blueprint for a reformed parliament and a civilised, representative voting system. It was also agreed to present the petitions to parliament when it re-opened a few days later on January 28 1817.

Neither Hunt nor Cobbett was a member of a Hampden Club. Neither man ever joined or supported a political party or club, preferring to maintain an independent position in all events. Cobbett was deeply worried about a large meeting at such a time, fearing that it would present 'a most desirable mark for the shafts of Corruption'. In other words, it would present a perfect target for a government keen to see sedition and conspiracies at every turn. Cobbett was proved to be right. Nevertheless, both men agreed to attend as delegates. Hunt was upset when Cobbett told the meeting he was in favour of confining the vote to direct tax payers only. He described later in his *Memoirs* how furious Cobbett had looked when he reminded everybody that Cobbett had written in favour of one man one vote in the *Political Register* just a few weeks previously.

Cobbett ended up backing Hunt's amendment for universal (male) suffrage but attributed his change of heart at the Hampden Clubs' meeting to a speech by one of the northern reformers, Samuel Bamford. The episode gives another glimpse of Cobbett's jealousy of Hunt. The newspapers thought so too. *The Times* joyfully described how Cobbett called Hunt's remark about the article in the *Political Register* 'foul play'. The dispute between 'Messrs Hunt and Cobbett' might suggest to its readers the idea of 'two quacks quarrelling for the body of a patient', sneered the newspaper. A few days later, *The Times* reported Hunt's strong denials of reports that he and Cobbett had fallen out.

The Times knew it was on to something though and continued to look out for divisions between the two men. A month later, when Cobbett failed to accompany Hunt to a meeting in Westminster, the newspaper asked: 'Why was not Cobbett, the father, present?' Presciently, it went on: 'Cobbett has not yet begun to rake into Hunt's past life and actions; but he will soon. These gentlemen statesmen never agree long'.

The day parliament re-opened, about seventy people from different parts of the country were ready and waiting with their petitions. Some carried just one; others were in charge of twenty or thirty each. Hunt assembled everybody at Charing Cross, and the procession marched off down Whitehall and Parliament Street towards Westminster. The Bristol petition was carried at the head along with a bundle of oak sticks tied to an oak staff symbolising union and strength.

The procession finished up outside Lord Cochrane's house in New Palace Yard where a crowd of around 20,000 people had gathered. The Bristol petition was selected to be carried first into the Commons. It was a huge roll of parchment, nearly the size of a sack of wheat. An armchair was found and Lord Cochrane persuaded to get in. (Sir Francis Burdett had categorically refused to do the job himself, much to Hunt's everlasting fury.) The petition was loaded onto Cochrane's lap, the bundle of twigs were stuck in its side, and the bearers of the chair staggered off towards

Westminster Hall with Hunt triumphantly leading the way. The remaining petitions were delivered in three hackney carriages. Many more were delivered over the following weeks.

There was another big event the day that parliament opened. As the Prince Regent returned to Carlton House after the opening ceremony, he was hissed and booed by the crowds and his 'bullet-proof' carriage was pelted with potatoes, rotten cabbages and stones. A window was broken as the carriage was driving in a quiet spot between the gardens of Carlton House and St James's Palace. The news spread like wildfire that somebody had fired a gun, although in the House of Commons the same day, the prince's lord of the bedchamber, Lord James Murray, admitted that no bullets had been found and that the Prince Regent had refused to let anybody search the carriage. Lord Holland recorded in his *Memoirs* that he was told by the Duke of Sussex, the liberal-minded brother of the Prince Regent, that the latter had made up the whole story about the attack. It was a very convenient story, however, and was to provide the government with plenty of opportunity for spin in its fight against Terror.

The following day, Lord Cochrane struggled to present the Bristol petition amidst what *Hansard* primly described as 'noise'. (The hoots, howls and jeers can be imagined.) Cochrane battled on, reading out the part of the petition which referred to the distress of the country, the increase in the numbers of paupers and beggars, the lack of jobs and the general misery of the people. The petition was ordered 'to lie on the table'. As the days and weeks passed, more petitions were presented. They, too, were left to 'lie on the table'. In fact, the huge rolls of paper ended up on the floor. Cobbett reported in the *Register* on the night of the third reading of the Habeas Corpus Suspension Bill in the Commons a month later, that nearly six hundred petitions signed by more than a million people were piled up on the floor, filling the space of several yards from the Bar of the House to the Table.

Fuelled by the alleged attack against the Prince Regent, the alarming sight of bulky reform petitions arriving at Westminster and the general unease throughout the country, Sidmouth and Castlereagh set up secret committees in both the Lords and the Commons to investigate the mountain of documents crammed into the bulging green bag. It was clear that the committees would come up with enough evidence to justify draconian measures against what the government saw as dangerous unrest in the country, and the 'evil designs' to campaign for universal suffrage and annual parliaments. Radical reformers, printers and publishers felt the hot breath of an alarmed and vindictive government on their necks.

Hunt drew up his own petition, which was presented to both Houses of Parliament. There was a 'foul conspiracy' against his character and his life by people appointed by the Crown and paid by public money, he wrote, and offered to appear at the bar to give evidence and clear his name of all libels and accusations. He sent a letter to Sidmouth along similar lines. Cobbett published the petition and letter in full in the *Register* of 8 February 1817, which appeared just before the third Spa Fields meeting, in which he called Hunt '*Mr Hunt, Hunt the Great*'. Both Sidmouth, who sat in the Lords, and Castlereagh, who was leader in the Commons, declined to take up Hunt's offer.

The reports of the secret committees were presented to the House of Lords and Commons over 18 and 19 February 1817. They made terrifying reading. The peers shivered in their ermine as they heard about the arrangements for the Spa Fields meetings, which were to lead to plunder and riot, rebellion and revolution. Prisoners were to be freed, barracks set on fire and soldiers persuaded to revolt. The Tower of London and the Bank of England, conveniently close to Spa Fields, were to be attacked. Pikes and arms had been provided. The members of the Hampden Clubs were largely a bunch of dangerous revolutionaries. Their aim was universal suffrage and annual parliaments, in short 'a total subversion of the British constitution'. The outrageous attack on his royal highness was 'additional and melancholy proof'.

The House of Commons was stunned to learn that not only were the people looking for a reform of parliament but 'a total overthrow of all existing establishments'. The contents of the green bag clearly revealed that gunsmiths were rushed off their feet with orders; pike-heads had been made, 250 of them, and more had been commissioned. It was plain to see that the intention was to create general confusion and lead on to plunder and bloodshed. MPs were asked to give their serious attention to the dangers of the situation and the inadequacy of the existing laws to deal with it.

A Bill was drafted to suspend the Habeas Corpus Act. Cobbett warned his readers that parliamentary Acts 'of the most tremendous importance to us all' were about to be passed. He wrote a fine explanation in the *Political Register* of what the phrase 'Habeas Corpus' meant. It came, he explained, from two Latin words. These meant that any man, who was imprisoned or confined in any way without knowing why, could apply to a judge for a writ so that he could be brought to court to hear what his alleged crime was and be able to defend himself against it. In short, Habeas Corpus safeguarded every person's human rights:

For if Magistrates, or anybody else, can take up any man they choose and send him to prison without *evidence upon oath*, without his being *heard in his defence*, without his being *confronted with his accusers*, without *a written warrant stating the nature of his offence*, without *any limit of time* and without being able to get a writ to be brought out before a judge to *have the cause of his imprisonment inquired into* ... what man can possibly regard his *Person as being in Safety*?

'A Pugilisti[c]-Political Contest'
Hunt and Castlereagh are stripped to the waist. Hunt lies on the ground, held up by his second, Cobbett, and is given a drink by the devil. Sidmouth holds out his watch to Hunt.
© *The Trustees of the British Museum*

Hunt once again petitioned both Houses of Parliament to call him to
the bar so that he had the opportunity to prove that the allegations
contained in the secret reports were false. Cobbett printed his petition in
full. In it, Hunt clearly accused Sidmouth of trying to ensnare him in the
Spencean plot. His lordship had known all along about the plan to adjourn
the first Spa Fields meeting, wrote Hunt. The home secretary had had the
chance to inform him about what was going on when he had called to hand
over the petition for the Prince Regent, but Sidmouth had chosen to say
nothing. His lordship had even congratulated Hunt on his control of the
crowds. It was obvious that Sidmouth had positively wanted the second
meeting to go ahead!

Hunt's petition also picked up on the detail about those 250 sinister
pike-heads. He had a letter in his pocket that had been sent to him
anonymously, he wrote. It said that a man dressed as a gamekeeper had
ordered the pikes from Mr Bentley, a blacksmith of Hart Street in Covent
Garden. The man said they were to be used to fence in a fishpond. He later
ordered a second batch. The Bow Street Police had asked Mr Bentley to
make a replica pike-head to prove that he had indeed made them. (There
was certainly a very fishy smell about the orders of pike-heads. Was it a
government plot? Had one of their spies ordered the pike-heads? Was it a
real gamekeeper? Whatever the truth, the radical *Black Dwarf* loved the
story of the pike-heads. 'Is it not ungenerous in the proprietors of *the
loaves* and *fishes*, to condemn these *guardians of the fish* as traitors?' mocked
its youthful owner, the journalist Thomas Wooler.) Hunt's petition failed
once again in both houses, neither of which had any desire to hear him
shoot down the contents of the green bag nor hear about his anonymous
letter about the pike-heads.

The Bill to suspend the Habeas Corpus Act was rushed through both
Houses of Parliament and given the Royal Assent on 4 March 1817. Any
person could be considered an enemy of the state and imprisoned at any
time, without bail, without a trial and without knowing what they stood
accused of. Cobbett wrote the following solemn words in the *Register:*

I have no scruple to say that this is the most important event that has taken place in the
world for hundreds of years ... When our children's children shall read of this event, they
will be all anxiety to know *what was the cause of it,* what was the cause of putting ... *the*

Personal Safety of every man, however innocent he may be, within the *absolute power* of a Secretary of State or of Six Privy councillors.

The Seditious Meetings Prevention Act was passed shortly afterwards. It was made up of a whole set of new draconian laws. Cobbett referred to this Act and the suspension of Habeas Corpus as the 'Gagging Bills'. The Seditious Meetings Act restricted the right to hold mass public meetings and censored the radical press. Magistrates were given the powers to ban any gatherings of more than fifty people. There were to be no more unauthorised crowds yelling for reform in New and Old Palace Yards or anywhere else within a mile of the Palace of Westminster. Magistrates were also given powers to monitor all lecture rooms, coffee houses and inns. If they found any reading material they considered to be seditious, they could withdraw licences and close the premises. As Hunt phrased it in his *Memoirs*, 'A system of terror was now the order of the day'.

The spies and informers rubbed their hands with glee as they envisaged the mounting piles of pound notes they could now earn. They began to haunt pubs and clubs to try to catch out people reading those nasty radical newspapers and journals, like those of that William Cobbett. Home Office records for March 1817 reveal that there were almost daily reports submitted. On one day at the Mulberry Tree in Long Alley in the Moorfields area of London, shock horror, Cobbett's *Register*, Thomas Wooler's *Black Dwarf* and Robert Southey's poem about the medieval revolutionary, Wat Tyler (written in Southey's radical days and re-published much to his fury), were being read and discussed.

It is also of interest to note here that the Northampton family, the owners of Spa Fields, began to lease the land for development. There were to be no more dangerous open spaces near the City of London and the Tower. Wilmington Square and the streets around it were constructed a few years later. Merlin's Cave was swallowed up in a late Georgian suburbia.

Hunt and Cobbett were deeply alarmed at what was going on in the country. Lord Holland noted in his *Memoirs* that both men went to see him and that a letter was sent to Lord Grey about the possibility of coming to some kind of political agreement to get the Whigs back into power. Cobbett suggested they could co-operate in public meetings and offered to support Whig policies in the *Register*. In return, the Whigs could offer protection against the iron fist of the Tory government. Cobbett stressed, however, that he would maintain his political independence and never join the party. No deal was made. Lord Holland admired Cobbett's writing but regarded both Hunt and Cobbett as extreme radicals. He wrote in his *Memoirs* of Cobbett's 'able mischief' and Hunt's 'brawling eloquence'. He also noted that Cobbett was personally alarmed by the suspension of the Habeas Corpus Act: 'He very unaffectedly acknowledged his distrust of his own nerves and a dread of behaving meanly and basely if arrested. He hinted an intention, which he afterwards executed, of retiring to America.'

Cobbett did not share his thoughts about exile with Hunt, who had no idea what was going on in his friend's mind. Hunt assumed that they were going to continue their work together, battling against the state and all its ills. They had an opportunity to do so on 11 March 1817 at a meeting of the leading Tories of Hampshire. It was one of many across the country called to congratulate the Prince Regent on his lucky escape after the 'outrageous and treasonable attack on his life'. (Hunt scoffingly called it the Prince Regent's miraculous escape from the potato.)

It was one of the most chaotic of meetings. The people stood in the courtyard of Winchester Castle. The speakers packed in to the Grand Jury Chamber overlooking the courtyard. There were at least a hundred people in the chamber jostling each other to gain access to the windows from which they could address the assembled throng below. Cobbett and Hunt were there together with Lord Cochrane. The Tories had agreed a plan in advance that none of the reformers would be allowed to speak, and had primed their supporters who were packed into the chamber. Cobbett described how they used sticks, umbrellas, heels of shoes, shouts, groans and hisses to harass the three men and separate them from each other. They were even spat at. Ominously, in an indication of the new mood of the authorities in the country, the under sheriff threatened them with arrest if they continued to speak.

Cobbett only mentioned Hunt once in his report of the event for the *Political Register* of 22 March. 'Mr Hunt seconded the amendments (drawn up by Cobbett) and was heard very well for about half an hour', he wrote. Otherwise he concentrated almost entirely on himself, his own contribution to the meeting and how he was chaired away amid triumph and applause afterwards by people in the crowd. It was almost as if he were putting a distance between himself and his friend. Cobbett wrote of the Hampshire event as the last public meeting to be held under the old laws of the land before the Gagging Act came into effect. It also turned out to be Cobbett's last meeting in England for at least two and a half years. Cobbett knew it but nobody else did, except his immediate family.

When a similar meeting was called at Devizes in Wiltshire for the end of March, the pair agreed to attend. Cobbett promised to ride down from London to meet Hunt at the Castle Inn on the day appointed. Hunt arrived on the day and was surprised there was no sign of Cobbett. He was convinced Cobbett had been delayed and would not disappoint him. Loyally, he continued to wait at the inn, sending a companion to find out when the business of the meeting would start. The companion rushed back to announce breathlessly that he had bumped into the sheriff who had laughed in his face. The sheriff had just received his copy of the *Courier*. The newspaper had a major scoop. Cobbett had gone to Liverpool and set sail for America.

Poor Hunt. For once he was lost for words. He sat riveted to his chair, unable to think or move. He simply could not imagine that Cobbett could have done this to him, with no warning. At first he insisted it was an 'infamous lie'. He wrote bitterly of the moment a few years later in his *Memoirs*:

I was thunderstruck for a moment as Mr Cobbett had never given me the slightest intimation of his intention, and till I saw the Courier I could not believe it possible that any man could act so treacherously towards one for whom he had expressed, not only in public but in private, the most unbounded confidence.

As Hunt would eventually find out, the story was true. In the early hours of Saturday, 22 March 1817, Cobbett had slipped out of his rented house at 9 Catherine Street in London, accompanied by his two eldest sons, William and John, and taken a coach heading northwards. Five days later, at Liverpool docks, they boarded an American ship, the Importer, and set sail for New York.

Like everybody else, Hunt had to wait impatiently to read what

Cobbett had written in the issues of the *Political Register* to understand what he had done and why he had done it. The articles had been carefully written in advance and left with Cobbett's publisher. Although they did not explain or even admit Cobbett's dramatic departure, they contained clues to his state of mind. Cobbett chose to unfold the news gradually. The first of these issues was on sale the Saturday Cobbett left London for Liverpool. In it, Cobbett continued to stress the terror and fear that the people of England were now living under:

Every man and woman is now liable to be seized at any moment and to be put into a prison and kept there for any length of time, cut off from all communication with friends, wife, children or anybody else whatever and also from pen, ink, paper, books. In short any man, or woman, may now be taken up, sent to any prison in the kingdom however distant, without any charge being made known to them, without their knowing what is alleged against them, without having any idea of who adjudged felony.

The following issue, published on 29 March 1817, still gave no explanation. Cobbett even dated the articles as if he were still at home in Botley in Hampshire.

Two days later, *The Times* published a few paragraphs written to the public by Cobbett at Liverpool. The newspaper prefaced them with the dramatic words: 'Mr Cobbett is really gone and has left the following farewell ... ' In the terse note, Cobbett had written that he was not prepared to live under a government that had the absolute power to imprison people at its pleasure. He promised a full statement in the *Register* of 5 April. He had not said goodbye to his many friends in London and in the country because he knew he would have been made too unhappy 'by their importunities and the expressions of their sorrow'. There was one other line. It stands out: 'My departure will surprise nobody but those who do not reflect'. Did Cobbett write this line especially for Hunt? He may well have done.

Hunt rushed to get hold of a copy of the *Political Register* on Saturday, 5 April 1817. It was a special issue. The banner headline read: 'MR COBBETT'S Taking Leave of his Countrymen'. In it, Cobbett explained and justified what he had done. He began solemnly:

Soon after this reaches your eyes, those of the writer will, possibly, have taken the last glimpse of the land that gave him birth, the land in which his parents lie buried, the land of which he has always been so proud, the land in which he leaves a people, whom he shall to his last breath, love and esteem beyond all the rest of mankind.

Everyone, Cobbett wrote, was entitled to pursue the path to his own happiness. He himself had to be blind not to see that he would be thrown into a dungeon if he continued to write as he had been doing. If he remained in England, he would have to stop writing. He had decided to go to America where he would be able to continue his journalism with perfect freedom, and offer important and lasting services to the cause. He was no coward. He was just being practical. If he stayed, he faced being imprisoned, without even a hearing and for an unlimited time, in any prison in the kingdom, without the use of pen, ink and paper and without any communication with any soul but the keepers. It would be madness to try to struggle against such a power. 'No! I will go where I shall not be as the shoes upon Lord Sidmouth's and Lord Castlereagh's feet', he wrote. He could not bear 'the horrid idea of being silenced'. He knew he would be attacked on all sides for having abandoned his friends and country at such a critical time. He would even be called a coward. He trusted his countrymen would not believe any of it:

Every species of falsehood, deception, imposture will Corruption now resort to, in order to blacken my character, to disfigure my motives and to diminish the effect of my writings. But, my Countrymen, if you have witnessed so much of all these while I was *present,* I need not fear that you will believe in them when I am absent.

Cobbett implicitly asked for understanding in this emotional piece of writing. He did not get it. His contemporaries fiercely attacked him for deserting the cause. Almost without exception, all the radicals ended up in prison for sticking to their principles. The extreme radical and publisher Richard Carlile spent six years in Dorchester gaol between 1819-1825, defiantly running his business from his prison cell. Cobbett's enemies and future critics used his flight to America as a stick with which to beat him. From Cobbett's point of view, he decided he could not face the risk and stay in England. He had already spent two years in Newgate and still had large debts. He believed the government's dictatorial measures were directed against him personally and that his arrest was imminent. (It is believed that Sidmouth offered Cobbett £10,000 to close the *Register*, which he refused to do.) He was unable to face another term in gaol, possibly unlimited. He wanted to continue publishing the *Political Register* in his own way and on his own terms.

For Hunt, this was all beside the point. How could Cobbett, 'unkind, unfeeling and treacherous', have done such a thing without telling him, raged Hunt. If there was a coded message in Cobbett's words about how those who reflected would not be surprised, Hunt did not get it. As far as he was concerned, Cobbett had not given him the slightest hint of his intention to flee to America. Hunt was also furious that Cobbett had not made 'the slightest allusion to me in his leave-taking address, any more than as if he never had such a friend.'

In his *Memoirs*, Hunt re-lived the moment on that dreadful day in Devizes when the news of Cobbett's departure first broke. He had jumped out of his chair and headed off for the meeting, although he was still in a state of shock as he reached the Town Hall in the Market Square. His head had reeled as he recalled and analysed a thousand conversations with Cobbett and he miserably began to doubt the man who had been his trusted hero. He tried to describe how he had felt that day, but it was too difficult:

> It is much more easy for the reader to imagine what were the sensations which I felt as I walked to the meeting, than it is for me to describe them. I had for many years acted in strict union with Mr Cobbett ... I had placed implicit and unbounded confidence in him and I thought that on his part such feelings had been reciprocal; but a thousand occurrences which hitherto had made no impression on me now rushed upon my mind, and half convinced me that I had been deceived.

The action in the Town Hall at Devizes jolted Hunt into forgetting Cobbett's flight. It was packed with people and the crowds were still pushing and shoving to try to get in. Many were standing outside. Hunt had the meeting adjourned to the market square. The sheriff took up position on the steps of the market cross, the landmark graciously erected by Lord Sidmouth in 1814 to thank the voters of Devizes for unanimously choosing him six times to be their MP. (It still stands today.) Hunt described how the sheriff was surrounded by 'a gang of desperados as never disgraced a meeting of highwaymen and pickpockets in the purlieus of St Giles's.' His old enemy, the wealthy Wiltshire landowner, John Benett, was in command of the gang. Hunt described how Benett signalled when they should 'bellow, hoot, hallow and make all sorts of discordant vulgar noises, such as would have degraded and lowered the character of a horde of drunken prostitutes and pickpockets in the most abandoned brothel in the universe.' Lord Pembroke, the Lord Lieutenant of Wiltshire, had also ordered his tenants and tradesmen to shut up shop and attend the meeting to shout Hunt down. A butcher tried to plead a previous engagement but was told in no uncertain terms that if he did not attend the meeting and join in, he would never sell another joint of meat to his lordship ever again.

Although Hunt wrote his account of this Wiltshire meeting some years after the events, the writing has a clarity and crispness about it. The language is violent and forceful. It is just as if he used his pen to jab out all his fury and anguish at Cobbett's betrayal. The gang 'raked together' against him, he wrote, was led by the usual leaders. There was 'Black Jack, alias the Devil's Knitting Needle' and Bob Reynolds, 'a scamping currier of Devizes who was a sort of lickspittle to Old Salmon, the attorney'. There was 'a jolter-headed farmer' who was captain of 'a gang of little dirty toad-eaters of the corporation'. In fact, there was:

Every scamp who lived upon the taxes – every scrub who had an eye to a place – and every lickspittle of the corrupt knaves of the corrupt and vile rotten-borough of Devizes ... every expectant underling, every dirty, petty-fogging scoundrel showed his teeth, opened his vulgar mouth, and sent forth the most nauseous and disgusting ribaldry.

John Benett blamed Hunt for all the disturbances that had taken place in London. Hunt was even responsible, said Benett, for the hanging of Mr Cashman outside the gunshop in London. Hunt was shouted down when he tried to reply. The sheriff read the Riot Act and Old Salmon ordered Hunt's arrest. A riot broke out. The crowds rushed to help Hunt. They formed a phalanx around him, which shielded him from all assaults. He was hoisted onto the shoulders of a group of men and had a grandstand view of what was going on. He was able to see how the police officers, bullies and blackguards repeatedly charged the crowds with staves and clubs, although the people stood firm. Two ruffians then seized hold of Hunt's deaf and dumb youngest brother, William, who was looking on. At first William Hunt smiled, but when he realised they were serious, his Hunt blood rose and he let fly with his fists. Hunt was gratified to see that the two bullies 'fell like slaughtered calves upon the ground'. He himself was carried off to the safety of the Castle Inn. The Riot Act was once again read out under the window but no further attempt was made to arrest him. Later that evening, one of Hunt's tenants, who had attended the meeting and spoken up for him, was attacked and smashed on the head as he drove home. His high-crowned hat, which was cut in two by the blow, probably saved his life.

All in all, it had been a traumatic and violent day, foreshadowing what was to come. As Hunt headed back home to Middleton Cottage near Andover, he reflected on what he saw as the critical situation he had been left in. Cobbett had deserted him and stolen away to America. His friend, hero, rock and staunch supporter had left him without a single word. He simply could not believe what had happened:

As I drove home in the evening from the meeting, I could not avoid seriously reflecting upon the critical situation in which I was placed by my friend Mr Cobbett having deserted me and stolen away to America. I had been constantly and faithfully acting with him for many years, up to the very hour of his flight, for I had now no doubt in my mind that the report in the Courier was true. I felt indignant and mortified in the extreme at this desertion on the part of my friend, at such a moment, and without his ever having given me the slightest reason to suspect him of any such intention.

Hunt resolved that come what may, he would never desert his country or his countrymen in the hour of peril. He described in his *Memoirs* how he prepared for the time when it would be his turn for the knock on the door in the middle of the night. Many of the reformers from Lancashire, including Samuel Bamford, had already been imprisoned. Their houses had been broken into during the night and they had been dragged away in irons. Hunt made sure he took a brace of loaded pistols and a double-barrelled shotgun when he went to bed. Armed with these weapons, he was confident that he could deal with up to four men at a time and was quite prepared to shoot them dead before they could get into the house. If they came for him in the daytime, he would accompany them quietly and peacefully.

It was not to work out quite like that. Hunt's turn was not yet to come. It came just over three years later, when the government finally got Hunt and shut him up in Ilchester Prison which, they hoped, he would not leave alive. There, Hunt brooded over the events of 1817, what Cobbett had done and how he had done it without telling him first. Cobbett's actions, Hunt wrote, had been 'most unkind, unfeeling and treacherous.' He comforted himself by deciding it was the highest compliment Cobbett could have paid him. It clearly proved Cobbett knew that he, Hunt, would never have sanctioned 'so dastardly, so thoroughly unmanly a proceeding as that of flying from my country and abandoning the Reformers to the uncontrolled malice of their enemies'.

Hunt also consoled himself with how he had tried to find some excuse for Cobbett's behaviour. He had ridden over to Cobbett's farm in Botley to find out what was going on and how the family was coping. He was saved having to speak to Mrs Cobbett. Nancy, together with the rest of the children, had gone to live in the family's rented house in London. Hunt discovered that all Cobbett's farming stock and household goods in Botley had been seized and sold to pay off debts. His rented farm had been repossessed. Cobbett, Hunt wrote accusingly, had decamped, leaving his debts behind him. He had backed the idea of one of Cobbett's local friends to raise a subscription to pay off the debts, but the London reformers squashed the plan. They did not want to raise money to pay the debts of a man who had deserted the cause of the people.

Reading Hunt's retrospective account of this dramatic point in his life, his loneliness, bitterness and sense of betrayal are still palpable two centuries later. 'The great literary champion of the Radical Reformers' deserted England and fled to America, wrote Hunt. He recalled how other radical writers and publishers moved in, keen to fill the gap. Among them were the publishers and writers, Thomas Wooler, William Hone and Richard Carlile. In his newspaper, *Black Dwarf,* Wooler mercilessly criticised Cobbett for leaving the field. In his *Memoirs,* Hunt was proud all over again as he remembered how he had stood up for Cobbett – and had been attacked in turn by Wooler for doing so: 'I lost no opportunity to vindicate the character of my absent friend, and in doing this I attacked Mr Wooler as violently as he attacked Mr Cobbett, for which Mr Wooler denounced me as a spy of the Government!'

It was, indeed, a horrible time.

8
Separation

In a time of universal deceit, telling the truth is a revolutionary act.
George Orwell

So in the spring of 1817, Henry Hunt was left stewing in a cauldron of emotions as he embarked on what was to be one of the most difficult periods of his life. By contrast, despite his hasty departure and the uncertain future, William Cobbett appeared to leave England to seek exile in America feeling calm and in control. It was the second time he had sought sanctuary in the land of the free. At the age of fifty-four he was accustomed to unexpected disruption and disturbances in life, far more so than the friend, ten years younger, whom he had left behind. Moreover, Cobbett was not going alone. His two eldest sons, William, aged eighteen and John, sixteen, were going with him, and the rest of the family were to join him later in the year.

As the coach bowled along heading for Liverpool docks, Cobbett looked out of the window and observed the lovely countryside passing by. In his inimitable prose, he shared what he had seen with his readers in the issue of the *Political Register*, which appeared some three months later on 12 July 1817. The most delightful stage of the journey, he wrote, was between Dunchurch and Coventry. Fine trees and beautiful whitethorn hedges lined the road, while rows of ash and elm divided the fields. Cobbett admired with pleasure the fat cattle and sheep and the well-kept homesteads, a pleasant picture of England – until the carriage drove through Coventry teeming with its 8,000 paupers. Cobbett lost no opportunity to make his political points.

The sailing ship took six weeks to arrive in New York, docking on 5 May 1817. There were the usual thrills and spills of such journeys in those days. Lightning killed one man, and after three weeks one of the eleven passengers sharing the Cobbetts' cabin died of a smelly, lingering disease. Cobbett and his sons spoke French together so they could 'talk and laugh about all sorts of things quite at our ease'. On arrival in New York, Cobbett rented the big, rundown house and three to four hundred acres of farmland at Hyde Park, near North Hemstead on Long Island. Cobbett called it North Hampstead. The rest of the family, his wife Nancy, their three daughters, Anne, Susan and Ellen, and their two other sons, James and little Richard aged three, sailed out to join them a few months later. They stayed just one year. Anne wrote a short note in her *Account of the Family*: 'We left London on our way to Liverpool for New York in September. We came back the next summer. 1818 November Landed from New York.'

The emphasis and brevity of Anne's words suggests that the family was unhappy that Cobbett chose to stay on for a further year. It is likely their displeasure was fuelled by the fact that, although the Habeas Corpus Act was reinstated in July 1818, Cobbett chose to stay in America until October 1819 before sailing home. His family were not alone in their feelings. Hunt and the other reformers also urged Cobbett to return to England sooner than he did. Cobbett may have been waiting until the period of his seven years of 'good conduct', which the court had imposed on him as part of his sentence for the Ely flogging story, had safely expired. He also enjoyed his free life in America.

Cobbett left the organisation and publication of the *Political Register* in the not very capable hands of William Jackson, a former secretary to Lord Cochrane. Jackson was to betray both Cobbett and Hunt by delaying the publication of articles until the Westminster Rump had had the chance to read them, and altering or refusing to publish articles by Hunt. Cobbett continued to write his own articles for the *Register*, dispatching them back to England in the first available ship. He relied on visitors and the letters and parcels of newspapers that were sent out to him to keep abreast of the news. It meant that there was always, at the absolute minimum, a three-month turn around between events and the publication of Cobbett's comments in the *Register*. Sometimes it was much longer, and Cobbett frequently complained that he had had no news for months.

Cobbett now had to fight to retain his hold on his readers in England. His style as a political writer lent itself to the occasion, however, as he tended to repeat and re-analyse events, often years after they occurred. It kept episodes and their significance before the public eye, hammering them into the collective memory. It was the perfect technique for his stay in America. Nevertheless, there was no getting away from the fact that Cobbett's comments in the *Political Register* about news stories were largely out of date, and a drop in circulation was inevitable. Despite this, the *Register* held its own. Early in 1818, Cobbett claimed that weekly sales were around 25,000. A report at the Home Office in October 1819 put circulation at 8,000. This would still have been pretty good particularly as the actual number of readers would have been much higher. The journal still made excellent reading. Cobbett's relationship with the popular, golden-voiced Hunt back home, with whom he was now inextricably linked in the public mind, could have helped. Many of the events Cobbett chose to re-visit featured Hunt. While Cobbett was in America, Hunt was to take a starring role in the *Political Register*, although Cobbett chose to ease him slowly back in – for a variety of reasons.

In England, Hunt battled on with his work as a Liveryman of the City of London. He continued to hope for news, a letter or at least a personal message from his old friend, although he refused to make the first move himself. In short, Hunt sulked. In America, Cobbett waited to hear from Hunt, although he knew perfectly well how Hunt would be feeling. In the event, it was Cobbett who would make contact first. He would do so on 17 October 1817 when he wrote his first letter to Hunt from America. The letter was penned on the same day that Cobbett also wrote his first public address to Hunt. This appeared in the *Political Register* on 3 January 1818 and included these gently reproachful words: 'I am at a great distance from you. I have neither heard from you nor written to you till to-day since I left England'. Cobbett excused himself two months later in a second private letter to Hunt. The long silence on his part, he wrote, was because he was convinced (quite reasonably) that any mail addressed to Hunt and sent through the post would be intercepted. He had preferred, he said, to wait until a visitor arrived from England who could take letters back home and deliver them personally.

To begin with, however, the waiting was done on both sides. After the sensational leave-taking, publication of the *Political Register* was suspended. The first issue after that was not until Saturday, 12 July 1817. How eagerly Hunt scanned the pages for some reference to himself and how disappointed he was that there was nothing. Then, in the issue of

2 August 1817 came a mention by Cobbett of Hunt's house in Hampshire: 'I remained at Middleton Cottage and wrote that Essay, which is entitled, "What *good* would a Reform of Parliament now do?"' And just in case Hunt missed the reference, Cobbett repeated it: 'This was No. 15 of Volume 31 and is dated at Middleton Cottage, 12th of October, 1816'. There was no mention of Hunt himself, but two weeks later, his name popped out of the issue of August 1817. There he was at the head of the triumphant crowds that had gathered at Charing Cross at the end of January 1817 to begin presenting the petitions for reform to parliament. Hunt must have devoured the pages hoping for more, but that was it, just one tantalising name check.

Cobbett calculated it all, dangling these titbits in front of Hunt, hoping he would be jogged into contacting him. In vain. The weeks went by but there was still no word from Hunt to Cobbett. So Cobbett turned his pen to other matters in the *Political Register.* Issue after issue was devoted to exposing the 'Sons of Corruption', the 'Green Bag Plot' and the 'Extraordinary Conduct' of that 'salamander in the fire', Sir Francis Burdett.

Still there was no response from Hunt, and Cobbett was forced to give in. Hunt finally took centre stage in the issue of the *Register* published on 4 October 1817.

It was done so casually; first, a joke about Hunt being a coward because he did not go to a fourth Spa Fields meeting and then, a full tribute. 'Mr Hunt', wrote Cobbett, was the man 'who, in presence of mind, in a public meeting, yields to very few persons that I have ever seen'. It was 'with no small pleasure' that Cobbett could report how Mr Hunt had gracefully persuaded one of the aged conservatives at the City of London's Common Hall to resign to allow a more active man to take his place. He had been attacked by the press, which had written the usual lies about him, thus making it all a greater triumph.

It was all so matter of fact, just as if no time had elapsed at all. Hunt must have cut the article out and stuck it on his wall. Although Hunt still failed to get in touch, Cobbett reinstated his friend in the *Register.* It was almost as if Cobbett enjoyed the distance between them. He could miss Hunt and praise him as his golden boy without those sneaky, creeping feelings of jealousy that had begun to stir. In America, Cobbett was in control. There was no Sidmouth, no gagging laws and no government spies. Cobbett could belabour the British establishment in perfect safety and enjoy his relationship with Henry Hunt.

Through October and November 1817, Hunt was back in the *Register* in all his glory, triumphing at Spa Fields and dodging the traps laid by Sidmouth with the help of his noxious agent, John Castle. 'How the bloodhounds must have hung their tails when they found that they were disappointed', wrote Cobbett for the *Register* of 11 October. He firmly believed that 'the most black-hearted miscreants that ever existed' hatched the Spa Fields plot mainly to get at 'the blood of Mr Hunt'. Cobbett hugged himself with glee all over again as he reminded his readers of the part he, himself, had played: 'I took infinite pains to convince him of the existence of a conspiracy against his life and he will remember my concluding words: "Hunt, your life is not safe for a month unless you are in a situation to *prove* an *alibi,* for every moment of your life."' Oh how Hunt had clenched his fists and sworn that a man had better be hanged than live such a life. Cobbett laughed to himself on Long Island as he recollected how it was his advice and his alone that had saved Hunt. His affection for his friend soared undiminished as his pen moved across the pages. Hunt, wrote Cobbett, had an undaunted personal courage and a perseverance that no discouragement could check. He made mistakes and was often carried away by his own ardour. He was not lacking in ambition either, but where was the man 'without spot or blemish'. Cobbett had never been able to discover 'any base selfish motive' in Mr Hunt. He had shown more zeal in the fight than any man Cobbett had ever met – apart from Major Cartwright. Hunt's main talents were quickness and presence of mind in difficult and dangerous circumstances. He was a man 'worth the powder and shot of the Boroughmongers'.

And so, even as he waited to hear from his friend in England, Cobbett continued to praise him in the pages of the *Register*. Sweetness and light blew from Cobbett across the Atlantic towards Hunt in England. Even Sir Francis Burdett had not been able to fault Hunt's character, wrote Cobbett for the *Register* of 25 October 1817. When Hunt left Wiltshire to go and live in Sussex, all his servants had followed him. In the *Register* the following week, Cobbett suggested that Hunt would be a suitable candidate to challenge the Tory MP for Bristol. Hunt's name, embellished with a thousand compliments, poured from the pages.

None of this soothed Hunt's later wounds and when he was writing his *Memoirs* in his cell in Ilchester gaol a few years later, he was grossly unfair to Cobbett: 'My friend, Mr Cobbett,' wrote Hunt, 'seemed to have almost entirely forgotten that there was such a person as myself in existence for more than five months ... He scarcely ever mentioned the name of his friend even accidentally.' In his lonely prison cell, Hunt ignored or forgot his appearances in the *Register* from July through to December 1817. In retrospect, he considered that the issue of 20 December 1817 was the one in which he made his comeback.

Cobbett's contribution had been prepared more than two months earlier in America, on 10 October 1817. His diary entry for that day

'Transatlantic Luxury'
Cobbett writes to 'My Dear Hunt'. Illustration for Cobbett's *Long Island Journal*, written in America, 1817-1819.
by permission of the British Library

reveals that he had been out at the crack of dawn inspecting his vegetables. He had observed how the leaves of the kidney bean were slightly curled by a touch of early morning frost, while the fences had protected the cucumbers and melons. The day, however, had turned into a fine one, a comfortable 59 degrees Fahrenheit in the shade. What Cobbett did not report in his diary was that it was a year to the day since he had stayed with Hunt at his home at Middleton Cottage near Andover – but he remembered. Was it chance or design? He sat down at his table under the tree in the farmyard, his straw hat slouched as usual over his eyes, and began a lead article for the *Political Register*. It would be published just over two months later in England in the issue of 20 December and would bring great joy to Hunt.

Cobbett began his article with the following words: 'This day twelve-month, at Mr Hunt's at Middleton, I wrote ... the *first* of those Essays at the end of the *fifteenth* of which the Boroughmongers were brought to a state of desperation'. And so Cobbett's nostalgia continued. It was very flattering to Hunt indeed. If ever Cobbett grovelled, he did so here. Any whiffs of jealousy flew out of the window. Hunt had been 'RIGHT' about Sir Francis Burdett letting the radical reformers down so badly, wrote Cobbett. He remembered Hunt's 'squeezing almost to dust' a letter from Burdett in which the baronet declined to present the Spa Fields' petition and address to the Prince Regent. (In the letter, Burdett had rudely written that he did not want to be Hunt's 'cat's paw'.) At the time, Hunt had threatened to go and confront him at once, but Cobbett had calmed him down. An open quarrel with Sir F. would do more harm than good, he had argued. Cobbett now sorely regretted that he had stopped Hunt going down to Brighton and having it out with Burdett. The world might then have known sooner just what kind of a man Burdett was.

Was it nostalgia, strategic planning or both? Whatever it was, it worked. How Hunt rejoiced as he read what was for him a riveting issue of the *Register*, but he was mean in his *Memoirs* about Cobbett. 'He had at length discovered that I was neither literally nor politically dead', Hunt grumbled, his bitterness against Cobbett during his imprisonment in Ilchester gaol between 1820 and 1822 obscuring what was in 1817 balm to his soul.

More was quickly to follow, both public and private. Exactly a week

later, on 17 October 1817, after the frost had killed the cucumber and
melon plants as well as the kidney beans, Cobbett sat down to write his
first private letter to Hunt since his flight from England. The letter was
relatively short but did the trick. Cobbett congratulated Hunt for his work
in court on behalf of the deluded Spenceans. (Hunt had exposed the work
of the spy, John Castle.) Cobbett also mentioned the possibility of a vacant
parliamentary seat in the Westminster constituency and the intrigue going
on to find a replacement. Hunt had to stop the plot and Cobbett would
shortly address a public letter to him in the *Register* to help. Cobbett
signed off his letter, 'God bless you. Wm Cobbett.' (In fact, he began the
public address to Hunt as soon as he had finished writing the letter, and
it was published in England on 3 January 1818.)

Hunt was delighted. Cobbett's private letter was delivered to him in
England shortly after the glowing 20 December 1817 issue of the *Register*
appeared. Hunt described it all in his *Memoirs*. He did it with the same
mixture of pride and excitement with which he wrote of the beginning of
his relationship with Cobbett:

Very soon afterwards I received a private letter from him full of professions of friendship
which correspondence was continued up to the period of his return from America. He also
addressed to me, in the Register, twelve public letters, beginning with 'My dear Hunt' and
ending with 'your faithful friend,' occasionally complimenting my zeal, courage and
fidelity in the cause of Reform and declaring that he was 'in no fear as to the rectitude of
my conduct but always in anxiety for my health!'

For the next two years, the partnership between the two men remained
strong and vital despite the physical separation. Hunt was an important
part of Cobbett's life and Cobbett missed him emotionally. He also
needed him. Hunt was to be Cobbett's weapon, his tool in England.
Cobbett used his friend to keep a grip on events back home and to
influence and shape them. He ran his business from America, pulling
Hunt's strings in England. Cobbett even boasted about 'his long arm,
reaching across the Atlantic'. The phrase appeared in the *Political Register*
of 28 November 1818. *The Times* was to put it more crudely, calling
Hunt 'the cat's paw' of Cobbett. 'Cobbett thrusts the hand of the other
into the fire to pull out the hot chestnuts, but Cobbett himself fled from
the heat', the newspaper commented in January 1819.

During these years, 1817 to the end of 1819, Cobbett linked himself repeatedly with Hunt, freely building on the public perception of the two men as a pair. He did this publicly through the *Political Register* and privately in personal letters, only three of which survived. 'You will be aware that all sorts of wheels have been set in motion to detach me from you', wrote Cobbett in his second private letter to Hunt, 'Some pretty decent lies have been hatched and brought out to me. All in vain!'

The issues of the *Register* were filled with Hunt and Cobbett standing together side by side. Cobbett did it so cleverly. On the one hand, given Cobbett's famed independence, the references were strong public displays of affection. On the other, they were vehicles to allow Cobbett to make his political points. The Englishmen who established America could be compared with both himself and Hunt, wrote Cobbett in one of his public addresses to Hunt in the *Register*. They were 'as foully calumniated by Corruption in their day as you and I now are'. They included the English Quaker and founder of Pennsylvania, William Penn, who was falsely accused of sedition and blasphemy. Happily for Penn, he was saved by a jury who 'snatched him from the fangs of a prostituted Attorney General and a savage Judge', wrote Cobbett.

In the *Register* of 11 April 1818, Cobbett happily quoted an article in a Prussian newspaper published in Berlin and re-printed in the *Courier*. The Prussian paper warned that there were 'HUNTS and COBBETTS' in the opposition party, 'who will not fail to interfere in all differences, for the purpose of inflaming and aggravating them'. Cobbett wondered how the newspapers could not see that 'in their attempts to vilify, they always exalt the object'. More followed. A woman had written to Cobbett about her husband and son, who were being held in gaol along with scores of other radicals detained indefinitely under the suspension of Habeas Corpus. She could find nobody to present their petition to parliament. 'I dare say', Cobbett wrote loftily, 'she will find no Member to call the parties to account until Mr Hunt or I shall be in Parliament'.

Cobbett was full of praise for Hunt who, alone among the Westminster reformers, attended the trial in Derby in support of the men who took part in the Pentrich Rebellion of 1817. Led by the unemployed stocking knitter, Jeremiah Brandreth, they planned to overthrow the government, unaware that the man who aided and abetted them was the Home Office spy, William Oliver. Yet, at the trial, the prosecution blamed both Cobbett and Hunt for having incited the men to riot. Cobbett described in the *Register* of 25 April 1818 how the occasion was used 'to make the nation believe that *we*, that your *speeches* and my *writings*, had been the cause of the commission of those acts which were called *levying war against the king*'. It was such rubbish but it was to be expected. As his and Hunt's lives were directed towards exposing 'Corruption', it was natural they should be 'honoured with an uncommon portion of her malice.'

The link with Hunt was a powerful way for Cobbett to keep his own name and deeds before the public, even though he was thousands of miles away from the cause, but Cobbett did it with generosity and admiration for Hunt. He reported in the *Register* of 11 April 1818 that a 'People's Memorandum Book' was to be compiled, listing the names of people who had made a 'conspicuous figure' or done great things. It would start from November 1816 so as to include Hunt's speech at the first Spa Fields meeting, which 'produced more effect in the world than all the orations of Demosthenes and Cicero'. (This project failed to materialise.)

Cobbett repeatedly demonstrated his attachment to Hunt. It is there when he returned to Hunt's part in the acquittal of the Spenceans after Spa Fields and the speech Hunt gave at the celebratory dinner afterwards. For some reason, Hunt had referred to the abundant harvest of 1817. Cobbett remembered this tiny oblique detail and recorded it in the *Register* of 10 January 1818. 'There is no man in England a better judge, as to such matters, than Mr Hunt', cooed Cobbett fondly. This time there was no political point to score. It was purely a coded message of affection for Hunt to enjoy, and conjured up the many occasions on which he and Cobbett had swapped farming notes, compared the merits of various species of sheep and talked about good old Jethro Tull.

How Cobbett missed Hunt. At the end of July 1818, he wrote his seventh public address to Hunt and finished it off with a glowing description of the delights of American sporting life. It appeared in the *Register* in England on 3 October 1818 and is a fine example of Cobbett's brilliant ability to hold several threads at a time in his hand. He effortlessly combined sharp political points with what read like a private conversation with Hunt, all written in the best Cobbettian prose. It would be enough to cause an exodus today, let alone in the early nineteenth century when farmers and disaffected working families were emigrating from a dreary England in droves. It is like a breath of clean air blowing away the intrigues and corruption of British politics and, at the same time, celebrates the two men's friendship.

The woodcock shooting had just begun, Cobbett told Hunt. Any kind of a shot would kill '*ten or twelve brace a day.*' Every farm had its own wood, anything from ten to a hundred acres, teeming with birds. They were flying about like bats in the evening. How Hunt would love it. '*You* would kill 100 brace every day', wrote Cobbett. The beautiful setter Hunt had given Cobbett's son James, together with Cobbett's own spaniels from Botley were galloping happily around, making the woods 'ring with their shrill voices'. There were uncountable numbers of partridges, plovers and deer. The season lasted three months and the game never failed. Why don't you come over Hunt, Cobbett urged. 'What say you to a shooting party here':

If you were to set out, I should not wonder if the Borough-mongers, to their other suspensions, were to add a suspension of the prayer for those that 'travel by water.' However, I hope you will not let the fear of this stop you. For I can assure you, that the danger is not half so great as that of going from Portsmouth to the Isle of Wight. Think of it. A hundred brace of woodcocks a day! Think of *that!* And then to see a free country for once and to see every labourer with plenty to eat and drink! Think of *that!* And never to see the hang-dog face of a tax-gatherer. Think of *that!* No Alien Acts here ... No hangings and rippings up. No Castles and Olivers ... No Cannings, Liverpools, Castlereaghs, Eldons, Ellenboroughs or Sidmouths. No Bankers ... No Wilberforces. Think of *that!* No Wilberforces!

The last reference was to the anti-slavery campaigner, William Wilberforce, whom both Hunt and Cobbett despised as the leader of 'the canting Saints'. Neither thought he did enough for what they considered to be the 'white slaves' in England. Wilberforce had also been a member of the House of Common's Secret Committee in 1817 and had backed the suspension of Habeas Corpus. The feeling of antipathy was mutual. In a letter to his family, Wilberforce described Hunt as 'a foolish, mischief-making fellow but no conspirator, though the tool of worse and deeper villains'. He called Cobbett 'the most pernicious of all'.

Cobbett's public displays of affection for Hunt are startling. He wrote about no other man in such a way. Sadly, it was what Cobbett had written about Hunt in the past that made the Westminster election of June/July 1818 an even bigger disaster for Hunt than it might have been. The subject dominated the *Political Register* and the private letters between the two men for many months. As in Bristol in 1812, Hunt battled away without Cobbett at his side. But this time around, owing to the separation of thousands of miles, the power of Cobbett's pen was delayed and, thanks to the dirty tricks brigade, poisoned.

It all started so well with the arrival at the end of 1817 of that first long-awaited letter to Hunt in which Cobbett suggested that Hunt should get involved in the Westminster election where there was to be a vacancy. The sitting MP, Lord Cochrane, was going off to South America to command the Chilean Navy in the fight for independence from Spain. There was a rumour that an Irish friend of Sir Francis Burdett, Roger O'Connor, was being groomed for the post.

It was a ridiculous idea. Roger O'Connor was an unstable Irish nationalist, but Burdett owed him a favour. A few months previously, O'Connor had appeared in court in Ireland, charged with organising the hold-up of the Galway coach. His object was to secure a packet of love letters written by Burdett to his former mistress, Lady Oxford. These were to be used as evidence against Burdett in court. (The daughter of a vicar, Lady Oxford had a string of lovers including Burdett, who probably fathered her eldest son. Her children were known as the 'Harleian Miscellany', after the family collection in the British Museum donated by the second earl of Oxford, Edward Harley.)

In his letter to Hunt, Cobbett made a joke that he knew his friend would ruefully appreciate given the media's exploitation of Hunt's own relationship with Mrs Vince. 'I should not wonder if Lady Oxford were proposed next to be the colleague of the worthy Baronet', he wrote. The whole intrigue ought to be exposed and no man could do it so effectually as Hunt.

To the dismay of both men, it was to be the complication of Hunt's private life with Mrs Vince and Cobbett's own written words about it that blew up Hunt's attempt to take the Westminster seat. For now, they were blissfully unaware of this and Hunt read the letter's concluding promise

with pleasure. Cobbett would that very month write an address to Hunt
for publication in the *Political Register* to start to lay the ground for the
defeat of the O'Connor intrigue.

Cobbett was better than his word. He began the address that same day,
17 October 1817, and it was to occupy the entire issue of the *Register* of
3 January 1818. The address began with the intimate words, 'My dear
Hunt,' just as Cobbett addressed Hunt in his private letters. The electors
of Westminster had to be warned about the plot being hatched by Sir
Francis Burdett, who had slunk out of his prison in the Tower by a back
entrance in 1810 to avoid the crowds, wrote Cobbett. How Hunt, unjustly
confined in the King's Bench Prison at the time, had felt let down, but,
despite his own ambitions, he had continued to support Burdett loyally.
'You have kept your eye steadily fixed upon the public good', wrote
Cobbett. 'I have known you most intimately for fourteen years ... I have
always found you the same man from the first to the last'.

Those words were to echo discordantly back and forth across the
Atlantic during the election just a few months later. For now, Hunt got all
the support and back up from Cobbett he could have wanted. The ground
was laid. Burdett felt the full force of Cobbett's pen from America in the
run up to the election in England. Hunt was bathed in light by the
contrast. Cobbett did it all in torrents of picturesque prose that is a joy to
read. No wonder the *Political Register* kept going, despite all the odds.

Cobbett laid it out before the public in issue after issue. During the
run up to the general election, he wrote, Sir Francis should be closely
questioned on a whole range of subjects including the kind of reform of
parliament he wanted. If he himself were not there to do it, the man for
the job was Henry Hunt, and Cobbett addressed Hunt sonorously: 'I
know well that you will do your duty ... I know well that you will not be
induced to remain silent while any deception or any mummery is going
on'. Everybody had to remember how Burdett had failed to oppose the
Corn Bill which kept cheap corn out of England, and how hard both he
(Cobbett) and Hunt had worked against the Bill, even though they were
also landowners and farmers relying on income from their own harvests.

Cobbett backed up his support in the *Register* with private letters
which were filled with encouragement and advice. His second letter to

Hunt was dated 8 January 1818. Hunt would have received it around March. The letter was long and written in passion to keep pace with the writer's tumultuous thoughts. There were several crossings out and many underlinings. Cobbett was worried that Hunt might not have received the first letter he had sent the previous October, and began with deep affection:

You will not, I am sure, my dear Hunt, ascribe my silence by private letter to any abatement in my attachment to you, but it is right that I explain why you have not heard from me in this way. I have always until now thought it impossible that the vile miscreants and traitors would suffer a letter to reach you by post. I wrote to you in the summer by Mr Harding but perhaps he had no opportunity of putting the letter in the post. I now write through our friend Jackson and I am told you may depend on getting my letter.

Cobbett's letter advised Hunt to announce immediately his own intention to contest the Westminster constituency seat. Although it was Lord Cochrane's seat that would be vacant, Hunt was to challenge and expose Cochrane's co-MP, Sir Francis Burdett. Hunt should write an address to the Westminster electors for publication in the *Register* for which Cobbett had enclosed a suggested script. Hunt was to accuse Burdett of abandoning the cause of reform and failing to oppose the 'cruel Corn Bill'. He was also to charge Burdett with remaining silent when the secret parliamentary committees had accused both Hunt and Cobbett of being revolutionaries.

Cobbett swiftly followed this letter to Hunt with a third just a month later. Hunt should make a move without delay, he wrote. Burdett was frightened of Hunt and his popularity. The baronet would prefer to raise his head under the petticoats of his mistress, Lady Oxford, nay, even under his own wife's, rather than face Hunt, Cobbett joked, and went on even more crudely: 'Take any shape but that!' The time was critical, urged Cobbett, Hunt should seize hold of it.

They were powerful letters and Hunt found them exciting and encouraging. As instructed, he sat down to pen his address to the Westminster electors. Part of Cobbett's suggested script for Hunt survived, so the two versions can be largely compared. Cobbett's script included the following line which Hunt copied exactly: 'I am very far from presuming that no man is so fit as I am to fill ... ' The rest of Cobbett's script did not survive, but it can be seen how his sentence continued from Hunt's address which was eventually published in the *Register*: 'I am very far from presuming that no man is so fit as I am to fill that post unless he has *diligence* and *resolution*, and unless he be firmly resolved to assail Corruption on all occasions that offer and by all the means in his power.' Hunt also made free use of Cobbett's phrase, the 'cruel Corn Bill'.

Assuredly, Hunt would have started work on his address as soon as Cobbett's second letter, together with the suggested script, reached his hands, at the best in March 1818. Yet his address did not appear in the *Political Register* until Saturday, 23 May 1818. This was very close to the election which was to take place the following month. The culprit was Cobbett's publisher, William Jackson. To Hunt's fury, and Cobbett's too when he eventually got to hear about it, Jackson not only delayed publication, he also edited and cut the address, deliberately omitting any direct attacks on Burdett. He also buried it at the end of the *Register*.

Hunt battled on, holding meetings and canvassing support. He was also loyally canvassing on behalf of Cobbett, whose name had been put forward as an MP for Coventry, even though he was still in America. Just a week before the elections began, Hunt went to a meeting at the Eagle Tavern in City Road to speak to 377 freemen of Coventry, who lived in London but had the right to vote in Coventry. Hunt was in the chair and filled with importance. The meeting, he declared in ringing tones, had been called by an advertisement in which he, Hunt, was described as 'The Friend of Mr Cobbett'. He gloried in the name, for he had indeed known Mr Cobbett for fifteen years as the friend of liberty (hear hear). He had no hesitation in saying that Mr Cobbett had enlightened men's minds on the subject of politics more than any other man (hear hear). An account of the meeting appeared in the *Register* on 13 June 1818.

Back in America, the would-be Coventry MP was struggling to keep things going. As he sat on Long Island in early April 1818, writing articles for the issue of the *Register*, which would be published in England on 20 June, two days after the Westminster election had begun, Cobbett wrote plaintively that he had received no news from England since early February.

It would take months before the news of what happened would reach him. So what did happen?

As the general election approached, Hunt believed he was set fair to becoming MP for Westminster. Until the dissolution of parliament on 10 June 1818, he and Burdett were the only nominees for the two seats. After that date, however, a whole host of people, from radicals to liberal Whigs, were put forward to fight the Westminster seats. The Westminster Rump had no intention of letting 'pistols and lamp-post' Hunt get in to the House of Commons. Hunt realised he had no chance of success, but decided to keep the poll open for the full fifteen days. At least, he said, he would have the honour of being the first man to offer himself as a candidate genuinely committed to the principles of one man one vote, annual parliaments and voting by ballot, and he would make the other candidates spend a lot of money in the process.

The contest began on 18 June and continued until 4 July. The hustings were set up as usual in the portico of St Paul's Church facing onto the piazza of Covent Garden. Following Cobbett's instructions, Hunt faithfully set out to question Sir Francis Burdett (who refused to appear on the hustings) to show him up as the most un-radical of reformers. In doing so, as Hunt reported in his *Memoirs*, he exposed himself to the wrath of most of the newspapers in England. The reptiles wrote their stories without the slightest regard to truth or fair play, he said. The usual dirt was brought out against him, and he was crudely heckled about the separation from his wife and his relationship with Mrs Vince, his 'mistress'. (By then the couple had lived together faithfully and lovingly for sixteen years.) The piazza rang to the screams of the various rentacrowds. 'Go home to your wife, where's your wife, Hunt?' they yelled. As Hunt starkly and bitterly wrote: 'During this contest, I was baited like a bull'.

On the fourteenth day, The Westminster Rump's general secretary, Thomas Cleary, ('the little contemptible reptile', as Cobbett called him) self-importantly mounted the hustings. With a triumphant flourish, he produced a piece of paper – a letter – and began reading it out to the crowds jammed into the square. To the delight of Hunt's enemies, it was Cobbett's infamous 'whore on horseback' letter written by Cobbett privately to his publisher John Wright ten years earlier in 1808. In it, Cobbett wrote that he had heard nothing but praise for the merits of Sir

Francis Burdett and that it was essential not to mix with men of bad character, men such as '*Hunt*, the Bristol man. Beware of him! He rides about the country with a whore, the wife of another man, having deserted his own. A sad fellow! Nothing to do with him.'

The piazza erupted. The yells and screams of triumph and the howls, hisses and boos of disapproval echo down through the centuries. Hunt was thunderstruck. His upset and confusion deepened as he was pelted with cabbage stalks. He tried to concentrate on maintaining his dignity in the midst of the chaos and see the election through to the bitter end. He came last with 84 votes. His consolation was the knowledge that he had been the darling of the vote-less crowds and had been cheered as he walked to his carriage at the end of each day, the people jostling for the honour of pulling him home themselves. On top of that, Sir Francis Burdett polled fewer votes than in previous contests. But this was small comfort. Hunt began to write frantic letters to Cobbett in America, begging him to confirm that he had not written the horrible letter and to return home at once.

Cobbett was unaware of what had happened. Without any newspapers or the arrival of any letters, he wrote his articles filling space as best he could. In one issue, which appeared in September 1818, Cobbett made fun of the farmer members of the Wiltshire yeomanry. He imagined them blaming Hunt for the state of the country and the failure of the Corn Laws to guarantee them a good price for their own home-grown corn. Cobbett cleverly mimicked their accent as he had them gathered around the Bible to swear that:

It were aal a long a thick thayer Hunt who's aalways a taaken about the poor, dam un and a maken the thayer fellers as sacey as highwermen. Why did n't hur zay that carn ought to be zold cheeup? Did n't hur zay that cheeup carn was a good thing, dam un! Come, I'll gee ye a toast: Zoshal Arder and Deer Carn!

With no news, Cobbett had to guess the outcome of the Westminster election. His guesses were typically shrewd, his support of Hunt, nevertheless, vastly generous. In a public letter to Hunt in the *Political Register*, published on 3 October 1818 months after the election had taken place, Cobbett wrote that he knew there was no hope that Hunt could have been elected. The great majority of the press would have been against

Hunt, but his friend could take pride in knowing that the mass of people supported him:

The *cause* of this confidence has been, in some degree, your own real merit ... your zeal, disinterestedness, industry, vigilance and great activity, your strict adherence to all your engagements with the people and your fidelity and kindness towards every one who has been oppressed and whom you have been able to assist or console.

There was more in this public letter to Hunt. Every living thing that was notoriously corrupt hated Hunt, Cobbett wrote. He alarmed nobody, except those who were afraid of seeing justice and freedom prevail. Ah, but wait a minute. He did not live with his wife! This was 'a thumping charge', although the Prince Regent did not live with his either. Of course, mocked Cobbett, when baronets (Burdett) or lords (most) were concerned, intrigues, divorces, fornications and adulteries made no difference to their reputations. 'Though we, your friends, may deeply lament that this circumstance should exist,' Cobbett wrote, addressing Hunt directly, 'we have no right to presume any fault in you on this score. Besides this, it is a matter with which the public has nothing to do'.

As the readers of the *Political Register* eagerly read this loyal defence of Hunt by Cobbett, they must have wondered at the paradox or accidental irony of which Cobbett himself was, of course, unaware, that Cobbett's own condemnation of Hunt's immorality had contributed to the hustings' disaster. There is something thrillingly poignant today about reading Cobbett's defence of Hunt. The age-old arguments about public and private lives are still chewed over every time the newspapers dig up unpleasant or embarrassing details about people in the limelight. Is it an infringement of human rights or justifiable information? The twist in those lines written nearly two hundred years ago is that the writer, Cobbett, had himself condemned Hunt for immorality in his fateful letter of 1808, arguing that the facts ruled out Hunt for public life.

Eventually Cobbett found out what had happened. His reaction came in the issue of 28 November 1818. Cobbett being Cobbett, there were plenty of surprises. The week's public letter was to the old reform warhorse, Major John Cartwright, and it began: 'The events of the General Election are now before me and I find them much more satisfactory to me than I anticipated'. WHAAATT, his readers must have screamed as they eagerly scanned the pages. Such a low-key beginning must have taken everybody by surprise, just as Cobbett would have brilliantly calculated. There were no radical reformers elected, he went on, but their time would come. He promised to expose the intrigues of the corrupt Rump and compare the conduct of Mr Hunt with that of Sir Francis Burdett in the next issue. In the meantime, Cobbett went on calmly, he was including a copy of a letter which he had just penned to the editor of the *Evening Post* in New York for publication.

The letter made sensational reading. The *Evening Post* had been following the election story using articles from the London *Courier*, and had republished the 'whore on horseback' letter, remarking that it would 'serve to show, pretty clearly, *Mr Cobbett's opinion of that arch-jacobin, Spafields' Hunt.*' The newspaper, declared Cobbett dramatically, had told lies and re-published a forgery. How could it be anything else when he, Cobbett, had just recommended 'that brave and public-spirited gentleman, Mr Hunt' to the people of Westminster in the strongest terms? Hunt was the man with whom he had been co-operating for almost ten years. He was the most popular man in England. And Cobbett proceeded to list Hunt's attributes. Mr Hunt was in dress, in manners, in mind and in fortune, a gentleman, Cobbett wrote. He was never drunk in his whole life. He was remarkable for his decency of language, economical in his mode of living and abstemious in his diet. He was gentle and kind to all who were dependent on him and always ready to help the oppressed. He was a faithful and zealous friend and braver than the bravest. Cobbett's simple and stark prose clearly revealed the depth of his emotions.

By and large, Cobbett stuck to the claim that the letter was a forgery, although his former publisher, John Wright, successfully sued him over the issue a couple of years later. Historians and biographers have debated about why Cobbett did so, whether he was panicked and told an untruth or had simply forgotten all about the letter. It had been written a decade earlier, one of thousands despatched by Cobbett's busy pen. By 1818, Cobbett and Hunt had enjoyed a long and successful friendship over many years. Hunt had become Cobbett's best friend and closest ally on the political dunghill. Cobbett had grown to respect and admire Mrs Vince. The 'whore' had turned into an elegant, clever and faithful lady. The

violent Hunt of the 'whore on horseback' letter was nothing like his own
dear Hunt. The letter had to be a forgery, didn't it?

Whatever the story, it was a bravura performance. Hunt seized on
Cobbett's denial and held on to it for as long as he could. He also
remained loyal to Cobbett. When the newly-elected Westminster MP, Sir
Samuel Romilly, committed suicide a few months afterwards, Hunt
backed Cobbett's nomination to fill the vacant seat. The *Manchester
Observer* reported that at a rowdy meeting at the Crown and Anchor in
London in November 1818, Hunt leaped on to a table to shout his
support above the din. Cobbett was a great character and political writer
with abilities to serve the public. 'You will find him an Englishman and,
I will say superior in intellect to any man in the country', roared Hunt.
Two months later, in Manchester, Hunt paid tribute to Cobbett's pen
which had defended him against the enemy press. It was a rod Cobbett
used, Hunt said, to render impotent the malice of the scribes of the
boroughmongers.

Cobbett bounced back from the letter episode with a perfect example
of the inventiveness of his pen. The subject ended, at least for the time
being, with a grand finale in the *Political Register* published on
5 December 1818. It was one of Cobbett's most extraordinary bits of
writing, taking the form of a burlesque of Shakespearean plays and
starring Cleary and Burdett. After the shock came mocking gales of
laughter. Here are some choice extracts:

Messenger: Comfort take, I pray you
Dear my Liege, 'tis nought but noisy mob with
Breath most foul that cry for Hunt and real Reform.

Cleary: Are you a man?
Baronet: Yes and a bold one, what man dare, I dare:
Approach thou like the ragged Russian bear,
The arm'd rhinoceros or Hyrcanion tyger,
Take any shape but Hunt's and my firm nerves
Shall never tremble.

Cleary: We'll Hunt, my Liege, attack by forgery,
And make him black as ...
Baronet: Hell, you'd doubtless say.
Ah! Dearest Cleary, that's the only way!

But, who'll believe?
Cleary: 'Tis Cobbett's name we take.
Baronet: The sound, dear Cleary, gives my nerves a shake.
But, can you blacken absent Cobbett too?
Cleary: We'll try, my Liege, what your bank-notes will do ...

Cleary: My Liege, I haste your wishes to obey;
And blacken'd Hunt shall rue the provocation
Given by his ruffian band. Into
His affairs most private will we enter;
His debts and dues, the treatment of his wife,
And his amours at every stage of life;
And though *he* still may act the patriot's part,
We're sure at least, to wring a *woman*'s heart.

There was much more, including lewd allusions to Sir Francis Burdett's own private life and his old affair with Lady Oxford. It was an unusual and witty way to hit back at Sir Francis Burdett and his Westminster Rump friends, although it is not possible to say how hard – if at all – Hunt laughed.

Cobbett's burlesque was mockingly echoed in England in a newspaper called the *Rump Chronicle* in March 1819, when it published a fake theatre bill. Henry Hunt was to play 'Mar-all'. Committee men and hired agents etc would be played by pupils of 'the celebrated Mister Wm. Cobbett'. The other characters included 'John Cleary (Sneak)'. The play was to conclude with 'the Farce of Universal Suffrage or Hell Upon Earth'. (This 'theatre bill' can be found tucked away in the collection of papers of the contemporary reformer Francis Place in the British Library.)

Hunt continued to beg Cobbett to return to England. He felt beleaguered and abandoned. His elder son, Henry, aged eighteen, and Hunt's brother, William, lured by reports of the good life, had left for America shortly after the Westminster elections. Cobbett answered Hunt through the *Register* on 12 December 1818. 'I hear and attend to all you say about my return home', he wrote, but he would not go, not just yet. He did, however, send home his own eldest son, William. Cobbett's treacherous publisher, William Jackson, was sacked shortly after William's arrival. Jackson had been openly colluding with the Westminster Rump. He had even allowed them to use the pages of the

Register to counteract attacks by Cobbett and Hunt. Jackson had also published his own accusations against Hunt, informing the readers, for example, that Hunt was not 'in a fit state of mind to appear before the public'. Jackson was replaced by Thomas Dolby, and William Cobbett junior began to accompany Hunt to dinners and meetings.

From America, Cobbett could hear the clock ticking in England. The cotton spinners of Manchester, 14,000 of them, were on strike over a wage claim. He was sure '*something* is about to take place'. The *Courier* and *The Times* were calling for dragoons, he wrote, and dragoons would come. Given that Peterloo was now just months away, it was prescient writing.

Hunt's letters from England were filled with news of the banks going bust. Cobbett was convinced the economy in England was tottering, owing to the overuse of bank notes, nasty 'paper money', as he called it, as opposed to proper gold and silver coins. He believed that if the economy did collapse, a reform of parliament would be inevitable. He also thought he could speed things up with his 'long arm' from America and came up with the idea of a massive forgery of bank notes to undermine Britain's finances and push the economy over the edge. He asked Hunt publicly through the pages of the *Register* to send over specimens of any bank notes that the Bank of England claimed were 'inimitable'. The notes, he wrote, could easily be forged in America and sent to England to be scattered around the streets. Mischievously, Cobbett announced that he would send a parcel to the Prince Regent.

Cobbett called his scheme the 'great Puff-Out'. The rumour spread that Hunt was going to organise the distribution of the forged notes in England. Unsurprisingly, Hunt did not entirely approve of this idea. The penalty for forging bank notes was, after all, death by hanging. Hunt chose more orthodox methods and took over a meeting of top bankers, merchants and politicians at the London Tavern in Bishopsgate on 18 May 1819, He routed them all with his own warnings about the economy and argued for an immediate return to gold and silver coinage.

Cobbett was probably not entirely serious about his Puff-Out plan. The poet, Percy Bysshe Shelley, however, was among those who loved the idea. He wrote to his fellow poet, the novelist, Thomas Love Peacock, to tell him so: 'Cobbett still more & more delights me, with all my horror of the sanguinary commonplaces of his creed. His design to overthrow Bank notes by forgery is very comic.'

Home Office papers show that the government took the forgery threat very seriously. So did the people. The *Manchester Observer* published a letter in June 1819 from the inhabitants of Wigan begging Cobbett to get a move on with his 'PUFF-OUT' to bring down the system. 'The monster can only be choked by giving him plenty of paper', they wrote.

Cobbett's Puff-Out plan hit a nerve. The people of England were desperate for a change of system. Cobbett knew this clearly in America, although he himself had no desire for a revolution. He knew that a reform had to come from democratic and non-violent efforts. The people, he wrote, had to be 'uncommonly active'. '*Good, large meetings*; good

[Imitation Bank Note]
Engraving of a fake bank note, following Cobbett's 'Puff-Out' plan. The three naked figures at the top, 'Quintessence of Revolution', are Cobbett, Hunt and Hone about to be flogged. Cobbett and Hunt are also on the side, pulling the cart. 1819
© *The Trustees of the British Museum*

speeches; good petitions; all these would do infinite service'.

Cobbett, of course, could not know that Hunt was about to do just that with disastrous consequences, but he felt uneasy for a variety of reasons. In the *Register* of 11 September 1819, he told Hunt that he would strike his tent that 'fall'. He meant it literally. Hyde Park house had burned down and Cobbett was living with his 17-year-old son, James, in a thatched tent lined with copies of the *Morning Chronicle* and *Courier*. This may have had something to do with his decision to go home. Here though, Cobbett wrote with sudden anxiety. He hoped that the people were not plotting to destroy the government. They were to stick to their text: 'Reform and nothing but Reform', otherwise England would be ruined. How Cobbett wished he had been with Hunt at the London Tavern meeting. What a glorious scene. How different was Hunt's conduct from that of the Shoy-Hoy (scarecrow) Burdett! 'What could that stuffed-with-straw have been at, while you were thus active?' jeered Cobbett. Was he like 'the God of the Baalites', asleep or gone on a journey or was he looking with his noon-day lantern for a public? What a triumph! And how clever he, Cobbett, was. Here he was, cut off from information in America but still using his 'long stick' to beat down 'the cowardly butchers'. It was again, sharp writing from Cobbett. He had no idea about the Peterloo Massacre which had happened just three weeks earlier: 'Why could not these shoy-hoys have done something *in* parliament, seeing that you could do so much *out* of it? Oh! what confusion we could have covered the reptiles with, if the people of *Coventry* had sent *me* into the House!'

The use of the word, '*me*', rather than 'us' stands out. Was Cobbett suddenly worried about Hunt and his increasing popularity among the radicals in England? Hunt had become 'Spa Fields Hunt', 'Orator Hunt' and the 'People's Man'. Was Cobbett concerned that by now he, Cobbett, was being sidelined? Were others filling his place, for example Hunt, who was handling the political scene so magnificently? He, Cobbett, was the teacher. The paper money saga was his story, yet Hunt was getting the glory. Cobbett continued to heap praise on Hunt who, he said, had not been subdued, despite all the conspiracies and the 'legal rascallites' against him. Cobbett also paid implicit tribute to the woman who loved and supported Hunt, Mrs Vince:

I beg you to remember me most kindly to all those who are dear to you, and who in any way whatever have assisted in supporting your spirits under such unheard of persecutions ... That they have not subdued you is to you glory more than enough for one man. You could not, with all your wonderful courage, have stood under such an accumulation of disheartening circumstances, had not some kindred heart come to your consolation and support; and the person whose bosom contains that heart, shall ever be held in honour by me.

Generous words for Hunt's achievements, yet there was an ambivalence in Cobbett's pen as he celebrated at the same time his own influence in England through the *Register* and anticipated his own success as an MP with the backing of Hunt outside the House of Commons. It was 'enough' glory for Hunt that 'they' had not 'subdued' him, wrote Cobbett. (Could he really have thought that the ambitious Hunt would be satisfied with that?) What was more, Hunt had not done it alone. A kindred heart (Mrs Vince) had been essential to Hunt's success. He could not have done it by himself (unlike Cobbett).

Cobbett's words were ambiguous. He could have had no idea, however, how horribly ironic his article was to sound when it was published in England after the Peterloo massacre, when 'they' finally did subdue Hunt.

9
Peterloo

Stuff happens.
US Defence Secretary, Donald Rumsfeld, 2003

Visitors to Manchester on the trail of the Peterloo Massacre have to look long and hard to find out where the infamous event took place and what exactly happened. The site of St Peter's Field can be located around St Peter Street, which runs eastwards off Deansgate in the city centre. The famous field itself long since disappeared under roads, tramlines and buildings. St Peter's Church, which was built just twenty-five years before Peterloo, could have provided an important clue to the location, but it was pulled down in 1907, although, ghost-like, its shape still survives. The church walls are marked out on the ground in the area occupied by the Cenotaph and memorial garden in what is now St Peter's Square.

People will no doubt stroll around the streets and admire the splendid buildings, largely Victorian, that have survived. These include the former Central Station, now the GMEX events centre, the splendid pile of the Midland Hotel and the former Free Trade Hall, today a luxury hotel. The latter occupies the spot on the southern edge of what was St Peter's Field where the hustings were positioned on the fateful day in August 1819. The first Free Trade Hall was built twenty years after the massacre. Discerning visitors admiring the imposing stone façade may notice a small plaque on the left-hand corner of the building. Until the end of 2007, this is what it said:

The site of St Peter's Fields where on 16th August 1819 HENRY HUNT RADICAL ORATOR addressed an assembly of about 60,000 people. Their subsequent dispersal by the military is remembered as PETERLOO.

The information was surprisingly cursory and misleading. The crowd figure of 60,000 was given by the city magistrates at the time. It was, of course, the lowest estimate. The radical *Manchester Observer* estimated a figure of 153,000. Hunt thought the numbers could have been higher, anything up to 200,000. Hunt was indeed the principal speaker although he never managed to make his speech. He was interrupted after just a few minutes when the Manchester and Salford Yeomanry charged into the crowds with sabres at the ready. Michael Bush estimated in his book, *The Casualties of Peterloo*, that the 'dispersal by the military' resulted in around fifteen deaths and that taking into account the deaths caused by further action the following week, the number of people killed as a result of the Peterloo event was at least eighteen. Bush also estimated that the number of people injured exceeded seven hundred. The plaque omitted to mention the numbers of casualties and also gave no hint of the reason for the meeting, which was to call for a reform of parliament and the abolition of the Corn Laws. The plaque neatly airbrushed the facts from history.

In 2008, after a protest campaign, another plaque was put up over the first:

The Peterloo Massacre – on the 16th August 1819, a peaceful rally of 60,000 pro-democracy reformers, mostly impoverished workers and their families, was charged by armed cavalry resulting in 15 deaths and over 600 injuries.

The words are slightly altered and some important numbers revised, but the plaque still fails to mention that the 'armed cavalry' were local people who cut down the crowds. And now there is no mention of Henry Hunt.

Hunt was uneasy in the run up to the meeting. His family had urged him to turn down the invitation to speak. They were right to be concerned. Home Office papers show that around this time, Sidmouth authorised the interception of letters addressed to Hunt. A letter from Henry Hobhouse, permanent under-secretary in the Home Office and a cousin of John Cam Hobhouse, reveals that the authorities were looking for a reason to pin a charge of treason on Hunt and have him hanged. The government was blaming the messenger rather than understanding the message. Since Spa Fields, the country had been in a state of continuous and violent unrest. There were riots, demonstrations and protests, including the March of the Blanketeers in which a group of country weavers set out to walk to London to ask for a minimum wage. Desperate men went on strike over starvation wages. The repeal of the Gagging Acts had allowed public meetings to resume, but, in an unprecedented step, the Prince Regent issued a proclamation just two weeks before the Manchester meeting. This included a warning to anybody calling meetings or writing articles to beware of treason and sedition. It also threatened the new, fairly desperate practice of the radical reformers to hold quasi-elections for mock MPs, a grass-roots dummy-run for a democratic, reformed House of Commons. The prince, who was guided by ministers, urged magistrates to use all the available laws to stamp down hard on anything they decided might be against the interests of the state. Long after Peterloo, when Cobbett received news of the proclamation, he described the prince's move as 'something new'. It convinced him that the system was about to collapse and added urgency to his feeling that it was a good time to return to England.

The Manchester radicals selected a day for a big meeting to be held on St Peter's Field, rashly advertising that they were going to hold one of the mock elections. The city magistrates promptly posted placards all over the town denouncing the meeting as illegal and warning people not to attend. The meeting was rearranged for 16 August 1819 and this time it was called 'to take into consideration the best and most legal means of obtaining a Reform in the Commons' House of Parliament'. Hunt was still uneasy, especially when he learned of a rumour that the magistrates planned to arrest him and charge him with a concocted political offence. He drove down to the city to receive a denial from the magistrates. He thought he had done all he could.

The day dawned. 'Monday arrived, and a beautiful morning it was', wrote Hunt in his *Memoirs*. It was indeed a perfect summer's day, with sunshine, warmth and a gentle breeze to cool the brow. Hunt was staying with one of the northern radical reformers, the brushmaker Joseph Johnson, in his cottage in Smedley, which was then outside the city. Hunt watched from his bedroom as men, women and children, accompanied by flags and bands, streamed by, heading for St Peter's Field. The conduct of the people was such that none but devils in human form could ever have premeditated to do them any injury, Hunt wrote bitterly in retrospect. Tens of thousands of people were similarly making their way into Manchester from the many villages and towns surrounding the growing industrial city, since swallowed up in the urban sprawl. There was a holiday atmosphere. People were wearing their best clothes for the occasion and they danced and sang along the way. They carried beautifully embroidered banners. The Oldham banner was of pure silk and bore the words: 'UNIVERSAL SUFFRAGE, ANNUAL PARLIAMENT, ELECTION BY BALLOT, NO COMBINATION ACTS, OLDHAM UNION'.

Wearing what became his trademark white bowler-style hat for 'purity', Hunt drove in his barouche (an elegant, light open-air carriage) to St Peter's Field, where he found an immense multitude waiting. As he drove on to the field, bands struck up the same tune, 'See the conquering hero comes'. Flags were unfurled and a roar of welcome went up. Hunt was overwhelmed. He described it in his *Memoirs* almost as if it were a religious experience. 'Every one appeared to me to be actuated by a similar feeling ... namely, the performance of an important, a sacred and a solemn duty to ourselves and our country.'

Hunt and his entourage were met by the Manchester Committee of Female Reformers, who were led by Mary Fildes carrying in her hand a white silk flag. She joined Hunt in the barouche and accompanied him onto the platform. (Mrs Fildes was to have her clothes torn away and her body slashed by a yeoman's sabre.) Her ladies, dressed all in white, followed in pairs behind the carriage up to the hustings, a platform placed over two carts.

Hunt mounted the platform and prepared to address the expectant crowds. He had hardly uttered a few sentences when the Manchester and Salford Troop of Yeomanry appeared on the field. Their members were all local business people who had volunteered to join up. It was fun to be in the yeomanry. It gave a good excuse to buy a fine horse and enjoy excellent drinking sessions. This troop included farmers, butchers, cotton workers, mill owners, cheese mongers, watch-makers, tobacconists, a lawyer, a farrier and a dancing master. Many in the crowds knew the men well, but as they rode on to the field jam-packed with people, there was a stir and panic.

Hunt called for the crowds to give three cheers in an attempt to defuse the alarm. He recorded in his *Memoirs* that before the cheering had even stopped, the yeomanry troop, led by its trumpeter, 'charged amongst the people, sabring right and left, in all directions, sparing neither age, sex nor rank'. Hunt's description was corroborated by the journalist Edward Baines, no friend of Hunt or Cobbett although he was also on the hustings that day. Baines described the scene decades later in his biography of his father: 'The yeomanry dashed furiously into the midst of an unarmed multitude, whom they trampled down and struck with their sabres ... Several persons were killed and hundreds wounded by this military outrage.'

The horsemen headed for the hustings. Eye witnesses said it was obvious the men were drunk because they were rolling around on their horses which were running out of control. It was also known that, unusually, their swords had been sharpened before the meeting. There was general panic. In the confusion, many people were trampled under hooves. Others were crushed in the press to escape. Many were slashed with those sharpened blades. The cavalrymen cut their way up to the hustings, and Hunt was arrested. As he was hurried away, two tried to slash him with their swords. Hunt quickly grasped hold of the arm of Manchester's deputy constable, Joseph Nadin, to use him as a shield, although he was still cut at several times. Two strokes pierced his hat and his hand was injured. Nadin also failed to prevent an army general from smashing Hunt's head twice in a double-handed blow with a heavy club. Hunt believed he was going to be murdered. His hat saved him from serious injury.

The magistrates sent in the 15th Hussars to clear the field. There was more panic. Hundreds more people were trampled and crushed as they tried to get away. There were further deaths and terrible injuries. The situation was made worse by the fact that the authorities had ringed the whole area with soldiers who blocked up roads and escape routes. People found themselves trapped, with the yeomanry cutting them down from behind. Bodies piled up against walls.

It took between ten to fifteen minutes for the field to be cleared except for the yeomanry wiping their blades and easing their horses' girths, the injured people who were unable to run away – and the dead. The reformer, Samuel Bamford, described the awful scene in his autobiography:

The hustings remained, with a few broken and hewed flag-staves erect and a torn and gashed banner or two dropping; whilst over the whole field, were strewed caps, bonnets, hats, shawls and shoes and other parts of male and female dress; trampled, torn and bloody ... Several mounds of human beings still remained where they had fallen, crushed down and smothered. Some of these still groaning – others with staring eyes were gasping for breath and others would never breathe more. All was silent save those low sounds and the occasional snorting and pawing of steeds.

Along with several others, including Bamford, Hunt was charged with high treason and locked up in Manchester's New Bailey Prison which squatted on the Salford side of the river bank of the Irwell, just over Bridge Street bridge (later re-named Albert Bridge). All the men were held in solitary confinement for eleven days before appearing in court. The initial charge of treason was dropped for one of seditious conspiracy to overturn the government. Hunt was given bail, although he was transferred to Lancaster Castle and briefly locked up in one of the towers before he had time to get it organised.

The events of 16 August 1819 quickly became known as 'Peterloo'. The name was coined shortly after the event by the *Manchester Observer*. Protest meetings were held across the country. Sir Francis Burdett wrote a passionate letter calling for a meeting in Westminster to demand that the men responsible for the atrocities committed on St Peter's Field should be put on trial:

What, kill men unarmed, unresisting & gracious God, women too! Disfigured, maimed, cut down and trampled on by Dragoons. Is this England? ... Whether the penalty of our meeting will be death by military execution I know not; but this I know, a man can die but once & never better than in vindicating the laws and liberties of his country.

The letter was to earn the baronet a three-month prison sentence for seditious libel. It was one of the finer moments of Burdett's career – although his letter failed to make any reference to Hunt.

Before going home, Hunt issued a farewell address to 'the brave reformers of Lancashire', in which he pledged himself not to taste one drop of taxed beer, spirits, wine or tea until the Peterloo murderers had been brought to justice. He arrived back in London on Monday, 13 September 1819, arriving at Islington via the Holloway Turnpike in the middle of the afternoon. Vast crowds had been waiting for hours to cheer him on his arrival. It was a beautiful day. Hunt looked pale and tired but revived when he saw the crowds. In his post chaise were 'two females elegantly dressed'. One of them was Catherine Vince. Together with Hunt, she had attended a stormy meeting of the reformers in Barnet the night before, when Hunt was urged to ditch the dodgy Spenceans, including Arthur Thistlewood and Dr Watson, and agree to work with Sir Francis Burdett and the Westminster Rump. The story was leaked to *The Times* a few days later.

Hunt's triumphal journey that afternoon took him from Islington to the City, along City Road and Sun Street, into Bishopsgate Street, up Cornhill and past the Mansion House from where the Mayor of London was watching. This was the only place where the military was deployed. He continued along Cheapside, past St Paul's Cathedral, along Ludgate Hill and Fleet Street, through Temple Bar (now to be seen in the precincts of St Paul's churchyard) and into the Strand to the Crown and Anchor where a dinner had been arranged. The journey took more than three hours.

Hunt travelled in the procession alone in a carriage drawn by six handsome bays decorated with scarlet ribbons. He was wearing his favourite tight white 'jeans', as *The Times* reported. His head was uncovered – he held his white bowler hat in his hands – and he bowed to the crowds as he passed by. Occasionally he lifted up the hat to show the crowds the sabre marks it bore. Behind him stood a man waving a large red flag over his head inscribed with the words, 'Liberty or Death'.

Hunt was followed by a long, colourful procession; bands of music played and hundreds of footmen carried branches of oak, poplar and other trees. *The Times* said it looked just like Birnam Wood coming to Dunsinane. Horsemen carried scrolls and banners. One scroll bore the words, 'Magna Charta and Bill of Rights'. There were scores of colourful silk flags, some commemorating the victims of the Manchester massacre, others calling for Universal Suffrage. Most flags had small pieces of black crape fastened at the ends, out of respect for the people who had been killed.

More than 300,000 people, many of them with knots of red ribbons in their hats, were on the streets to salute Hunt and enjoy the spectacle.

They had either walked to get there or, as *The Times* reported, arrived
using any and every kind of conveyance they could find, 'from the glass
coaches and landau, to the humble tax cart or cumbrous coal-waggon'.
The houses, windows, doors, eaves and roofs along the route were packed
with people. Among the crowds was the poet John Keats who was
overcome by the event. He described it in a letter on 18 September 1819
to his brother and sister:

You will hear by the papers of the proceedings at Manchester, and Hunt's triumphal entry
into London. It would take me a whole day and a quire of paper to give you anything like
detail ... The whole distance from the Angel at Islington to the Crown and Anchor was
lined with multitudes.

London was brought to a standstill. 'It is impossible to describe the
enthusiasm with which Mr Hunt was received as he passed along', wrote
The Times with uncharacteristic enthusiasm, given that the newspaper
was one of Hunt's most bitter enemies. The scene was unprecedented;
there had been nothing like it in living memory, the newspaper reported:

The waving of hats and handkerchiefs, the clapping of hands, the shouts of applause
mingled with the sounds of musical instruments and the voices of some thousands who
accompanied them in the national air of 'Rule Britannia,' presented to the eye and to the
ear such a combination of scene and sound, as we believe has seldom, if ever, been equalled
in London.

Four hundred people attended the dinner at the Crown and Anchor.
Fresh from the meeting in Barnet the night before and with a new mood,
Hunt said it was time to hold out the olive branch rather than throw down
the apple of discord. All animosities and former causes of disagreement
should now be buried in oblivion, he said solemnly. Everybody needed to
join hand and heart to fight for the one great object, a reform of
parliament. Everybody, he urged, should stand together.

Over in America, Cobbett was unaware of the momentous events in
England. He continued to fill the *Political Register* as best he could as he
made preparations to return to England. He continued to address Hunt
in the *Register*, but there was a palpable change in his tone and manner of
writing. It was as if Cobbett had mentally taken a step backwards away

from Hunt and everyone else and was preparing the ground to proclaim his own independence. At the end of July, he sat down to write his lead article for the issue of the *Register*, published in England on 2 October 1819. It took the shape of another public letter to Hunt, No 12, the last to be written in America. It filled the entire issue. Cobbett could not know it, but it was written just days before Peterloo.

Cobbett addressed his friend as usual as his 'dear Hunt', and concluded the address with the sign off: 'I am always most faithfully yours'. But it was a very different public letter from the ones that had gone before. Cobbett picked up again on the London Tavern meeting and paid tribute to Hunt in the opening paragraph:

Well may the tyrants hate you! Well may you be hated by the tribes of little envious wretches like the Burdettites of Liverpool! Well may all the hordes of lawyers, spies, and blood-money men seek your life!

As Cobbett continued writing, however, it became clear that the opening lines were not as straightforward as they seemed, and his praise of Hunt became cooler. Cobbett now realised that Hunt had not tackled the issue of paper money in quite the way he, Cobbett, would have wanted. And as the paragraphs turned into pages, Cobbett moved the spotlight away from Hunt, whom he patronisingly referred to as 'my good fellow', to shine brightly and unwaveringly on himself. He, Cobbett, had been the only one to reveal the inadequacies and dangers of the bank note system. He, alone, knew that a return to payment in gold could not be done without reducing the national debt and cutting spending on the army, sinecure pensions and salaries. He believed that the measures had been ruled out '*only because they have been proposed* BY ME'.

The tone was set, and so Cobbett continued. All those years ago, he wrote, he had set out as a 'self-dependant politician'. His opinions were his own and he had dashed at all prejudices. Before his time, every talented writer enlisted under the banners of one party or minister. He, alone, had stood free from all such connections. He had crouched to no power. He had drawn down upon himself the mortal hatred of the press and the men in power. All had hated him and all had desired to keep him down.

Cobbett used the word 'hatred' repeatedly here, and also the even more corrosive phrase, 'hatred and envy'. His return to England was to be 'a new epoch' in his life, he said. Great events would take place. Great changes had to take place. He had it in his power to propose the means of 'complete restoration' of the country. He had made up his mind as to the part he should act. 'Let it be our business to expose their follies and their crimes', he wrote, offering a token hand to Hunt. He looked forward to being back with Hunt after Christmas, he said, but this personal note was overwhelmed by the egotistic roar of what had just gone before.

A few weeks later, there were more signs of this fierce, almost paranoid independence in the issue of the *Register* of 30 October 1819, which had been written in America on 5 September. It came in a sudden diatribe in which Cobbett rejoiced in his triumph over Sidmouth, Canning and Castlereagh, who all thought they had got rid of their greatest danger, his writings. How busy they had been in crying down his 'trash'. They would have been better employed studying it. The boroughmongers used to laugh at Cobbett's predictions. They were not laughing any longer:

> Has *any* man, or any body of men, succeeded in their attempts to pull me down, or to keep me down? Where are *now* Gibbs and his set? Where are the hundreds of hirelings, set up to write me down? Where are Burdett and his Rump Committee? Where are all the host of foes that ... have assailed me with a species of hostility?

Cobbett again referred to the envy, hatred and hostility against him from the 'gabblers in parliament' and the reporters who had written about the evils of the paper-bubble, 'using my arguments in my very words'. It was clear that Cobbett was getting ready to turn his back on all of them, although he penned a postscript to his 'dear Hunt' to say that he was due to sail back to England on 10 October 1819. He urged Hunt to be cautious in language as well as movements. Cobbett was sniffing the winds from England, although his words were, unfortunately, too late. By then Hunt was busy dealing with the aftermath of Peterloo. Was he aware of what was going on inside Cobbett's head? He might have made a diary note of the date on which Cobbett's ship would be docking in Liverpool – but he would not go to meet it.

Cobbett had left Long Island and was in New York waiting for his ship. He left Hyde Park in August about six weeks before his departure, to establish an office for his 17-year-old son, James, who was to stay behind and run Cobbett's publishing and seed business there. By 10 September 1819, Cobbett had all the details about the Prince Regent's proclamation. It made good copy for the *Register*. He could guess that a crisis was approaching, and more news was coming in even as he was writing. There was a thrilled note in the postscript for the issue of the *Register* that appeared in England on 6 November 1819. 'We have just heard of the Battle of Manchester', Cobbett wrote urgently and with some confusion. He did not know the details, but it had obviously been a 'mere downright act of unlawful violence'. The authorities had thought any 'odium' was preferable to the holding of meetings. Cobbett urged people to remain cool and rely on the collapse of the economic system to achieve a reform of parliament, rather than on a revolution against the status quo.

By 26 September, as Cobbett was putting the finishing touches to the issue of the *Register* which would be published in England on 13 November 1819, he received more news. 'We have just got a short account of the *Manchester Murders*', he wrote to Hunt in the *Register* in great excitement. The news had come from a couple of paragraphs taken from articles in the Irish press and re-published in the New York press. The people must get their rights or the government would have to lay aside all laws and impose a military dictatorship to quell the unrest, Cobbett wrote. He was relieved to read that Hunt had been in prison – because that meant he had not been killed.

I pray God to preserve your life and your health; for, I am fully convinced that your life is, at this moment, of inestimable value to our unhappy country, in whose cause you have made so many and such great exertions and sacrifices.

These rather stiff and formal lines came after a lengthy passage filled with meandering jokes and insults against the Whigs and Hunt's enemies in the City of London. Cobbett's usual sharpness was missing. He gabbled and rambled and then pulled himself together to hope that Hunt would be preserved from 'all conspiracy, murder and sudden death'. There was a note of ghoulish excitement in the postscript Cobbett then added. They were waiting anxiously for news from England, he wrote, and wanted to know what Sidmouth's Manchester men would do with him. They would probably decide to imprison him for some time. It was likely that the blood spilt at Manchester was just a start. If the assailants went unpunished, England was under '*military government now.*' And Cobbett added with high melodrama, 'Adieu; take care, what you *eat* and what you *drink*. Remember *Emperor Paul* and *Baron Gortz*! You are of more consequence than either of them ever was.'

Dramatic stuff and there was still more, written just two days later. Cobbett was still without any of the English newspapers, but the American press was reporting that Hunt had been detained on a charge of '*High Treason!!!*' This was just what Cobbett had expected. 'You are an object of hatred with every thing cruel, base and treacherous that England contains', he wrote happily. He was sure that Sir Francis Burdett would view what had happened to Hunt with feelings like those of Satan, when Job's flocks, herds and children were dying. Cobbett was sure nobody would do anything, even call a public meeting to protest.

In fact Burdett had done so, and at the meeting in Old Palace Yard, Westminster, on 2 September, had (at last) praised Hunt for his 'wisdom and propriety'. The reformers were continuing to urge Hunt to unite with Burdett and the Westminster Rump. Cobbett knew about Burdett's post-Peterloo letter and his call for a meeting before he left America, because he later said so in the *Register*, weeks after he got back to England. He must have pondered on events as the ship sailed to England, brooding over the implications. It doubtless fuelled his fears that Hunt would join Burdett and that, he, Cobbett would be side-lined. His fears were unnecessary. Hunt declined to co-operate with Burdett, but Cobbett's jealousy was not to be assuaged.

With a note of envy, Cobbett continued his article, comparing Hunt to the Puritan, William Prynne, who had defied William Laud, the archbishop of Charles I, and had his ears – and later the stumps – cut off as a result. Cobbett also compared Hunt to the seventeenth century anti-royalist in the civil war, John Hampden, who died of his injuries received in battle and was the inspiration for the Hampden Club. 'Your name will be honoured for ever', wrote Cobbett reassuringly to Hunt and warned him on no account to go further than calling for a reform, certainly not even to think of '*republicanism*'. He himself would soon be there. His writings from America had done their work. The people of England now knew everything they needed to know about the question at issue. Nobody could cheat them any more into believing that they should be wretched:

There is no *guessing* at what may happen. There must be a *great change*, but many of us may be destroyed during our efforts to preserve the crown and restore the nation to happiness. The Borough-Moloch may take my blood, perhaps. But I think that the time is at hand when I ought to be ready to assist, with my best abilities, my suffering countrymen and our insulted king.

What a perfect moment to go home. The words 'insulted king' were written to underline Cobbett's rejection of republicanism. On no account did he want a French-style revolution. He was absolutely unconscious of how the lines that followed undermined this reassurance to the dying George III and his Prince Regent son.

To make his return to England even more perfect, Cobbett wrote dramatically, he was returning with the bones of Tom Paine. He had found

'The Political Champion turned Resurrection Man'
Cobbett flies home to England with the bones of Tom Paine to be welcomed by a riotous mob, one holding a red flag, 'HUNT and COBBETT'. Bonaparte in exile on St. Helena behind says: 'Ah! Ça ira'.
Isaac Robert Cruikshank, 1819
© *The Trustees of the British Museum*

Paine's bones 'lying in a corner of a rugged, barren field!' His expedition
had set out from New York in the middle of the night, arriving at the spot
at dawn. He had done it on behalf of the reformers of England, Scotland
and Ireland. He planned to write a complete history of Paine's life, labours
and death. At last Englishmen would honour Paine's name and memory.
It was Paine who had so brilliantly exposed the truth about Britain's
economy. Cobbett might not agree with Paine about everything (in
particular with his republicanism and deism which was seen as atheism)
but he was a friend of freedom and that was enough for him.

Cobbett was scribbling furiously away up against a deadline. His copy
had to be deposited safely in a ship that was about to sail away to England.
There were six more days to go before he himself was due to board his ship

'The Radicals'
Cobbett as the Hampshire Hog dragging Tom Paine's skeleton. Hunt
follows on behind wearing his white top hat and holding a bag labelled
'The Weekly Penny Radical Subscription'.
© *The Trustees of the British Museum*

to go home. He had no sense of the paradox in the final paragraph he wrote. Hunt should demand nothing else except a radical reform of parliament. Under the circumstances, any man who proposed republicanism as the ultimate object would have to be nearly mad. All they had to do was keep steadily on and they would see 'a long series of happy and glorious days'. Cobbett wrote this with a final flourish as he looked proudly at the case into which he had packed the arch-republican's bones to take back home, as he thought, in triumph to England.

Cobbett's ship docked in Liverpool on Sunday evening, 21 November 1819. The passengers were not allowed to land until 2 o'clock the next day. Cobbett was desperate to see Hunt – although the latter had now become 'Mr Hunt' again. In a private letter to his son James, who had been left behind in New York, Cobbett revealed that as soon as the ship docked, he was leaning over the side shouting for information: 'No communication, except by bawling, has yet been suffered between us and the shore. But Mr Smith came alongside last night and from him I learnt... that Mr Hunt was well and was to be sent for when I came'.

Cobbett was in a state of high excitement and he received the reception he hoped for. Crowds had gathered on the wharfs to greet him. As he left the ship, there were many cheers and much shaking of hands. A public meeting was arranged in Clayton Square in Liverpool, followed by a dinner at Castle Inn in Lord Street. A government informer sent a report of the dinner from the radical *Manchester Observer* to the Home Office, where it can still be found in the files. At the dinner, Cobbett was called upon to forget any differences between himself and 'other eminent leaders of reform'. Cobbett replied that he was ready 'to bury all that had occurred in oblivion, and to make every sacrifice for union'. If he found there were 'empty promises', however, he would be unable to do so, and he referred, ominously, to 'nasty, envious dispositions'.

Cobbett headed off for Manchester where the Female Reformers were to present him with a silver writing stand and pen, but the magistrates refused him entry into the city. Cobbett made much of their refusal in the *Register*. He turned back to Warrington and took the road to London via Coventry, where thousands more people turned out to greet him. At

Coventry, Cobbett referred to the 'fatal results' of 16 August, but the reports of his speech do not show that he mentioned Hunt by name.

The reception he was given should have been balm to Cobbett's soul and told him what was obvious, that he had no need to be concerned about his position in England. Nobody could equal his powerful pen, and his enemies still cowered before him. As soon as his ship docked, the little spies and informers were busy watching Cobbett's every move, reporting back to the Home Office in London. The government scrambled to bring in new repressive legislation. Parliament was convened especially to pass the infamous Six Acts. Public meetings were restricted, even more severely than they had been in 1817. Only people living in the parish where the meeting was held would be allowed to attend. Those who were convicted of seditious libel for the second time faced banishment. (Cobbett already had one conviction for his comments on the Ely floggings.) The radical press was also hit with an increase in the tax on political pamphlets. This was aimed mainly at Cobbett's publications. Almost as soon as he got home, he had to increase the price of the *Political Register*. This affected circulation and reduced his income.

Despite all this proof positive of his power and influence, the poison of envy had dripped into Cobbett's soul. It was plain from the issues of the *Register* which direction he was heading, and it was away from the reformers and Hunt. *The Times* took great delight in foreseeing what was going to happen. Almost as soon as Cobbett had landed, the newspaper cautioned Hunt to 'beware' of Cobbett, and dredged up yet again the 'whore on horseback' letter. The newspaper chortled that 'my dear Hunt' would soon be grossly 'blackguarded' again by 'my dear Cobbett'. It would not be long, said *The Times*, before Cobbett's pen attacked Hunt again for some cause or other.

The pair met in London as soon as Cobbett arrived. Did Cobbett 'send for' Hunt? Did Hunt rush to Cobbett's side? It is impossible to say. After nearly three momentous years apart, these two proud and sensitive men once again faced each other. It would have been an interesting meeting on which to eavesdrop – possibly a restrained and rather formal encounter, both men moving cautiously, wondering, almost as they had at their first meeting in 1805. There was so much to say, to ask and discuss, yet so many emotions to hold them back. Hunt may have bitterly remembered how he heard the news in Devizes of Cobbett's flight to America. In Cobbett's absence, Hunt, now aged forty-seven, had gone from being the Spa Fields Orator to the hero of Peterloo. Cobbett, ten years older, fresh from the freedom and wide-open spaces of America where he had been king in his own domain, may have looked at Hunt, a growing paranoia and suspicion peeping out of his ever-watchful eyes. Hunt, having read the last few issues of the *Register*, may have returned the gaze, hoping against hope that his powerful friend could be persuaded out of ploughing a lonely furrow and would realise instead that there was strength in unity.

Cobbett only made a brief reference to Hunt in the *Register* of 4 December 1819, the first issue to be published after his return to England. It took the form of a public letter to his son James. Cobbett was happy to say, 'Mr Hunt is well, and that, with the exception of the very ignorant and the very corrupt, his conduct has the hearty approbation of this whole nation'. Cobbett also mentioned that people were being urged to boycott beer, wine, spirits, tea, coffee and tobacco, all of which were heavily taxed. 'This is a measure strongly recommended by Mr Hunt', he wrote. And that was all.

A public dinner, with Hunt in the chair, was held on 4 December 1819 at the Crown and Anchor to celebrate Cobbett's return. Nothing but water was drunk all evening. Gratifyingly for Cobbett, the dinner was a sell out and many people had to be turned away. Significantly and unsurprisingly, Sir Francis Burdett declined to attend. Among the diners was Thomas Wooler, editor of *Black Dwarf.* Wooler had criticised Cobbett mercilessly for deserting the cause in 1817 and taking refuge in America, although he had afterwards repeatedly urged him to return home where his pen was needed. As soon as Wooler walked into the Crown and Anchor, Hunt rushed over to him and guided him towards Cobbett in order that the two men could shake hands and make peace. The *Manchester Observer* reported that the action produced a sudden and spontaneous burst of applause from every corner of the room. Wooler apologised to Cobbett for anything he might have said to his disadvantage and recommended 'a general oblivion of all private feuds between the real friends of reform'. Hunt called for a toast. They had seen union, he said, and with such a union the 'Radical Reformers might defy the whole world!'

There were more loud cheers, but Cobbett himself missed the point and arguably passed up what could have been an historic opportunity to support a union of the radical reformers to press for a democratic parliament in the wake of Peterloo. He spent most of the evening talking about his plans for the bones of Tom Paine. This was a subject which was not well received by the diners. The radical publisher Richard Carlile had just been found guilty of blasphemy for re-publishing Paine's *Age of Reason* and sent to prison, where he would remain until 1825. Cobbett was never to get the public support he wanted over the bones of Paine and was to find himself ridiculed and mocked. The poet Lord Byron was among the scoffers:

In digging up your bones, Tom Paine,
Will Cobbett has done well;
You visit him on earth again,
He'll visit you in hell.

One artist, thought to have been Isaac Cruikshank, was to draw Cobbett cruelly as the Hampshire Hog with a boar's head and a forked tail, dragging behind him the grinning skeleton of Tom Paine draped over his back. Hunt in his white hat marched behind, smiling sardonically. The mockery increased when Cobbett tried to sell rings made with Paine's hair. It all added to Cobbett's feeling of isolation. (The bones themselves went missing and have never been found, but in 1964 Americans gave the town of Thetford in Norfolk, Paine's birthplace, the gold-painted statue of Paine that now stands outside the civic buildings.)

At this stage of the game, Cobbett still linked himself with Hunt – just. Following the Crown and Anchor dinner, Cobbett addressed the prime minister, Lord Liverpool, in the issue of the *Register* published 11 December 1819. Unless there was a reform of parliament, Cobbett wrote, it was as clear as the 'noonday sun' that the miseries of the country were just beginning. It was not he or 'Mr Hunt' who had caused the people to become discontented. Liverpool's government could not blame them for what was going on. In this issue, however, Cobbett made no secret of his hostility towards the other radical reformers. At the recent dinner, he wrote, he had only recognised four or five faces, and, he continued sneeringly: 'All the tribe of little envious beings that used so to infest me are gone and are no more heard of'.

Cobbett included a brief note about a gathering to be held a few days later at the Crown and Anchor to promote 'Sobriety, Frugality and an Abhorrence of Gaming', which were good for the health and also good for depriving the government of taxation. He reported on the event the following week. It had been a 'most glorious meeting', wrote Cobbett. Everybody agreed that he, Cobbett, should draw up a strategy to promote the message across the country. He made no mention of Hunt, even though the latter had chaired the meeting, nor the fact that the whole abstinence idea followed on from Hunt's personal declaration after his arrest at Peterloo.

Cobbett continued to promote himself and all his works. He took inordinate pleasure in publishing congratulatory addresses to himself from reformers in the north, and wrote a public letter in reply. It included the following lines: 'It is very certain that I have been the great enlightener of the people of England. Had I not written, it is hardly possible to conceive the base and dejected state in which the nation would have been, at this time.' It was in this issue, published on Christmas Eve 1819, that Cobbett at last revealed that just before he had left New York for England he had read all about Sir Francis Burdett's angry letter against the perpetrators of the Peterloo Massacre, and of the baronet's organisation of the Westminster protest meeting. Cobbett had seen it as proof of the baronet's desire to co-operate with Hunt. He had decided that he would forget all about Burdett's past deeds, and had been encouraged to do so by many people on his arrival back in England. Although the wish was very general, Cobbett went on, he had categorically refused to be the *under-worker* of Burdett, or ever to consult with him again, unless Burdett would immediately use his 'great heaps of money' and pay his and Hunt's election expenses so that they could fight and win seats in parliament. But Burdett, whose adherents were 'a little nest of grovelling vermin,' had refused. The baronet was 'like Gulliver tied down by the Lilliputians ... a sand-bank which the sea has left', wrote Cobbett; and this was his proud and lonely resolution:

I shall pursue my own course singly. My banishment ... taught me to *depend upon myself.* I am resolved to walk in the trammels of nobody; and to have no intimate connection, as to public matters, with any man ... I never will again have to complain of having been betrayed or abandoned.

10
The Split

Wrath is cruel, and anger is outrageous, but who is able to stand before envy.

Proverbs

And so Cobbett separated himself off from everybody, including Hunt, just when he needed the backing of Cobbett more than ever. Cobbett withheld his powerful pen as Hunt continued with his struggle to clear his name, press charges against the 'butchers' of Peterloo and get a public inquiry into what happened on St Peter's Field. There was no consolation or support from Cobbett, who continued to celebrate his decision to go it alone. As the new year began, 1820, he repeatedly rejoiced over his resolution in the *Political Register*, starting in the issue of 6 January:

I have shaken from me at once all the crowd that used to hang upon my skirts, hamper me by their intrigues and vex me by their selfishness and folly ... I now know that I have associates whom neither gold nor blandishments can seduce and who will not act the part of those who stab in the back every one whose talents pushes him on before them.

The smallest of incidents was enough to set Cobbett off. The landlord of the Crown and Anchor refused to let him rent a room for a large party to celebrate Tom Paine's birthday (29 January 1737), no doubt worried that he might end up in gaol for aiding and abetting revolutionaries. Cobbett's fury was crazily intense. Bitterness and paranoia oozed from his pen as he raged in the *Register* of 27 January 1820: 'Envy, hatred, malice, revenge, fear; but above all, Envy, mean black dastardly Envy interfered to prevent the triumph of reason and of truth.' His reaction was way over the top but it gave an indication of what was going on in Cobbett's mind. Everybody was jealous of him. Everybody had become an enemy. By the issue of 19 February 1820, the mania was almost out of control. He accused his enemies in the press of publishing malicious stories about his debts and what was more:

Private letters, written in confidence many, many years before, obtained from a base and treacherous agent and published to the world and that too in a partial and garbled state. Was a thing like this ever heard of in this world before?

Ooops. Cobbett was so furious, he inadvertently let slip here that he, and no other, had written the 'whore on horseback' letter. Apparently unaware of what he had just revealed, Cobbett dashed on. He felt so sorry for himself that he included an account of his life beginning when he was an 'extraordinary boy' (as indeed he was), and listing in painstaking detail all his good points. He had always refused to take one single penny from the government. He had never abandoned England (despite two periods of exile in America). He had never hit any of his children in anger. He was the kindest of masters to his servants. He had never eaten or drunk in a public house except when he was travelling. The public loved him. His family loved him. He knew he would be accused of 'disgusting egotism' but, really, what had he done to earn the reproach of any man?

Tom Paine, Cobbett and Hunt are attacked by rats. Paine carries his *Age of Reason*. Cobbett is carrying a coffin inscribed 'Paines Bones'; Hunt holds a banner inscribed 'Reform' with a cap of Liberty under his foot.
© *The Trustees of the British Museum*

The issue was a bumper production and one feels for this extraordinary man as he wrote it. During this period, Cobbett's family was indeed offering him every consolation and support. They all loyally supported what 'the Governor', as his children called him, was doing. Nancy Cobbett, in particular, was surely thrilled at her husband's turning his back, at last, on that bad man, Henry Hunt. Anne described what was going on in her letters to James in America. On Christmas Eve 1819, she wrote with approval of her father's actions, the same day the issue of the *Register* was published in which Cobbett said he would have no intimate connection as to public matters with any man. Anne described it thus:

He has cut the Old Major [Cartwright], as he ought, and there is a fair prospect of his cutting somebody else too, our friend Chasse [Hunt]; Papa begins to be sick of him, and to find out that he is envious as well as the rest. As long as that fellow sticks to Papa's shirts, he will pull him back.

Immediately following on from this, Anne continued with great pride in her father: 'You will see in the papers mention made of a silver inkstand given to Papa by the Lady Reformers of Manchester.'

It sounded like a *non sequiter*, but Anne may have subconsciously linked Hunt with Manchester in her mind and been jealously gratified at the honour paid by the city's ladies to her father. She made no mention of Peterloo in the letter to her brother. Her written words reveal the envious state of mind of the Cobbett family, now led by Cobbett himself, and cheered on by Nancy. They were all delighted that Hunt was being cut out of the picture. A few months afterwards, in April 1820, Anne sat down to write another letter to James. It was in the same tone. She mentioned Hunt, again calling him 'Chasse'. (This could have been a safeguard against any prying eyes which might have been intercepting and reading Cobbett letters, or simply a private joke):

We suspect, that a fellow, whom we always hated, and who has always been supported by Papa, will go out to America. Monsieur Chasse I mean. Pray, be on your guard against him and against every body else! This country is full of traitors and villains; and Papa has been deceived by them all. He is, however, now free from them all; and he will do well for him and ourselves, in spite of all that can be done against him.

Anne's comment about Hunt going out to America is an interesting one. Could Hunt have been thinking about fleeing Britain to escape what he probably feared was going to be a lengthy prison sentence? There is no other evidence for this. It could have been wishful thinking on the part of the Cobbett family. They may have thought Hunt might have been considering going to help his elder son, Henry, and his own deaf and dumb brother, William, in Illinois, where they were struggling to make a living out of farming. Uncle and nephew were in desperate straits. Letters and money sent out to them had failed to arrive, possibly, as Henry junior feared, because they were intercepted. William Hunt was to die of fever in June 1820 just as his brother would begin his lengthy sentence in Ilchester Prison. It was a terrible time for Hunt.

Nevertheless, Cobbett split himself off from Hunt both publicly and privately, although he did not do it without pangs of sentiment. He was not having a very nice time of it either. 'Sir, Good God almighty!' he began in a short, sharp note to Hunt on 24 February 1820, and continued:

Yet, I must believe my own eyes! I cannot bring myself to do so degrading an act as to address a denial to you. When your letter shall appear in print, which, I suppose, it shortly will and which it may as soon as you please, I shall not fail to do my duty towards you, my sons, myself and the public.

At the end of this incandescent note with its threat of possible violence against Hunt, Cobbett signed himself off in his rudest way possible: 'I am, Sir, Your most obedient and most humble servant,' although Cobbett made it even ruder than usual by actually writing: '... obedient and most hum servant'. And the word 'servant' was scribbled so hard, it looked like 'sert'.

Hunt must have shot back a letter giving as good as he got and defending whatever it was he had said that had made Cobbett so angry, because the latter had second thoughts. The following day, on 25 February 1820, Cobbett followed his abrupt note to Hunt with a more conciliatory letter. He still began with the abrupt form of address, 'Sir,' but the lines that followed had a plaintive ring about them. If anybody had told Hunt that Cobbett had been busy criticising him in some way, why, Cobbett had merely been getting his own back:

All I did was to defend myself against what they said you <u>complained</u> of in my conduct, which has invariably been that of sincere friendship and evincing a constant desire to see you prosper both in private and public affairs ... In my note of last night I said nothing offensive ... my conduct towards you will never be influenced by anything that you may think proper to do, in the <u>law</u> way against my son, who is able to defend himself. I have always been, and I still am

    Your sincere friend

    Wm Cobbett.

Reading this correspondence from Cobbett to Hunt, it is clear that both men were involved in a fairly childish exchange over who had said what to whom. But Hunt was also furious about something else that had happened, something that was much more important. Both Cobbett's note and letter to Hunt mentioned Cobbett's sons. The letter also mentioned a man called Mills. This was one, James Mills, who had persuaded the *Examiner*, the Sunday newspaper run by the Hunt brothers, to publish a letter in which Mills claimed that Hunt, 'this itinerant demagogue', had gone to Peterloo with a government letter of protection in his pocket. Outrageously, Mills also said that the killings by the Manchester Yeomanry on St Peter's Field were all Hunt's fault.

Hunt chose to deny Mills' 'extraordinary as well as most malignant attack' in a letter which was published in *Cobbett's Evening Post*. The newspaper had been set up by Cobbett at the end of January 1820 to give him a medium in which to publish daily news, and also to try to make some money. His eldest son, William, was printer and publisher. Cobbett junior accepted for publication Hunt's letter in which he denied Mills' allegations. To Hunt's fury, however, William then allowed Mills to have the last word, and used a lengthy letter from him in the *Evening Post* on 17 February, in which Mills ramblingly and illogically amplified his allegation and added a few more for good measure. When Cobbett wrote to Hunt on 25 February, he justified his son's action and claimed that Mills had had the right of reply. 'I do not see how he could refuse insertion to Mills' letter after he had inserted yours', wrote Cobbett.

But Mills' letter in *Cobbett's Evening Post* had been very nasty indeed. Apart from his repeated claims about Hunt's supposed government protection, his letter made a host of other cheap and petty jibes at Hunt.

They included the fact that Hunt was selling a coffee substitute and making a profit of tenpence out of every shilling. It is interesting to note that the Excise men must have read Mill's letter in the *Evening Post* because the very morning after it was published, the premises in London of various vendors selling Hunt's coffee were raided and many sacks seized. Among the vendors were Cobbett's former publisher, Thomas Dolby, and the wife of the imprisoned publisher, Richard Carlile. Mrs Carlile got wind of the raid, filled a sack with ashes and dirt and sprinkled coffee powder on top. The Excise men staggered off with the sack of dirt. An account of the event was later published in *Cobbett's Evening Post*.

Mills sneered at Hunt and his coffee substitute although it was a very important subject. The radical reformers were trying to earn some badly needed money, strike a blow against the government tax on imported coffee and supply poor people with an affordable drink. It was Cobbett, with his marvellously practical mind, who had come up with an alternative to real coffee. He devoted pages to the subject in the Register, describing in minute and copious detail how roasted wheat could be used as a coffee substitute and how to prepare it. Hunt, whose bank balance had been seriously eroded by his attempt to win the Westminster seat and the prolonged legal battles over Peterloo, had taken a leaf out of Cobbett's book and set up a business making his own coffee substitute. He named it 'Hunt's Breakfast Powder' and capitalised on his own well-publicised declared abstinence from certain taxed goods including real coffee, until the perpetrators of Peterloo were brought to justice. Mills jabbed at Hunt in his letter in *Cobbett's Evening Post* for daring to call it his beverage, when, Mills wrote, it was in fact Cobbett's. But Hunt's false coffee was indeed his own. He was busy making it out of a recipe of roasted rye, as opposed to Cobbett's roasted wheat. Cobbett never forgave him, and the bitter subject of their alternatives to coffee was to be used as a battle weapon between the pair. They would fight over the issue blisteringly and bitterly in the full glare of the public until they died.

On the same day that Cobbett wrote his letter to Hunt defending his own and his son's conduct, while stressing his continuing sincere friendship for Hunt, Cobbett also wrote a letter to John Cam Hobhouse. In it,

Cobbett asked the Whig politician for a contribution of £10 towards a subscription fund to help him fight the Coventry parliamentary seat. A similar letter, he said, was being sent out to seventy other gentlemen. Despite his request for money, Cobbett stressed his own political independence. He would not join any political party nor would he be bound to anybody. He had returned to England for the express purpose of saving his country from 'a bloody revolution.' And, Cobbett continued, 'I am now bound up in politics with NO MAN. My mind is my own. I will pursue what that mind shall dictate.'

Cobbett's declaration to Hobhouse meant what it said. Despite his pledge of 'sincere friendship' for Hunt, and his wish to see him prosper 'both in private and public affairs', Cobbett's 'NO MAN' line now included Hunt. Even as Hunt's sensational legal battles against the 'butchers' of Peterloo filled the daily newspapers, the *Political Register* remained a Hunt-free zone. Admittedly, Cobbett's *Register* was not a newspaper as such. It was published every Saturday and commented on public affairs rather than reporting the daily news. Nevertheless Cobbett's silence in the weekly *Register* about Hunt and his trial spoke volumes. Cobbett had so often hammered Sir Francis Burdett for not attending controversial and significant court cases in order to lend his support to the defendants. Yet Cobbett does not appear to have attended Hunt's trial at any stage.

Cobbett's Evening Post followed the trial using reports from correspondents and other newspapers. In the edition of 14 February 1820, there was a lengthy report of a hearing at the Court of King's Bench to decide Hunt's request that all the trials of those arrested on St Peter's Field should be moved from Manchester to York. Hunt hoped, wrongly as it turned out, that they would get a fairer hearing in Yorkshire. The judge agreed to the trial being moved. The report in the *Post* commented on how Mr Hunt had addressed the court 'with an unusual degree of ability, an acuteness, and in the course of his observations made some palpable hits at the Learned Law Officers of the Crown'. These kind words, however, were not from the powerful pen of Cobbett.

Later that month, it appeared that Cobbett himself broke his self-imposed silence on Hunt's trial to wield his pen for the *Evening Post*. The newspaper chose to re-publish on 24 February 1820 a letter to the editor of the *Courier* as well as a comment paragraph. Both excoriated Hunt for daring to request that the trial be moved to Yorkshire. With a whiff of old times, the Cobbett newspaper hurled abuse at the writers on Hunt's behalf in an article under the dramatic headline 'Thirst for Blood'. Although Cobbett did not put his name to the piece, it had all the hallmarks of his invective. It poured scorn on the 'blood-hunting' author of the letter and, ironically, the 'congenial' editor of the comment paragraph. One would have thought, thundered *Cobbett's Evening Post*, that even the enemies of Mr Hunt would be glad that the trial was not to take place in Lancashire, where it had already been decided that none of the Manchester Yeomanry should be prosecuted but only the very people who had escaped with their lives from their sabres. It was obvious that Hunt could never have a fair trial in Lancashire. If people did not have confidence in the justice system, the name of government was worthless. Men who lived under misrule and a corrupt court system would try to throw off the burden as soon as they could. The piece continued with these marvellously resonant lines only Cobbett could have written:

As long as every innocent man can say: '*There*, at last, *there* I *know* I am safe. *There* I *know* I shall have *justice*. *There* I know there will be no *foul play*.' As long as a man can say this, the state is in no danger; but if the time were ever to arrive, when *men could not say this*, there would, in fact, be *no government*.

Hunt must have read these words like a thirsty man stumbling across an oasis in the desert. Sadly, the spell was broken two weeks later, when *Cobbett's Evening Post* ran the kind of tittle tattle about Hunt that readers of the day would have expected to find only in the reptile press, never in a paper owned by his friend, Cobbett. An article in the edition of 7 March 1820 reported that Hunt had been charged with trespassing on land next door to his home at Middleton Cottage near Andover in Hampshire. The land belonged to a Colonel Iremonger, who said that he had repeatedly tried to stop Hunt shooting game in his woods. Hunt tried, but failed, to have the court case postponed so that he could appear in person to defend himself. The jury was directed by the judge to find Hunt guilty in his absence, and he was ordered to pay 45 shillings to the colonel. There was nothing in *Cobbett's Evening Post* to enlighten the readers that it was just like the old tricks played on Hunt nearly two decades ago by his neighbours in Wiltshire.

There was an echo of happier times, however, in the edition of the *Evening Post* of 10 March 1820, when the Cobbetts graciously decided to publish a report of the election in Preston in which Hunt stood as a candidate. (The general election followed the death of King George III.) When Hunt arrived in the village of Wallan, two miles from Preston, he found 20,000 people waiting for him. They formed a procession, took the horses out of the carriage and pulled Hunt themselves into town, where 'an immense concourse of people' was there to greet him with the most enthusiastic cheers ever heard. Hunt addressed them in an animated speech in the market place in front of the Castle Inn for an hour. He was applauded so loudly, it made 'the welkin ring'. Nothing but the justice of his cause, said Hunt, could have enabled him to bear up against the foul unmanly calumnies and attacks incessantly made upon him. He repeated his pledge not to receive, directly or indirectly, one shilling of public money either for himself or in favours for his family. The report continued: 'He paraded the town accompanied with thousands of his friends in the afternoon and candour obliges us to say that he received a most cordial and unanimous welcome in every street through which he passed ... Every hour seems to increase the popularity of Mr Hunt.'

Yet there was nothing about Hunt's campaign in Preston in the *Political Register*.

Cobbett himself was busy contesting the Coventry election and having a harder time of it, as he reported extensively in the *Register*. His supporters were literally beaten off by hired thugs, and he and his eldest daughter were violently harassed and attacked. Anne later wrote of her conviction that both she and her beloved father were going to be murdered, both on the way to the hustings and during the election itself:

I expected him to be shot every minute ... It was a frightful time to us even in the house for at one time a savage mob burst in, calling out for the 'miscreant' to kill him. We were in the bedroom and heard the noise and we pushed the bedstead against the door and hid the fire-irons. Downstairs they were so frightened that Mrs Sergeant ran down into the cellar with the knives.

Anne's *Account of the Family* reveals that despite the chill winds blowing between her father and Hunt, the pair were speaking to each other up to the elections. As she and Cobbett were about to leave London for Coventry, the story of the Cato Street Conspiracy made the headlines. The conspiracy by the Spenceans, led by Arthur Thistlewood, was a Guy Fawkes-style plot to blow up members of the cabinet. Hunt called at the inn where Cobbett and his daughter were staying. He referred to this short visit in his *Memoirs* as the last occasion on which he had any communication with Cobbett. (It was, of course, the last before Hunt was jailed. After he left prison, the relationship would resume.) Anne marked Hunt's visit with this perfunctory note: 'The Cato Street plot had just been discovered. Hunt came abusing them all. Told me that his name and Papa's were on the list of persons to be killed. Papa said he did not believe it.' Despite Cobbett's scepticism, it was quite true that Thistlewood had threatened to kill Hunt, at least after the gang had blown up the cabinet. Thistlewood had hated Hunt since the Barnet meeting when he had broken off all contact with the Spenceans.

Neither Cobbett nor Hunt was successful in the elections. Hunt battled on at his trial in York in his vain attempt to win justice. Still there was nothing in the *Political Register*. From around mid March 1820, *Cobbett's Evening Post* carried reports most days, many of them lengthy ones. In those days trials were covered in copious detail. It took a couple of days for the news happening a distance outside London to get into the newspapers. The *Evening Post* re-published selections. On 17 March, William Cobbett junior used an extract from a letter published in one of the Yorkshire newspapers. Did the Cobbetts have a pang of conscience? It was extraordinary to see the great popularity of Mr Hunt in every part of the country, the correspondent had written. When Hunt passed through Leeds on his way to York, up to twenty thousand people waited all day just to catch a glimpse of him. Torches blazed and the applause was overwhelming. Cries of 'Hunt and Liberty' and 'Yorkshire will save England' resounded from every quarter. The slogans were even chalked on the walls. Many witnesses to the Peterloo Massacre walked from the Manchester area to York. They marched behind a banner on which was written, 'The Truth, the whole Truth and nothing but the Truth'.

The next day, Saturday, 18 March 1820, *Cobbett's Evening Post* devoted its front page to reporting the crush to get into court, and there were yet more columns the following Monday. The court had been besieged. Among the members of the public were 'several ladies of rank and fashion'. (Was Catherine Vince there, maybe with her sisters?) The Cobbett newspaper also published an article from the *Morning Post*, which said that it would avoid any 'premature opinion or observations', but then went on to quote selectively from hostile witnesses, who claimed to have heard the reformers say they intended 'to make a *Moscow* of Manchester' (i.e. burn it down), and that Hunt had urged the crowds to 'put the soldiers down'. Cobbett's evening newspaper poured scorn on the *Morning Post* and its report. The witness statements, it scoffed, had been leaked by the prosecution and would be absolutely contradicted by witnesses for the defence. A prosecution witness had already contradicted them in any case. He had revealed that when Hunt urged the crowds to 'get them down and keep them down', Hunt had not been referring to the soldiers but to unruly people in the crowd. Was the *Morning Post* journalist not 'a wretch more detestable and vile than pen can describe or language express?' thundered the Cobbett pen.

At the end of the month, the Cobbetts decided to publish a favourable cameo of Hunt. It reads just like a diary story today. On 27 March 1820, Hunt and four others were found guilty of unlawful and seditious assembly for the purpose of exciting discontent. Hunt returned to London to await sentencing. *Cobbett's Evening Post* reported that a crowd of people, who were attending a funeral, spotted Hunt 'walking up the Strand with a Lady' (surely his beloved Mrs Vince). The scene of solemnity, reported the Cobbett newspaper, 'changed into one of long and loud cheerings.'

The next day, *Cobbett's Evening Post* published a full report on the conviction of Hunt and his co-defendants. The newspaper was guarded in its comments, keeping an anxious eye on the Six Acts. (The *Manchester Observer*, a radical newspaper and pro-Hunt, was similarly cautious. It said it was difficult and dangerous to comment on the verdicts of the juries.) This is what the Cobbett paper said:

It is useless for us to enter into any particulars of the charge, the mode of prosecution or the trial itself; and prudence teaches us to refrain from expressing our opinion of the conduct of the Judges or of that of the Jury ... The Judge is reported to have sharply reproved Mr Hunt, several times, for heaping praises on him. We shall profit from the hint and take great care, whatever our feelings and wishes may be, not to give offence in the same way.

Yet in this same edition, the Cobbett newspaper also used a report from the *Morning Herald*, which revealed that Hunt intended to press for a new trial. The *Herald* article listed the seven grounds on which Hunt was going to make his case and reported them in full. They included the fact that the killings and injuries had been caused by the yeomanry, and that the jury had consisted of magistrates 'procured and packed by the Master of the Crown Office.'

Curiously, the next day, 31 March 1820, *Cobbett's Evening Post* published a report from the *Courier* about Hunt's intentions to seek a new trial. This time around, the Cobbett paper decided to censor Hunt's claim that the jury had been knobbled. The Cobbetts left out the words 'procured and packed', and replaced them with a row of dots. 'We *copy* the above, leaving out three words, which we do not think it prudent for *us* to insert', said the *Evening Post* virtuously, even though it had printed the words just twenty-four hours earlier. It also nitpicked at the other six arguments for a new trial, sneering that Hunt had praised the judges and yet was now implicitly criticising them with his demand for a fresh hearing.

On the one hand, this edition of *Cobbett's Evening Post* appeared to support Hunt. 'We anxiously hope that a new trial may be granted. We watched the progress of this trial with uncommon attention and anxiety.' On the other, the newspaper undermined several of Hunt's arguments that a new trial should be called. It also got in yet another dig at Hunt for his politeness in court: 'We should now be taught, if past experience had not already taught us, to avoid *bestowing praise* with almost as much care as we would avoid meriting condemnation.'

Pompous words, and also specious ones. Everybody reading the lines would have remembered the praise Cobbett had lavished on Hunt in the past, before this very public split between the two men. The Cobbett evening newspaper's coverage of the conviction was altogether bitty and messy and its comments petty and woolly.

The tone was not much better in the issue of the *Political Register*, which appeared the following day, Saturday, 1 April 1820. Cobbett's brief comments about the trial appeared right at the end, almost as an afterthought. They were very unlike his usual trenchant writing, even circumscribed as they might have been by fears of legal action. 'To make *remarks* upon this affair is much *too delicate* a task for me', he wrote. The judge had reproved Mr Hunt more than once for praising him, 'I will take good care not to expose myself to reproof *on the same ground.*' Some of the newspapers talked of a new trial, but Cobbett did not know for what reasons. The place of trial was the place '*chosen by the defendants*' and Hunt had praised the conduct of the judge '*to the skies*'. Cobbett concluded thus: 'However, there may be other grounds for a new trial; and, at any rate, I hope, that I may, without exposing myself to the chance of banishment, express my deep *sorrow for the result of this trial.*'

There is no doubt that Cobbett genuinely meant those last few words, but it was mealy-mouthed stuff and this very complex man might well have felt remorse. The following week, Cobbett showed just what his pen could do when he chose to wield it. He tore into the hard-liner, George Canning, who had just been elected MP for Liverpool, and described what he called Canning's 'insufferable nonsense' in defence of the Six Acts, in particular the act to restrict public meetings. On what grounds had the meeting at Manchester been unlawful? Cobbett asked. There had been no law in place at the time to prevent it. All the people assembled on 16 August 1819 had had the right to be there. 'Away, then, with all your hypocritical, your scandalous pretexts about the danger of large public meetings', roared Cobbett. There was nothing so odious as the use of tyranny, nothing so truly detestable as the tyranny which compelled an opponent in dispute '*to hold his tongue*' while the tyrant keeps on speaking:

The *Six Acts* are passed. The press is nearly silent, except as far as *praise* goes. We cannot meet freely to speak to each other, *even in a room.* If we say that which may TEND to bring the parliament into contempt, we may be *banished* for life ... Yet you talk of a *struggle for all that is dear to us!*

There were pages of it. It was brilliant. If only Cobbett had not turned his back on Hunt, just when his old friend needed him most. A week later on 15 April 1820, there was one small reference to Hunt, blink and you missed it. Everybody agreed, wrote Cobbett, that the government would need wisdom and firmness, together with the cordial goodwill of the people, to get the country back on its feet. Yet this was how it was to be done, by preserving the rotten borough of Old Sarum, and exulting that Sir Francis Burdett and Mr Hunt were to be locked up!

And that was all. Should Cobbett be forgiven? He himself was under extreme pressure at this time. He was still recovering from the experience of the Coventry election during which he had been threatened with murder. He was also trying to shake off the effects of a severe chill he had caught on the hustings. There were also business pressures. These were the last days of publication for *Cobbett's Evening Post*. After just a few months, the new venture was failing. Cobbett's creditors were harassing him and he was being repeatedly arrested for debt. He was forced to declare himself bankrupt and take refuge in the village of Westerham in Kent on the border with Sussex in order to avoid further arrests before his surrender. There, he could escape by simply crossing over the county boundary where an arrest warrant for Kent was not valid. His daughter Anne poignantly described the scene in her *Account of the Family*: 'A fine moonlight night, clear, and *so* cold.! Papa coughing all the time. Neither of us so warmly clad as we ought to be. Somehow there was never money for those things.'

Cobbett surrendered himself at the end of April 1820, and went into the so-called Rules of the King's Bench Prison, an area next to the Southwark gaol where privileged prisoners were allowed to rent rooms and houses as long as they followed certain rules of conduct. He found lodgings at 15 Lambeth Road and spent the following five months there with Anne and his son John, until he was cleared of debt. As Cobbett moved into his lodgings, he announced that in future issues of the *Register*, he would write about all the ongoing trials for sedition. He did not do so, even though there were many. By mid 1820, practically all the radical speakers, journalists, publishers and their distributors were behind bars. In fact, Cobbett directed most of his energy between June and November 1820 campaigning obsessively for Queen Caroline during her trial in the House of Lords. This was set up to prove that the queen had carried on 'a licentious, disgraceful and adulterous intercourse' with Bartolomeo Bergami, and that her husband George IV, therefore, was entitled to dissolve the marriage. Despite his abhorrence of adultery, Cobbett viewed

Caroline as a victim of an oppressive government. Paradoxically, he mentioned the reformers' court cases in the *Register* almost in passing.

Cobbett's silence over the Peterloo Massacre, the subsequent court battles, Hunt's incarceration in Ilchester Prison and what happened there, speaks volumes. He occasionally used the facts of Peterloo and Hunt's conviction as weapons in his battle against the establishment. Hunt himself, however, largely disappeared from the pages of the *Political Register*. The Cobbett household was jubilant. At last Cobbett stood triumphantly alone, as Anne wrote in a letter to James later in the year on 6 December 1820:

> Papa did never a better thing than cutting the old Major, Hunt and the whole tribe calling themselves Reformers. He has never until now, been able to do anything, or go anywhere without having to drag some of them along with him and they always kept him back, but now that he is rid of the whole swarm, he is able to do more for himself, for the cause, and is of much more consequence in himself.

Cobbett claimed that they were all jealous of him. But just who was jealous of whom? There is no evidence that Hunt, up to this point, had been jealous of Cobbett. He had written to Cobbett endlessly asking him to return to England. He repeatedly acknowledged Cobbett as the greatest political writer of all times and the man who had taught him so much. Hunt needed Cobbett. He was not jealous of him. It was the other way round, although Cobbett could not see this. Even Sam Bamford, the Lancashire reformer who disliked Hunt, observed that Cobbett was so jealous of Hunt's popularity that he could not bring himself to write about Peterloo and the aftermath, choosing instead 'to neutralize his powerful pen on the subject of the Manchester meeting and the extraordinary proceedings at York.' In his autobiography, Bamford recalled that one of Cobbett's sons visited the King's Bench Prison in which the Peterloo defendants were temporarily held after they were sentenced. He failed, however, to visit Hunt, who wrote to Bamford expressing his anger. Hunt believed that it was Cobbett himself who had visited the prison:

> What a melancholy thing that Cobbett should suffer his envy to destroy his character ... I understand he came into the King's Bench to see and spend the day with Johnson. Did you see him and if so did you not call him to account for either his <u>cowardice</u>, his <u>supineness</u>, or his <u>treachery</u>, in neglecting the cause of those that he so long pretended to

HENRY HUNT, ESQ.ᴿ

Engraved by T. Woolnoth, from a Drawing
taken in the Kings Bench Prison
the Morning after Judgement was given.

Published June, 5, 1820, by T. Dolby, 299, Strand.

Hunt in the Kings Bench Prison after sentencing in 1820, before being
taken to Ilchester Prison.
Bristol Library

advocate ... How did he account to Johnson for his worse than neglect in not noticing the trial at York. Does he not know that what he said was well watched by the tools of the system our persecutors. He blamed Sir F. Burdett for coolly looking on and silently encouraging the Ministers to pass the Suspension Act in 1817. What then is to be said of his conduct now?

Hunt and his co-defendants were sentenced in the Court of King's Bench on 15 May 1820. Hunt was given the longest sentence, two and a half years in Ilchester Prison. It was among the worst prisons in England. In 1812, Cobbett had written in the *Political Register* about the terrible conditions in Ilchester gaol, eloquently describing the solitary confinements, the use of heavy iron manacles, the freezing conditions, straw beds, bread and water diet and the 'shocking severities' inflicted on the prisoners. Nothing had changed by 1820.

When sentence was pronounced, Hunt's younger son, 17-year-old Thomas, passed out. One of Hunt's female relatives (possibly a sister or Hunt's daughter, both of whom were sickly and both of whom died while Hunt was in gaol) became temporarily paralysed by the shock. In the issue of the *Register* published five days afterwards, Cobbett merely included Hunt's name in a list of those gaoled. Astonishingly, he wrote: 'There is not room this week to say more on the subject.' He allowed himself to make one typically pungent comment, although it hardly reflected the magnitude of what had happened. 'What a pity it is that the National Debt cannot be paid off as easily as these sentences can be passed.'

And that was all he said.

11
Ilchester Bastile

And now predict the outcomes when we part
Acid rain, nuclear fallout, broken heart.
Robert Wallen

Hunt went into the black maw of Ilchester Prison on 17 May 1820 with his head held high. He was the first political prisoner to be incarcerated there. If he could only be sure of obtaining happiness and justice for his poor, suffering, insulted fellow creatures, he wrote to Sam Bamford shortly after his arrival, they could lock him up in a dungeon for life. He would laugh with scorn at all their malevolent and impotent attempts to punish him. What was more he far preferred his situation than having to watch the antics of the drunken inmates in the King's Bench Prison (where Cobbett was being held until his bankruptcy was discharged).

These were brave words. The reality was that the authorities chose to incarcerate Hunt in a prison which they hoped would either kill him or wreck his health and spirit to such a degree that he would no longer be any kind of threat to the establishment when he emerged at the end of the two and a half years. Cobbett's stay in Newgate Prison twelve years earlier had been a picnic by comparison, as Hunt would point out so bitterly. Ilchester Prison, which had been re-built in the early seventeenth century, was notorious. Nothing had changed since Cobbett condemned it in the *Register* in 1812.

The foul wreaking prison of cold stone, which Hunt immediately dubbed 'Ilchester Bastile', loomed up on the north bank of the river Yeo on the west side of the ancient town of Ilchester near Yeovil in Somerset. (Part of the exterior and some of the interior walls remain to this day.) One of Hunt's friends described Ilchester Prison as an 'Old Hulk moored in a swamp where two hundred people huddled together like pigs in a sty.' Hunt's 'dungeon', as he himself called it, was a cold, damp, dark cell in an isolated part of the prison, overhanging the river and facing north. There was a grated window but it opened into a small yard enclosed by a blackened wall nearly twenty feet high, which blocked out light and air. The well in the yard was contaminated by the dilapidated sewerage system, as were all the water sources throughout the prison. To make matters worse, the river regularly flooded the site.

Visitors to the prison had to use a so-called felons' conversation room. This consisted of two cells facing each other four feet apart through iron grating. The prisoners were crammed into one cell and their visitors herded into the other. They were then expected to communicate with each other as best they could. The prisoners included men and women who made the most of the visits in other ways. Hunt said the scenes in their cage were 'too revolting to mention'. Throughout his stay, he battled with the authorities to be able to receive visitors in his cell. Sometimes he was successful; other times, he was expected to see his female visitors, including Catherine Vince, whom the authorities classed as a 'prostitute', in the public area. Hunt refused to do so. This meant that Mrs Vince often made the time-consuming and expensive journey to Ilchester to visit Hunt, only to be denied access. For much of the time, Hunt was held in solitary confinement at the whim of the prison authorities. They arbitrarily decided who could and who could not visit him. Hunt's sick daughter was permitted to see him in his cell. It is likely the shock of seeing her father's plight hastened her death. One of his sisters also asked to be able to visit Hunt. It was her dying wish. The authorities refused and she died without seeing him.

As soon as the door of his cell clanged shut behind him, Hunt began to write. It is puzzling why the authorities allowed him to do so, but most of the radical reformers continued to write and even run their publishing businesses while they were behind bars. Despite poor health and the damage caused to his eyesight as he strained to see in the bad light, Hunt wrote continuously over the following two and a half years of his sentence. As well as the story of his life in his *Memoirs*, Hunt wrote regular political pamphlets, which he called *Addresses to the Radical Reformers of England, Ireland and Scotland*. He also conducted a sensational campaign to publicise the abuses carried out against the prisoners, force the prosecution of the gaoler William Bridle, and have the place condemned. Throughout his writing, Hunt paid one of his greatest compliments to

Cobbett by continually echoing and imitating his style and methods.

The instalments of Hunt's *Memoirs*, the *Addresses* and the revelations about the prison were published and sold by Thomas Dolby, one of Cobbett's disaffected former publishers. The income was useful. The authorities made it very difficult for Hunt to sort out his financial affairs from gaol, and he suffered heavy losses. He also had to pay the legal fees incurred by his campaign against the prison and all its works.

Hunt's writings were widely read and editions sold out quickly. Hunt fondly recalled in his *Memoirs* the beginning of his friendship with Cobbett and the good times together, before lapsing into bitterness and resentment over Cobbett's flight to America in 1817, how ill 'Mr Cobbett' had behaved towards him ever since his return, how he had deserted Hunt at a time of danger and difficulty and how he had neglected to aid him with his pen. It may be remembered that Hunt was also rude in his *Memoirs* about Nancy Cobbett and her inability to retain her servants, and how she hated and worked against him. He made it quite clear that he blamed her for the collapse of his friendship with her husband. There might be faults on both sides, he wrote:

It is a lamentable truth, however, that the strongest mind is not always proof against the insinuations of false friends, of go-betweens, and the eternal workings and worryings and sly malignant hints, of the low pride and cunning of those who are always at a person's elbow.

Judging by what Cobbett and his daughter Anne wrote, the family read Hunt's writings with the same avidity as Hunt read the *Political Register*. Yet Cobbett, eaten up with the jealousy which had begun to consume him in America, largely ignored Hunt's plight, the vile conditions he endured and his campaigns against the system. That did not mean he cut Hunt out completely. On the contrary, despite the rift in their relationship, the pair continued to loom large in each other's life. Reading Cobbett's *Register* and Hunt's writings during the Ilchester years, the connection is clearly visible and a pattern emerges. Both men continually reacted to or had their memories jogged in some way by what the other wrote

At the end of 1821, for example, Cobbett reported in the *Register* on his 'pilgrimage' to the former farm of the agricultural pioneer, Jethro Tull, at Shalborne in Berkshire, whom Cobbett admired so much. He announced a plan to re-publish Tull's books and include details of his own Tullian experiments. It can be seen from Hunt's *Memoirs* that this wrung his sentimental heart as he remembered how he had read Tull's works 'with great pleasure, on the recommendation of Mr Cobbett', and how the pair had experimented with Tull's farming methods. He may even have recalled writing the letter to Cobbett in which he proposed the formation of a Tullian society to bind his friend more closely to him. As Hunt sat writing in his cell, however, his fond memory turned into fury against the friend who had betrayed him, and he cautioned people 'not to be led away with the beautiful theory of Mr Tull'. Both he and Cobbett suffered heavy financial losses because they had followed Tull's theory too minutely, he wrote bitterly.

Hunt's pen also hammered Cobbett in his *Addresses*, although at times he was very gracious towards his former friend. It all added to the piquancy of Hunt's writing for his eager readers. Messages of support and gifts flooded in from across the country and petitions for his early release were sent in to parliament. The conditions in which Hunt was held and the sensational revelations about the tortures carried out in the prison were repeatedly discussed at Westminster. One peer told the House of Lords that the country was greatly indebted to Hunt for exposing the atrocities of Ilchester Prison. Throughout 1820 to 1822, Hunt's imprisonment was a major national story. There was plenty of material in his writings and campaigns for Cobbett to have used in the *Political Register* had he so wished, but Cobbett largely withheld his pen, although his conscience occasionally pricked.

By August 1820, after just three months of being locked up, Hunt was calling for an inquiry into Ilchester Bastile and describing the cruel mental torture and extreme physical discomfort which had been inflicted on him right from the start. He was already suffering from severe rheumatism. In his *Address* for this month, Hunt revealed that one of the members of the grand jury, which oversaw the prison and was responsible for the disgusting and degrading conditions in which Hunt was being kept, was none other than the wealthy Somerset landowner, Sir John Cox Hippisley, the 'cunning old fox' and enemy of Hunt and Cobbett. Hunt would have remembered how fiercely Cobbett had attacked Hippisley in the *Register* in 1811 and 1815, and would have reflected on how silent his pen had since become.

Hunt was more kind to Cobbett. In this August *Address*, he warmly praised Cobbett's pamphlet, *A Peep at the Peers*, which Cobbett had just published in his campaign of support for Queen Caroline in her battle in the House of Lords to prove her innocence against the accusations of debauchery by George IV. His *Peep at the Peers* listed all the jobs, sinecures and pensions, funded by the tax payers, which the aristocratic members of the House of Lords and their many relatives enjoyed. Hence their devout support of the new king and their readiness to help him discard his wife. Hunt was lavishly generous in his praise of Cobbett's *Peep*. Everybody should buy a copy, he wrote. It had been written by the only man in the country capable of doing justice to the subject. The author deserved a statue of gold to be erected to his memory. Hunt would not be without his copy for twenty guineas. He himself had learned more from the author than from any other writer, he went on gushingly. If the author had never written another line, he was entitled to the thanks of every lover of his country: 'It conveys more real, substantial and unequivocal knowledge about the state of politics in the country than all the books that have been published in the last century.'

Hunt patently wanted to contrast his own generosity towards Cobbett with Cobbett's meanness towards him. Hunt believed what he wrote. He still saw Cobbett as a hero and the greatest political writer in the country. He wanted to show Cobbett that there was no need to feel jealous, and that he, Hunt, was badly missing Cobbett in his hour of need – although Hunt could only bring himself to refer to Cobbett throughout this eulogy as 'the author'.

Cobbett could hardly bring his pen to write down the name of Hunt or even to refer to him obliquely. Instead, he lavished praise on the reformers. In the *Register* of 12 August 1820, by which time he would have been fully aware of the vile conditions under which Hunt was being held, Cobbett mentioned the trials and imprisonment of a group of the radical reformers, including Thomas Wooler and Major Cartwright. They ought to feel consoled by the reflection that the cause of truth and justice would finally triumph, wrote Cobbett. They were among those who would thereafter be objects of national gratitude. A year later, in the issue of 22 September 1821, he launched into a lengthy – and unfulfilled – pledge to

obtain justice for the reformers who had been persecuted and imprisoned
between 1817 and 1821. He would never cease to oppress or annoy, as far
as he legally could, anybody who did not do the same, he wrote. To this
he would hold and from this he would never depart:

If justice be not done to these men, I care not who suffer ... This is my solemn
determination, that under all circumstances, at all times, and in whatever situation I may
be placed, I never will cease to endeavour to obtain justice for the basely persecuted
Reformers ... Upon this score I submit to no compromise.

Maybe Cobbett could not see, or pushed the thought to one side, that
by ignoring Hunt, whose situation was among the worst, if not the worst
in terms of physical conditions, he was undermining his own pledge. It is
impossible that Cobbett could have written those words without a
thought about Hunt. The latter desperately needed his powerful pen to
obtain justice, but Cobbett was withholding it. It is true that Cobbett used
the subject of Peterloo to rain down blows on the establishment. He
devoted a section of the issue of the *Register* of 23 September 1820 to the
yeomanry cavalry, reminding his readers that they were volunteers and
members of the community whose praises were sung by the establishment.
Yet everybody had seen what sort of services they had offered at
Manchester on 16 August 1819. It was a day, never to be forgotten, any
more than Sidmouth's letter of thanks to the yeomanry for their work on
that occasion should be forgotten. Nevertheless, Cobbett made no
mention of the calls being made, by Hunt and others, for an inquiry into
the Peterloo Massacre.

A week later, he got close to it when he hit out at the clergy, always one
of his favourite targets, noting the reward given to one, Parson Hay, who
was among the Manchester magistrates who sat on the jury that convicted
Hunt and his co-defendants. After the court case, Hay was given the living
of Rochdale, which was worth the princely sum of £2,500 a year.
Cobbett's pen dripped ironic venom:

A Parson will say that it was singularly humane in the Ministers, while they were
applauding the Magistrates and the Yeomanry, to refuse all inquiry into their conduct, and
at the same time to prosecute a considerable number of the injured parties with all the
weight of crown law and before special juries.

Cobbett was not shy here to repeat, albeit obliquely, Hunt's claim and one of his reasons for demanding a second trial that the juries were knobbled by being packed with magistrates. He even managed a mention of Hunt by name. A parson, Cobbett went on, would swear it was not even cruel to shut up Mr Hunt for '*two years and a half*' for presiding at a meeting whose object was to agree on the way forward to achieve the reform of parliament. It was Cobbett's usual brilliant, coruscating writing. What a difference he could have made to events. The conscience of this passionate man, with deep and complicated emotions, was pricking him. On the one hand, he was walking firmly down his solitary path; on the other, his old friend, the man whom he had treated like nobody else, was having a terrible time of it – and Cobbett was not helping him.

In the middle of November 1820, Hunt published an affidavit detailing the horrors of his confinement in Ilchester Prison and the conditions he and the other prisoners were having to endure. It made gripping reading. On his arrival in England's worst prison, Hunt wrote, he had been put into a cold, damp and smelly cell with two ordinary convicts. His bed was a straw bag. He was not allowed to make a fire and

Ilchester Gaol
Ilchester Museum

was confined to a small yard in which to take exercise. His health began to deteriorate. His friends were only allowed in for three separate hours a day. Early in July 1820, visiting restrictions were eased, but, a month later, a magistrate had arbitrarily ordered that no female visitors should be allowed to visit Hunt in his cell. They could only use the felon's conversation room and speak to Hunt through the grating which separated the common prisoners, who included murderers and people convicted of bestial crimes, from their visitors. Hunt had been locked up in solitary confinement. The bolts, which allowed him to lock his door from the inside, had mysteriously been removed, and he was fearful for his own safety. His mental and physical health was suffering. His co-defendants from the Peterloo meeting were in prisons elsewhere and enjoying infinitely better conditions.

Hunt's affidavit was presented to the court at a hearing four days later, when his lawyer appealed for a writ of Habeas Corpus so that his client could appear in person to plead his case for better treatment and beg to be removed to a less awful prison. (Hunt did not get a writ and was later billed for his request to the court.)

Cobbett's conscience gave another ping and he published the affidavit in full in the *Register* of 25 November 1820. It appeared out of the blue towards the end of the issue. There was no reference to it in the index for this volume of *Political Registers*. Cobbett confined his pen to a terse paragraph as a preface. It was headed 'MR HUNT', and continued: 'The following article will speak for itself. It is useless to waste *words*. But, base is the man, who will *forget* what is here recorded. What I have so often recommended, "*a Peep into the Dungeon,*"must be published.'

And that was all Cobbett could bring himself to write. Cobbett referred to the Dungeon Peep several times through 1820. His idea was to publish a list of all the people who had been prosecuted for political offences since 1792, their alleged offences, lawyers, judges, names of jury members, sentences, and the prisons in which they were confined. It was another project that never happened.

In the last month of 1820, Cobbett repressed all twinges of conscience and displayed just how insensitive he could be to the feelings of others, when he celebrated what he saw as his success in a libel trial brought against him in the Court of King's Bench by Thomas Cleary. The case centred around Cobbett's 'whore on horseback' letter that Cleary had used against Hunt in the Westminster election of 1818, the letter Cobbett swore to Hunt was forged. Cleary had sued Cobbett for libel, claiming £2,000 in damages. After listening to a *tour de force* defence by Cobbett, the jury awarded Cleary nominal damages of just forty shillings.

Every detail of the entire affair was brought up and used as evidence in court, and Cobbett chose to re-print practically every single word. His coverage in the *Political Register* included all his best insults against Cleary, 'the little contemptible reptile, a thing here today and gone tomorrow'. It also included the exact words Cobbett had used against Hunt and Mrs Vince in his letter and the wickedly witty, mock burlesque Cobbett had written and published in the *Register* in 1818. Readers 'of an attentive turn of mind', as Cobbett would say, may recall that the burlesque featured Cleary and Burdett devising the plot on how to shame and torment both Hunt and Mrs Vince, by reading out Cobbett's letter on the Westminster hustings:

Burdett: Into
His affairs most private will we enter;
His debts and dues, the treatment of his wife,
And his amours at every stage of life;
And though *he* still may act the patriot's part,
We're sure at least, to wring a *woman*'s heart.

Cobbett enjoyed himself re-publishing every word of the burlesque, as did the newspapers, including *The Times*. Hunt, locked in his gloomy dungeon and battling against a vindictive establishment, was definitely not laughing. Once again, the letter, so insulting to himself and his beloved Mrs Vince, was the centre of attention; those horrible words, written by Cobbett, were in public yet again: 'There is one *Hunt,* the Bristol man. Beware of him! He rides about the country with a whore, the wife of another man, having deserted his own. A sad fellow! Nothing to do with him.'

To add insult to injury, Cobbett went through most of it again just a week later, in the *Political Register* of 16 December 1820, when John Wright also took Cobbett to court for libel. Wright won his case and was awarded damages of £1,000. (This was paid by one of Cobbett's friends.) Cobbett, totally unabashed, reported the details that had emerged during the trial, how Sir Francis Burdett had been an intimate friend of Hunt from 1810 to 1815, and was often his guest enjoying his hospitality (and that of Mrs Vince) at shoots and parties. Burdett, wrote Cobbett accusingly, would have known exactly how much pain the production of the letter would have brought. Cobbett's pen dripped fury:

The lady's heart was to be wrung. She was to become the subject of scandal with every scandalous tongue in the kingdom. She, who was innocent of all offence against Sir Francis Burdett, was to suffer this in order to get vengeance on me because I had dealt my blows upon the Baron. And, if you can, in the annals of malignity and cowardice, find anything equal to this, I beg you to refer me to the page.

It was all about Catherine Vince – and Cobbett! There was nothing about the acute anguish to Hunt caused by the whole affair. There was no consideration of the pain Hunt, languishing in a vile prison cell, might have been feeling to have the whole subject dredged up again, nor was there any embarrassment from Cobbett about his own persistent claim that the letter had been forged. Even here, he tried to wriggle out of responsibility. If part of a private letter were left out, then it had been altered and was therefore a forgery, he insisted defiantly. He then had the colossal cheek to point his finger accusingly at the Westminster Rump. Look at them, he wrote, no word of commiseration for any of the people locked up in prison, including 'Mr Hunt'.

Hunt never got over Cobbett's claim of forgery. He went over it again and again in his *Memoirs*, marvelling how he had believed and trusted Cobbett and had been so badly let down. He returned to the subject in one of the last instalments before leaving Ilchester Prison at the end of 1822, his old bewilderment and hurt ringing through the words:

In his letter to me as well as his letter in the New York paper, he solemnly declared that the letter ... was a FORGERY ... My having implicit reliance upon the word of my friend, who in the most solemn manner declared it to be a forgery, made me have no hesitation in pronouncing it as my belief that it was such.

On the subject of Burdett, it is interesting to notice that during this last month of 1820, Hunt turned out two *Addresses* in which he too criticised the baronet. Hunt was motivated in his anger by Burdett's repeated delays in calling for a public inquiry into the Peterloo Massacre. He remembered how jealous Burdett had been of him post-Peterloo at the Westminster meeting, how Burdett had turned pale when he heard the shouts of support for Hunt, how his lips had quivered and how he had shaken with envy and jealousy. It was all down to '*Jealousy, the green-eyed fiend jealousy*', wrote Hunt accusingly. He was certainly furious with Burdett, but the baronet was only second fiddle. Hunt's message about 'jealousy' was directed, consciously or unconsciously, at Cobbett, for him to read and reflect upon. Hunt needed allies in the House of Commons and was certainly upset that Burdett was letting him down. Far far more devastating for Hunt, however, was the fact that Cobbett had turned his back on him.

The year, 1821, unfolded with Hunt beginning to face the fact that Cobbett was not to be won over. The iron entered his soul. At the end of January, Hunt looked back at the suspension of the Habeas Corpus Act fours years previously, and the wholesale arrests of the radical reformers. 'Mr Cobbett, our great literary champion, had taken flight to America', Hunt wrote bitterly in his lonely, gloomy cell. Their great public writer had been driven not only out of the field but also out of the country. Although, he, Hunt, had expected to be thrown into gaol at any moment too, there had been no question of him deserting the cause. 'I was determined to stand my ground. I would have lost my life before I would have fled', he wrote in his January 1821 *Address*.

Hunt told his readers that he had received many letters from people inquiring about a reform meeting, which was planned in London. The inquiries had possibly arisen, he wrote, because of the news in the *Political Register* at the beginning of the month that a reform dinner was to be held after the re-assembly of parliament. His readers had written to Hunt asking for further details. He could only reply that he was no longer in the confidence of 'Mr Cobbett' and had no information. Readers of the *Political Register*, Hunt sniffed bitterly, would remember Mr Cobbett's announcement after his return from America that he would have no political connections with anybody except his own sons. Shortly

afterwards, Mr Cobbett had published a violent, scurrilous and
unfounded attack against Hunt by James Mills, although he had known
it was all a lie. After that, Hunt went on: 'Mr Cobbett went to Coventry
and I went to Preston and we have neither spoken nor communicated with
each other since.'

The extraordinary thing about the relationship between Hunt and
Cobbett was that they were, in some curious way, 'talking' to or about each
other all the time. They were constantly aware of each other, what the
other was doing or saying, even thinking. Cobbett might not have used
Hunt's actual name very often in the *Register*, but Hunt was still there, like
a ghostly spirit. Half way through this year of 1821, Cobbett suddenly
remembered with great pleasure Hunt's deaf and dumb brother William,
who had died in Illinois of fever a year earlier. Cobbett described William
Hunt fondly in the *Register*. He had been an Englishman and a sportsman,
with health, strength and activity 'in an *extraordinary degree*', he wrote. It
sounded just like Hunt himself. Cobbett omitted to mention that William
Hunt was Hunt's brother. His very silence about his former friend was
significant. Cobbett might have cut Hunt out in name, but Hunt was ever
present in his brain and, of course, in the mind of the knowing readers. It
was like a game in which both players pretended they were not looking at
each other although they were both looking all the time.

Cobbett was all disdain and scorn in the *Register* of 17 February 1821
when Burdett's Westminster MP colleague, John Cam Hobhouse,
announced that Burdett, who had finally been gaoled for three months for
his post-Peterloo letter, planned, as soon as he was released, to submit a
motion to the House of Commons calling for a parliamentary inquiry into
the massacre. Cobbett had a field day:

Keep your countenance, reader! Never ask how this motion comes to have remained
unmade during three Sessions of Parliament. Never ask how it happens that so distant a
notice of it is necessary just now. Hold your tongue as to those or the Rump will knock
you down!

He also cautioned the Manchester reformers. They should on no account
get excited either by any 'big bawling speeches' made by some Don
Quixote.

Hunt lapped up Cobbett's words and took up Cobbett's theme in his very next *Address*, sneering at any idea that Burdett would keep his word. 'The mountain is to be in labour again, is it?' he jeered. And then he continued with more of his own financial troubles. He reminded his readers that when he was about to set off to York for his trial, excise officers swooped on his business premises and seized his Breakfast Powder made from roasted rye. Soon after he was imprisoned, he was notified that he was to be given a fine of £100. He applied for a writ of Habeas Corpus so that he could attend the case in the Court of the Exchequer and contest the fine. His request was refused and the fine was doubled. Hunt informed the world that his son was now busy packing up his remaining stock into pound and half pound packets, which were to be sent free to the king, the queen, leading lawyers and members of parliament. In the meantime, Hunt planned to manufacture his own British Herb Tea and he was going to call it the 'Ilchester Mixture'.

Cobbett seized on the subject for the *Register* of 10 March 1821, although he could not bring himself to write Hunt's name. He was merely 'the Defendant'. The trial took place in the Exchequer, wrote Cobbett. 'The Defendant' was unable to speak in his own defence because the authorities would not allow him to leave his cell in Ilchester Prison. An Act of Parliament caught him out over the adulteration of coffee. The Act had been drawn up to prevent beans and acorns being used. If 'the Defendant' had not called his product by the equivocal name of '*Breakfast Powder*', wrote Cobbett, he would have got away with it.

Cobbett's mention of 'the Defendant' was brief and passing. He cold-bloodedly used the article largely to make political points, observing that the use of wheat to make imitation coffee could help the farmers. They could grow more wheat and thus create more jobs. Instead, the money was going out of England to buy coffee from overseas. The land-owning members of parliament were unable to see that their 'hostility towards the Radical Coffee People' was hurting nobody but themselves, Cobbett went on. He said nothing about how the establishment was vindictively trying to ruin Hunt.

Hunt set out to get his own back. In his *Address* published on 25 March 1821, he had more praise for *A Peep at the Peers* but was critical of Cobbett's twin pamphlet, *Links of the Lower House*, which had followed. It

was totally unworthy to be called a companion of *A Peep at the Peers,* Hunt
wrote scornfully. Like the mountain in labour, a mouse had been produced.
It was deficient in every page and many names had been omitted. He
accused 'the compilers' of being 'fearful' of government retribution. (As a
matter of note, GDH Cole believed that *A Peep at the Peers* was almost
certainly written by Cobbett's publisher, William Benbow, and that *Links
of the Lower House* was not the work of Cobbett. George Spater, however,
attributed both pamphlets to Cobbett and his daughter Anne. If so, she
would have been most upset by Hunt's comments.)

In this March 1821 *Address,* there were more ghastly details about the
prison. After ten months of complaining, Hunt wrote, he had persuaded
the authorities that another well should be dug in his courtyard. During
the work, they had unearthed a corpse just a couple of feet below the
surface, grotesquely severing the head and shoulders from the rest of the
body. Hunt promised more details in his next *Address.*

Cobbett did not bite on this sensational titbit, but returned just two
weeks later in the *Register* to the gritty subject of the substitute coffee and
promoted his own use of roasted wheat (as opposed to Hunt's use of
roasted rye). But Hunt was there, in this issue of 14 April 1821, tucked
away in a small corner at the end of the *Register* in the shape of an
advertisement.

After years of resolutely refusing to take advertisements, Cobbett
decided that to survive financially he had to do as most other publishers
did. This issue was the first one in which advertisements appeared.
Cobbett being Cobbett, they were as much a joy to read as the magazine
itself. He had obviously decided to favour anything anti-establishment
with a whiff of reform and subversion about it. The latest works of the
radical writer and publisher William Hone were there, including 'THE
SPIRIT OF DESPOTISM', which, the advertisement rejoiced, was being
read 'with the greatest avidity' in post-revolutionary France. There was
also 'THE TORY FACTION UNMASKED'. This advocated a union
between the Whigs and the Radicals to 'save the country from the effects
of military Despotism or a bloody Revolution.'

Some of the advertisements were very whacky. For the price of a
shilling, readers could purchase 'A NEW CARICATURE ...

CLARENCE'S DREAM or BILLY BARNACLE receiving an unwelcome Visitor from the other world.' Despite Cobbett's support for Queen Caroline, his readers were informed that the latest publications detailing the salacious scandals about her alleged illegitimate child and adulterous affairs were now on sale. Readers should 'be careful' to order all three volumes of the new edition. There was also 'THE CHRONICLE OF THE KINGS OF ENGLAND,' including their religious and political crimes, follies, vices and amours, all in all, 'a faithful picture of the indescribable blessings of monarchical government'. There were several advertisements for the latest caricatures of the engraver George Cruickshank, including 'A GROAN from the THRONE' and 'A FROWN from the CROWN.'

Amongst all these was a large advertisement for the 'MEMOIRS OF HENRY HUNT, Esq. written by himself, in his Majesty's Jail at Ilchester'. Hunt's publisher, Thomas Dolby, would have written the words. The *Memoirs* were:

A plain and unvarnished History of the events of his own life ... interspersed with original Anecdotes ... expected to throw much light upon the intrigues and movements of Political Parties as well as upon the principal Political Characters who have figured before the Public for many years.

Volume 1 was already completed in boards (fine and expensive stiff front and back covers) at a cost of 10s 6d. The next instalment, Number 13, was just published. Meanwhile – and this was given three stars – Number 14 was to be published that very day and would contain a full account of 'a most important and interesting event in the Author's Domestic History.' (It was, of course, Hunt's sensational account of how he met, fell in love with and eloped with Mrs Vince.)

There was more, namely *A Peep into Ilchester Gaol.* (The '*Peep*' title was commonly used, but Hunt was obviously inspired by Cobbett's various *Peeps*.) This promised to reveal 'the Barbarities, the Oppressions, the Extortions and the Indecencies carried on in that sink of iniquity; with an ENGRAVING of the different methods of torture practised therein.' There were also petitions to the government from two of the inmates, together with Hunt's latest correspondence to the High Sheriff of Somerset. The advertisement dramatically concluded with a quotation from the Old Testament: 'Tell it not in Gath – proclaim it not in the streets of Askelon.' This must surely have been borrowed from Cobbett's practice of using quotations and references, often Biblical ones, in the *Register*. It was also a sly hit at Cobbett and his silence about Hunt and his situation in prison.

Two weeks later, on 28 April 1821, out of the blue Hunt popped up by name in the *Register*. Cobbett was jeering and sneering about a dinner organised by the moderate reformers at the London Tavern. Suddenly his old friend was in the forefront of his mind as he recalled the fiasco of the 1818 Westminster election, and how it was Hunt who had been the darling of the people even though he had come bottom in the election. 'How came it, that MR HUNT had the *show of hands;* and that he got only about *four-score votes* out of ten thousand; and that Sir Francis Burdett, who was rejected by the show of hands, was elected by the *votes?*' roared Cobbett's wonderful pen. A blast from the past. Did Hunt eagerly pore over these lines, hoping for more?

On 5 May 1821, the fourth edition of the *Ilchester Peep* was advertised in the *Register*. The contents of Hunt's *Address*, meanwhile, published by Dolby that same day, were truly sensational. His readers were informed that Hunt had been successful in getting an inquiry set up to examine the conduct of William Bridle, the gaoler of Ilchester Bastile. The High Sheriff of Somerset, together with the magistrates, was holding the inquiry inside the prison. Hunt was himself paying the expenses of former inmates who had been asked to return to the gaol to give evidence. A picture of what was going on in the prison was beginning to emerge. Cruelty and torture were endemic. Hunt described some of the cases, including the story of the weaver boy John Wheeler, who had been found guilty of stealing a pair of worsted stockings and sentenced to hard labour for two years in Ilchester gaol. He was just eleven years old at the time. The boy was severely ill-treated. He was held in solitary confinement for sixteen days during which time his hands were shackled behind him with iron hand-bolts. The bolts ate into his hands and wrists and pulled his muscles until they were over-stretched. Afterwards, the boy was unable to swing his arms back into a normal position and lost the use of his hands and arms. This meant he could no longer work as a weaver.

Hunt followed this excruciating story with a mass of evidence against William Bridle. The gaoler refused to allow prisoners to organise clean supplies of water for themselves, although he knew the water within the prison was contaminated. He had fathered children using the female prisoners, and also forced them to have sex with the male prisoners. He was regularly drunk, swore and ran gambling sessions inside the prison. He stole both from the local authority and the prisoners. During elections, Bridle would fling open the prison gates and invite the locals in for a big party. There were flags, colours and bands. The gaoler debauched the women and everybody danced and drank themselves senseless.

In this *Address*, Hunt also printed up some of the letters and addresses he had received from his adoring public. They were enough to make Cobbett green with envy. The Radical Reformers in Leeds had written to Hunt to tell him that the people loved him for having exposed 'the vile machinations of the people's enemies'. They loved him even more now because of his sufferings in their common cause. They knew that his noble conduct would sweeten the bitter cup of his oppression and that the benignant rays beaming from Hunt's virtues would light up the gloom of his dungeon. They were also glued to his *Memoirs*:

The active and impressive scenes you there delineate, accompanied by the reflections of experience and written in language at once simple, eloquent and convincing, cannot fail to entertain, instruct and improve your readers ... The ardent glow of Liberty which pervades your manly bosom, now animates the breast of millions of your fellow countrymen.

Yes, millions. How Cobbett must have squirmed to read those fulsome tributes, a red rag to a bull. Just a week later, in the issue of the *Register* of 12 May 1821, Cobbett smashed back. The year 1819 was the most disgraceful year that England had ever known, he declared. Why? First, because of the reception given to him on his arrival back in England from America by the Manchester magistrates who had barred him from entering the city. Second, because of the gaoling of the Bolton town crier, John Hayes, for ten weeks for proclaiming the safe arrival of Cobbett at Liverpool docks, and thirdly, because of the Six Acts. There was not a single word about Peterloo. But Hunt was still there, leaping up and down in the advertisements. No 15 of his *Memoirs* was now available together with an *Address*, and *A Peep into Ilchester Gaol* was into its fifth edition.

Cobbett chose to address the entire issue of the very next *Register* of 19 May 1821 to the famous Bolton town crier. Towards the end he drifted off into self-congratulatory mode, describing how he had been hanging on like a bulldog for nineteen years, beset by persecutors, all of whom he now graciously forgave. (His temporary forgiveness resulted from the government's decision to re-introduce payments in gold coins, something Cobbett had long pressed for and which he believed would benefit the working classes):

As for me, who has so much to *forgive* as I have? Who has been so persecuted by this long train of Pittite Ministers? Yet, so grateful do I feel for the good now done to the Labouring Classes, that I freely forgive them, yea, *Sidmouth* and all.

Let England's Glory (Sir Francis Burdett), Cobbett continued, chuckle at the comparison between his own three months in the King's Bench Prison and Cobbett's two years in Newgate. Let Burdett 'promulgate private letters.' Let him wallow in his money. All Cobbett wanted was the happiness of the labourers. He only needed the reward of an approving silent look from them. Only let the 'Labouring Classes' be happy and his own happiness would be complete. Cobbett turned to Proverbs for a suitable quotation for this issue and found what he considered to be the perfect one: 'Open thy mouth, judge righteously and plead the cause of the poor and needy.'

Poor Hunt must have thought that was exactly what Cobbett should be doing with regard to him. The battles he was fighting on all fronts were making him ill. He complained bitterly of the stress he was under in an *Address* in July 1821. The inquiry into the deeds of the gaoler William Bridle was over. In its last phase, Hunt had sensationally persuaded the magistrates that the tortures should be re-enacted using the original iron hand bolts and manacles. One former prisoner, Thomas Gardner aged eighteen, had returned to the prison to give evidence. He had put on the strait jacket he had been forced to wear at the time, got into the crouching position he had been made to adopt in his cell, and graphically described how his head had been deliberately burned and blistered with hot irons several times.

Hunt celebrated the fact that already improvements had been made.

The torturing had stopped. Letters to the prisoners were delivered unopened, and they were allowed to have good bread and clean water brought in from outside. He was now even more convinced that the authorities were plotting to kill him, however. The inner bolts on his dungeon door had still not been replaced and, he wrote dramatically, he was sleeping with a carving knife by his side.

Hunt's waves of misery may have penetrated Cobbett, who may have felt another pang of conscience. The theme in the *Register* of 21 July 1821 centred around the collapse of country banks and the ruin of people whose deposits had been in paper bank notes as opposed to gold. Cobbett recalled that when he was in prison in 1811, 'while the THING had me in Newgate', he had written his celebrated pamphlet, *Paper Against Gold* (which Hunt had so much admired). Cobbett remembered how he urged people to go to their country bank to demand gold in exchange for their paper bank notes. '*Mr Henry Hunt*', he recalled, (how sonorously the name rings out from his pen) went to the Hobhouse Bank in Bath to change his notes into gold. They refused to allow him to do so. 'Mr Hunt' began an action against the bank but before it could go to court, an Act of Parliament was passed to protect country banks against any demands for payment in gold.

There was absolutely no need for Cobbett to mention Hunt like that out of the blue, but he did.

In this issue of the *Register*, an advertisement announced that Hunt would be publishing weekly instalments of his evidence to the Somerset Magistrates in their inquiry into the running of Ilchester Prison. 'This sink of Iniquity has been brought to light through the individual exertion of Mr Hunt under every disadvantage of ill-health and inconvenience', it carolled triumphantly. There was more triumph for Hunt, and more coals of fire for Cobbett, in Hunt's next *Address* published on 26 July 1821 (two in one month), in which Hunt revealed the glorious news that the prison gaoler William Bridle had been sacked as a result of the inquiry, he, Henry Hunt, had instigated.

There was not a whisper of this sensational news in the *Political Register*, but it had fuelled Cobbett's jealousy. Two months later, he gave an extreme example of what could only be a latent insecurity, in the

Register of 22 September 1821, when he referred to a meeting of yeomen farmers from Worcester. The meeting had been called to discuss the distressed state of the country. At the end, the farmers had passed a grovelling resolution thanking various people, including government ministers, whom they toasted. They did not mention Cobbett. Cobbett's pen spluttered out the following lines in the *Register*:

What! *Forget Cobbett!* Not thank him, without whose writings these resolutions could not have been passed ... What! Not thank *him* who and who alone has taught the principles upon which these resolutions are founded, who has put into the mouths of this Meeting, even the very words that they make use of ... Not thank him on whose pen these Yeomanry must still rely for success in their endeavours to preserve themselves from ruin and who has only to take part against them to cause their Petitions to be blown to the Devil ... to thank *them* while not a word is said of him, who has the power to make that cause succeed or so to mar it as to render the distress of the complaining parties a hundred times greater than it now is.

These toasts were taken very seriously. The newspapers and journals scrupulously reported – or significantly missed out – the names of the people who were toasted at meetings. Cobbett and Hunt used toasts as part of their armoury of weapons against each other. Hunt was livid when Cobbett, along with the mainstream press, missed out the fact that Hunt was unexpectedly toasted at a Whig meeting in Preston the following month. The meeting in October 1821 was attended by a group of lawyers from the north of England. Cobbett heaped sparkling insults against the tribe of 'black bodied and grey-headed foxes from the Assizes at Lancaster' and the 'cackling geese' who invited them. The headline for his article in the *Register* was 'Festival of the Geese and the Foxes'. Cobbett did mention – and condemn – a toast to James Scarlett, the prosecutor of those who '*escaped*' the sword on the 16 August 1819 in Manchester, 'Messrs Hunt, Johnson and Bamford'. If the people of Preston did not disavow the act of the toast, they merited lashing and starvation for the rest of their lives, wrote Cobbett, with a holier-than-thou hat on. Nevertheless, he carefully omitted to mention the surprise toast to Hunt.

Hunt complained bitterly. Cobbett's headline was very witty, he wrote in the next *Address* that followed hot on the heels of Cobbett's *Register*, but, Hunt continued indignantly, Cobbett had played the fox himself by keeping the most important feature of the entire meeting totally out of sight. The main fact was that a toast had been drunk to Hunt 'with a degree of enthusiasm seldom equalled upon any similar occasion'. This was despite strong resistance from the chairman, who had been unable to prevent one of Mr Hunt's strenuous admirers boldly standing upon his seat and, undaunted, calling for the health of Henry Hunt Esq. with '*three times three*'. There had been an instant burst of applause, and nearly everybody had jumped on to the chairs and tables to drink the toast amidst rapturous and repeated cheers never witnessed before at a public meeting, squeaked Hunt's pen furiously.

This October *Address* concluded with the joyful news that Hunt's pamphlets detailing the gory evidence against William Bridle were selling out. Those who wished to complete their sets should rush to get them while stocks lasted. The issues of the *Memoirs* had also sold out and more copies were being printed. Meanwhile, letters and gifts were pouring in. Hunt had been sent a half hogshead of the finest cider. He was going to get a piece of plate from the ratepayers of Somerset in gratitude for his investigation into the prison. A cheese made from ewe's milk by farmers on the banks of the river Coquet in Northumberland had arrived, as had a beautiful length of flannel sent by the Radicals of Rochdale in Lancashire. The tub of herrings from Mr H Martin, Junior, of Yarmouth had also been gratefully received. Subscriptions were being raised and money sent in. Two small hamlets near Ashton-under-Lyne had sent Hunt £2 10s 6d towards his expenses, and branches of the Great Northern Union, that Hunt had been busily organising from his prison cell, were being formed. (The aim of the Union was to raise money to sponsor an MP. The first one was to be Hunt himself. Cobbett studiously ignored any mention of the union. Hunt furiously attributed Cobbett's silence to 'great jealousies and heart-burnings'.)

The public support helped Hunt to battle on, but it was still hard work and his mood had changed by the time of the next *Address* which was published on Christmas Eve 1821. There was still another year to go locked up in Ilchester Bastile and, despite everything he had achieved, he was still locked up for fifteen hours out of every twenty-four. Winter loomed and his cell was colder than an ice-house. Hunt was bitter about

Cobbett's treatment of him. He could not recollect Cobbett mentioning his sentence, his sufferings or his work to expose conditions in the prison. 'I have never seen or heard whether he approved or disapproved of my labours during the Investigation into the abuses of this Gaol', Hunt wrote plaintively. Of course he had been much too busy in any case to notice what Cobbett said or had not said about the investigation, but it must surely have deserved either censure or approbation. He 'understood' that Cobbett had never even bothered to notice the Great Northern Union although thousands of people had now enrolled, Hunt went on, pretending he was not glued to the *Political Register* every week but giving himself away as he went on to list all the topical subjects Cobbett was writing about. He continued wistfully: 'As he knows that we are going on very well without him, he is directing his powerful pen and his powerful energies in another direction, all tending to the same end.'

They were revealing lines. Cobbett obviously did not read them properly or he might have stopped being jealous and got back together with Hunt much more quickly than he eventually did. The true meaning was quite clear. Hunt needed him. He needed Cobbett's energy, praise and approbation. He needed Cobbett's powerful pen. It did not matter what anybody else said, thought or wrote if Cobbett were paying no attention. What was more, Hunt knew they were on the same side and working for the very same cause.

As Hunt rambled on in his lonely cell in the run up to Christmas 1821, he was sunk in depression as he remembered the glory days with Cobbett, the petitions for reform and the great meetings, his own ongoing battle against the horrors of the prison and his achievements, all unacknowledged by his old friend. There were pages of it. Hunt practically wept with rage and misery at his treatment by Cobbett and everybody else, including the reptile press, which had had the cheek to accuse Hunt of having a 'disgusting egotism'. How could they accuse him of that, the man who had run a campaigning investigation single-handed, spending hundreds of pounds of his own money while being persecuted by the government? How could they accuse a man of being an egotist who was labouring night and day to expose tyranny and oppression, up to his knees in water? It was the third time the gaol had been flooded within the past six weeks! He was worried too that he could be murdered at any moment or even burnt alive by the fires that kept breaking out throughout the prison.

One can see his point.

12
Down with the Bastile

We are not ashamed of what we have done, because, when you have a great cause to fight for, the moment of greatest humiliation is the moment when the spirit is proudest.

Christabel Pankhurst

As Hunt entered his final months in Ilchester Prison, Cobbett got away from it all on the first of his glorious travels around the country on horseback. Sometimes accompanied by his youngest son, Richard, Cobbett rode up hill and down dale, observing the countryside with an acutely critical eye. He noted down what was thriving, what was blighted and why, and how the ordinary people lived. He wrote about the villages, market towns, fruit gardens, hop and hayfields. Peering over walls, looking under hedges and observing the flow of the rivers, Cobbett read the soil, the air and the skies, and studied hearts and minds, from the rich to the destitute, peers, bishops, farmers, labourers, the cruel overseers of poor relief, the bishops in their castles and the absentee clergy raking in the tithes. He did it all in some of his best lyrical prose. The accounts of his journeys were published in the *Political Register* and were eventually turned into his two eminently readable volumes, *Rural Rides*.

While Hunt shivered in his freezing cell, Cobbett breathed in the frosty air and bathed his soul in the wide open spaces on top of the steep hills in the Forest of Dean in Herefordshire, along the River Medway in Kent and through the rich valley of Sevenoaks in Surrey. Near Marlborough in Wiltshire, Cobbett saw a group of poor girls reaping in the bitter cold, 'ragged as colts and as pale as ashes'. Their blue arms and lips would have made any heart ache but that of a seat-seller or a loan-jobber, he observed.

Cobbett's *Rural Rides* present an intimate and detailed picture of how Britain was in the early nineteenth century in the post Waterloo slump, as the last of the common land was enclosed, and before the so-called Great Reform Act of 1832. In his own time, Cobbett's writing clearly spelled out the injustice and inequality of a system that threw people into poverty, allowing them no escape route, nor any effective means of protest. Cobbett's travels included a visit to Burwash in Sussex where he discovered that the landowners, farmers and clergy were petitioning parliament over the distressed state of the parish. They blamed the slump in market prices, which meant that farmers could not afford to employ labourers who were, in consequence, riotous, turbulent and ready for extreme acts of desperation. Premises and property had been set on fire and anonymous letters written threatening murder if something were not done. Half the population was receiving parish relief so the poor rates were high. They all looked set to be ruined. The petition was printed in the *Political Register* of 8 June 1822. It was a prescient piece of reporting on Cobbett's part, foreshadowing what was to happen in the Last Labourers' Revolt of 1830 – for which Cobbett and Hunt would be so unjustly blamed.

During these years, instead of arguing with the farmers as he had done at public meetings with Hunt a decade previously, Cobbett sympathised with their plight, and now, instead of booing, they listened. In the 'fine city' of Norwich, as Cobbett called it, in December 1821, 2,000 rich farmers took off their hats and bowed to him as he walked through the market place. It was the ultimate accolade. With loving pride, Anne described the scene in a letter to her brother James in New York: 'If he had shown his nose there years ago, he would not have got away with a bone unbroken. He was received with unbounded applause ... and those who were near enough pressed forward to shake him by the hand.' The applause and homage her father was receiving was pleasing for him after all his troubles, she wrote. It was 'equally galling to his enemies, amongst whom are the Baronet, the Old Major and that snarling lean Hunt', she added sourly.

Cobbett was travelling for a purpose. His rural riding reinforced his confidence and position as the country's leading political writer. It was also almost a psychological reaction to the claustrophobic, solitary confinement of Hunt in Ilchester Bastile. And Hunt was trotting closely behind Cobbett in spirit, if not in body. In his *Address* of 12 January 1822, Hunt enjoyed Cobbett's triumph among the farmers:

O, how they used to guzzle ale, gin and wine and drunk damnation to the Reformers! But now the case is altered. They are as meek and as mild and as quiet as possible and to see

them come sidling and whining to the Reformers to claim their compassion and solicit
their aid to help them out of the mire, is quite pitiable.

Cobbett may well have laughed on reading those words. Hunt was very
generous to his estranged friend in this *Address*. He referred to a meeting
of farmers in Battle in East Sussex, which Cobbett attended as a member
of the audience. Afterwards, reported Hunt, the farmers honoured 'Mr
Cobbett' with an invitation to sit at the head of the second table. They
listened with great attention to his eloquent and comprehensive speech
on the reasons for agricultural distress and toasted his health with great
applause, wrote Hunt proudly. As Hunt jolted along, figuratively
speaking, in Cobbett's hoof prints and in his family's thoughts, so
Cobbett himself could not quite get Hunt out of his mind. As he rode
through Faversham in Kent, he mused over the idea of Joseph Hume, the
pro-reform MP, doing his best in the House of Commons to pare away at
government spending, and how there would still be others, 'the Hunts,
Cobbetts and Carliles, who would always want the expense to be less.'

At a public dinner in King's Lynn, Cobbett's speech moved from the
agricultural distress in the countryside to the need for a reform of
parliament. He published his speech in the *Political Register* of 2 February
1822. Hunt's name popped up again. Cobbett told the farmers that they
should remember all the people, 'with Mr Hunt at their head', who were
persecuted because they encouraged people to use corn to make a
substitute coffee. Cobbett even referred to it here by Hunt's own name of
'Breakfast Powder'. The farmers were only too glad to see imported corn
being used in the process, he said. They should demand a repeal of the Act
which made it a crime to make coffee powder.

As Cobbett's speech developed at King's Lynn, he selected the
constituency of Ilchester in Somerset as an example of some of the bad
practices a reform of parliament would stamp out. He described how some
people had had the roofs of their houses removed when they had been bold
enough to vote for the man they wanted to represent them in parliament
instead of their landlord. When they still refused to leave their homes, the
'landowner boroughmonger' (Sir William Manners) dumped a load of
dung alongside so that they were eventually forced out by the stench. Had
Hunt again wafted through Cobbett's mind? If he had, he continued

wafting. The first task of a new government would have to be the repeal of the Six Acts and the release of the 'suffering' reformers from prison, Cobbett informed the farmers. A toast was drunk to Hunt – but Cobbett left that bit out.

Like a panther in a cage, Hunt seized on Cobbett's omission. Although he was ill with chest pains and violent spasms of the heart, he was still monitoring the newspapers. He found out about the toast at the King's Lynn meeting from the radical *Stamford News*. The newspaper's publisher, John Drakard, reported that toasts were drunk to Hunt at two public dinners attended by Cobbett, the one at King's Lynn as well as another at Huntingdon. Hunt pounced on the information with furious triumph. In his *Address* of 11 February 1822, he solemnly drew up two lists side by side to compare what Cobbett had said in the *Political Register* (nothing), with the words printed in the *Stamford News*. In his account of the King's Lynn meeting, Drakard reported that 'the brave Captive of Ilchester' was among the imprisoned reformers to be toasted; at the Huntingdon meeting, it was Mr Cobbett himself who had called for the health of Mr Hunt and all the persons suffering in the cause of Reform, and he had wished that 'the massacre at Manchester might never be forgotten or forgiven till amply atoned for'.

Hunt laughed hollowly in his cell. 'Do not look grave, my friends but laugh with me', he wrote bitterly. The editor of *The Times* had forecast that Cobbett would attack his friend, Hunt, when he got home from America. It would be manlier for Mr Cobbett to do just that, wrote Hunt, rather than presenting his readers with false statements about public meetings. Hunt was distressed and depressed. He informed his readers that he was ill with chest pains and experiencing violent spasms of the heart. The authorities were refusing to allow him medical aid and all family visits were once again banned, despite a petition presented to the House of Commons from his younger son, Thomas, aged nineteen.

Thomas' frantic petition complaining about the way his father was being treated and his family's lack of access to him had been presented to the Commons just three days earlier. The petition sparked a debate in which Sir Francis Burdett, whose conscience was being jogged by Hunt's plight and the conditions he was enduring in prison, spoke up forcibly on his behalf. Hunt's sentence was more severe than any that had been delivered since the infamous time of the Stuarts, Burdett said. It had not been applied to the offence but to the individual, and Burdett accused the state of using Ilchester Prison to pay off old scores against Hunt.

In this *Address* of 11 February 1822, Hunt gave Burdett 'most unqualified and grateful thanks' and implicitly compared the baronet's behaviour with that of Cobbett. Bitterly, Hunt quoted St Paul who upbraided his friends for neglecting him in his adversity: 'I was in prison and ye visited me not.' This must have been greeted with cruel laughter in the Cobbett household. In the first year of Hunt's imprisonment, it had been suggested that any radical who visited him in gaol should be given a 'knighthood' according to the order of 'St. Henry of Ilchester' to keep Hunt's plight in the public eye. The idea was laughed out of court and died a death. Now, here was Hunt, comparing himself in his misery to St Paul. Meanly, Cobbett noted the allusion and filed it away for future use.

Two weeks later, Hunt was in his 34th day of solitary confinement and feeling abandoned and alone. He penned another *Address* to his readers in which he looked back at his great triumphs at Spa Fields, the suspension of Habeas Corpus, and, yet again, the flight of Cobbett to America. In this *Address* of 25 February 1822, Hunt also published his own petition to the House of Commons in which he outlined the frightful prison conditions, his fight to expose them, how he had paid the expenses of his witnesses in the inquiry into the prison and how some of the former prisoners had been too intimidated to attend. He described the contaminated water supplies and the miserable deaths of imprisoned debtors. He himself was ill, yet medical aid was being refused him.

Alongside his *Addresses*, Hunt continued the theme in his *Memoirs*. Since Mr Cobbett's return from America the latter had behaved very ill towards him, he wrote. The silence of Mr Cobbett had made things worse and encouraged his enemies in their attempt to destroy him. Mr Cobbett could not expect many partial words to flow from his pen when he had failed to help his former friend in his hour of need, wrote Hunt miserably.

His desertion of me at a time of danger and difficulty and his neglecting to aid me with his pen, in the herculean task which I have had to perform in this bastile, must to every liberal mind appear unpardonable ... Such a struggle and made by a prisoner under such circumstances too, to detect, expose and punish fraud, cruelty, tyranny and lust perpetrated within the walls of an English gaol, surely deserved the assistance of every enemy of oppression.

Did Cobbett experience another pang of conscience? At the end of the *Register* of 9 March 1822, he wrote a terse comment piece. He had read 'Mr Hunt's Petition,' and it had moved him to the core:

If any man can read, or can hear read that petition, without feeling his *blood boil*, that man is a tyrant and a base and cowardly villain! Such a series of atrocities, *of base atrocities*, and of so many distinct kinds, never were stated on one piece of paper.

He had no room to insert the petition in this issue, he wrote, but he would print it in full in the next, 'with such remarks on the matter as I deem proper and as I dare publish.' He did observe that the high sheriff had sent word that the treatment of Mr Hunt should be relaxed. This, Cobbett pointed out, was curious. Previously the high sheriff had claimed that he had no powers to intervene with what was going on in the gaol. And suddenly, there was a flash of Cobbett's old style towards Hunt: 'How came the Sheriff to find that he *had power* on *Saturday last?* Faith, the THING is growing more *tame* than it was! Some time back the THING would have *laughed* Mr Hunt's petition to scorn.' It almost sounded like the spring was being coiled up ready for a quick devastating release, but, sadly, the flash petered out, Cobbett's pen spluttered and then rambled off at a tangent.

Cobbett did not keep his word about publishing Hunt's petition with 'remarks', and it did not appear in the *Register* as promised. Instead, Cobbett wrote that he had intended to use it but again he had had to delay publication. 'It should be read and carefully kept, by every man in the kingdom', he intoned. Yet, there was nothing about it in the following *Register* either, and Cobbett never published Hunt's petition.

Cobbett's lack of coverage of Hunt's treatment in Ilchester was altogether disgraceful. There were several debates in the House of Commons about Hunt's plight in gaol, some of which were triggered by the pro-Hunt protests across the country and the petitions that poured in to parliament demanding his early release. The events taking place in

Ilchester Prison remained national news. People read with horror Hunt's own description in his *Memoirs* of an operation carried out on a tumour in his eye, after doctors were finally allowed in to his cell. Hunt was attended by three surgeons. One held his eyelids open. The second squeezed the eye almost out of its socket. The third seized hold of the tumour with a sharp crooked needle and cut it out. The House of Commons heard how Hunt's younger son, Thomas, had been refused permission to be there with his father. In desperation, the teenager had taken a boat and rowed out onto the River Yeo to the prison towering over the north bank. There was a small gap in the wall of his father's cell that overlooked the river. By manoeuvring the boat on the water, father and son had managed to shout to each other through the gap.

Hunt bitterly resented the lack of support from Cobbett during this critical period of his life. On 16 March 1822, around the anniversary of the time Cobbett had fled to America five years previously, Hunt wrote a miserable letter to one of his friends: 'I have ever since March 1817 ... been accustomed to rely <u>entirely upon my own opinion</u>, never having had <u>one Friend</u> whose judgement and principles I could depend upon, that I could consult.'

Hunt's spirits sank and soared. In his *Address* a week later, on 25 March 1822, Hunt celebrated another triumph in his campaign against the prison. He had won the release of Charles Hill, aged seventy-six, who had been locked up in Ilchester Bastile for a debt he was not responsible for, and kept there for sixteen years. Hunt exulted. The gaoler William Bridle had told him not to bother with Mr Hill, 'a sad fellow, a sad fellow! Have nothing to do with him, Mr Hunt.' This was a palpable hit by Hunt at Cobbett, and a reminder to his readers of Cobbett's own treacherous 'whore on horseback' letter that he had written against Hunt and denied as a forgery.

Ten days later, Cobbett published an account of another meeting in Norwich at which he had addressed the farmers and tradesmen. There had been a toast to Hunt and this time Cobbett published the fact.

There was no question of hostilities by Cobbett against Hunt ceasing, however. The *Political Register* of 20 April 1822 began on an unusual note. Cobbett had been getting complaints that supplies of the *Register* were irregular. Instead of getting their copy on Saturday, as people did in

Norwich, Bristol and Portsmouth, for example, all of which were an overnight journey away, many were having to wait until the Monday or Tuesday. Cobbett blamed the middle man who was responsible for sending the journals into the country, and who had 'perhaps *other things to send*, about which he is more anxious than about the *Register*, which latter, therefore, he *keeps back*, in order to save the expense of two coach-parcels instead of one.' In future, agents were asked to write directly to Cobbett for supplies and he would pay for the carriage of the parcels.

Hey presto, Hunt's publisher, Thomas Dolby, included a foreword in Hunt's *Address* a few weeks later on 15 May. The '*other things*' Cobbett had mentioned were in fact copies of Hunt's *Addresses* and instalments of his *Memoirs*. The latter were published every fortnight and were proving to be very popular, wrote Dolby. They were being sent out from London across the country in the same parcels as Cobbett's *Register*. Now Dolby was concerned that Cobbett's new system would overturn the arrangements and disrupt supplies of Hunt's work. He did not want to cause a quarrel between Hunt and Cobbett 'between whom there is, unhappily, already a coldness which it may, ere long, be necessary to explain and account for', wrote Dolby (cleverly whetting people's appetites so they would continue to buy Hunt's works). Mr Hunt had justly attained an eminence 'too dazzling not to excite a little envy in the breasts of those who may heretofore have fancied themselves peculiar objects of popular regard'. (In other words, Cobbett was jealous as hell.) Dolby was sure that country booksellers would be far too generous to fall in with any plans that might prevent the free flow of information, but if '*any attempts*' were made to '*exclude*' Mr Hunt's *Memoirs* from the customary channels, Dolby wanted to know, sharpish.

There was more from Dolby on the subject in Hunt's next *Address* of 25 May 1822. From what Dolby wrote, it can be inferred that supplies of Hunt's *Memoirs* had indeed been interrupted and that Cobbett was busy claiming it was all because Dolby was not sending him enough copies to dispatch along with the *Register*. Dolby furiously pointed out that Mr Cobbett could '*always*' have enough copies of the *Memoirs* to make up the orders. He only had to ask. If Cobbett failed to dispatch them, it was entirely from the 'ungenerous motive before stated [jealousy]... all the *excuses* he makes for not sending Mr Hunt's *Memoirs*, however his ingenuity may disguise the matter, are false', Dolby raged.

While the battle was going on, it can be seen what Cobbett's family was saying about Hunt from a letter Anne sent to James. Hunt had just written and published the instalment of his *Memoirs* in which he declared that Nancy Cobbett was a bad mistress to her servants and unable to keep them for very long. James was due to sail home from New York later in the year. Anne wrote her letter to him on 30 May 1822. It included the following lines:

> You will be here just about in time to see that scamp of all scamps Hunt come out of his den. He has been for a long time abusing first Papa, then William and John, in his periodical publication, and lately he has fallen upon Mama, telling the reformers of England that Mrs Cobbett was always changing her cooks and housemaids, did you ever hear of such a fool?

Anne also mentioned the sudden friendship between Sir Francis Burdett and Hunt: '[They] are making all the world sick by <u>praising one another</u>. What a set of rogues Patriots are!'

Anne was referring to the new twist in the Hunt/Burdett saga. Burdett's own conscience had been doing some pricking. The baronet was now repeatedly speaking out in the House of Commons against the length of Hunt's sentence and the conditions in which he was being held. He even proposed his own motion calling for Hunt's early release. During the debate, one MP spoke of the gross immorality of the adulterous relationship between Hunt and 'his mistress' (Mrs Vince). Another compared her to a prostitute. Deeply embarrassed, Sir Francis declared there was more immorality and scandal in unnecessarily dragging the circumstances before the public, than in allowing it to pass unnoticed.

Hunt was pathetically and grovellingly grateful to Burdett, and wrote glowingly of him in his *Memoirs*, excusing his own past behaviour towards Sir Francis. He had only criticised Burdett in the past out of public duty, not because of any personal feelings. He was sure that the baronet bore him no malice for performing what had only been Hunt's painful duty. Since he had been locked up in Ilchester gaol, Burdett had behaved most nobly towards him, squeaked Hunt's pen. (After Hunt left prison, it was to be hostility between the two as usual.)

Hence Anne's disgust in her letter about the sudden good relations between Hunt and Burdett. Interestingly, her letter to her brother also reveals that it was the Cobbett household who were vociferous against Hunt, NOT Cobbett himself. He was not saying anything about Hunt to his family. 'All this has never provoked Papa to say one word about him, either good, bad or indifferent', Anne wrote.

So Cobbett, it seems, did not join his wife or his children in their abuse of Hunt. He kept his thoughts to himself. Maybe he could not bear to join in his family's attacks against the man he had been so proud to call his 'dear Hunt' and whom he secretly missed. Nevertheless, at the same time, Cobbett was creating problems over the circulation and distribution of Hunt's works, and continuing to jostle with Hunt in the *Register*. It may, for example, be recalled that Hunt bitterly resented how the newspapers criticised what they called his 'disgusting egotism'. In the *Register* of 1 June 1822, Cobbett reflected on his own – and smugly justified it:

I have long since passed that point within which a man can with propriety be accused of what is called egotism. If I were not, it would be impossible for me to separate, at this time of the day, a great deal of that which closely concerns myself, from that which must now be interesting to the Country at large.

Those words opened this particular issue of the *Register*. There is no question, of course, but that both these men, William Cobbett and Henry Hunt, were terrific egotists. They may be forgiven. They had to be egotistic or they probably could not have done and achieved what they did against such odds. Cobbett was being very disarming in this issue of the *Register*. He wrote those words after a visit to his home town of Farnham in Surrey, during which he reflected once again on his obscure origins, what he had become and what he had achieved. It was, also, a very subtle swipe at Hunt.

A week later, on 8 June 1822, Cobbett offered a small olive branch. It came in a notice in the *Register* from Cobbett to his 'Country Booksellers'. He knew, he said, that some of the booksellers wanted parcels of '*other pamphlets*' sent together with the *Register*. There had been some delay to those '*other pamphlets*' because of the change in the system of distribution. But sales of the *Register* had risen, which proved that the new system was better for Cobbett. He would, however, offer a concession. The publisher of the *Political Register* would accept '*other pamphlets*' from publishers, if they were packed up in parcels, sealed and taken to Cobbett's office before 12 o'clock on Friday, and if those publishers paid their share of the carriage.

Cobbett's conciliatory offer was too late to mollify Hunt's vitriol which poured out two days later in his *Address* of 10 June 1822, in which he celebrated the passing of an Act that legalised the sale of his Breakfast Powder. It should be called 'Hunt's Bill' *and* 'Hunt's Breakfast Powder', he wrote triumphantly. He had every right to the claim, he crowed. Why, if he had not revived an old French recipe for producing a coffee substitute, the Act would never have been passed. Hunt's guns now blazed against Cobbett: 'There were those connected with the Radical press – those to whom I had rendered great and important services – those to whom I had been most devoted and most faithful at all times and under all circumstances – who were taking every base and underhanded means to injure me', he wrote. 'Instigated by the most malignant passion of jealousy,' Hunt continued, they were trying to destroy the sale of his Breakfast Powder by claiming that he was making too large a profit. He would venture to say that 'the party' would never write another line upon the subject if it were not to gratify his own passions. Those people who had been induced to use common roasted wheat had been completely '*sickened and surfeited*' by it. Even a half-starved pig had turned up her nose at it, snorted Hunt. He wished to inform his readers that production at the Hunt Breakfast Powder Manufactory in Broad Wall on the south side of Blackfriars Bridge was now in full swing under the supervision of his son Thomas.

Cobbett must have promptly withdrawn his olive branch, or it was not good enough, because a fortnight later, on 22 June 1822, Hunt included a furious note in yet another *Address* that month. He had been inundated with complaints that numbers of his *Memoirs* had not been delivered. His publisher, Thomas Dolby, had told him that Mr Cobbett was directly responsible for interrupting supplies. Hunt's pen spluttered with incoherent rage: 'Does Mr Cobbett think to put me down *by such* or *by any means*? If he does ―――― But we shall see!!! I am my friends, Your's steadily and faithfully, H Hunt.'

This was a shame because it spoiled what had just gone before in the very same *Address*. Hunt had written of his delight at the success of Mr Cobbett at the Kent County Meeting in Maidstone on 11 June, and how he had galled both the Whigs and the Tories. Not many people had attended, although if they had known that Mr Cobbett was going, the place would have been packed out. Hunt was full of praise: 'Mr Cobbett is as good a speaker as he is a writer and I need not say more to convince every one who has read his writings what a powerful influence such a man must have over any meeting that he addresses.'

So in one *Address*, Cobbett went from being a marvel to a low down dirty rat, with which Hunt would deal as soon as he got out of gaol. Hunt, half-demented by the horrors of Ilchester Bastile, was swinging between depression and bitterness. On the one hand, he wanted to hurt Cobbett as much as he could, on the other, he still wished so hard he could get his friend back. The ambivalence was mutual, but Hunt's bitterness now overwhelmed him, and it was to be the last compliment he paid to Cobbett while he remained in Ilchester Prison. From then on, in the last half of 1822, Hunt banged on against his old friend in both his *Addresses* and *Memoirs*.

Cobbett's sniping against Hunt continued in both the *Political Register* and the London evening paper, *The Statesman*, in which Cobbett had bought a share and to which he contributed articles from 1822 to 1823. During 1822, Cobbett used both outlets against Hunt. In particular, he undermined Hunt's campaign against the prison gaoler, William Bridle, claiming that he was innocent of Hunt's charges. Even *The Times* noted that the newspaper had 'become the apologist of BRIDLE'. Cobbett also began to praise the Somerset MP, Sir Thomas Lethbridge, 'old leather breeches', as Hunt disgustedly called him. Lethbridge refused to believe a word Hunt said about his treatment in Ilchester Prison and dismissed all the evidence against Bridle. He also repeatedly told the House of Commons that Hunt should stay in prison until his sentence was completed. Cobbett ignored all this and in the *Political Register* of 8 June 1822 chose to compliment Lethbridge for his conversion to the idea of a reform of parliament. Lethbridge had become, wrote Cobbett, 'a man of sincerity and integrity', and had spoken with 'manly language'.

Hunt picked up the ball and ran with it. 'Hold, hard, a little Mr Cobbett', wrote Hunt furiously. They all knew Sir Thomas Lethbridge too well to believe in his conversion now. He supported the system, he persecuted the reformers, and he was an apologist for the authorities of Ilchester Bastile. 'Have a care, Mr Cobbett, you may deceive yourself, but you will deceive no one else by praising Sir Thomas Lethbridge', Hunt wrote angrily.

Hunt screamed loudly with rage, fury, misery and passion against Cobbett. The latter wielded his pen and his wit to hurt Hunt more subtly, with an insidious cruelty. As Hunt said, there was no contest as to whose pen was the most powerful.

The points of conflict remained the same. The row over distribution of the *Political Register* and Hunt's works continued unabated. Thomas Dolby included a note in Hunt's *Address*, published at the end of June 1822, which said that if Cobbett continued to hold up delivery of the *Memoirs,* he was obviously determined 'to contravene the great maxim of all morality and all religion and REFUSE to do by others that which he compels others to do by him!'

The saga of the Breakfast Powder also continued. Cobbett took great delight in telling his readers that it was possible to grow their own rye, roast it and grind it into powder at a cost of three farthings for every pound in weight. Hunt hit back. Those who recommended people to roast their own corn over the fire were nothing more than common impostors. Nobody would envy him his profits, 'unless it be some selfish, mean-spirited, dirty grovelling wretch'.

Cobbett continued to avoid mention of toasts to Hunt at public dinners and meetings. Hunt accused Cobbett of declining to go to radical dinners <u>because</u> of the toasts, for example the dinner to celebrate the release from prison of Thomas Wooler, editor of *Black Dwarf.* When Cobbett declined an invitation, having previously accepted it, Hunt carolled in triumph that that meant there would be no 'envious snake in the grass' amongst them to disturb the harmony of the day or mar the universal feeling of pleasure. Why? Because 'there will be no selfish "I myself I."'

This last remark referred to Cobbett's practice of writing articles in *The*

Statesman under the pseudonym 'I MYSELF I'. Cobbett, of course, was using the name to take a rise out of Hunt the 'egotist'. For a while, Hunt naively believed that Cobbett was referring to himself – which no doubt made Cobbett laugh the harder.

Hunt's fury over Cobbett's treatment of him boiled over in his *Address* of 23 July 1822 in which he revealed some joyful news. The *Address* began with these triumphant words 'ILCHESTER BASTILE IS TO BE RAZED TO THE GROUND!!!' Thanks to Hunt's persistence, the stinking gaol had been condemned and was to be demolished. (It was pulled down in the 1840s.) It should have been a time for celebration. Hunt had scored a rare, major triumph against the system. The *Address*, however, turned into a scream of rage against Cobbett who had ignored everything. The floodgates opened and Hunt's pent up fury and bitterness poured out.

Incredibly, he jumped straight to the subject of his Breakfast Powder. He had arranged, he wrote, to have half a ton sent over to Ireland to be sold at a low cost to raise money for the people who were suffering one of their periodic famines. His good deed, Hunt went on furiously, had obviously stuck in the gullet of 'a certain person, who had very properly christened himself "I myself I," alias William Cobbett.' This person was Hunt's 'old friend', who had written an article about the offer in his newspaper, *The Statesman*, in which he said the Irish people did not want to be insulted by a 'feeling heart' that shipped them off half a ton of rye-meal, costing 'THREE POUNDS'. That was a bare-faced lie, Hunt raged. It had cost him a lot more than £3 and the 'person' would have known that perfectly well. The Irish were very satisfied with Hunt's subscription. 'I myself I' might hold his malignant tongue till he had equalled Hunt's contribution. Why had Cobbett not reported the fact that the Ilchester gaoler, William Bridle, was to be prosecuted for torturing prisoners? All Cobbett could do was tell lies about Hunt's Breakfast Powder.

He had often been asked what motivated Cobbett to write such bare-faced falsehoods, Hunt howled on. It was, of course, his second nature, although this time: 'envy, hatred, and malice, and all uncharitableness, drives him thus to expose himself.' Cobbett could never get over the fact that Sir Francis Burdett had visited Hunt in Ilchester gaol. Cobbett would never forgive Hunt for his reconciliation with Burdett. Mr Cobbett had told several of Hunt's friends that he would not openly attack him while he was in prison, but the moment Hunt left, he would fall foully on him. Let him do it as soon as he wanted to, wrote Hunt. 'It would be much more manly for him to attack me openly at once, than it is to take every dirty opportunity to injure me privately, by dark and cowardly insinuations.'

Hunt's mind flew back to 1820 as he remembered how Cobbett had allowed the claim that there had been a government protection in Hunt's pocket in Manchester to appear in his *Evening Post*. (Hunt was so upset he called it the Morning Post.) Why did Cobbett do it when he knew it was a lie? Hunt raged. He had gained thousands of friends since Cobbett's cowardly attacks upon him, shut up in Ilchester Prison. Cobbett could never accuse him of denying his own hand-writing and swearing that it was a forgery. Cobbett could never accuse him of deserting his friends and fleeing the country. Cobbett could not accuse him of having become a bankrupt to cheat his creditors. As soon as he got out of prison, roared Hunt, he would lose no opportunity to meet with Cobbett face to face. He could choose his own dunghill, and Hunt would meet him on it. He knew Cobbett was a most powerful writer, who could make black appear white or vice versa, as it suited his purpose. Cobbett's writings would always be read. He had done much good by them, but also much harm with his 'insufferable vanity and selfishness'. The boroughmongers would have been brought to a standstill, and the people would have got a reform of parliament long before, 'if it had not been for Mr Cobbett's incessant labours, which put our enemies upon their guard, and made them avoid those rocks which they would otherwise have split upon.' Look at what Cobbett had written on the 'puff out'. The government and the Bank of England had been put upon their guard, which had totally defeated the purpose. Cobbett had wrecked everything with his vanity and cupidity.

All Hunt's hurt and misery poured out. He must have been drained after writing this issue. It is exhausting to read. Hunt had no guile. He wore his heart on his sleeve. Cobbett harassed Hunt in more subtle ways, apparently remaining controlled and calm, although his passions ran so deep. Cobbett was a past master at studied insults, and clever blowings-up and underminings. His style worked so well against the system. It hurts to read it when it was turned against Hunt.

In the *Register* of 17 August 1822, Cobbett reported on the suicide of the hated Lord Castlereagh and the grief of his widow. It only served to remind him of the anguish of the poor dead wife of the radical brushmaker Joseph Johnson, wrote Cobbett, rather ludicrously. It was, of course, another ingenious way to get at Hunt. Johnson was Cobbett's new, guided weapon. He was the man who had invited Hunt to speak in Manchester in August 1819, and with whom Hunt stayed for a week. Hunt detested Joseph Johnson for a variety of reasons. He blamed him for the death of his favourite and famous horse, Bob, who was unaccountably poisoned while in Johnson's care. Even more importantly, Johnson had offered to hand over to the authorities Hunt's letters written before the Manchester meeting. Now, Johnson was busy attacking Hunt in public letters, blaming him for Peterloo, accusing him of bad debts and insulting Hunt in any way he could. It was obvious that Johnson was doing so with the full backing of Cobbett. The latter did not re-print the actual letters (there were two), probably because he was worried that Hunt would sue him if he did, but he gave Johnson copious advertising space in the *Register* to publicise them. The letters contained resonances, language and links that only Cobbett could have thought of. Johnson addressed Hunt as the 'Saint' – reminding everybody of Hunt's failed order of St Henry of Ilchester and his comparison of himself to St Paul in prison. Johnson's language was grotesquely vicious:

Now 'St Henry of Ilchester' I have waded through the filth of about 15 months of your life; and from the longest life of the worst man that ever lived, could such a heap of infamy be collected? ... I have shown you to be the meanest wretch and the basest monster that ever poisoned the earth on which he crawled.

There were pages of the stuff. Hunt was 'crouching to those you had before pretended to despise', (a reference to his sudden friendship with Burdett). Hunt was sunk so low 'that to all honourable men his slander was praise, and his praise was quite sufficient to cast suspicion upon all those who might be the objects of it'. Pettily, Johnson noted that Hunt had arrived in Manchester with 'a very indifferent wardrobe'. It included white breeches, 'the things by which you say you offended Mr Cobbett', Johnson wrote, referring to the wrong trousers scene at Newgate Prison as described by Hunt in his *Memoirs*. He also accused Hunt of using 'malignant private slander ... to sully the character of Mr C——t merely because he wished you to sell your breakfast powder to the poor reformers who were its consumers, at 6d, instead of a shilling per pound'. In short, Johnson concluded, his strings viciously pulled by Cobbett, 'all persons with whom you have been connected for any length of time, you have attempted to blast with your pestiferous influence.'

In his second public letter to Hunt, or as Johnson cruelly phrased it, 'Second exposure of the character of the Saint of Ilchester', Johnson revealed that Cobbett's pseudonym 'I myself I' referred to Hunt. Johnson also accused Hunt of lying, in words that horribly echoed Cobbett's former burlesque about Burdett and Cleary: '"Lie on," thou saintish puffing knave, For by such tricks thou think'st to save Thyself: – Whilst my revenge shall be Unmasking thy hypocrisy.'

Hunt was livid. He accused Johnson of being used by his 'patron', Cobbett, in his own war against Hunt. Johnson had become 'the tool and agent of a more artful scoundrel than himself', scribbled Hunt in anger.

Cobbett, meanwhile, continued with the joke about Hunt's sainthood. On 2 September 1822, *The Statesman* published a satirical poem by Cobbett to 'Saint Henry of Ilchester'. The poem mocked everything, from Hunt's Breakfast Powder and the death of his horse, Bob, to Hunt's battles at Ilchester Prison, his support of the prisoners and his eye operation. The poem compared Hunt with the eighteenth century Baron Munchausen of Hanover, whose extraordinary tales of his travels and feats were turned into a best-selling book of exciting tall stories. Cobbett's poem was a crude and cruel piece of writing. Here is a taste:

Munchausen long has borne the prize
From all the Quacking 'Squires;
But, what are all his heaps of lies
To thine, thou prince of liars!

How t'would have made the German stare
To see *thy* wires and pegs!
How blush, to see thy loving mare
' *Trot on with broken legs!*

The '*operation*' on thine eye,

Great Saint, we've all a heart in,
Oh! could'st thou hear us, how we sigh,
'My eye and Betty Martin!'

The Times joyfully seized on the whole saga. On 4 September 1822, the newspaper not only reported on all the exchanges between Cobbett and Hunt, it also re-printed the poem. Hunt fought back in his *Address* published just five days later. He had received letters from gentlemen authorising him to use their names to disprove 'the atrocious, barefaced falsehoods published by Joseph Johnson'. He was obliged to them for their offers, but he had 'other fish to fry', than to bother to notice the falsehoods and malignant calumnies of 'Squire Brushmaker'. Of much more importance, he was able to tell his readers that Johnson's own neighbours, the Female Reformers of Manchester, had called a public meeting to raise a subscription to buy a piece of plate to be presented to Hunt on his release from gaol. Johnson had issued a notice to stop them, but the ladies had resolved unanimously that he was a 'mean, pitiful paltroon, a dastardly liar and slanderer', who 'merited the contempt, detestation and abhorrence of every part of mankind.'

Bravely, Hunt re-printed Cobbett's poem to St Henry of Ilchester. It was, he said, nothing more than a 'precious contemptible mass of ribaldry'. What was more, Hunt had his own poem in reply. It had been written by a friend, was called 'Cobbett and his Man Bristle or Buying a Brush', and it should be sung to the tune: 'I've kiss'd and I've prattled with fifty fair Maids.' Here is an extract:

When a trickster is foil'd, and hemm'd round ev'ry way,
And his projects no further can push,
His only resource, in the slang of the day,
Is said to be 'BUYING A BRUSH.'

When grim *danger* threaten'd, did HUNT ever *bend*,
Or peep at his foes through a bush:
Did he e'er fear a tyrant, bamboozle a friend,
Or quit them, by 'BUYING A BRUSH.'

Hunt had this published in a pamphlet, price 'One Penny or 100 copies for Three Shillings', and available to ballad singers 'on still more liberal terms.'

It was incredible. The most famous political writer and the best-loved public speaker were slugging away at each other in public, through the press and in poetry and prose, like a pair of fighting cocks. As Hunt approached the end of his long, hard sentence, he gave his readers a taste of how the battle of words was being viewed by members of the public. He re-published on 14 October 1822 an address written by his 'Admirers from Preston', in which they sharply castigated Cobbett. Although the admirers did not mention Cobbett by name, it was obvious to whom they were referring. The detail is impressive and reveals that people were following every move in the Cobbett/Hunt game with great attention. Hunt had no need to worry, said the Admirers of Preston: 'There are so many of the noble acts of your long political career impressed on our minds, that leave no place there for the voice of the *green-eyed fiend* jealousy, embittered by vindictive *malice.*' Oh how the Preston admirers laughed when they thought of beings such as '"I myself I" and "Squire Bristle" ... setting themselves up to attack a man who is so deservedly engrafted on the hearts of his countrymen!' The first had fled his country to escape persecution, leaving behind those to whom he pretended friendship, and had remained in America 'till the blast had passed over his suffering country'. The admirers only feared that Hunt would degrade himself by taking notice of such '*reptiles*'. The country would do the job for him and condemn 'the unfounded and slanderous falsehoods' which had been used to injure the character of 'one of the most illustrious advocates of the inherent birthright of every rational son of nature'.

This view of the two men was confirmed four years later when Cobbett would stand for a parliamentary seat in Preston and be rebuffed by the electorate, which was, at the time, one of the most representative in the country. (All men over twenty-one and who had lived in the town for six months had the vote.) Hunt, by contrast, would achieve a stunning victory in Preston in a by-election in 1830 when his win would prove to be the final straw for jealous Cobbett.

Hunt's release date drew near. The authorities tried to make him go quietly at midnight when his sentence formally expired. Hunt refused, although as the clock struck twelve, his friends and supporters outside the gaol lit bonfires and let off rockets to mark the moment. A cannon roared from the nearby village of Mudford. Hunt emerged from Ilchester Bastile on the morning of Wednesday, 30 October 1822 to the cheers of thousands of people who had gathered for the occasion. He blazed forth from the black hole in triumph and style, wearing the Argyle tartan cloak sent to him by the reformers of Greenock, and the gold medal and chain given to him by the female reformers of Leeds after his trial. He headed straight for the Castle Inn in the town (now a private house called Castle Farm) where a public breakfast was held. No doubt Mrs Vince was at his side. The town was jam-packed with people, some of whom had travelled hundreds of miles to be there to welcome him. There were festivities and celebrations throughout the country, including bonfires, dinners and processions.

There was not a word about any of this in the *Political Register*, but Hunt was on Cobbett's mind, and he made a reference to Hunt in a private letter written to an acquaintance twelve days after Hunt's release from Ilchester Prison. The House of Lords, Cobbett wrote, remained 'terrified out of their wits at Hunt, who is really as inoffensive as Pistol or Bardolph.'

13
The Thaw

Forsake not an old friend; for the new is not comparable to him.

Ecclesiastes

Hunt resumed his life with Mrs Vince at 36 Stamford Street in London, just south of the River Thames in what was then Surrey. There was easy access into both the West End and the City of London over Blackfriars Bridge and the bridge over the Thames into the Strand, which had been named after the Battle of Waterloo. He was also only a few steps away from his Breakfast Powder factory with its busy roasting furnaces, at 65 Broad Wall, just around the corner in an industrial area. There, with the help of both his sons (Henry junior had returned from his unfortunate experiences in America), Hunt produced his substitute coffee made from rye. The customers who visited their rented shop in Pall Mall included buyers for King George IV over the road at Carlton House, as well as government ministers. Hunt also began to develop his own 'Matchless Blacking' solution to render leather shoes waterproof. He worked hard to claw back the money and time he had lost while locked up in Ilchester gaol, although he still managed to fit in his radical politics and his often unexpected but always flamboyant appearances at political meetings.

Cobbett was busy as ever, running his publishing empire from 183 Fleet Street with help and contributions from his three eldest sons, attending county meetings and public dinners, and riding out on his great rural journeys across England. He was living with his family on a rented four-acre small holding in west London. It was situated just about where High Street Kensington station rumbles and roars today. Here, Cobbett lovingly nurtured his precious Indian Corn (maize or corn on the cob), together with his trees, shrubs and cuttings and a huge variety of seeds, much of which was imported from America. He sold specimens via friends, agents and buyers throughout the country. Cobbett's horticultural interests, including his instructions on how to plait straw bonnets, took a starring role in the *Political Register*, alongside the political questions of the day. These included the return to using gold instead of bank notes, the spiralling national debt and the so-called 'Sinking Fund' (bottomless pit of money) to pay it off, the vicious Game Laws and Catholic Emancipation.

The other great question of the day was what the state of play would now be between Cobbett and Hunt.

Towards the end of January 1823, Hunt slipped sweetly, albeit briefly, back into the pages of the *Political Register* after attending a meeting in Wells in Somerset. 'Mr Hunt' moved an amended petition which was carried almost unanimously, wrote Cobbett in the closing pages of the issue of 25 January. The matter and circumstances were of great interest and it would all be found detailed in the *Statesman*; Cobbett had no room for anything further about it in the *Register*.

It is likely that despite everything that had happened, Cobbett itched to be back with Hunt. A year before, Cobbett had written a letter to his friend in Norfolk, Samuel Clarke, telling him what 'famous fun' he had been having in Sussex, how 'the Bull-frogs of the South Downs' had been stirred up and how he had 'beat the cocks upon their own dunghill.' Cobbett also admitted that he had been very glad that his eldest son had been standing behind him, and that a friend had been on his right-hand side during the debate.

It was a rare admission from the resolutely independent solo operator. Cobbett was surely missing Hunt. He had been Cobbett's best companion. The pair had worked well together. Nevertheless, as Cobbett admitted in his letter to Clarke, he still wanted to be the top cock on the dunghill. This overwhelming desire continued to shine through in the *Political Register*. If Cobbett did refer to the other reformers during these years, it was largely to criticise and undermine them, apart from Richard Carlile, who remained in prison and out of whose situation Cobbett made political capital.

Through February 1823, Cobbett obsessively promoted himself in the *Register* as the teacher and the people's 'political master'. The 'baleful press', he wrote triumphantly, now beheld him with 'that ENVY, that passion which the poet calls the eldest born of hell'. He, Cobbett, was the man who clearly foretold all the evils despite 'the endless list of persecutions and abominations' practised against him:

Nature made me for great and incessant labour. She gave me a clear and quick understanding. And she never gave to any human being a more ardent love of country and a stronger desire to promote its interest and cherish and preserve its renown.

Hunt stopped writing his *Memoirs* and *Addresses* after he had shaken the mildewed dust off his shoes from Ilchester Prison. Unfortunately for posterity, he never resumed his autobiography. He would not write his *Addresses* again until 1831, although he continued to pen letters and political pieces for the newspapers. He was still rushing to read his weekly copy of the *Political Register* and studying it hard for any references to himself. He would no doubt have been pleased to read in the *Register* of 14 June 1823 an abusive letter from Cobbett to Sir Thomas Lethbridge, who had persecuted Hunt in prison and whom Hunt had scoffingly nicknamed 'old leather breeches', the man whom Cobbett had so unfairly praised at the time. Lethbridge had just withdrawn notice of a motion in the House of Commons on agricultural distress because, he said, he had noted a rise in the price of farm produce and decided that the distress 'appeared to have ceased'. What rubbish, snorted Cobbett. The distress in the country was certainly not over, and if food prices continued to rise as they were doing, the days of the Manchester massacre would come again. Lethbridge's dream was nothing more than the 'dream of an idiot'.

The strings vibrated with some intensity after a reformers' meeting in the London Tavern on 13 June to protest about the invasion of Spain by France and to consider how the Spanish could be helped to establish a constitutional monarchy. 'Humbug', snorted Cobbett in the *Register* 21 June 1823. The real object, he wrote, was 'to *uphold that system, under which the English have so long groaned* and which now oppresses them more severely than ever'. Hunt had played his old trick of turning up at the last moment, and Cobbett simply could not resist commenting on the dismay of the reformers at his unexpected arrival. They included Joseph Hume, John Cam Hobhouse 'the little son of the old fat placeman', Henry Brougham and Francis Place. They had been even more disconcerted when Hunt suggested that a letter should be sent out to everybody on the government's pay roll – which would include the Hobhouse family –

asking them to donate to the Spanish cause. Cobbett loved the uproar produced by Hunt's performance. 'No wonder that this crew took the alarm', he chortled. He noted that Hume quickly told Hunt that there would be a resolution about a subscription later in the evening. What that had to do with Hunt's motion was unclear and it was not even true, Cobbett mocked. No motion was put and how could it have been, given that they would have been sending out letters to themselves! (Although history wrote them down as such, neither Cobbett nor Hunt considered any of these men to be true radicals. 'Their very *names* have an *awkward sound!*' Cobbett commented.)

Hunt's performance at the London Tavern was just as Cobbett would have wanted, and he made sure that Hunt's name was included in the index of the quarterly collection of the *Political Registers* for the year.

The Times also reported the events at the London Tavern meeting. It warned people not to be frightened about going to public meetings in case they had to mix with such men as 'Hunt and old Cobbett'. If others did not attend, warned the newspaper, the public might start calling for 'Hunt-and-Cobbett meetings' only. Despite the rift between the men, in the public eye Cobbett and Hunt were still a team and their names were still linked together. Three months earlier, *The Times* had reported that a sheriff of Devon refused permission for a county meeting on a reform of parliament because he did not want 'such demagogues as Hunt and Cobbett' to take the lead over the respectable freeholders of the county.

There were a couple more concessions from Cobbett towards Hunt later in this year, 1823. In the issue of the *Register* of 11 October, Cobbett noted that John Benett of Wiltshire, another of Hunt's old enemies, had been forced to sell off some of his land because of the disastrous slump in farming that had bankrupted thousands of farmers. 'Oh! Ho! Mr Benett! And so you are hooked into the puffs of the Nabob!' Cobbett crowed triumphantly. 'I remember you, Mr Benett, petitioning for a Corn Bill and promising to pay taxes cheerfully if you could but get high prices'. (There must have been cheering and laughter from 36 Stamford Street.)

The following month, on 15 November 1823, Cobbett made one of his many references to the Manchester massacre, reminding his readers how the people had been chopped, hacked and trampled upon and that many of them had been killed and hundreds wounded. The attackers had been thanked for what they had done, he wrote, while some of the 'persons' attending the meeting had been punished 'with almost unparalleled severity'. He did not mention Hunt by name, but Cobbett must have been thinking about him. The full weight of the law had, after all, fallen most heavily on his former friend and political colleague.

The next year, 1824, there was just one fleeting reference to Hunt by name, in the *Political Register* of 18 September. It came in an article written by William Cobbett junior, who recalled how he watched Lord Cochrane being carried in triumph into Westminster Hall on the opening of parliament, and how 'Mr Hunt' had, with his own hands, assisted in putting him into the chair in which he was carried. William was remembering the events of 1817 and the presentation of the petitions for reform. There was a whiff of Cobbett nostalgia about the unexpected mention of Hunt's name.

At the beginning of April 1825, the mercury in the thermometer suddenly leaped from cool to very warm when Cobbett re-published a newspaper report of a meeting in the piazza at Covent Garden. It had been called by the two Westminster MPs, Sir Francis Burdett and John Cam Hobhouse, to petition parliament over the window tax. Hunt turned up and took over proceedings. The window tax was indeed a bad one, he told the crowd, but why had the two members waited nine years after the end of the war before trying to do something about it? It could easily be abolished if the chancellor of the exchequer cut the government's pay and pension list, which included Hobhouse's father, Sir Benjamin – Hunt meant no offence to that gentleman – who had been paid for years to do nothing. Enraged, Hobhouse junior fought back. His father had been a respectable commissioner of estates in India, he spluttered. He had not been doing nothing. His father had been perfectly entitled to take a percentage whenever he facilitated loans and the collection of debts.

Hunt continued to twist the knife and raised the question of Catholic Emancipation. The thorny subject of the lack of civil rights for Catholics, including the six million in Ireland, was being debated in the House of Commons. It was also filling up issue after issue of Cobbett's *Political Register*. The Protestant establishment was worried that if the Catholics were allowed to take up seats as freely elected members of parliament, there would be a flood of them into the House of Commons. A plan was being worked out to modify the bill to prevent this from happening. The property qualification would be raised so that freeholders worth forty shillings a year would lose their right to vote. At the same time, salaries of thousands of pounds would be paid to Catholic priests to keep them from objecting to the loss of people's voting rights. As Hunt bluntly put it to the meeting, the priests were to be bribed into silence by English tax payers' money. He knew perfectly well that raising the subject would embarrass Hobhouse and Burdett as they stood before their voters. The master orator, he played on the people packed into the Covent Garden piazza. Were they willing for this to happen when it would deprive half a million Irish men of their voting rights? he asked. 'No! No!' came the cry from the crowd. Hunt was sure that Burdett (squirming next to him) would never agree to it. Cries of 'he never will.' (Burdett voted for it a few days later.)

The crowd refused to raise their hands to support the official petition against the window tax because Hunt's clever resolution on Catholic Emancipation was not included. The apple cart had been well and truly upset.

Cobbett loved the fact that Hunt was battling away on the political platform, using all his, Cobbett's arguments and doing so very effectively. He devoted pages of the *Register* of 2 April 1825 to justify everything 'Mr Hunt' had done and said. Readers were not to be surprised at any press reports of Mr Hunt being hooted and scorned at the meeting, he wrote. The newspapers hated Mr Hunt because he did not pay them (as other people and government ministers did to keep them 'on side'). All the shouting and clamour against Mr Hunt came from a group of bawlers who were put there especially for the job. Sir Francis Burdett and his Westminster Rump had no right to leave out Mr Hunt's resolution. Mr Hunt said it was a gross insult to the meeting to refuse to include it, and he had been quite right to say so. The people of Westminster had shown they would prefer to continue paying a window tax than not be able to express their own opinion about removing the voting rights of the freeholders of Ireland. Cobbett crowed over Hunt's success: 'Was there ever anything more decisive than this? Was there ever a fouler attempt to mislead the people? Did people ever show more good sense and more public spirit? Was ever foul play more justly and more signally punished?'

Just two weeks after Hunt's triumph at the Westminster meeting, he was yet again in the *Register* of 16 April 1825 at a dinner for 'the Friends of the Freedom and Happiness of Ireland' in the City of London Tavern in Bishopsgate. Cobbett re-printed a newspaper report of the proceedings in full. Hunt had been unanimously elected chairman and had spoken at length. If Irish freeholders had to lose their right to vote so that Catholics could sit as MPs, he would prefer them to remain excluded from parliament, he said.

The ice was thawing. Unfortunately, as this very issue of the *Political Register* was being printed, Hunt was giving evidence in the trial of Parkins v Byrne.

By 1825, most people in the country would have been fully acquainted with the story of the Irish Catholic, James Byrne. The story began in Dublin in 1811 when Byrne complained that Percy Jocelyn, the Protestant Lord Bishop of Ferns, had made a pass at him. Byrne was taken before the mayor of Dublin and charged with libel. At the trial, Jocelyn was described as 'one of the most benevolent, most virtuous, most spotless, most pious of human beings'. By contrast, Byrne was 'a horrid and unprincipled villain'. He was found guilty of the charge, gaoled for two years, fined large sums of money and sentenced to be whipped in public three times.

Nobody thought any more about it until eleven years later when on 19 July 1822, Jocelyn, by then the Rt. Rev Father in God, Lord Bishop of Clogher and a member of the Society for punishing Vice and Immorality, was caught literally with his pants down in the act with a private soldier of the Foot Guards in a back room of the White Lion pub. Cobbett put it more colourfully in the *Register*. The 'Father in God', he wrote, was caught in 'the *actual commission* of that horrid and unnatural crime which drew down God's vengeance and brought destruction by fire and brimstone on two whole cities in times of old'. The 'Father in God' and 'the Father in God's *mate*', Cobbett went on, were taken, amidst the execrations and peltings of the indignant populace, to the local watchhouse with their middle garments hanging about their heels, just as they had been found.

From there, the pair were hauled off to the police station and given bail.

(At this time, homosexuality was considered to be a heinous offence. Cobbett's views were fairly extreme. He believed that no foreigner should be allowed onto British territory until it was absolutely confirmed he was not homosexual, although he did not say how this could be done.)

As a result of the Rt. Rev Father in God's very imprudent behaviour in the parish of St James in Westminster, the newspapers revived the sad story of James Byrne. Cobbett reminded his readers of every detail of Byrne's whipping in 1811, how he had been taken from gaol, stripped naked to the waist and his hands tied to a wagon. This was pulled by a horse slowly from Dublin gaol to the College, a distance of a mile and a half, during which time Byrne was whipped continuously by the prison hangman using a cat o' nine tails. Half way along, the whip broke and had to be mended. By the time the wagon reached the College, Byrne was practically dead. His half-flayed carcass was thrown into gaol and there he had languished for two years.

Byrne's story was a terrible one and it provided the radicals with the perfect stick with which to beat the establishment over the whole of the Irish question and the plight of the Catholics. At the end of 1822, Cobbett invited Byrne over to England with his wife and four children, and a subscription was set up to compensate him for the past injustice. This was organised by Joseph Parkins, a former sheriff of London, who happened to be an acquaintance of Hunt. Cobbett had a tin box to collect money for Byrne at his premises in Fleet Street. The Cobbett household showered Byrne and his family with hospitality, and Cobbett wrote about him in the *Register* as 'The Martyr of the Unnatural Bishop Jocelyn'.

And then the complications started. Parkins lent Cobbett a horse that turned out to be nothing more than 'an old broken down nag' and cost Cobbett a fortune to feed. Cobbett fell out with Parkins as a result. So when Byrne complained that Parkins was keeping back some of his subscription money, Cobbett urged him to sue Parkins and offered to appear as a witness. Parkins wrote a letter to Hunt asking for evidence he could use to discredit Cobbett, including details about his debts:

If you are able [I] will thank you to let me have the date, or about the time, that Squire Cobbett, as the *Chronicle* stiles him, borrowed £700 from Squire Clement, and also let me

know the date of the Squire's flight to America and the date of his famous equitable
adjustment with the Foxhunting Baronet. [Burdett]

There is no record of a reply from Hunt.

The first trial of Parkins v. Byrne was in February 1824. Cobbett was
called and gave evidence about how Parkins had withheld Byrne's
subscription money. Parkins lost the case and was ordered to pay Byrne
nearly £200. He appealed, and there was a second trial more than a year
later. This time, both Cobbett and Hunt gave evidence: Cobbett, once
again, on behalf of Byrne, Hunt, reluctantly, on behalf of Parkins.

The trial took place on Friday, 15 April 1825. Cobbett did not stay in
court to hear Hunt tell the judge about a visit James Byrne had made to
Hunt's house. During the visit, Byrne had accused Cobbett of
withholding subscription money, and spoken in the most favourable
terms of Parkins. Nevertheless, on another visit, Hunt continued, Byrne
had accused Parkins of ill treatment. Hunt had become so sick of the Irish
man abusing his friends, he told Byrne never to visit his house again. Hunt
told the court that he was only appearing as a witness because he had been
issued with a subpoena.

Reading the reports of the trial, Hunt was obviously deeply
embarrassed that he had been made to appear as a witness for Parkins and
report tittle tattle against Cobbett. Cobbett, however, would not let it go
by. He was furious to hear of Byrne's accusation against him and, ignoring
the fact of the subpoena, was also furious that Hunt had appeared in court
to repeat it. He consulted lawyers and returned to the subject in the
Political Register published on 14 May 1825. He had been amazed by
Hunt's evidence, Cobbett wrote. Any money he had received for Byrne's
subscription fund had been handed straight over to Parkins. After the first
trial, Cobbett had paid money to Byrne weekly, before he had even
collected any subscriptions. When Byrne went back to Ireland, he had left
his daughter in Cobbett's house. When Byrne was in England, he and his
family regularly visited and dined with the Cobbett family, sometimes
three times a day, and always drank tea at Cobbett's house in Kensington
on Sundays. It was 'the strangest thing in the whole world that Byrne
should have complained to Mr Hunt of me', snorted Cobbett.

To prove it all, Cobbett published the contents of an affidavit made by

Byrne that had appeared in the *Dublin Morning Register* just a few days previously. Byrne had sworn 'an Oath on the Holy Evangelists' that despite what Henry Hunt told the court, he, Byrne, had never abused Cobbett. Hunt's assertion was false and unfounded. Byrne would be guilty of the blackest ingratitude if he had spoken disrespectfully or injuriously of Mr Cobbett. He and all his family had treated him with a generosity and kindness which would remain engraved on his heart to the latest hour of his existence.

Cobbett said that he believed every word of Byrne's affidavit. There were later accusations, however, that the affidavit had been drafted by one of Cobbett's sons. These were firmly denied by the Cobbett family. Hunt stuck by what he claimed Byrne had told him, accused Cobbett of calling him a perjurer, and decided to sue Cobbett for libel. The thaw was over for the time being, and Hunt disappeared from the pages of the *Register*.

Around nine months later, on Wednesday, 1 February 1826, Cobbett wrote to his old friend, the London master-baker Silvester Sapsford. Cobbett's letter invited Sapsford to his home for dinner on the following Tuesday to discuss arrangements for 'the business' to be held the day after at the Freemason's Tavern in Great Queen Street, Lincoln's Inn Fields. Cobbett added a postscript: 'The gentleman whose arrogance so offended us all on Sunday last, shall have no hand in this affair, of any sort or degree.'

Could Cobbett have been referring to Hunt? There is no way of telling. It is not known when the two men met after Hunt's release from Ilchester gaol. It may be assumed that as they were both living in London and were both prominent on the political scene, they might have sometimes coincided at meetings and functions. If Cobbett was referring to Hunt in his letter to Sapsford, he was to be disappointed. Despite his hopes of a trouble-free meeting, the two cocks certainly did confront each other at 'the business' at the Freemason's Tavern in Great Queen Street on Wednesday, 8 February 1826, when, much to Cobbett's fury, Hunt turned up like the thirteenth fairy and, despite Cobbett's best attempts to stop him, took a starring role.

The 'business' was a meeting to launch a subscription to fund Cobbett's bid to win a seat in the House of Commons. The idea had come from Cobbett's new young friend and admirer, Sir Thomas Beevor, the wealthy third baronet of Hargham Hall near Attleborough in Norfolk. It was an important day for Cobbett, hence his excitement and his nervousness that it could be spoiled by 'arrogant gentlemen'.

The first mistake was the underestimation of the public interest the event would attract. The room booked at the tavern was only big enough for about three hundred people. Ten times that number turned up. (Hunt must have got there long before the start time of one o'clock to secure his seat.) The room was packed and the narrow staircase and passageways leading to it were also dangerously crowded. People were spilling out into the street. By the time Cobbett arrived with Sir Thomas, who was going to chair the meeting, they were unable to get into the building. They decided to hold the meeting outside in the north west corner of Lincoln's Inn Fields where there was an empty coal-wagon they could use as a hustings platform. As Cobbett described in the *Political Register* of 11 February 1826, he was lifted into the wagon by the willing arms of the crowd as if his weight had been that of a feather. 'It was indeed a proud day for me', he wrote with disarming simplicity.

The people, including Hunt, who had managed to jam into the room at the tavern, were unaware of what was going on outside. A reporter from the *Morning Chronicle* described what happened. Cobbett reproduced the entire article in the *Register*. Time ticked by and Mr Burridge, a frequent petitioner to the House of Commons, gave an impromptu lecture on 'Dry Rot in the Navy'. The people became increasingly uncomfortable and began to chant, 'Cobbett, Cobbett'. Hunt took control, pedantically reminding everybody of the protocol and rules that they should follow. Sir Thomas Beevor had called the meeting, so they could not legally act without him, said Hunt. A messenger should be sent to tell him that the gentlemen were assembled, and to ask what was going on. At that point, people near the window said they could see Beevor and Cobbett in the courtyard below. Amid gales of laughter, a note was scribbled and dispatched: 'You ought to be here and you are not here – here we are in anticipation.'

The waiting went on and there were calls to adjourn to Lincoln's Inn Fields. Hunt again addressed the squashed assembly. It was against the law to hold a meeting in the open air without permission from the sheriff, he said. The law's expired, shouted the crowd, but Hunt was obdurate. The meeting had been called by Sir Thomas Beevor, and therefore he was the chairman. By law, Beevor had to come and tell them what to do. And who was this Sir Thomas anyway? He, Hunt, had never heard of him before. Hunt's following words were reported in the newspaper: 'If anybody knows this Sir Thomas, please would he come forward and tell me the state of the case. This Sir Thomas is quite unknown to me – a new man, I believe. At least I have never heard of him twice in my life before.'

The newspaper report gives it away. Hunt was clearly jealous of Cobbett's new, much younger and richer friend, and upset that Beevor was at Cobbett's side on such an occasion instead of Hunt himself. If the news was that Sir Thomas had gone to Lincoln's Inn Fields, Hunt continued, why, the very next message might be that he had gone to Smithfield! (laughter) 'They are gone to drink roasted corn', said a person in the crowd (shouts of laughter). All he knew, Hunt cried, was that 'they should not stay roasting there any longer (continued laughter).' They needed to know what was to be done in accordance with the rules, Hunt insisted.

The pantomime went on. There was booing, hissing and laughter. Although he himself was not 'on terms with Mr. Cobbett', said Hunt, he would take the liberty of moving that Mr Budd, a highly respectable gentleman of Newbury and a friend of both Mr Cobbett and Sir Thomas Beevor, should take the chair.

The arguments continued. At last, word came from Sir Thomas that neither he nor Mr Cobbett had been able to get in through the crowds and everybody should come to the meeting outside. Hunt gave in and moved 'that the meeting do adjourn to Lincoln's Inn Fields.'

Everybody poured out of the tavern and stampeded towards the large wagon on which Cobbett and Beevor and their supporters were standing. The wagon was already surrounded by a crowd of around three thousand. People driving past in their carriages had pulled up their horses to watch the fun, and passers by had stopped to listen. The arrival of Hunt provided yet more entertainment and, after a speech by Cobbett, the crowd clamoured for Hunt to speak. To Cobbett's fury, Hunt forced his way through the crowds and managed to squeeze onto the wagon. He got as close to Sir Thomas Beevor as he could. The newspaper report described the tell-tale scene: 'Mr Hunt was here loudly called for and with some difficulty procured standing-room in the well of the wagon, close to the Chair.'

It sounded suspiciously as if Hunt wanted to crowd Beevor out. Having apparently succeeded, Hunt took over proceedings. He regretted that he had missed the resolutions and the speeches. He supposed there had been resolutions and speeches (laughter). He had managed to hear a part of Mr Cobbett's speech and had listened, admiring his talents as he had done for the last fifteen or twenty years. Mr Cobbett was not only a powerful writer but also a powerful speaker. He, Hunt, approved of what was going on, and he would be contributing his 'mite' to the subscription to get Mr Cobbett into parliament. (A man wondered aloud, Cobbett later reported, if Hunt had not meant 'spite'.) They should not, however, appear to be the bigoted disciples of Mr Cobbett, Hunt continued, but his sober and rational supporters. He himself wanted to remind everybody, including Mr Cobbett, of the pledge he had made to the electors of Honiton in June 1806 and again to the electors of Hampshire in 1812. Mr Cobbett had said that as long as he lived, he would not receive either for himself or for any member of his family, any salary, place or pension, not one single farthing of public money, nor would he give a farthing to anybody so that they would vote for him. Hunt now called on Mr Cobbett to confirm his promise. Parliament did not need men of talent so much as men in whom the people could place their confidence, men who would pledge themselves not to meddle with the public money. Mr Cobbett, a man of 'transcendent talents', would have all Hunt's support – so long as he first made this necessary declaration.

Cobbett was livid. What a man had sworn in 1806 was surely binding twenty years later, he fumed. It was the greatest act of self-degradation to repeat an oath already sworn. He hoped the meeting would spare him so great a humiliation as to call upon him to repeat it. There his oath was, and there it would continue, as strongly binding on him now as then.

There was no reason for Cobbett not to have repeated his oath again at the meeting. There was no reason, however, for Hunt to have humiliated

Cobbett on his big day. Over the years, Cobbett had repeatedly promised in the *Political Register* that if he were elected to parliament, he would not wish to profit in any way. Could both men have been pecking at each other because of Hunt's pending libel case against Cobbett? Could both men have descended to such a level? Cobbett obviously thought Hunt was being petty. He also obviously bitterly resented the fact that Hunt had taken over the meeting and stolen some of the limelight. What was more, Hunt had done it by making the kind of powerful political points that Cobbett himself had taught him to make. His former protégée and once dear friend had upset Cobbett's day and had publicly told him what to do.

Cobbett got his own back in court just two weeks later.

The case of Hunt V. Cobbett was heard by the Lord Chief Justice in the Court of King's Bench on Monday, 20 February 1826. The case attracted wide public interest. Hunt was represented by the attorney general, Sir Charles Wetherell. Both Hunt and Cobbett were so well known by the public, said Wetherell, they needed no introduction. Hunt was not asking for damages. He only wanted to clear his name of the 'unmerited and foul aspersions' cast upon it by Cobbett, who had accused him of perjury. Hunt had been concerned about Byrne's inconsistency and had been reluctant to be called as a witness for Parkins. Nevertheless, he had attended the trial and reported Byrne's remarks. It was quite obvious, went on Wetherell, that Byrne's later affidavit, in which he claimed that he had never spoken ill of Cobbett, had been drawn up by somebody else, probably by Cobbett or his son who was at that time in Ireland. If Byrne's affidavit were true, why had he not been called in court as a witness to prove that what Mr Hunt had sworn was false?

Hunt must have been pleased with the clear case as presented by Sir Charles Wetherell, but the plain-speaking attorney general could not match the irony and wit of Cobbett's lawyer, Charles Phillips. Mr Cobbett had meant no offence to Mr Hunt in what he had written, said Phillips. If Mr Hunt thought the publication was likely to cause anyone to revise their opinion of his character, he must be one of the most timid men in nature (laughter). There had not been a single expression of an offensive nature towards Mr Hunt. It was impossible that Byrne would have praised

Parkins and abused Cobbett. How could the oppressor be praised by the
oppressed? He would as soon believe that snow and fire would unite or
that the tiger and its prey would lie down in peace together! Mr Hunt
would leave the court with as fair a character as ever he had. (Oh heavy
irony.) Where was the proof of libel, and what damages could possibly be
sought as compensation? Had Mr Hunt's character been injured? There
might possibly be something like a passing cloud moving over it, but it
would soon be gone. Just like Hunt's jet blacking for boots, nothing could
obscure for long the polished surface thus produced (laughter). There was
not the slightest imputation cast upon Mr Hunt's character. The charge
of perjury had not been proved. 'Mr Hunt's character would stand as fair
in the public estimation *as it did before the charge was brought.*'

The entertained jury found Cobbett not guilty, and Hunt was ordered
to pay costs of £25.

Cobbett reported the trial in the *Political Register* the following
Saturday, 25 February 1826. He headlined the whole section under the
witty phrase: '"THE UNNY MAN" For Matchless Blacking and for Law',
cleverly imitating Hunt's own flamboyant advertising style and echoing
his voice with its strong West Country accent. (Hunt must have called
himself 'the only man' to do something on countless occasions. Cobbett
was as successful at conjuring up the essence of his victim through a
nickname or a phrase as the caricaturists were in their satirical pictures.)
When the 'Unny Man' appeared at the meeting at the Freemason's Tavern,
wrote Cobbett, people were puzzled to know what he was up to:

Some thought that he was only anxious that my *purity* should be preserved; but, when he
said that he was ready with his '*mite*,' 'with your *spite*, you mean,' said a gentleman in the
crowd, and he said it quite loud enough for the 'Unny Man' to hear him. The following
report of a trial, which took place on Monday last, may serve to explain all this ...

And Cobbett triumphantly presented his readers with the verbatim report
of the trial as it appeared in the *Morning Herald*. There were pages of the
stuff and Cobbett followed it with his own comments. Hunt had gone to
the expense of hiring a special jury for the occasion, even though he, like
Cobbett, had so often said 'a great deal about the institution', (criticised
it). He, Cobbett, would have been quite happy to be tried by any twelve
men in the country. Hunt's choice of the attorney general as his lawyer

showed that he was as matchless in his taste as in his ingredients for his blacking. Cobbett had been so confident that a man could not be punished for defending his own character, he had not even asked when the trial would take place.

Hunt would not give up. In desperation, he wrote a letter to the *Morning Herald*. The newspaper printed it but left out the nasty bits, substituting stars where Hunt accused Cobbett and his lawyer of lying. 'I rely upon your justice and love of fair play, for the insertion of the following facts to show how easy it is for an ingenious Counsel to xxxx and an xxxx writer to xxxx', wrote Hunt furiously. The evidence he had given in court about what Byrne said about Cobbett and Parkins had been true. One man had even written to Cobbett when Hunt's action had begun to say that he had been present when Byrne criticised Cobbett. The latter had only taken up Byrne's case because of his own row with Parkins over a horse. What was more, Cobbett had even offered to pay Byrne four shillings a week to accompany him on one of his rural rides as an exhibit for the farmers, but Byrne had indignantly refused his offer.

Cobbett slammed the ball back over the net in the *Register* of 4 March 1826. He re-published Hunt's letter and printed his own in reply. He roundly condemned, denied and refuted everything. None of Hunt's dates matched up. Byrne had only declined to ride out with him around the country because he was ill at the time. Had not he and his family loaded Byrne with favours and hospitality? There was the doctor his son had called to attend Byrne's wife, who had eye trouble. He, Cobbett, had himself taught Byrne's eldest daughter to plait and knit straw to make bonnets. Cobbett absolutely and utterly refused to believe that Byrne could ever have spoken badly of him. What was more, just to nail this thing down once and for all, Hunt's friend, who had indeed written to Cobbett confirming that he was present when Byrne had allegedly spoken badly of him, had written a song in praise of Hunt's Matchless Blacking. It was written to the tune of '*Scots wha hae wi' Wallace bled*'. How could you trust anybody who had done something like that! (Hunt might have sniggered at this crack.) Not another word would ever be necessary on this subject, Cobbett declared.

But there was another word or two on the subject a fortnight later, when Cobbett happily re-printed an article from the *Dublin Morning Register*. The newspaper had categorically denied that Cobbett or his son had written Byrne's affidavit for him. It had been written in the newspaper's office at Byrne's own request. The whole thing had taken about ten minutes and had as much connexion with the Cobbetts 'as the transactions that are at this moment going forward in the "celestial Empire."'

A few months later, Cobbett came last in the Preston election of June 1826. There was the usual gross intimidation of voters by the establishment candidates with their sackfuls of cash and their dirty tricks brigade. The brigade exploited the war of words between Cobbett and Hunt, 'the gentleman whom Cobbett has so often addressed in his Register as My Dear Hunt,' and re-published some of Hunt's past diatribes against Cobbett. These included an accusation that Hunt had made in a letter to the *Morning Herald* that the bones of Tom Paine, which Cobbett brought back from America, were in fact the bones of a black man. The undated letter was published in full and made entertaining reading:

'I trust,' says Mr Hunt, 'that my trade of selling matchless blacking, which sticks confoundedly in William Cobbett's gullet, is full as respectable as that of digging up dead men's bones and endeavouring to raise the wind by offering for sale a few hairs from the skull, for a guinea a lock, to make rings of Matchless jewellery! I flatter myself that my trade is quite as respectable and a little more profitable than his bone and hair scheme or I shall soon follow him into the Gazette.'

One of Hunt's *Addresses*, penned during his imprisonment in Ilchester Prison, was also quarried for insults. He was often asked what motive Cobbett could have for writing barefaced falsehoods about him, Hunt had written on 23 July 1822:

I generally answer that habit is a second nature, but in this instance, envy, hatred and malice and all uncharitableness drive him thus to expose himself. The fact is, he knows I am in possession of certain facts, for which he will never forgive me.

Cobbett would never be able to accuse him of denying his own hand-writing and swearing it was a forgery, Hunt had continued, nor of deserting his friends and fleeing the country. Cobbett might lie and swear all sorts of things against him, but he could not accuse Hunt of raising large subscriptions all over the country, or of becoming a fraudulent bankrupt to cheat all his creditors.

It was perfect material for the Whigs and the Tories to use against Cobbett at Preston. That was the 'matchless language' used by Mr Hunt to describe the merits of the town's candidate, they mocked.

Cobbett consoled himself with the overwhelming enthusiasm with which he was greeted by the people both in Preston and on the journey there and back from London: 'I put my arm over the side of the carriage and sometimes both arms together and let them squeeze and pull my hands about just as they pleased, till my hands were sore from my wrists to the points of my fingers.' His right arm was shaken so many times between Blackburn and Bolton, Cobbett wrote, he was unable to tie on his cravat the next day. He also got a sneaky blow in against Hunt. In the *Political Register* of 19 August 1826, Cobbett listed the subscribers who had contributed to his campaign in Preston. The list included 'Mite from a few Friends.'

A few days later, Cobbett saddled and bridled up and rode off to Burghclere in Hampshire. He had chosen one of his favourite villages. He lovingly studied the dry chalk and flint topsoil, the hard roads, the high bare hills and the deep dells, and watched the rooks skimming over the lofty trees. He headed west into Wiltshire, straight into Hunt country, riding along the River Avon past the pretty villages of Netheravon and Upavon. Among the many fine sights, he wrote, were the wheat, barley and hay ricks he counted in the stack-yards in the splendid Chisenbury Priory. Cobbett did not mention that this had been Hunt's fine home at the turn of the century. Hunt must have been in his mind though because, despite everything Cobbett said and despite the ridiculous court case between the two men, Cobbett wanted an end to the war between them. He was not a sentimental man. His thoughts and feelings were profoundly deeper than that. But, plainly speaking, he had had enough of going it alone. He needed the support and companionship once again of the man whom he had honoured every time he called him his 'dear Hunt'.

So, gradually, Hunt was reinstated in the *Register*. Cobbett's *Rural Ride*, during which he admired the ricks at Chisenbury Priory, appeared in the issue published on 16 September 1826. Just two weeks later, Cobbett reported that he had had the 'inexpressible satisfaction' to read in the newspapers that Hunt had taken over a pro-Corn Laws meeting organised by landowners and farmers in Andover and had defeated and covered 'the Jolterheads' with disgrace. Cobbett promised he would publish the entire article the following week on 7 October about 'this signal triumph of justice over greediness'.

And this time, Cobbett kept his word, 'agreeably to my promise'. (Did he remember the times he had not?) His purrs of pleasure can be heard through his prose. To the landed gentry's fury and dismay, Hunt had walked in with one of his friends to interrupt what they had hoped would be a 'snug' meeting in the George Inn with nobody to interrupt them. The pair unveiled an alternative petition which blamed the use of bank notes, the immense national debt and high taxation for the unhappy state of the country and the wretchedness of the labourers. Hunt gave a vintage speech, swiping not only at the Corn Laws but also at the greed of the landowners. He also called for the abolition of the Game Laws. His points and witty asides were greeted with cheers and laughter. By the time he finished, several farmers were shouting against the Corn Laws. (Cobbett loved that bit. 'Renting farmers begin to see that *Corn Bills* are *no good* TO THEM', he commented with immense satisfaction.)

There were pages of it. The landowners objected to the idea that ordinary members of the public at the meeting should be able to vote for Hunt's petition. Nobody was allowed to vote except the farmers and themselves. Ah ha, said Hunt to more laughter, they had said anybody who was 'interested' could attend the meeting, had they not? There was not a man there who did not either eat bread or wish to eat it. They all lived in houses and were entitled to vote. That was 'interest' all right. The chairman objected, did he? If the meeting voted for the alternative petition, he would refuse to sign it, would he? Never mind, said Hunt, no one paid any attention to petitions in parliament anyway (laughter). The vote was taken and a forest of hands shot in the air amid loud cheering. Hunt proposed an ironic vote of thanks to the gentlemen who had called them all together. There was a vulgar saying, Hunt said, the devil raises a storm but another power gives it a direction.

Hunt may or may not have known it but his rude figurative words mirrored the very unpleasant storm that was going on in the Cobbett household as Cobbett inched closer and closer to making things up with Hunt.

14
Two Cocks on the Dunghill

'History,' Stephen said, 'is a nightmare from which I am trying to awake.'
James Joyce

'My dear Nancy,' wrote Cobbett in a letter to his wife on 16 April 1827, he was sending her all the asparagus there was. It was a 'Black-thorn Winter', and things were not growing as well as they should, although there would be some rhubarb shortly. The birds had either stopped singing or were singing 'less merrily.'

The letter was penned at Barnes Elms, or Barn Elm as Cobbett called it. At the time, Barnes Elms was a rural area of farmland and market gardens near the village of Barnes, south of the river Thames in what was then Surrey. When Hammersmith Suspension Bridge opened in October 1827, it took Cobbett an hour to walk there from the family establishment in Kensington. To start with, Cobbett rented some garden plots at Barn Elm. He later leased a neighbouring farm of around a hundred acres. The rent was more than £600 a year, which was a small fortune. (He did not renew the lease in 1830.) As well as telling his wife about the cold spring and slow growth of the vegetables, Cobbett also urged Nancy not to worry herself about his affairs. If she did, he wrote, he would never know happiness or quiet again. It was 'monstrous' that Nancy mistrusted his judgement: 'The truth is the presumptuous talk about my 'crochets' has become so habitual, that it seems to be almost impossible to eradicate the idea, or to prevent it from breaking forth into sarcastic criticism.'

Poor Nancy. Life with William Cobbett was no picnic. It was more of a white-knuckle ride, wondering where and what he was going to do next. Nancy was ever concerned about her husband's ventures and the family's income. She was also deeply upset that Cobbett appeared to be moving towards reconciliation with Henry Hunt, the man she most hated and feared. The whole family was against the idea. Cobbett later recorded in a legal briefing, which was never made public, that his son John said that men of questionable private character should not be befriended by men of good private character. John particularly regretted his father's renewal of his friendship with Hunt 'considering what they had said of one another'.

Much as Cobbett loved his family, however, he was the 'master', as he so often told them to their deep resentment. Cobbett was sniffing the air and detecting a change, not just in the weather but also in the political climate. As he said, the birds were singing less merrily. For at least a year he had been vividly documenting the warning signs in the pages of the *Political Register*. Much of what he described he had seen for himself on his rural rides throughout the country. In the Avon valley, he had been deeply ashamed, he wrote, to see 'the general *extreme poverty*' of the labourers. Dogs, hogs and horses, Cobbett observed, were better treated. In Lancashire, the people were reduced to eating oats. 'Oh horrible system! Horror of all horrors, that can cause starvation of thousands in the midst of plenty!' Provincial banks were going bust. Many people had lost their savings. The great machines in the factories were silent. In Manchester, Leeds, Glasgow and Paisley 'misery walks abroad in skin, bone and nakedness'.

The plight of Britain was even being discussed overseas. Meetings were being held in America to discuss 'the continued and almost unparalleled sufferings of a large portion of the inhabitants in England, Ireland and Scotland from causes altogether beyond their control'. There was talk of sending cargoes of flour over to Britain, although as Cobbett grimly pointed out, the Corn Laws would prevent any foreign relief from entering the country. People were once again petitioning for a reform of parliament. In the *Register* of 28 April 1827, Cobbett re-printed the memorable petition of 1793 of the Whig politician, Charles Grey. This had called for reform and questioned the monstrosity of a system that allowed Cornwall and Wiltshire to send more borough members to parliament than Yorkshire, Lancashire, Warwickshire, Middlesex, Worcestershire and Somerset combined.

Despite the winds of change, Sir Francis Burdett, who had initially won his independent Westminster seat in the House of Commons on a ticket of 'Purity' (no bribery or corruption) had just sensationally abandoned his independent position to link himself with the new hard-line coalition government of the Tory, George Canning. This was despite Canning's pledge that there would never be parliamentary reform in his lifetime. Cobbett was triumphant. It proved everything he and Hunt had ever said about the 'shuffling' baronet. He described Burdett sitting in the Commons behind the mortal enemy of parliamentary reform, 'tickling the shoulders of Canning with his Knees'. Cobbett used this marvellously evocative phrase at every opportunity, even after Canning's death just a few months later, when he varied it slightly and wrote how 'the Daddy had stuck his knees into poor Canning's back'.

As far as Cobbett was concerned, he told his readers in the issue of the *Register* of 5 May 1827, something had to be done. Somebody would have to quiz Burdett, 'Westminster's Pride and England's Glory', for an explanation of his behaviour. Somebody would have to do it at the annual 'Purity of Election' dinner to celebrate Burdett's success in the Westminster constituency in 1807. This was due to be held later that month. It was going to be a big occasion as it would mark the twentieth anniversary. Cobbett's words rang out sonorously from the page:

Someone will, to be sure, ask for such explanation, inspite of the howlings, the wands and the nails of the Rump ... if someone do not demand this explanation, if someone do not ask what can be the meaning of this change, Westminster is sunk for ever and is baser than any rotten borough in the kingdom.

The 'someone' was, of course, going to be Cobbett – but he was not going to do it on his own. As he revealed to his readers the following week on 12 May, he was going to do it with Mr Hunt.

It was a cliffhanger of an issue. As a build up, Cobbett launched into a stinging attack against Burdett and the Whigs, pouring scorn on them for favouring a coalition with the Tories at such a time, and, despite all their fine words and promises, deciding that parliamentary reform was no longer a priority on the political agenda. They had chosen to forget the long imprisonments, horrible ruin and terrible sufferings of hundreds of men dedicated to the cause of reform, 'the choppings and shootings and tramplings at Manchester'. How could 'this old rump of politicians' betray the cause to join Canning, the bitter and everlasting enemy of reform? Behold the paupers swarming like the lice of Egypt all over England, rotting upon straw, packed together so closely there was no room to turn over in this starving, this tread-mill country. If his readers thought about 'the brass' of Burdett, their rage would be so great they would have to look around for consolation. He could offer that consolation – but they would have to wait for several pages more before finding out what it was, wrote the master of suspense and timing.

Finally, he got to the point – almost. A meeting had been called in Covent Garden at twelve o'clock on the coming Monday, wrote Cobbett. His language was thrilled and thrilling. 'At that meeting I shall be; and I understand that *it is the intention of* Mr Hunt *to be there also.*' As he himself detested 'roundabout ways', Cobbett continued disarmingly, he would now explain everything, and he proceeded to do so in one of his best roundabout ways.

The previous Sunday he had asked a gentleman to call on Mr Hunt to ask him if he had the same views upon the subject as Cobbett and, if he did, would he meet with Cobbett the following day to discuss how they could defend the cause of reform together. The go-between, however, had left London suddenly. So Cobbett had picked up his pen and written to Mr Hunt himself to request a meeting that very day, 'if he chose to co-operate with me for such purpose'.

Hunt did. The two met, and everything was settled in ten minutes. A notice for publication in the *Morning Herald* was drawn up. It announced that both Cobbett and Hunt were to attend the Purity of Election dinner at the Crown and Anchor on 23 May 1827 at which they hoped to find out why 'certain quarters' (Burdett) had betrayed the cause of the people. The pair believed it was their right, a duty they owed to their country, to attend the dinner and find out why the very men who professed to be the most zealous defenders of the people's rights were now choosing to betray them. If Burdett were not censured at the dinner, the assembled company would have become 'so base, so entirely worthless and infamous, so rotten, so corrupt and so degraded', they would deserve to be 'trodden into dirt and dung, like the spawn of those filthy reptiles from which the eye is turned and the touch recoils'. All real and earnest friends of reform had 'a very sacred duty to perform' on this occasion. In the meantime, he would be at Covent Garden in two days' time along with Mr Hunt.

One thing Cobbett did not tell his readers was that his wife was so distressed about her husband's reconciliation with Hunt, she had threatened to commit suicide if Cobbett went to the Covent Garden meeting with him. It took place, however, as planned on 14 May 1827. Despite Nancy's threat hanging over him, Cobbett went along with Hunt. It was business as usual, just like old times. The high sheriff had tried to ban it, and the two Westminster MPs, Burdett and Hobhouse, ignored their invitations to attend. When Cobbett and Hunt arrived, they found the police tearing down the hustings platform which had been set up in the usual spot outside the east front of St Paul's Church on the piazza. Hunt promptly sent to his factory in Broad Wall for one of his blacking vans. When the van galloped up, Cobbett and Hunt climbed in and drove defiantly to the exact spot where the hustings should have been.

A large crowd had gathered in the meantime to see the fun. They were not disappointed. As the van was being manoeuvred into position, a ticket inspector arrived armed with his note-book. In the *Register,* Cobbett called him a 'Commissioner of Pavements'. The man insisted that under the Paving Act, even though there was no market that day, the van could not park there, nor anywhere else in the parish of St Paul, because it was an 'obstruction to travellers on the king's highway'.

Cobbett blamed this intervention on Burdett, but there was nothing to be done except to drive off in the van around the corner, down Catherine Street and into the Strand. They parked in the 'wide and quiet' area of Lancaster Place, just north of Waterloo Bridge, where the meeting finally got underway. Hunt gave a speech of 'considerable length' (as Cobbett shortly described it) and then proposed an address to be sent to King George IV. Cobbett seconded it. The address congratulated the king on his choice of Canning as his new prime minister, but expressed deep regret he had chosen someone with a never-ending hostility to parliamentary reform. There was not one dissenting vote from the crowd.

Cobbett and Hunt walked away from the meeting arm in arm. When Nancy Cobbett learned about the meeting from the newspapers the next day, she cut at her throat with a knife. The wound was not fatal but Nancy was left dangerously ill. Two years later, in an unpublished legal brief, Cobbett would miserably describe what she did as 'a most violent and tragical deed'. At the time, however, he carried on public life in exactly the way he wished to do so. His account of the Covent Garden meeting appeared in the *Register* five days later, when he repeated that both he and Hunt continued to look forward to the Purity dinner at the Crown and Anchor on the following Wednesday. As Cobbett had said, the pair had a sacred duty to perform. Nothing and nobody was going to get in their way.

Predictably, the Purity of Election dinner on 23 May 1827 turned into a huge occasion. The dinner was held as usual in the famously large meeting room of the Crown and Anchor, which was on the east side of Arundel Street running south of the Strand. (It burned down in 1854). The tavern's so-called 'great room' was 84 feet long and more than 35 feet wide and could seat 2,000 people. Such was the excitement about seeing Cobbett and Hunt back together again that the dinner was heavily over-subscribed. The organisers managed to pack in more than twice the number that usually attended. As Cobbett said, there were 'great expectations' about what was going to happen. The reptile journalists were out in force, pencils sharpened, certain it was going to be a big story for the newspapers the next day. The 'stewards' were also ready and waiting.

Cobbett helpfully explained to his readers who these stewards were. Organisers of events, in this case the Westminster Rump, employed these hand-picked men to manage proceedings. They were armed with seven-foot long, stout sticks, which were discreetly called 'wands'. The wands were used to control rowdy diners by giving them, as Cobbett described, a good thrust in the stomach, putting out an eye or, with the butt end, knocking a man down. The stewards mingled with the people and stood by to prevent anybody speaking anything 'inconvenient'.

The tables had also been carefully arranged. There was a cross table running the width of the room at one end. Five tables were positioned length-wise. The chairman and his henchmen sat in the middle of the cross table. Two days before the dinner, Hunt had applied for two seats for himself and Cobbett at the cross table from where it would be easier to address the whole room. Unsurprisingly, his request was turned down, although the stewards promised that the pair would get a fair hearing, a promise they found hard to believe. They managed to reserve seats at the top end of the long table on the left of the chairman, Sir Francis Burdett.

One can imagine the buzz of excitement as Cobbett and Hunt strode into the room side by side to take up their seats.

On the dot of 5 o'clock, in marched Burdett, 'Sir Glory' as Cobbett called him, with a crowd of Whig aristocrats and landowners, including 'Daddy Coke' (the famous Thomas Coke of Holkham in Norfolk) and Lord John Russell, together with 'a whole band of placemen, pensioners, sinecures and notorious expectants'. The dinner ended, the plates were cleared away, more bottles of wine were brought out and everybody could look forward to the toasts when they knew the fireworks were likely to happen. Just before it did, the stewards unexpectedly ushered in about twenty more 'Lord Charleses', as Cobbett scoffingly called them, to sit behind the top table as extra reinforcements.

Cobbett had thoughtfully prepared a resolution in advance. He read it out. A toast to the good health of Sir Francis Burdett should on no account be drunk, he said, and began to give a critical account of Burdett's entire political life. The noise was so great that Cobbett had to stop, even though there were many who agreed with him, he later wrote. He changed tactics and began to propose amendments to the toasts called. One of the amendments included a request to George IV to sack his prime minister, George Canning. This was greeted with more yelling from Burdett's supporters whom Cobbett disdainfully referred to as 'the hired crew'.

After another amendment in which Cobbett linked the baronet to Canning, whom he called 'the opponent of parliamentary Reform', the place erupted. 'Now arose a row, a yelling, a noise, a hurly burly, a confusion and uproar, enough to stun any man, but, far sweeter to the ears of Burdett than a hearing of my speech would have been', Cobbett informed his readers. Burdett asked for Cobbett's amendment in writing. Cobbett handed it over, but the baronet did not dare to allow a vote, 'even upon his own dunghill'. Oh how Sir Glory wriggled and twisted and shuffled as Cobbett continued to shout at him. Hunt joined in with Cobbett, but whenever his remarks became too pointed and hit Burdett too hard, the 'myrmidons' yelled so loudly, even 'Mr Hunt' was drowned out.

Cobbett then called a toast, barbed with insults, to the health of the other Westminster MP, the short and stocky John Cam Hobhouse, 'my dear little Sancho' (to Burdett's Don Quixote) as Cobbett loudly called him. Hobhouse furiously grabbed a steward's stout stick, jumped onto the table and ran towards Cobbett threatening to knock him down if he called him names again. Hobhouse looked just like 'a Gulliver swaggering on the table of the Brobynagians', Cobbett wrote later with malicious delight. There was laughter from all sides.

Then it was Cobbett's turn to erupt. Although he wrote about the event with a light touch for the *Political Register* of 26 May 1827 (the whole dinner episode took up most of the issue), he was in a state of deep excitement at the time. Leaping onto the table, he confronted Hobhouse, who later commented in his diary that Cobbett had been very drunk. Newspaper reports described Cobbett as shouting, swearing, waving his arms around and gnashing his teeth. The laughter turned into shouts against him: 'Out with him! Turn him out! Down with him.' A dozen or so stewards advanced brandishing their wands. One poked Cobbett in the stomach. Another aimed at his eye, until a friend intercepted the stick, broke it in half and turned the big end back against the steward's throat.

Cobbett was pulled off the table on which he was dancing. The white waistcoat he was wearing was torn to shreds. Friends rushed to help him. Hunt overturned the chairs to set up a barricade, and Cobbett leaped back onto the table. Others joined him. The battle was in full swing when the table collapsed with a smashing and crashing of bottles and glasses. A steward narrowly missed clouting Burdett on the head. Instead the wand went straight through a window just behind him.

Hobhouse, meanwhile, surrounded by his friends and supporters, was standing on another table trying to make a speech, when it too collapsed, taking with it more bottles, decanters and glasses. There were howls of glee from the Cobbett and Hunt faction. The scene, reported the *Morning Chronicle* the next day, beggared all description. Full credit may be given to Cobbett for re-printing every word of its lengthy article in the *Register*. The newspaper reported the screaming, howling and hissing on the one hand, and the cheers and clapping of hands on the other. The noise was deafening. Cobbett continued to bellow at the top of his voice. His opponents shouted, 'Oh, you old bone-grubber, why don't you pay Sir Francis Burdett his three thousand pounds.' 'Go to Hell', screamed

Cobbett's friends. According to the *Chronicle*, Hunt behaved 'manfully and honourably' and preserved the utmost coolness of temper throughout.

What an evening it had been. Cobbett reported triumphantly in the *Register* how 'the fallen Baronet' and other diners, including 'Daddy Coke' eventually retired from the fray. They went relatively early at 11 o'clock. He described with amusement how they marched off 'amidst the clapping of the hirelings, the rappings of the stewards' wands on the floor and the hissings and booings of the rest of the assembly'. Many who remained had called on Mr Hunt to take the empty chair, but he declined to do so. He would not disgrace himself, he said, by sitting in a chair Sir Francis had just sat in. The party went on to a late hour. The *Morning Chronicle* reported that Cobbett and his friends put up with the pushes and elbowing they received when they at last called it a day and retired.

Cobbett did not mention Hunt at the end. It can only be assumed that they left the dinner together. Cobbett took all the credit for his victory in what he called the 'battle' at the Crown and Anchor, and continued to proclaim it through the pages of the *Political Register*. 'I remained upon the top of the dunghill', he crowed. 'I kept the field'.

The day after the night before, John Cam Hobhouse penned a lengthy entry in his diary. It makes interesting reading. Surprisingly, it appears that the Westminster dinner was the first occasion at which Hobhouse had seen Cobbett in person:

I had never seen Cobbett before. He looked to me like a higher sort of respectable country shopkeeper or church warden of a parish. He was neatly dressed in a white waistcoat and chocolate-coloured coat. Except that his brow was rather contracted and overhung, I saw nothing forbidding in his face.

As the evening went on, Hobhouse's diary entry continues, Cobbett behaved 'like a madman', drinking several glasses of wine during his first speech against Burdett. He 'called us bad names and swore tremendously.' Afterwards, Burdett sent him a note telling him to keep quiet about what had happened. And then Hobhouse made a crucial revelation in his diary:

It is certainly true that Mrs Cobbett made an attempt on her life the other day and is lying now very dangerously ill. She has been on bad terms with her husband some time and told him if he went to the Westminster meeting on May 14 she would destroy herself. On reading the account of that meeting in the Herald she tried to commit suicide.

These lines in Hobhouse's diary clearly reveal that the events going on behind closed doors in the Cobbett household were common knowledge. It can also be inferred from his words that everybody also knew that Hunt was the major reason for Nancy Cobbett's fury.

Despite his public behaviour, Cobbett was privately deeply shocked and sorry about his wife's actions. When Nancy went to Brighton later in the year to recuperate in the sea air, he dispatched quantities of partridge and young hare, and peaches and squashes for her to enjoy. No cost was spared. Nevertheless, he remained unyielding. Cobbett was back together with Hunt, although he continued to refer to him as 'Mr Hunt' in the *Political Register*. In his private letters, however, he continued to use the fond and intimate style of address, 'My dear Hunt'.

A few weeks after their very enjoyable 'battle' at the Crown and Anchor, Cobbett wrote his 'dear Hunt' a short note from his farm at Barn Elm on 16 June 1827. He enclosed a separate letter he had written to the Lord Mayor of London on behalf of the voting freemen of the City, the Liverymen of London. Both Hunt and Cobbett had been liverymen for years, and Hunt was active in City politics. Cobbett's letter asked the mayor to call a meeting to organise a petition to the government. The petition should call for action to save the labouring millions, who had been stripped of nearly all their political rights and who were now being reduced to nakedness and famine. In his note to Hunt, Cobbett said his request was bound to cause a stir and asked Hunt to set the wheels in motion: 'I send you the thing; as you will copy it, of course, pray mind all the points very exactly. The last three lines will let us into famous matter.'

It was just like it had been fifteen years previously, Cobbett was in the driving seat, telling Hunt what to do and how to do it. And of course Hunt did do it because Cobbett still wielded the most powerful pen in the world and was once again, as he had signed his note to Hunt, 'Yours most faithfully, Wm Cobbett.'

Everything was sweetness and light between the two men once more. Cobbett sang Hunt's praises in issue after issue of the *Political Register*. He remembered how he, together with Hunt, had battled away more than a decade previously against the Corn Bill; Wiltshire had been the only county to call a regular meeting, Salisbury the only city to host such a meeting and Mr Hunt had had the honour to call it, Cobbett wrote proudly. A week later, in the issue of 30 June 1827, Cobbett had just read in the newspaper that Mr Hunt had been voted an auditor of the accounts of the City of London by 'a majority of ten to <u>one!</u>' and was determined to put an end to the 'guzzling and gormandizing' that was going on. 'Never did I hear anything that gave me much more pleasure', wrote Cobbett. 'I have no scruple to say that I regard this as of a thousand times as much importance as the making of Burdett or any other man, a peer'.

And so it continued. On 11 August 1827, Cobbett reminded everybody how 'that same vile old Times' that pursued poor Cashman to the gallows had also called for '*the destruction* of Mr Hunt'. The following week, he chuckled all over again at how Mr Hunt had prevented the Scottish lawyer and MP, Henry Brougham, from speaking at the Westminster meeting in 1816. The memory was so comical that Cobbett fondly resorted to his old intimate way of addressing Hunt in the *Register*:

It was observed by Hunt, who was an old sportsman, that he never saw a fox slide along through a thicket with more dexterity and cunning than Lawyer Brougham stole away from the hustings and got his brush safely within the door of Westminster Hall ... 'He is safe there,' said Hunt. 'There we cannot dig and into that hole our terriers dare not enter.'

The battle of 23 May at the Crown and Anchor remained in the news. Cobbett had been banned from the tavern by the long-suffering owner, who decided in the September to auction off the battered furniture together with what survived of the plates and crockery. There was more chortling from Cobbett in the *Register*. The owner was only doing it, he wrote, to prevent 'a repetition of the last dismal scene'. The auction was to include the big chair in which so many Whigs had sat. Poor chair, wrote Cobbett, it was time it sought refuge in the fire. It needed the weight of sin taken off its feet. The sale was to be in a few days' time. He intended to be there and bid for the chair, 'a poor degraded mass of wood, hair and gold leaf', which had suffered long enough. If the auction included the '*name*' of Burdett, there would be no bids unless the sale also included the baronet's '*money*', he joked.

As Cobbett joyfully related in the issue of the *Political Register* published on 22 September 1827, both he and Hunt turned up at the Crown and Anchor for the sale in the spacious dining room – Cobbett called it 'the grand theatre of dunghill Glory'. Hunt wanted to buy the chair but wandered off as it was about to go up for auction. So Cobbett leaped on a stool and bid eightpence. The auctioneer put the price up to fifty guineas. It finally went for forty-five guineas, although Cobbett thought the bidding was faked.

He and Hunt had more success with the famous or infamous 'wands'. These were also auctioned off, and the two men bought the lot between them. Cobbett happily remembered how the heavy sticks had been used 'to put ME out of the room'. He informed his readers that he was going to put some of his wands on show at his office in Fleet Street so that everybody could see with their own eyes the way Glory's opponents were kept in order. He would also use some of them in his gardens, dressed up in old clothes as 'shoy-hoys' (scarecrows). Others would be 'turned to all manner of vile uses'. He would keep some of the sticks to make a fire 'to broil an old *dunghill cock* at the next feast of the Gridiron'. (Cobbett always said he would submit to being cooked over a fire on an iron grid if his predictions over the collapse of the economy were wrong.) Sadly, Cobbett did not reveal what Hunt planned to do with his haul.

Cobbett's family life was under strain, but it was fun to be back together with Hunt. The press noted their antics. *The Times* ran a story about their appearance together at the auction, referring to the pair as 'the two notorious brokers in politics, Mr Hunt and the Bonegrubber', and sneeringly reminded its readers about the highs and lows in the Cobbett/Hunt relationship.

Over the following eighteen months, from 1828 to the middle of 1829, the partnership was back on track, although some underlying shufflings to be top cock may be detected. All in all, however, these were good months with the two men solidly supporting each other. There were fond private letters between the pair, and they continued to support each other in public. Hunt stoutly defended Cobbett against the frequent insults hurled against him by the Irish Catholic lawyer and politician, Daniel

O'Connell. At one point, O'Connell described Cobbett as a savage and a monster 'whose very home-inmates groan under the most afflicting domestic tyranny'. In August 1828, Hunt wrote an open letter to O'Connell, which was published in the newspapers: 'Your vulgar abuse of Mr Cobbett one day and your fulsome flattery of him the next and then your abuse of him again and vice versa, as the fit takes you, will be better answered by him than by anything that I can say.' In the letter, Hunt also attacked O'Connell for attempting 'to *traffic* in the liberties of your countrymen and to *prostitute* the religion of your forefathers'. O'Connell was a 'mere political weather cock', wrote Hunt, who had been earning money for so long by prostituting his talents to make the worse appear the better cause that he sometimes forgot what principles he had professed at his last meeting.

Cobbett, who warned Hunt to beware of O'Connell's political manoeuvrings, published Hunt's letter in full in the *Register* of 30 August 1828.

Hunt supported Cobbett and he, in turn, supported Hunt. Cobbett even made a rare reference in the issue of the *Register* of 21 February 1829 to the years that Hunt spent in gaol. The issue was addressed to Sidmouth (Cobbett left out the word 'Lord') and reminded him of all his horrid deeds and bills. Suddenly Cobbett snarled:

And now, Sidmouth, have you any recollection of one HENRY HUNT, who used to be so often a subject of debate in your noble House, and in that other place where the members are so much under the influence of public opinion, and who has of late years passed pretty nearly three years altogether in one of those receptacles for the bodies of Parliamentary reformers?

Cobbett proceeded to devote column after column informing Sidmouth about Mr Hunt's latest glorious political activities.

Out of the blue, a couple of months later, on 9 May 1829, Cobbett re-published a letter Hunt had written in February 1826 to the 'loan monger', Alexander Baring, after the money lender had sneered at him in the House of Commons as 'The Blacking-man'. Baring also said that Hunt went around 'with other itinerant *Patriots*' (Cobbett) telling lies to the people. In his letter, Hunt had thanked Baring for having publicly advertised his blacking within the walls of the House of Commons, and had given him a warning:

... when that crisis of National distress arrive ... then, Sir, the *Blacking-man,* as you in your elegant phraseology are pleased to call him, will be found quite as good and efficient a member of the community, whether within or without the walls of Parliament, as the *Loan Monger* or the *Stock Monger.*

Cobbett's re-use in the *Register* of Hunt's letter to Baring was really making amends. He had probably itched to use the letter the first time round, but had been locked in the ridiculous court case against Hunt involving Byrne and Parkins.

During these months, good will and compliments about Hunt flowed once more from the pen that Hunt eulogised as 'gigantic', just as they used to. Cobbett, however, was not averse to trying to pull one over on Hunt when it came to business. In a letter to his friend, Silvester Sapsford, written on 18 November 1828 from Kensington, Cobbett admitted that he had over-dried some of his corn which was going to be roasted and turned into his famous false coffee. He followed this with another urgent letter just a week later: 'For God's sake <u>say nothing</u> about the <u>coffee</u>! My wife and family can find <u>no difference</u> between it and Coffee.' Cobbett told Sapsford that he was going to carry on with the process, and sell it at a lower price. He was sure of an '<u>enormous sale.</u>' Hunt had sold 'his stuff' for a shilling. Cobbett would sell his un-ground roasted coffee for 3d and the ground coffee for a halfpenny more. He begged Sapsford, '<u>S</u><u>ay nothing about it.</u> <u>Smell</u>, <u>taste</u>, <u>colour</u>, everything <u>equal to coffee</u>.'

Overall, however, everything was harmonious on the dunghill. The two big political subjects keeping Cobbett and Hunt busy were Catholic Emancipation and Hunt's battles in the maelstrom of the City of London.

The latter kicked off in the *Register* in a spectacular manner on 10 May 1828 under the headline, 'City Gluttony'. In his article, Cobbett crowed over Hunt's triumphs in exposing 'the misapplication of the money belonging to the citizens of London'. When Mr Hunt was appointed one of the auditors, he, Cobbett, had known 'valuable disclosures' would be made. Everybody knew that Mr Hunt would not treat the post like a sinecure. They had been quite right. To prove it, Cobbett was re-printing in full a public letter to the 'Liverymen, Freemen and inhabitant

Householders of the City of London', written by Hunt and published in the *Morning Herald*.

In his letter, Hunt wrote that he had soon learned that one of the rules of the City of London's Court of Common Council was that people who were not council members were banned from having access to any of the relevant documents. Even the auditors could not get hold of them. When he had tried to see the paperwork in his capacity as an auditor, he had been 'vulgarly assailed' by some of the old council men and accused of lying. One councillor, 'a Mr Figgy' (Vincent Figgins), declared that everything was honestly managed because the accounts, 'forsooth', were laid every year before parliament, which regularly declared that the City of London's affairs were '*beautifully kept*'. They were indeed '*beautifully kept*', Hunt went on in his letter to the *Morning Herald*, the auditors were unable to track down where much of the money had gone. Hunt could tell them though. It had disappeared down the throats of councillors in 'guzzling and gormandising'. He promised he would give them a full report on Michaelmas Day.

Cobbett jubilantly piled on more comments to follow Hunt's letter. If the liverymen suffered these abuses to continue, they would be guilty of the most foul treason towards the inhabitants of the City. They would have broken their solemn oath. They would be a set of wretches who deserved nothing more than to work 'to stuff the maws of these gormandizers during the winter and to pay for their pleasures in jaunting about during the summer.' The cost for the 'guzzlings and gormandizings' in one year alone was more than £12,000! Yet the poor freemen's widows had to share a mere £100 between them. It was a scandal that had to be stopped. 'I dare say that Mr Hunt's letter may have tended to save us something by taking away their appetites,' wrote Cobbett.

The Court of Common Council got its own back when Hunt stood as a council candidate at the end of 1828. The dirty tricks brigade swung into action against both Hunt and Cobbett. The latter had also put himself forward as a candidate, although he ended up supporting Hunt 'as a *ferret* to be sent in amongst them'. The linking of the pair was enough to turn the election into a big occasion. Notices were posted up beforehand asking whether Hunt and Cobbett were:

'Catechising'
A bishop addresses five men who repeat: 'Thou shalt not buy Hunt's matchless Blacking, nor his Ink, nor his roasted grain, nor anything that is his.' In another scene behind, the bishop directs the birching of a young man, holding up a paper marked with a gridiron [Cobbett's Political Register] and shouts: 'How dare you read this vile Book Sir?'
Robert Seymour, 1828.

... such persons as you would like to introduce into the society of your Wives and Daughters? Would you present them as proper examples to your Servants and Apprentices? Would you place them in a situation to be mixed with the Magistrates and members of the Corporate Body of the first City in the World?

The anticipation about what was going to happen was enormous. Cobbett described it in the *Register* of 20 December 1828 as 'a great stir', just like that made by rats hiding in the corn as the mowers got closer and the vermin were able to hear the excited whining of the dogs approaching. A week later, he reprinted the lengthy and colourful *Morning Herald* report of what took place.

When the doors of St Andrew's Church in Farringdon Without opened, the newspaper reported, a huge crowd was waiting. People poured in, packing into every corner of the church. 'A number of respectable females' sat in the gallery. Cobbett managed to get a seat close to the chairman. The newspaper described him as busily writing throughout. There were loud cheers when Hunt walked in, and the cheering continued when he launched into a sensational defence of his own private character. Gross forgeries had been circulated against him making use of Mr Cobbett's name, said Hunt. The assertions were so gross and scandalous they were scarcely believable. His private character was as immaculate as anybody else's. He wanted to explain why he no longer lived with his wife (hear hear). He had now been separated from her for twenty-six years. He had given her four times her marriage portion (applause). Nevertheless, it had been said that he had turned his wife away. Since the separation, Hunt went on furiously, unlike other men he had never set foot within the door of a brothel and he had never been seen coming out of one; he had never frequented common pot-houses nor had he ever been heard singing songs of the most 'beastly and indecent description'. This was unlike Mr Figgins (Figgy), who was known to sit and laugh at them 'until his old rotten teeth almost dropped out of his head'. The songs would not even be tolerated by the lowest prostitutes. Was it by such 'immaculate' men as these that his morals were to be questioned? (shouts of 'hear hear'). These immaculate gentlemen, roared Hunt, were always talking of their honour and their honesty, but what would they say to know that one amongst them had been twice convicted at the Old Bailey for fraud, and another had been tried for a rape on his own servant. 'Such were the fair fame and fair characters of these gentlemen'.

When Hunt stopped his personal tirade and resumed his attack against corruption in the City of London, Cobbett stepped in to help him, and there was a sort of double act between them:

Hunt: When I first went to look over the City's accounts, would you believe it, there were no vouchers produced!
Cobbett: No vouchers?
Hunt: None. Nothing but four books.

It was a magnificent performance for the crowds, and there was a final flourish of fireworks when the decrepit and revolting Figgy got to his feet and accused Hunt of having seduced the wife of 'Colonel Vince' (cries of 'Off, off!'). Hunt hit back. That was 'a mere cowardly attack on a woman', he shouted. Figgins asked Hunt if the accusation was not true. At this, Hunt really lost his cool. 'Such a question was never put in any other Court than the Spanish Inquisition', he roared. As to whether Mr Figgins himself had ever been guilty of such an offence – why no man could possibly ever suspect him. The very appearance of the man was a denial to the charge!

Hunt lost the election, but he was more devastated by the very personal attack that had been made against him in public. He wrote miserably to Cobbett after Christmas asking his friend whether he would ever be able to dine with anybody ever again. His letter did not survive, but it can be guessed what Hunt wrote from the reassuring reply Cobbett sent to him on 9 January 1829 from Barn Elm: 'I was in the country when your note came; and did not see it till this morning, or else I should have been one of those to give you a dinner in spite of the qualms of the canting debauchees.'

Cobbett's letter to Hunt was intensely personal and fond. In it, he mentioned Hunt's younger son, Tom, who was living a low drunken life in London. Cobbett would write to Tom, if he could get hold of his address, and invite him for 'a good-humoured talk.' His own sons would be glad to see him. Cobbett himself could not but remember how fond they all were of Tom. 'Let him come here, and see whether I cannot laugh him out of a part of his folly', his letter continued. The last lines were reserved for Catherine Vince: 'My best respects to Mrs Vince, who has, I hope too much sense to feel that which all people despise.' In other words, Cobbett hoped that Catherine Vince, who could well have been among the 'respectable ladies' sitting in the gallery during the City of London meeting, was too sensible to class herself as a prostitute, as nasty old Figgy had clearly implied. Cobbett was trying to be reassuring, but it is difficult not to detect a note of ambiguity in that sentence, suggesting a slight struggle with his conscience. 1829 was to be the year when Cobbett would write in his *Advice to Young Men* that any woman who slept outside the marriage bed was a prostitute. It is a mark of how special Hunt was to Cobbett that the latter was prepared to accept Mrs Vince and continue with his public and personal friendship with Hunt, despite his own standards of morality – and the misery and fury of his own wife, Nancy.

Cobbett continued to back Hunt in his battles with the City of London. In the *Register* of 27 June 1829, Cobbett chuckled to his readers how Mr Hunt had been tickling trout in Wiltshire, while the House of Lords had been waiting for him to help them tickle the 'devouring *sharks* of London'. Under the headline 'TURTLE-EATERS', Cobbett then published a letter from Hunt to the Liverymen of London, which explained Cobbett's reference to the House of Lords.

Hunt had finally scored a major success in his battle against the maladministration of the City of London by its 'cabal of Common Councilmen'. A new London Bridge had been built to replace the medieval stone one. The final cost was double the original estimate. What was more, the bridge had been built twenty feet higher than necessary, and the approach roads forgotten. Either the people had to climb over the houses to get to the bridge, wrote Hunt, or the houses had to be knocked down so that a ramp to reach the bridge could be built. The council wanted parliament to allow it to continue to tax domestic coal to raise the necessary finance. This had infuriated two of the big coal mine owners, the Marquis of Londonderry and Lord Durham. The House of Lords had set up a committee of inquiry and called Hunt as a witness. He had returned from his trout fishing to give evidence. Oh what a field day he had. He told his Lordships all about the delinquency, such a mass of jobbing, such unquestionable proof of the most wanton, wicked and profligate waste of City money, such deception, fraud and plunder that would not only astonish their Lordships but the whole world. The result was that the Lords took management of the job out of the hands of the City's Bridge Committee and gave it over to the government!

Cobbett obviously loved Hunt's letter and rounded it off with his own remarks. As soon as he knew Mr Hunt had been made an auditor, he had said to himself 'there is an end of the 'gormandizing and peculation'. Thanks to the vigilance and industry of Mr Hunt, wrote Cobbett, the whole country now knew about the devious practices of the City of London. The base crew of Farringdon Without had tried to cover Hunt with degradation, but had failed.

The whole piece, with its opening sunny picture of Hunt *gone fishin'*, clearly illuminates the relationship between Cobbett and Hunt at this stage, their conversations, the issues, the political manoeuvrings and the enjoyment they were sharing.

The pair also threw themselves into the complicated question of Catholic Emancipation and the removal of the bars that stopped Catholics from becoming MPs, lords, judges and justices of the peace and from holding high positions in local authorities and the armed forces. Cobbett blamed everything onto Henry VIII and his Reformation. He argued that the demise of the Catholic Church and the loss of benevolent religious institutions had been a major factor in creating widespread poverty. Hunt loyally backed him up. In a letter published in the *Register* of 29 November 1828, Hunt informed the Irish leaders that Cobbett's *History of the Protestant Reformation* had done more to eradicate English people's prejudices against the Catholic religion than all the Catholic speakers since the Reformation. Yet the Catholic Association had never missed an opportunity to libel, calumniate, abuse and misrepresent him.

Both Cobbett and Hunt were appalled by the misery of Ireland and supported emancipation – but only if it were to be accompanied by the granting of equality of rights for all Christian sects and a reform of church and parliament. Therein lay the problem. In the shifting sands of Irish politics, the Catholic leaders, including Daniel O'Connell, or 'the big O' as Cobbett scornfully called him, were ambivalent about the question of reform. Cobbett and Hunt attacked O'Connell viciously for this. The Irishman revealed how he felt about both of them in a letter marked

'Private', written in March 1829 to his friend, Edward Dwyer. The radical reformers had no leader, no system and no confidence in either Hunt or Cobbett, wrote O'Connell. The reformers were powerless because of their leaders, 'who are despicable both from their characters and their vile jealousies and ill temper.'

This was not exactly how Cobbett would have described the situation, although in many ways, O'Connell had a point. Cobbett did believe, however, that the state of affairs in the country had become so bad that all sorts of politicians were starting to jump on the reform bandwagon to use it for their own advantage. The national debt was more than 800 million pounds. Vast sums of money were being spent on poor relief, yet people were still starving. Prisons had tripled in size but were still too small to cope with the numbers being sentenced by the courts. Banks were going bust; tradesmen, farmers and merchants faced ruin and people were emigrating in droves. Civil unrest loomed. Politicians had to be seen to be doing something. Cobbett was worried that whatever plan for reform they came up with, it would not be the kind of radical adjustment that was needed. He believed it would merely tinker with the system. Cobbett decided that he and Hunt should publish a declaration stating the situation. Cobbett would draw it up; Hunt could suggest any alterations. They would both sign it and get it published in as many of the newspapers as they could. He explained his plan in a private letter to Hunt on 15 June 1829:

I am sure there must very soon be a stir of some sort. Things cannot go on long in this way and I think that we should now put ourselves forward and take the lead in pointing out what ought to be done. The Declaration ... must state the nature and extent of the misery. It must trace it to its courses. It must show that these have sprung from want of reform and then show that no reform other than the real one can afford relief for the present and security for the future.

The following month, after Hunt's tickling of the trout in Wiltshire and those in the House of Lords, the declaration was published to the world. It turned out to be the last united attempt by Cobbett and Hunt to shape the radical reform movement in the crucial run up to the Great Reform Act of 1832.

15
The Fall Out

Dream after dream ensues;
And still they dream, that they shall still succeed,
And still are disappointed.
William Cowper

They drew up their declaration for 'a *Radical Reform in the Commons'
House of Parliament*', on 4 July 1829. The day was carefully chosen. As
readers were reminded, it was the anniversary of the day in 1776 when
America shook off forever the authority of the parliament and government
of England, which had wanted to tax their people without representation.
It was the day that had given rise to 'the great and glorious republic on the
other side of the Atlantic, that gave an example to the oppressed in every
part of the world, and that provided a place of refuge for the victims of
tyranny.' (The crown of the bloated and failing George IV must have
wobbled in fury and fright at these words.)

The declaration was presented to the public in the issue of the *Register*
of 11 July 1829. It was the lead item and was addressed to 'The Reformers
of the Whole Kingdom.' It began with the words, 'My Friends and Fellow
Countrymen,' although both men put their names to it. Hunt protested
about the use of the word 'my', because Cobbett later apologised and said
it had been an oversight.

The writing was strong and presciently foreshadowed the Last
Labourers' Revolt or Captain Swing riots that were to break out across the
country almost exactly one year later. The times, said the declaration, were
of soaring taxation, injustice, misery and ruin. To describe the distress in
both town and country was beyond the power of tongue or pen. It was felt
by every creature from 'the great landowner down to the most miserable
ditcher or weaver.' A House of Commons committee had just presented
its report on the state of the labouring classes. One witness had described
seeing in Kent (where the revolt would begin in 1830) around forty able
young men attached to carts and wheelbarrows filled with stones. The men

were dragging them around and using the stones to repair turnpike roads. This was not because there was a lack of agricultural work in the parish but because the farmers could not afford to hire them. A Wiltshire magistrate, whose name had been 'carefully suppressed,' stated that the parish supplementary relief granted to a man with six children earning nine shillings a week allowed him to buy bread for his family, but there was nothing left over for drink, fuel, clothing or lodging. Other witnesses said that convicts were better fed and clothed than honest labourers, that the crime rate was rising, and that magistrates were demanding powers to try cases of theft *without trial by jury!* In short, said the declaration, England, whose glory was once a well-fed and well-clad people, had become a nation of paupers and miserable creatures whose nakedness was hardly covered. Even 'the middle class of society' was being dragged down.

Lord John Russell was proposing that seats should be created in the House of Commons for the growing industrial towns of Birmingham, Manchester, Sheffield and Leeds. His lordship believed that the voters should be confined to people owning or renting property worth £10 or £20 a year. Yet that would merely put eight big manufacturers into parliament who would look after their own interests. Property should not be the basis of representation. A reform of the House of Commons should not mean 'shuffling the right of voting from one set of corrupt and dependent people to another of the same sort'. It should mean universal suffrage, annual parliaments and voting by ballot, 'in order that every man who pays a tax may have a vote'. No man should be taxed without his consent. This was the 'very essence of the laws of our forefathers'. Nobody should be deluded by the words '*moderate reform*'. That would be a cheat meaning half measures 'bearing the *name of reform*,' but really intended to prolong the people's oppression. They had to make sure they did not become instruments in the hands of the deceivers:

Listen not to those who may tell you that it is better to *get a little* than to get nothing and that tell you, in the old adage, that *half a loaf is better than no bread*. In this case half a loaf *is no bread*. It is worse than no bread. It can only deceive, only enthral, only prolong your degradation ... if you be deluded to be *content with a part*, you will, under the delusive name of reform, be, if possible, worse off than you now are.

The declaration's message was clear. The goal had to be, '*Annual*

Parliaments, Universal Suffrage, and *Vote by Ballot.*' Nothing else would do.

Ringing words. Yet, when it came to the crunch, Cobbett, whose adherence to one man one vote was never as strong as Hunt's, would water down his opposition to 'moderate reform', and accept 'a little' rather than get nothing. When the time came, Cobbett would agree to half a loaf of bread. Hunt, by contrast, would remain true to his principles and would be reviled and attacked for doing so, not least by Cobbett himself.

At the end of this issue of the *Political Register* was an advertisement for a meeting two days later, on Monday evening, 13 July 1829, in the Theatre of the Mechanics' Institution, Southampton Buildings (a street just off Chancery Lane in Holborn), for the Friends of Radical Reform. Hunt would be in the chair. Admission was on payment of a 'radical rent of One Penny.'

The meeting took place and a Radical Reform Society was launched. Hunt condemned the moderate reform proposals from the 'sham' reformers. Was there a man in the world who would be bold enough to look another in the face and say 'I am entitled to a certain right which you are not entitled to?' asked Hunt. He was supported by Cobbett, who attended, despite his mistrust of organised political organisations, and who was received with tremendous applause and waving of hats.

Almost immediately afterwards, however, cracks between the two men began to appear. Cobbett, the man who had brought back the bones of Tom Paine from America and who loudly applauded the American constitution, was worried about the impact on the image of the society if republicans such as the publisher Richard Carlile and the public speaker John Gale Jones were allowed to participate. His fears were reinforced the next day by the newspapers. *The Times* sniffed that 'the pure Tory blood' would not like 'association with their vulgarities'. Cobbett wrote a letter to Hunt on 16 July. From what he had read and heard, he wrote, 'respectable people' would stop going unless the reform society prevented such men from speaking at the meetings, particularly Gale Jones 'whose name ... is death to all it touches.'

Hunt complained about the suggestion to Cobbett's secretary, Charles Riley, in particular the proposal to ban John Gale Jones who was one of

Hunt's close friends. So Cobbett wrote a second letter to Hunt. Mr Riley had told him what Hunt had said about Mr Jones. He, Cobbett, assured Hunt that he had no reason to believe that there was anything at all objectionable in Mr Jones' moral character. Mr Jones was a speaker by trade and had been so for more than thirty years. A man had as much right to live by his voice as by his pen; but Cobbett was convinced that if he had to take part in any public discussion with Gale Jones, it would destroy any effect he might have on the audience. In short, Cobbett would not participate unless Mr Jones was excluded.

Cobbett ended his letter to Hunt on a positive note: 'Anything that I can do for you in order to further your objects, I shall at all times [be] ready to do just the same as if the impediment had not arisen.' He sent his kindest regards to Mrs Vince, and signed off even more warmly than ever: 'Yours <u>very</u> faithfully, William Cobbett.'

In fact, Cobbett had been uncomfortable about the entire meeting. There was a distinct grumpiness, even scepticism, about his report in the issue of the *Register* of 18 July 1829. Cobbett's lack of ease hinted at the differences that were beginning to emerge between himself and Hunt at this crucial period of history. Hunt, ten years younger, was by comparison a modern man, an organiser, ahead of his times and looking to the future. Cobbett, born in 1763, now aged sixty-six, was still steeped in the ways of the eighteenth century.

Cobbett reported in the *Political Register* that the object of the meeting had been to lay the foundation, 'as it were', of 'this Radical Reform Society', and map out the way it was to proceed. It had been suggested, he wrote, that the discussions at the monthly meetings should mirror the debates being held in parliament. This was a good idea. It would allow the public to compare the relative knowledge and talents of the members of parliament with those of the members of the society or, as Cobbett slightly mockingly called them, the '*out-of-doors collective*'. He also understood that the intention was to agree the subject in advance and so imitate parliament's Order of the Day. He further understood that the '*order of the day*' for the next meeting was to be the question raised by the home secretary, Robert Peel, at the end of the last session of parliament, that there was great inequality in the distribution of the country's wealth –

although whether that would be the order of the day was more than Cobbett could positively say.

The way Cobbett laboured these points in the *Register* is ambivalent. It reads as if he were observing events from a distance rather than being involved himself. He was, however, pleased with the meeting house. The venue was a good one, he wrote. It could hold a thousand people and had benches as in a theatre. It had a pit and a gallery, which was a convenient place for the reporters, and a stage-like platform for the chairman and the executive on which to sit. What was more, Cobbett could promise his readers a houseful of 'attentive, intelligent and well-behaved hearers!' (He expected to win his argument with Hunt over the exclusion of the republicans and, for a while, he did.)

At the end of this issue was a large advertisement for Hunt's latest invention. Hunt had taken out a patent for making a solution to strengthen leather. 'This unrivalled composition will, at a very trifling expense, render the Soles of Boots and Shoes, Aprons of Gigs, Harness and all Leather exposed to the atmosphere completely Waterproof', it read. Users would be protected from 'Colds, Coughs and the numerous train of ills arising from Wet and Cold Feet.' It would protect Health and promote the Economy. 'In bottles at 1s each', guaranteed to keep one person's boots or shoes dry for a Year. The address of the main point of sales was Cobbett's Fleet Street premises, No. 183, where he printed the *Political Register*.

Despite Cobbett's grumpiness about the meeting, the friendship appeared secure and Cobbett became enthusiastic about the Reform Society as he realised its potential – and that he could influence things. The last extant letter he wrote to Hunt was dated 21 July 1829 and was written from Barn Elm farm. Cobbett had had second thoughts about the topic for discussion at the next meeting. It should be sharpened up. Instead of discussing the inequality of wealth, the debate should be whether the distress in the country was the fault of the government or not. The last meeting had caused a buzz in Manchester and Leeds where it got full press coverage, and Cobbett once again signed himself off in his most affectionate way: 'I am my dear Hunt, yours very faithfully, Wm Cobbett.'

A few days later, on 25 July 1829, there was a lot more on Hunt's leather-strengthening invention in the *Political Register*. The subject took up more than half a page. Cobbett thought it was a '*duty to my readers*' to tell them how wonderful it was. He himself had shoes with soles three quarters of an inch thick. They weighed his legs down enormously and did not even keep out the wet. It took up to ten hours to dry them out. Thanks to Hunt, he could now wear a pair of thin-soled shoes for any length of time in wet grass, dirt and water, and his stockings were not even damp. He would only add, Cobbett went on with a sly, glinting sting in his pen, that if Hunt had been a 'bitter and unjust enemy' then he, Cobbett, would have made use of his 'Composition' and not said anything about it (reminding everybody that that was what he considered Hunt had done with Cobbett's substitute coffee recipe). Even if he had never heard of Hunt before, Cobbett went on, he would have said exactly the same about the product and allowed it to be sold, as he was doing, in his shop in Fleet Street. He was convinced that it was one of the most useful inventions ever offered to the public.

Just a week later, on 3 August 1829, at another meeting of the Friends of Radical Reform, Hunt paid generous tribute to his 'friend Mr Cobbett'. Everybody now knew, he said, that Cobbett had been right about the disastrous way the government handled the economy. The legislators were ashamed to acknowledge how right he had been.

Despite one or two little glitches, our two cocks were crowing happily together on the dunghill. Hunt could not have known that just three days before, a letter had been delivered to Cobbett that would wreck everything. The letter's subject matter was going to be a major scandal and it was all poor Nancy's fault.

The trouble began when Cobbett's secretary, Charles Riley, decided that he could no longer tolerate the drunkeness and adultery of his wife. One of her lovers was the Catholic barrister Daniel French, a radical reformer and a friend of Hunt and Cobbett. Beating his wife had failed to deter her, so Riley dispatched her back to her family in Yorkshire. To his utter amazement, Nancy Cobbett thought that Riley had got rid of his wife so that he and Cobbett could have gay sex together, or, as Riley explained to Cobbett in more nineteenth century terms in a horrified letter written on 31 July 1829, so that 'you may indulge with me <u>in unnatural propensities!</u>'

Nancy, he said, was suspicious about why Cobbett was spending so much time at Barn Elm and so little with her and the family in their Kensington house. Riley had been told this startling bit of news by Daniel French, in whom Nancy Cobbett had confided. Now, wrote Riley in his letter to Cobbett, she was bitter and implacable and resolved to persecute and annoy Cobbett through Riley.

The whole thing sounded unbelievable, but there was a history to it. Nancy Cobbett loathed many people, not just Henry Hunt. She resented and disliked Charles Riley, who had been her husband's secretary since 1826. In 1827, the year in which she had tried to cut her throat over Cobbett's renewed friendship with Hunt, Cobbett had withdrawn from his wife and children for seventy-five days, living in another part of the house altogether and allowing nobody else in apart from Riley. It was then that Nancy began to imagine all sorts of horrible things about her husband's secretary. She had hated him with a passion ever since, fuelled by the fact that Cobbett spent a lot of time at his farm at Barn Elm where he was attended by Riley.

As the days passed and the full enormity of the potential scandal hit him, Riley began to panic. He wrote to Cobbett again. He had been like a wild man all week, unable to sleep. They needed to 'think.' A storm was brewing. He feared that Nancy was going to use her suspicions to make Cobbett get rid of him, break with Hunt and abandon the Radical Reform Society and those she called the 'disaffected spouters' (the radical reformers). Riley was petrified that if Cobbett were made to do all of these things, particularly the last one, there would be 'the greatest possible public inquiry.' Meanwhile, Nancy was getting desperate. Riley had been told that she had gone down to Barn Elm the other day, asking where he, Riley was, and crying very much.

The letters continued. There were increasing complications. Nancy Cobbett did not know who had told what to whom, who knew and who did not. Then came more awful news. On the evening of 12 August 1829, three of Cobbett's sons armed with bludgeons ambushed Daniel French at Kensington gravel pits and beat him up. The next day, French wrote to Cobbett saying he would not press charges against them for their father's sake to avoid the scandal being made public. Cobbett bravely wrote back:

French could do whatever he wanted, he said. So French did. He went straight to Bow Street Police Station to get a warrant of arrest for Cobbett's three sons. This was reported in the newspapers.

To begin with, Cobbett was livid with his wife. But as time passed, Cobbett and his sons believed, or wanted to believe, that Daniel French had made the whole story up for some reason, and that Nancy was in no way to blame. The family presented a united front. In the *Political Register* of 15 August 1829, Cobbett included an advertisement for some travel books written by his sons. Anybody would understand him doing this, he wrote, 'if he be the father of sons for whom he justly entertains the greatest affection'.

Riley was furious. He bombarded Cobbett with letters. 'The infamous imputation' could only have come from Mrs Cobbett, insisted Riley. He had been to talk once more to French who had told him '<u>facts</u>' it was literally impossible he could have known, other than via Nancy Cobbett. He, Riley, would not be seeing Cobbett again until the whole affair had been sorted out.

Riley did, however, go and see Hunt, who wrote to Cobbett on Sunday, 16 August 1829. The letter was headed, 'my dear Cobbett,' although the tone was stormy. Mr Riley had told him all about Mrs Cobbett's allegation. Horror stricken, Riley had asked for his advice on what to do and how to behave. As Cobbett knew, Hunt was himself being tormented by a member of his own family (his younger son, Tom, drunk and down and out in London.) He had quite enough on his own hands without interfering in the affairs of others. What was more, he knew Cobbett's too well to want to get involved:

I excused myself to Riley from becoming his advisor on that account and I refused to become an arbitrator where Mrs Cobbett was one of the parties concerned, as <u>I know too much of her conduct to you, formerly as well as latterly, to think of it with any degree of temper.</u>

Hunt had read in the newspapers that Daniel French had applied to Bow Street Police station for a warrant against Cobbett's three sons. Riley was calling in again that afternoon, which was why he was writing the letter. He would give it to Riley to take to Cobbett, although Hunt supposed that Riley would only return to Barn Elm once the matter had been 'cleared up'. Hunt's letter continued: 'This <u>damnable charge will be before the public tomorrow</u> and whoever has made it ought to retract publicly or be <u>publicly punished.</u>'

Hunt was obviously referring to Nancy. Written in his fast flowing handwriting with much underlining, his letter shuddered with a mixture of disgust and shock about what had happened, dismay at the inappropriate behaviour of Cobbett's sons, and rage against Nancy Cobbett. His letter, however, concluded with the affectionate phrase: 'I am my dear Cobbett, Yours very sincerely H. Hunt.'

Cobbett's misery deepened the following day. His three sons were arrested on a warrant of assaulting Daniel French, and the post brought Cobbett yet another letter from Riley. This one was more assertive. Riley demanded that Nancy make a public apology to himself or to Cobbett, otherwise he would consider taking her to court. Even Riley's own wife with all her faults would not have done such a terrible thing to him as Mrs Cobbett had done to her husband.

Riley's language was suspiciously strong. It sounded rather like Hunt had given him some advice after all. What was more, Riley went to a magistrate a few days later to press for Nancy Cobbett's arrest. His request failed. The story was reported in *The Times*.

Manfully, Cobbett soldiered on and re-published an article from the *Morning Herald* in the *Register* of 22 August 1829. It reported the appearance of three of Cobbett's sons, William, John and Richard, before the Bow Street magistrate, Sir Richard Birnie, on an assault warrant obtained against them by Daniel French.

One week later, on 1 September 1829, Riley again wrote to Cobbett. The letter was written from 36 Stamford Street, Hunt's home south of the River Thames. Hunt was away on a business trip, Riley explained. He himself had been very ill with jaundice, which had been brought on by anxiety, and he had been invited to stay at Hunt's home while the latter was away. (It was clear that, despite his desire not to get involved, Hunt had every sympathy for Riley in a predicament caused by the hatred of Nancy Cobbett.)

Cobbett was outraged that Hunt appeared to be taking sides against him, harbouring Riley and continuing to blame Nancy. Nevertheless, he continued business as usual. The *Register* of 5 September 1829 advertised the next Monday meeting of the Radical Reform Society. Hunt would, as usual, chair the meeting, and Cobbett himself would also attend.

Come the Monday evening, the Theatre of the Mechanics' Institution in Holborn was besieged. Thanks to the scandal, the 2,000 seats inside quickly filled up, leaving 3,000 frustrated people outside. Cobbett spoke at length, warning the audience against republicanism. He reported his entire speech in the *Register* a few days later, although he did not mention the fact that he had spoken far longer than the half hour allotted, and that Hunt had ruled him out of time twice. He did report that Daniel French got up to speak as soon as he himself had sat down. According to Cobbett, French declared himself a republican, called for 'universal confusion' (anarchic chaos to bring down the government) and was hissed, hooted and booed for doing so. (Cobbett's claim was later denied by the society, which said it was a 'deliberate falsehood' on the part of Cobbett.) The next day, 8 September 1829, Cobbett wrote a letter to the society's secretary. He resigned his membership and said he would never attend their meetings ever again in any capacity.

On the same day, Hunt wrote to Cobbett. The letter began with one curt word of address, 'Sir'. It went straight to the point. Since his return from the country, he had been speaking to Mr French and others acquainted with Cobbett's family. They confirmed that Cobbett's wife was indeed the one who had made the 'horrible accusation' against her husband and Riley. Hunt had thought long and hard and had found not the slightest reason to alter the good opinion he had always had of the integrity, veracity and honour both of Mr French and Mr Riley. This was an opinion formed from Cobbett's own belief in the pair, which he had urged upon Hunt and even maintained right up to the very day before his sons' 'brutal and cowardly assault' upon Mr French. It was possible that Cobbett might have 'family reasons for sitting down quietly under the disgrace of such a dreadful charge' made by his wife, Hunt went on. Those reasons may have made Cobbett change his mind about making his wife acknowledge the enormity of her crime: '"<u>upon her knees before the Rev Mr Scott</u>" (your own words) that the charge which she had made against you and him was as unfounded as it was malignant.' Hunt believed Riley was innocent, but he had asked him to leave his house until he had taken steps to wipe the stain from his character. Riley had already begun legal proceedings against Cobbett's wife. As Cobbett himself appeared to be doing nothing to clear himself of 'such a detestable charge', Hunt was cutting relations with Cobbett:

... although I give not the slightest degree of credit to your wife for the truth of her accusation against you or him, yet under such circumstances, common decency and common prudence forbid me ever again to meet you in private, and I now beg to close all correspondence between us, requesting that in future you will refrain from calling at my door.

Such was Hunt's fury against the woman who had hated him for so many years, who had repeatedly tried to end his friendship with her husband and who looked down on his beloved Mrs Vince as nothing more than a whore. Because of his own bitterness against Nancy Cobbett, Hunt was unable to take into account the terrible anguish that Cobbett was enduring, torn as he was between his own extreme fury at his wife's behaviour, and the vain hope that somehow his own beloved 'little girl' was not to blame. Hunt was so upset when he wrote his letter to Cobbett that he dated it 8 August 1829. In fact the month was September. Cobbett's son, John, attached a note to the letter stating that it was brought from Fleet Street to his father in Kensington on 9 September 1829, that Cobbett opened the letter immediately and handed it straight back to his son.

It was almost certainly the last letter Hunt ever wrote to Cobbett. It survived along with Hunt's letter to Cobbett of 16 August. They are the only two letters Hunt wrote to Cobbett that are known to be still in existence. They survived because, unlike the rest of Hunt's letters to Cobbett, which were probably destroyed, these two were tucked away in the bundle of papers belonging to the lawyers Edward and George Faithfull, who handled the defence of Cobbett's three sons for their assault on Daniel French. The yellowing documents and papers, crisp dry with age, lie quietly in a box in The Library of Nuffield College, Oxford.

Also tucked away in the Faithfull paperwork is a document entitled 'Defendants' brief'. It runs to forty-one pages and was written by Cobbett in his pain, loneliness and misery sometime after he received Hunt's letter of 8 September 1829. Cobbett wrote the brief to help his lawyers defend his sons in their plea of justification for their assault on French. Some of it is incoherent and rambling. It hinged around Cobbett's wild and muddled belief that the reformers concocted the whole plot to blacken Nancy because they were worried that her hatred of Hunt would persuade Cobbett to leave the Radical Reform Society, thus wrecking the radical cause.

The plot began, wrote Cobbett, at a family tea party at which Daniel French was a guest. French listened as Cobbett's wife and son John criticised Cobbett's connections with Hunt, and the fact that he was mixing with 'bad men.' Afterwards, Cobbett claimed, French went to Riley, both went to Hunt and all three of them hatched the plot against Nancy. Cobbett could prove this from Hunt's last letter to him, in which Hunt 'spoke with the utmost malignity of my sons and anticipated with delight what he calls "public punishment of my wife."' Cobbett was sure that his wife would never have said anything to injure the character of her husband, 'all her anxiety having for years been the fear that I should injure that character by associating with Hunt'.

It is in this Defendants' brief, agonising to read, that Cobbett described how in 1827 Riley had witnessed Nancy 'committing a most violent and ... tragical deed solely because she had just read in the newspaper that I had walked away from the meeting in Waterloo Place arm in arm with this very man.' (Hunt) Cobbett also revealed something else that had occurred in that fateful year of 1827. 'There was, which had never before happened under my roof, a family quarrel,' he wrote. It had involved the children. Nancy took the part of one side, Cobbett the other. He had withdrawn from his wife and family to live in a study in an outhouse in the garden during the day, sleeping at night in a room at the back of the house. He had only communicated with his family by writing: 'I was carrying on a contest for mastership and what I had to guard against was being in the presence of my wife and hearing her plaintive voice and seeing her tears.' The split had lasted seventy-five days until Cobbett resumed family life. Nancy blamed Riley for influencing Cobbett to do 'unpleasant' things and had never forgiven him. It was an unending hostility and must have caused

Riley huge resentment, more than Cobbett could have imagined. That was obviously why Riley had decided to get his own back before he left Cobbett for a new job and had devised this 'villainous scheme'. It was impossible that Nancy had told French those things. Cobbett could clearly see that it was all 'a horrible lie, hatched for the purpose of effecting a separation of me from my family and of gratifying the base passions of the parties.' Riley went to talk to Hunt; Hunt thought that at last he had Nancy Cobbett, his old enemy of twenty years, 'safely within his grasp; black upon her, black upon me or black upon my sons, either was equally delectable to him.'

The brief went on for page after page. Cobbett had never answered Riley's letter. It was more foolish, spiteful and malignant than anything Riley had ever written. Cobbett had not the smallest doubt that the letter had been concocted by Hunt. Riley had become Hunt's 'complete tool'. It was all a 'rascally conspiracy against Mrs Cobbett,' who had expressed her detestation and abhorrence of Hunt to hundreds of people for twenty long years. If Cobbett needed proof of Hunt having been the grand mover, he could find it in the fact that Riley was in Hunt's service and now living in his house in Stamford Street. Cobbett was not sure what motive French might have had. It is plain from reading Cobbett's brief that his wife had vehemently denied that she had ever told such a thing to Daniel French. Cobbett needed to believe her: 'The bare idea of the effect of my believing the story plunged my wife into a state of misery not easy to describe.'

Cobbett's brief was never used or made public. He never made his suspicions about Hunt public either, although eighteen months after the event he made an oblique reference to the episode in the *Register* published 2 April 1831. In the few short lines, Cobbett falsely claimed that he had been the one to end his relationship with Hunt:

Now, my friends, prepare yourselves for real '*matchless black.*' In revenge for my resolution, taken about *eighteen months ago*, to have *nothing more to do with him*, he hatched a conspiracy, the detail of which will, whenever it shall come forth, astound even those most accustomed to contemplate deeds of villainy.

Cobbett's three sons appeared in court on 24 September 1829. The verdict was published in the *Register.* William, John and Richard were found '*Guilty*, but under STRONG PROVOCATION', and were fined for their assault on French. Riley subsequently tried to sue Cobbett and his wife. Nancy committed perjury and signed an affidavit denying she had ever made the allegation. The case never got to court.

Cobbett rode off on a rural ride to Tring in Hertfordshire where he took comfort and consolation from seeing bundles of straw for plaiting outside a shop, a scene just as he had imaginatively described in his *Cottage Economy*. He was also invited to a dinner at the Rose and Crown Inn for about forty-five gentlemen, and addressed them for an hour and a half even though he had a severe cold (the usual sign that Cobbett was run down).

Despite the break, Cobbett did not let the subject drop. Just a week after the trial, in the *Register* of 3 October 1829, he returned to the beating of Daniel French by his sons and blamed everything onto French who, Cobbett wrote, had lain what he must have thought was 'the corner-stone' of Nancy Cobbett's destruction. And then Cobbett wrote some words that must have made Hunt choke. Figuratively-speaking, Cobbett knelt before his wife and publicly grovelled:

If any apology for the boundless rage of my sons were wanted ... it would be found in the character of that MOTHER , the destruction of whose peace, and indeed of whose *life*, was aimed at; that life which had been a life of chastity, of sobriety, of industry, of frugality, of care, and above all things, of incessant, anxious and heroic devotion to her husband and children.

Cobbett's words echoed the sort of thing he had been writing in his *Advice to Young Men* which he was publishing in instalments. Like all Cobbett's writings, the copies sold out as quickly as they were printed. The work glorified his own family life and cast a rosy, apple-pie glow over the Cobbett household. It also crudely condemned women who left their husbands to live with another man. Cobbett can only be admired for writing and producing such a work while the newspapers were busy reporting the salacious details of the Cobbett family scandal.

Did this all add to Hunt's fury? It could well have done. *The Weekly Free Press* reported that Hunt was in the chair at a reform meeting on 21 September 1829, cruelly making many jokes at Cobbett's expense and mocking him for having resigned from the society. Cobbett had never even been a member, Hunt claimed. He had never paid his subscription, although he did not forget to claim his half guinea payment for advertising meetings in the *Register*. Hunt allowed Daniel French to address the meeting at great length and made no attempt to stop him making a derogatory reference to Cobbett's portrait of his wife in *Advice to Young men* as 'a great contradiction'. It was the audience who hissed French down, not Hunt the chairman.

Hunt continued to insult Cobbett at reform meetings. *The Weekly Free Press* followed the cock fight as Hunt attacked Cobbett with words of fire, derisively calling him 'the great hero of Reform', and 'the giant of the press'. Cobbett, he said, was the man to whom they had all looked up to with so much admiration and who, since his withdrawal from the society, had never mentioned the word, reform.

Cobbett could not stand it. He announced in the *Register* of 21 November 1829 that he himself was to give a series of independent lectures in which he would reveal to the people how they could escape the ruin that was menacing so many thousands of industrious families. He used the opportunity to take an oblique swipe at those who professed themselves to be an '*orator.*'

Far from me be the ambition to shine as what the Irish call an *orator*. I have the most thorough contempt for speech-making, having observed throughout my life that the most voluble speech-makers are the greatest fools ... I am for ... no ' *intense eloquence*;' plain matter in plain words, addressed to plain understandings: those are the things that I aim at.

Everybody would have known that Cobbett meant men such as Daniel O'Connell, John Gale Jones – and Henry Hunt.

Cobbett's first lecture took place five days later. The room was packed. Cobbett was overcome with emotion when he saw the audience assembled. The twenty years of calumnies, long and cruel persecutions, merciless, degrading and ruinous imprisonment, exile, bonds, his sufferings of all sorts were wiped away, he wrote subsequently in the *Register*. For the first time in his life, wrote this deeply emotional man, he 'felt his voice falter'.

The reference to the Irish, or to orators, or to both, however, had been extremely ill-advised. As a result, Cobbett's second lecture on 10 December 1829 turned out to be a complete riot. The people who witnessed the event must have dined out on the story for months. It was a pure 'I was there when ... ' occasion. In the *Register* of 19 December, Cobbett re-printed a report from the *Morning Herald* of what happened.

The lecture began at 8 o'clock in the evening. The newspaper described how people began arriving early, crowding against the doors to get in. When the doors opened, they poured in. Soon, every seat in the auditorium was taken, as well as those in the galleries and even on each side of the platform on which the speaker stood. The audience, which included many ladies, appeared to be respectable – except in the gallery to the left of and overhanging the speaker's table, where a particular group of men had taken up the seats. From their 'tattered costume and stupid looks', said the politically very incorrect newspaper, they 'appeared to be of the lowest order even of Irish labourers.' There were about forty of them.

Cobbett arrived attended by three of his sons and several good friends. His lecture lasted two and a quarter hours and included a half an hour of 'most extraordinary interruptions'. They began in the gallery, with first mutterings and then rude shouts. 'Silence! Silence! Turn him out!' shouted the crowd. It was impossible to tell who was doing the shouting because of the shades around the gas lamps. One of Cobbett's friends, followed by two of his sons, climbed up with the help of the audience to the gallery twelve feet above the platform. They hurled themselves over 'into the middle of the enemy's quarters', encouraged by the hissings, execrations and hootings of the audience. There was a scuffle and they fell back defeated, tumbling down into the crowds beneath. Cobbett tried to go on with his lecture but the uproar from the gallery resumed.

It was a scene of confusion and warfare. Another attempt at an assault on the gallery was made. Suddenly, a wooden partition at the end collapsed exposing some internal windows behind it. These opened out into an inner chamber. The windows were thrown open revealing two of 'Mr Peel's policemen!' (They had obviously been stationed there to eavesdrop on Cobbett's speech.) Two of the troublemakers were thrown through the windows, arrested and taken to Bow Street Police station. There were no more interruptions.

Cobbett thought he recognised the faces of many of the people who disrupted his lecture. He was convinced that they were some of the Irish labourers he had once hired to work for him. It had all been a plot, he wrote. He did not think it had been an establishment plot, but he was certain, 'the monsters were hired and paid: no doubt of that'. Rightly or wrongly, Cobbett pointed the finger of blame squarely at Hunt. The gang at the meeting, Cobbett claimed in the *Register* eighteen months later, had been 'hired by the VILLAIN par excellence, to interrupt me at one of my lectures.'

The tumultuous year, which had begun so promisingly with the pair in harmony, collapsed in sad disunity. 1830 arrived with Hunt continuing his attacks against Cobbett, and using his speeches at the Reform Society meetings to pummel him mercilessly. Hunt endlessly reminded his audiences how Cobbett had fled to America in 1817. Now, 'Doctor Cobbett', 'the great enlightener of the age', 'the monarch of the press', 'the literary Go-liar', had altogether lost sight of reform. 'Mr Cobbett is afraid to join us, and if there be any bustle, he will scamper off to America once more', jeered Hunt, who even chose to appear on the platform side by side with Daniel O'Connell. Such was the fury and disgust of Hunt against Cobbett, who had chosen to stand by his wife, the woman Hunt hated, instead of publicly humiliating her for her vile allegations, as Hunt had demanded and Cobbett had initially threatened to do. When Hunt told his audience in the Theatre of the Mechanics' Institution in Southampton Buildings that people were mistaken if they thought he was envious of Mr Cobbett, he was telling the truth. He was not jealous of Cobbett; he was jealous of his choice.

Once again, Cobbett ploughed his lonely furrow. In April 1830, he told readers of the *Register* that for more than twenty-five long years, he had been the one really sharp and efficient thorn in the side of the system. He alone had been the nation's teacher, the great source of political knowledge:

I have been the evening and the day star, the moon and the sun and the aurora of the press; that all the other parts of it have come twinkling behind me, shining now and then, indeed, but shining with a borrowed light.

It was inevitable that Cobbett and Hunt continued to bump into each other at public occasions. On 29 July 1830, *The Times* presented a bittersweet cameo picture of how both men had turned up early the previous day for a meeting of the City of London Liverymen in the council chamber of the Guildhall. The meeting had been called to draw up an address to the new king, William IV. (Cobbett had already written in the *Register* that there would be no 'slave-like crawling' from him!) *The Times* reported that everybody was astonished to see Cobbett there (he rarely attended City meetings). The newspaper described the mood: 'A great deal of amusement was expected, from the well-known animosity which each bears to the other; and those who attended for "the fun of the thing" were much gratified.' As soon as the requisition was read out, continued *The Times*, both men stepped forward together to speak. Hunt at once

A sign for a radical pub, featuring Cobbett's gridiron and a pot of Hunt's Matchless Blacking. 1830.
After a copy in the British Museum

objected to Cobbett addressing the liverymen, because he had not signed the requisition. Hunt did not press his opinion, and Cobbett was allowed to begin. To loud laughter, Cobbett explained that although he had been a liveryman for several years, he had never before addressed them, unlike 'Mungo here, and Mungo there and Mungo everywhere.' He was doing so that day, said Cobbett, 'prompted by a sense of justice and modesty (loud laughter, in which Mr Cobbett joined), well, by justice at any rate.'

(The reference to Mungo was an old in-joke within the City of London. 'Mungo' was a former Lord Mayor who was renowned for popping up at many public meetings and speaking at length. Cobbett used it to refer to Hunt on this occasion. In the past, he and Hunt had employed it against Sir Francis Burdett.)

Cobbett finally got round to reading out his proposed address to King William. Then it was Hunt's turn. Again *The Times* enjoyed the occasion: 'Mr Hunt stood forward amidst cheers and laughter. The manner in which he looked at Cobbett, who stood by his seat, was particularly amusing. The hall was frequently in a roar of laughter.' Hunt again explained why he had interrupted 'the modest gentleman who stood next to him' and who had no need to refer to Hunt, as 'Mungo here and there and everywhere.' The 'worthy gentleman' was more like Mungo, said Hunt to loud laughter. The gentleman had changed his mind and opinions many times over the years, while he himself had never abandoned a single principle in his life.

The Times reported with relish how Mr Hunt drew attention to Mr Cobbett throughout his speech in a 'very comical way'. The liverymen voted for Hunt's 'long and strong' address to the king by a large majority, and Cobbett left the meeting, reported the newspaper, 'greatly dissatisfied'.

The Times would have said that, wouldn't it, and Cobbett probably was displeased. He did not like to lose, but, surprisingly, he did not appear to bear Hunt any grudges. Two days later, he supported Hunt in the pages of the *Register* of 30 July 1830 in a battle he had had at a reform meeting at the Freemason's Tavern. The meeting had been called by the 'sham' reformers including John Cam Hobhouse, Sir Francis Burdett and Joseph Hume. Cobbett re-printed an article from the *Morning Chronicle* and told his readers to pay particular attention to the passages he had marked with italics. Some of them were about Hunt's reception and performance.

'*Mr Henry Hunt* had arrived a few minutes before and as he walked up to the table *was loudly cheered*'. When Mr Hunt rose, 'some *few persons* called him to order but the *great majority cheered him loudly*'. The chairman '*spoke in high terms of Mr Hunt*', although he asked the audience not to keep on cheering him. Somebody got up to thank Mr Hunt for his '*assistance*' in the cause of reform. Hunt opposed Burdett's proposal of any connection with the Birmingham Political Union, which wanted to confine the vote to householders, and proposed that '*all* Englishmen should *enjoy the right of voting at elections*'. The resolutions favoured '*universal suffrage*', with the '*protection of the ballot*', and that all elections should begin and close '*on one and the same day*'.

It was a novel way to praise somebody without wanting to appear to be praising them. In fact, just in case anybody had missed it, Cobbett then went on to tell his readers that it was all thanks to 'Hunt' that the resolutions were phrased the way they were. He also said that the newspapers should not have left out Hunt's speeches, and that overall the report had been, as usual, a 'foul' one in its discrimination against Hunt. It looked very much as if Cobbett was making subtle, friendly overtures to Hunt, and indeed he was, although Hunt was studiously ignoring all Cobbett's wavings of the flag of peace.

Later in the year, in November 1830, John Gale Jones spoke at the Rotunda meeting house just south of Blackfriars Bridge. (The Rotunda had become the fashionable venue for major political meetings.) He commented on the reconciliations and the quarrels between Cobbett and Hunt. It was a rare public reference by one of the radical reformers to the relationship between the two men. Gale Jones' words were reported in *The Times* on 22 November 1830:

Two suns could not, he said, exist in the same hemisphere and those two gentlemen could never long agree together. Like Peachum and Lockit in the Beggars' Opera, they were constantly at variance, but became reconciled as each considered the other necessary to him.

Gale Jones' cynical remarks were made just days after Hunt publicly disassociated himself from Cobbett, Richard Carlile and Gale Jones himself. There had been serious rioting outside the Rotunda, which had precipitated the resignation of the government of the Duke of Wellington. Hunt had no intention of being linked either to the rioting or to the radical speakers who were being blamed by the authorities for causing it, especially Cobbett, as contemporary Home Office papers reveal. This time the two men were never to be reconciled again, because, much to Cobbett's total and utter jealousy, Hunt was about to become a member of parliament for Preston in the incoming pro-reform Whig government of Lord Grey. Hunt's election swept away any attempts at any reconciliation Cobbett might have been hoping for. The two cocks resumed their public fight, jabbing and pecking at each other with vicious bloody beaks, even as they continued to mourn the loss of their friendship.

16
The Cock Fight

Hunt got his heart's desire to become a member of parliament without even trying. His election in December 1830 as an MP for Preston was completely unexpected. Wellington's government had collapsed in the November after the Duke, frightened by what he saw as the revolutionary unrest in London and the Captain Swing riots across the country, unwisely declared his opposition to a reform of parliament. A reform-minded Whig ministry led by Earl Grey was swiftly appointed at the beginning of December. As part of Grey's reshuffle of the government, Edward Stanley, son of the thirteenth earl of Derby and a member of parliament for Preston, was given the job as Ireland's chief secretary. This meant he had to re-submit himself to the Preston electorate in a by-election. When Stanley announced that he would not campaign against the Corn Laws or support a secret ballot, Preston's reformers decided to take a chance and put forward Hunt as a candidate, even though he had stood unsuccessfully for the seat only six months earlier in the general election that had followed the death of George IV.

Hunt was on a business trip in Somerset when he heard the news about his nomination. He rushed to Preston, arriving late in the evening on 13 December 1830. The polling was practically over and his win was assured. He was officially declared the winner just two days later with 3,730 votes. It was a marvellous moment in Hunt's life. He was unable to take up his seat immediately because of a delay caused by Stanley's quibbles over the vote count, so he enjoyed himself and travelled around the area where he was applauded, feted, wined, dined and cheered by crowds of enthusiastic supporters. The celebrations continued all the way back to London.

The one sour note, apart from those from the usual reptile press, of course, came from Cobbett. He sat down to pen a lead article for the issue of the *Register* published on 18 December 1830. It was addressed to the people of Preston and was filled with latent menace against Hunt. 'My Excellent Friends, That which you have now done has given delight to every good man in England who is a competent judge of the matter', wrote Cobbett. Amongst all the millions who were delighted, he went on, he believed there was not one man who felt '*half so much delighted at it as I do.*' It was altogether an enchanting picture, trilled Cobbett. The back of the picture at least had its charms and so did the wooden frame that went round it.

It all sounded promising, but this was not the writing of the Bristol election or Spa Fields. Cobbett's words dripped with irony. There was very little about Hunt and his qualities. The spotlight was focused on Cobbett. How pleased Cobbett was that the proud and insolent 'STANLEY', who had once referred to him as 'the *person* on my right hand,' had been cast down. It was a triumph against the rich employers, who had told their men not to vote for Cobbett on pain of starvation, when he had stood as a candidate in Preston. How embarrassed 'the fellows *in the House itself.*' – Hobhouse, Burdett and Baring – would be. They now faced having to deal with 'the Blacking-man' in the House of Commons. Once again, Cobbett re-printed Hunt's riposte to Baring's insults in the House of Commons in 1826 in which Hunt had warned Baring to watch out for the time when he might become an MP. 'There, Baring, take that,' Cobbett crowed. How would he get down 'the bitter bolus' and manage to call Hunt 'the *honourable gentleman*.' How would the others manage? Yet they would have to address Hunt in such a manner or they would not be able to reply to anything he might say in the Commons. How clever Cobbett was that he had documented everything in the *Political Register*. What a convenient thing it was. When any event took place, he only had to look back to the time when he had foretold it in the *Register*

It was Hunt's triumph, but Cobbett was stealing the credit and the limelight. There was, he knew, a question on everybody's lips in Preston, Cobbett continued triumphantly: 'WHAT PART AM I PREPARED TO ACT towards the man that you have chosen?' Cobbett would blot out of his mind anything injurious Hunt might have done to him, but only on

condition that Hunt '*do his duty*'. Cobbett would be ready to ask people
for their patience and indulgence towards Hunt when he met 'the *great
difficulties*' that he would have to deal with. The people expected a lot and
they had a right to expect it, but Hunt had to be given time. As Cobbett
would, they should put the most candid construction upon Hunt's every
act, 'whether of commission or of omission.' The London newspapers
were going to misrepresent him; they were going to hold him up in a
'ludicrous light', get a laugh against him, '*suppress* what he says,' Cobbett
continued, but they would not and should not succeed in any of those
things.

They would, of course, and Cobbett knew this perfectly well. What
was more, Cobbett himself was going to do it all too. Cobbett himself was
going to be one of Hunt's greatest enemies outside the House of
Commons.

Hunt was well aware of this. The same post that delivered to him his
copy of the *Register* also brought him a private letter written by somebody
who knew Cobbett very well. Hunt would make its contents public nearly
a year later in an *Address* written 29 October 1831:

> I was cautioned (which was not necessary) not to believe a word of what he had written
> in that Register, for it was all an hypocritical falsehood – adding that master, meaning
> the old ruffian, was raving about the room, tearing his hair and vowing vengeance against
> me, and damning and blasting all the men and women of *Preston*, as a set of ungrateful
> rogues and ————. His envy, hatred and malice were worked up to the highest pitch
> of frenzy imaginable. Thus you have, my friends, the real, the true cause of all his hatred
> to me.

As Hunt said, the letter had not really been necessary. Cobbett's fury
and jealousy oozed from the pages of the *Register*. Between Christmas and
the resumption of parliament in February 1831, Cobbett returned
obsessively to the subject of Hunt, MP for Preston. He re-published
newspaper articles describing Hunt's triumphant visit to Manchester on
New Year's day, how he was met by a barouche drawn by four horses with
out-riders dressed in scarlet liveries, and how he had addressed the
cheering crowds at St Peter's Field, promising to bring the perpetrators of
the Peterloo Massacre to justice. There was 'Mr HUNT'S Public entry
into London', the postillions in dresses of crimson silk with banners

preceding him, and the assembled multitude who accompanied him through the cities of London and Westminster to his house.

Far from being a celebration of Hunt's success, it was, in fact, a subtle way to undermine Hunt further. Mr Hunt should be careful, wrote the green-eyed Cobbett, those demonstrations merely added to the weight of the burden he was taking on. But then the Preston crest was a game-cock, was it not? At the end of the election, a victory flag had been raised. Hunt was represented on it as a 'RED COCK' crowing and clapping his wings, while a dunghill 'YELLOW COCK' (Stanley) ran away. So, went on Cobbett sweetly, Hunt was not bragging in his speeches. He really was resolved to do what he said he would do. Well then, he, Cobbett, approved and applauded all the cheers and processions. Let there be more of them. Hunt was too experienced not to know that the demonstrations by the people indicated '*proportionate expectations*'. His acceptance of them therefore revealed that he was prepared '*for the satisfaction of such expectations*', wrote Cobbett remorselessly.

Poor Hunt – and poor Cobbett. He itched to be there with Hunt, sleeves rolled up, doing it too. His frustration is palpable. He poured out advice, anticipating how Hunt would and should behave as an MP, and, willy nilly, complimenting his old sparring partner. It was a shame Mr Hunt had been unable to attend the end of the parliamentary session, wrote Cobbett. He would have challenged the length of the seven-week break while the farm workers (who were by now smashing up the new threshing machines in the Last Labourers' Revolt) were being hanged. Mr Hunt would have been calling for an inquiry into the unrest in the country.

Cobbett's bile returned a few days before Hunt was due to take up his seat, when Cobbett learned about his plan to set up a London office from which his campaign for reform could be co-ordinated. Hunt had begun to realise the magnitude of the task that lay before him. Before he had even begun the job, he said, his desk was piled high with paperwork that had flooded in from all over the country. The work was too much to get through on his own. (This was in the days long before MPs were paid salaries or expense allowances.) Hunt's idea was revolutionary. Cobbett jumped on it with malice. It was the chink he had been looking for. Let us hope, wrote Cobbett in the issue of the *Register* of 22 January 1831, that the people of Preston would not have to hear 'these faltering accents of anticipated failure; these sighs heaved up by conscious want of ability or want of something else, which it would, after all that has been promised to us and hoped by us, break one's heart to name.'

(Cobbett's words would come back to haunt him. He himself was to find out about the weight of parliamentary business. It was to contribute to a nervous breakdown, put the final nail in the coffin of his marriage and hasten the end of his life. Hunt survived his time as an MP, but his health was also impaired and towards the end of his term he had a stroke which presaged his death.)

When parliament resumed on 3 February 1831 after the Christmas holiday, Hunt entered the House of Commons in St Stephen's Chapel to take up his seat, his head held high, a proud man. There is a contemporary description of him as a 'comely, tall, rosy, white-headed' man. The political diarist Charles Greville gave a fine picture of Hunt: 'His manner and appearance very good, like a country gentleman of the old school, a sort of rural dignity about him, very civil and good-humoured.' It should have been Hunt's moment of triumph. In fact, he faced a bleak reality. Given the ticket of radical and uncompromising reform on which he had won his seat, he stood on his own in a sea of 657 other, largely hostile men. He also knew that his former friend and hero, William Cobbett, blinded by jealousy, was now ranked among his most powerful opponents.

After he had taken the oath, Hunt jumped straight into the fray, presenting petitions from Somerset and Manchester. The demands were largely pure Cobbettian in tone and included calls for a reduction in taxes, the abolition of sinecure jobs and the Corn Laws, and a reform of parliament in the shape of one man one vote and voting by ballot. Over the following days, Hunt spoke eloquently about the poor living in hovels and trying to exist on five shillings a week. He told of the inhuman conditions, high taxation and the inequality and injustice that had led to the labourers' riots across the country, disturbances for which he and Cobbett were being unfairly blamed. He described how the rioters had smashed the threshing machines of the Wiltshire MP, John Benett, (Hunt's old adversary) who had promptly said: 'I see how it is. Cobbett and Hunt are at the bottom of all this.'

This was a connection Hunt did not want. As he laid out his stall in the House of Commons, he explained how he planned to address the House. He was a new inexperienced MP, he said. He hoped his fellow members would make allowances and give him credit for wishing to avoid any personal offence or any lack of respect towards the House. *Hansard* reported what Hunt said thus:

He trusted that as he was so young a member, they would extend to him the indulgence his inexperience required and give him credit for every wish to avoid, in the delivery of his sentiments, anything approaching towards personal offence or any want of respect towards the regulations of that House.

Hunt followed this by once again dissociating himself from the fire-raising speakers at the Rotunda, including Cobbett. (The *Morning Chronicle* included Cobbett's name in Hunt's list. *Hansard* did not.)

Cobbett took up his cudgel. One would have thought, he snorted in the issue of the *Register* 19 February 1831, that Hunt was a 'diffident beardless boy, taking his station before his time amongst men.' In his speeches outside the House of Commons, Cobbett went on, Hunt had sworn all sorts of things that he would do to the '*rips*' and the '*drunken blackguards,*' all the men whom he was now so anxious not to offend. '*Is this the same man?*' howled Cobbett, as he laid into what he grotesquely called 'the hackerings, the stammerings, the bogglings, the blunderings and the cowerings down of this famous Cock'. As for Hunt's statement dissociating himself from Cobbett, 'the shaft at me is merely venomous', he wrote. Everybody would be rushing to congratulate him over the fact that Hunt had disclaimed all ties with him 'after the exhibition which he has made in parliament'.

Cobbett, of course, was half blind with jealousy. He also took exception to the position that Hunt adopted right from the start on the main question itself, that of parliamentary reform.

Earl Grey has gone down in history as the man who led the government that reformed the House of Commons through the Great Reform Act of 1832. It is quite true that the Act abolished the notorious rotten boroughs, including Old Sarum and Gatton, and gave representation to the big manufacturing towns. In the boroughs, occupiers of houses worth at least £10 a year in rental value got the vote. In the counties, the long-established forty-shilling a year freeholders kept their right to vote. Overall, however, the Act slashed the numbers of voters; there were many anomalies and pocket boroughs were still legion. The middle classes were made happy, but the labouring classes, who had petitioned so hard for one man one vote, were left out in the cold. Real power remained securely in the hands of land and property owners. The gravy train continued to rumble along the tracks. The concept of universal suffrage was never on the agenda nor was there any question of voting by ballot. The Act made no impact at all upon the potential for violence surrounding elections, or the practices of bribery and corruption. The bill was the minimum that was thought necessary to quell riots and disturbances. It was nothing more than a sop to paper over the cracks, keep the people quiet and avoid a French-style revolution. As Cobbett and Hunt had warned in their declaration of 1829, both Whigs and Tories hoped it would put the lid on the reform demands of the radicals forever. Lord John Russell, who introduced the reform bill in the House of Commons, earned the name of 'Finality Jack' because he said that it would settle the question once and for all.

When Hunt joined the House of Commons in February 1831, he was under no illusions about the shape any Act was likely to take; but he made an important pledge. He had always fought for the right of everyone to have a vote, he said. If the government's concept of parliamentary reform did not match his own, he would still vote for it at every stage. He would, however, continue to fight, argue and plead for the sort of parliamentary reform in which he believed.

It was not going to be as easy as that. Hunt himself would get bogged down and tripped up in debates over the minutiae of who exactly should get the vote, and the newspapers – and Cobbett – would wilfully twist and misinterpret what he said and did. Nevertheless, even as he voted with the government, Hunt remained true to the principle of one man one vote, although he came under attack from all sides for taking up this position. People failed to see how he could vote in favour of something he was at the same time arguing against. His main attacker was Cobbett who argued that Hunt's position handed ammunition to the opponents of reform. Cobbett even claimed that Hunt was being paid by the boroughmongers (in this case, the Tories who, needlessly, feared the loss of control over seats in the House of Commons) to prevent the bill's passage through parliament. In a letter published in the *Morning Herald* on 7 March 1831, Cobbett wrote that every sincere radical reformer should be contented with the Whigs' proposal. He himself had argued the principle of one man one vote for a decade, but its omission from the bill did not prevent him 'from entertaining a deep sense of gratitude towards those who, under the gracious sanction of the King, have tendered to the people this mighty good.' (And Cobbett accused Hunt of being obsequious.)

Cobbett needed to believe that it was one of the greatest moments in British history. He was the one who had been working so hard for so long to bring about a reform of parliament, writing away slavishly throughout the decades. He was the instigator of everything, the mover the shaker. It was his pen and his pen alone that was at last producing results. He had devoted his whole life to achieving it; he had gone to prison over it and been bankrupted and mercilessly reviled for it. The Reform Act had to be great, as he wrote in the *Register* of 12 March 1831:

This measure is one the adoption of which will form a really New Era in the affairs of England, aye, and of the *world* too. It will produce *greater effects* than any that has been adopted since the Protestant Reformation.

Hunt pressed on, a lone voice inside the House of Commons, sardonically offering throat lozenges to fellow MPs who dried to drown his speeches out by coughing. He himself had no need of his lozenges. His years as an orator had fine-tuned his voice. There was a description of his technique in *Blackwood's Magazine*:

He pauses for a moment, until the unanimous clamour of disgust is at its height, and then, re-pitching his note, apparently without an effort, lifts his halloo as clear and distinct above the storm, as ever ye heard a minster bell tolling over the racket of a village wake.

Hunt needed every technique he could muster as he kept his word to support the bill. He grimly presented petition after petition from towns, which had originally called for annual parliaments, one man one vote and voting by ballot, but which now said they were happy to back the government's plans for reform. As he did so, he continued to argue that the bill did not go nearly far enough, and bitterly decried the unjust accusations made against him by everybody, including Cobbett, that he was doing everything in his power to defeat reform.

Cobbett sniped and mined away at Hunt, repeating himself endlessly. How dared Hunt announce in the House of Commons that he was cutting all ties with him when Cobbett had nothing to do with republicans such as Richard Carlile or John Gale Jones, he wrote in the issue of the *Political Register* of 19 February 1831. Was this the man who was never intimidated? Was this the '*red game cock*,' who clapped his wings while the yellow dunghill cock ran away? 'Ooh! ooh! who-o-se afraid!' he mocked. Hunt's speech in the Commons calling for a pardon for rioting labourers had been received with roars of laughter and monstrous contempt. Not one argument he used was worth a straw, raved Cobbett, and what was the result? 'Motion negatived without a division.'

Cobbett's bile overflowed in the issue of the *Register* of 12 March 1831. He had known all along the people would be disappointed with Hunt. His triumphal journey back to London had been nothing more than an 'idle parade from Preston to London'. Hunt should have been dashing back down south to the aid and protection of the six hundred labourers then in prison in his own native county. Then, of course, there was the ridiculous proposal to establish a 'parliamentary office' to assist the Cock in his duties as an MP, to be paid for by the radical reformers! Meanly, Cobbett referred to Hunt's speeches, in which he pointed out the inadequacies of the reform bill, as 'stuff'. What was more, people were not to believe a word of it when Hunt declared he had never criticised the House. He had done so, many times, and violently too. To prove it, Cobbett extracted quotes from all the newspapers that he himself had always said told pure lies and were never to be believed.

At this stage of the game, Hunt had been in the House of Commons for just six weeks. Yet Cobbett had already diminished his election triumph, sneered at him as the Preston Cock, ignored or twisted his speeches, accused him of working for the Tories and charged him with undermining the reform bill. Hunt had had enough. Four days later, on 16 March 1831, he sat down at his writing desk. Dipping his pen into the ink, he began his reply. His attack took the shape of a public letter to the People of Preston. He called it a twopenny exposure of Cobbett's fourteen pennyworth of falsehoods. The letter was headed '*The Preston Cock's reply to the Kensington Dunghill*'. It was a sensational howl of fury. Hunt poured out all his frustration, misery and bitterness over the years against Cobbett, rooting into every closet he could find. He did it reluctantly, he said, but it had to be done.

> To attempt to controvert in detail the misrepresentations and falsehoods of a notorious and proverbial liar is a task that I have neither time nor inclination to undertake. But as this *backbiter* of every man that ever was acquainted with him, the *calumniator* of every one who ever rendered him a service has thought proper to put forth his impotent venom and to level his cowardly and malevolent attack upon me in an address to you, the People of Preston, in his last lying Register, I feel it a duty ... to state the reasons that have caused the wretched creature thus to assail me.

And Hunt did so in searing detail. He had known the 'cowardly being' since 1802, he continued (the year Cobbett launched the *Register*; their first meeting was in 1805). He knew Cobbett when he was prosecuted over the flogging of the Ely soldiers, when, 'to save his carcase from imprisonment', Cobbett had offered to stop writing if the government would stop the court action against him. When Cobbett was imprisoned in Newgate, Hunt had devoted a whole year to visiting him, and did all sorts of kind and friendly things. Cobbett's letters to him showed how grateful he had been, or at least had pretended to be. When he, Hunt, was himself locked up in Ilchester Bastile, how did Cobbett repay his kindness? So far from ever visiting him, the coward had taken every opportunity to abuse and vilify Hunt in his lying *Register*. Cobbett had even praised the gaoler who was prosecuted for torturing the prisoners.

Hunt had known Cobbett in 1816, when he wrote in favour of universal suffrage one week and then opposed it the next. He had known Cobbett in 1817, when, 'like a dastardly coward', he fled to America to escape his creditors, including all the little shopkeepers and tradesmen in Botley, and left everybody in the lurch. While Cobbett was in America, Hunt scribbled on furiously, he urged the reformers '*to forge Bank of England Notes* ... thus did the cowardly hypocrite instigate others to risk their lives by *committing forgery,* while he took care always to save his own filthy carcass from any risk whatever.' In fact, Hunt hissed, he knew enough of those sort of tricks of 'the Dunghill of Kensington' to fill a book as large as a Bible. He would reserve them for a future occasion. Despite everything, Hunt went on, friends had brought the two men together.

They had shaken hands and begun working together in public once more, although Hunt found Cobbett 'the most selfish and treacherous ally'. They continued together until the end of 1829 when Cobbett's wife, having previously cut her own throat, accused him to Daniel French of having committed a detestable and loathsome crime. Cobbett swore that she should beg his and Riley's pardon upon her bare knees in the presence of the Rev. Mr Scot, but then did everything he could to hush the matter up. Hunt had written to Cobbett telling him never to call at his door again. This was surely plain language that nobody could misunderstand. But 'the old dotard' did not give up:

... the mean, dirty, grovelling knave again cast his net, again put forth his slimy and pestilential web of sophistry, in order to get me once more within the grasp of his worse than deadly, his blasting fangs. I resisted all his attempts, public and private, whether put forth as feelers in his Register, or whether urged by those who professed to be mutual friends. My answer to all was the same – 'I have twice shaken the ruffian old beast from my back, he shall never fix his filthy carcass upon my shoulders again; I will have no connection with him privately or publicly.'

At the end of this ferocious public letter to Cobbett, Hunt included a copy of a petition he intended to present to the House of Commons a few days later. It was a list of complaints made against Cobbett by a group of Irish labourers whom he had hired a few years previously on controversial terms of engagement. Instead of paying them money, they claimed, Cobbett had paid them with daily rations of 'disgusting food'. This included coarse black filthy Indian corn and stinking cheese. The petition begged for the practice to be outlawed. 'Now, my friends,' wrote Hunt triumphantly, 'what will you say to such a thing having lived deluding the public for so many years, under the pretence of being a friend to the poor?' Cobbett, Hunt announced, was nothing less than a 'proverbial liar'.

The Preston Cock's reply to the Kensington Dunghill sold out repeatedly as soon as it was published. It was reissued at least four times in that month of March 1831 alone. The shouts of rage echo down the centuries. The fury and emotion that Cobbett felt when he read Hunt's 'Reply to the Kensington Dunghill' are almost palpable. He pored over every word, storing it all up for future reference. The Irishmen's petition convinced him that Hunt must have had a hand in organising the horrible disturbances at his lecture in December 1829. Cobbett also picked up Hunt's references to him as 'the thing' and a 'proverbial liar', and turned the insults mercilessly and relentlessly against Hunt himself. The gloves were off. Cobbett launched full-scale war on the man who had been for so long his 'dear Hunt,' and whom he had tried – and failed – to win back, as Hunt so humiliatingly revealed to the public. Cobbett outdid all the reptile press together in his attacks against Hunt, even the ones he so picturesquely called in the *Register* of 16 July 1831: 'the stupid OBSERVER, the savage OLD TIMES, the dirty puking thing called the GLOBE, the vagabond COURIER, the shuffling CHRONICLE'. These

'Old Grill and the Truck System'
Hunt drags Cobbett along by his gridiron. He points to a ration of bread and meat on the floor, on which a dog is peeing, and says, 'Here's a fellow that calls himself the poor Man's friend and makes his Labourers take a shillingsworth of bad Articles for a day's work.' In return, Cobbett says, 'Oh if I don't Register you for this.' It follows the presentation to parliament in 1831 by Hunt of a petition from some of Cobbett's labourers.
Robert Seymour, 1831.
© The Trustees of the British Museum

newspapers paled into insignificance compared with what Cobbett did to Hunt with the full force of his 'gigantic' pen.

As Cobbett had predicted, Hunt was hounded by the mainstream newspapers. They turned Hunt's integrity and steadfastness in his beliefs into a weapon to be deployed against him. Cobbett used their attacks and built on them. In the *Register* of 30 April 1831, he re-printed an article from the *Morning Chronicle*. It had been written after the dissolution of parliament and before the snap election of late spring 1831, and followed on from a visit by Hunt to Manchester and the site of Peterloo:

No popular idol, for a long series of years, has had such a tumble from the high pinnacle of his celebrity as the *ex-member for Preston*. Wherever he appears, he is pelted ... in one place they break his blacking bottles, in another they burn all his labels, in a third they burn a 'counterfeit resemblance' of 'the orator's person.'

Part of the report was misleading and the burning bit was untrue. Hunt had enjoyed a rapturous reception in the north of England, particularly in Manchester. But that did not stop Cobbett from re-printing the article and similar. Despite Cobbett's own attacks on newspaper lies, he freely quoted them in his war against Hunt.

In 1832, Hunt brought an action for libel against *The Times*. The trial took place at the Court of Exchequer on 9 February 1832. It was *The Times* that had first reported the claim that Hunt's effigy had been burnt in Manchester at the site of Peterloo. The line had been picked up and used in hundreds of publications – including Cobbett's *Register* – although Hunt did not mention it by name. Hunt launched into a general attack about the lies, disinformation and misinformation that were being published about him in the newspapers. His trade, he said, had been destroyed as a result of the Manchester story. His men dared not go through the streets and his family had been threatened by a mob which had gathered outside his house.

Hunt won £50 damages against *The Times*.

Cobbett shamelessly published a report of the court case two weeks later. He headlined it 'AMUSING TRIAL!' His report highlighted in italics Hunt's complaints about the impact on his personal life. Cobbett also re-produced yet again the lying lines that had appeared in *The Times*, a version of which Cobbett himself had used in the *Register*.

The recreant Hunt has been burnt in effigy on the famous field of Peterloo where he has appeared so often. There were more persons to be seen dancing about the ashes than ever attended him on the most popular occasions.

Cobbett knew exactly what he was doing. In a private letter written shortly afterwards to his daughter Anne, he gloated over how he had 'put down the scoundrel Hunt by making people ashamed to name him'. Cobbett stressed that his letter was to be read by the whole family (to make sure that somebody would read it out to his wife).

Cobbett's campaign in the *Register* against Hunt was indeed brilliant. The avalanche of insults from his pen became more twisted, manic and surreal as time passed. Hunt went from being the formal 'Mr Hunt' to 'THE LIAR', and the 'Preston Cock', to having no name as an amorphous diseased 'thing'. Cobbett jealously scrutinised every line of Hunt's speeches in the press, jabbing over words and pecking over phrases, even though Hunt endlessly complained that all his speeches were misreported by the parliamentary hacks. The more Hunt said in the House of Commons that was pure Cobbettian, the greater Cobbett's rage appeared to be. There were very few issues of the *Register*, through 1831 and much of 1832, which spared Hunt. Page after page was filled with Cobbett's bile against his former friend and political partner. Vitriol poured from his pen as he twisted and misinterpreted Hunt's speeches, often cutting Hunt out of debates altogether even when he had been the principal speaker. Cobbett rejoiced at how Hunt was treated with 'monstrous contempt' by his fellow MPs. When Hunt's cogent and compelling arguments were squashed flat and greeted with roars of laughter, Cobbett laughed too. In the *Register* of 2 April 1831, he poured scorn on the voters of Preston who had elected Hunt. They could not have chosen a greater fool, bully or coward as their MP, he wrote. Shakespeare or Ben Johnson might have given them his match in Pistol or Bobadil, but the Preston voters could not have found a greater 'LIAR' anywhere else in real life or in fiction. They were not to blame, Cobbett continued. Their deception had done everybody a favour:

You have lifted the senseless and malignant thing up, that he *might be seen by all* ... Such a thing can live only amidst troubles and strife. Instinct teaches it this. And therefore this *horrible* thing, which really ought NOT to be called a man ... is *raving mad* at the prospect of a state of *justice* and of *harmony*, which the Reform bill is so manifestly calculated to produce.

Cobbett's prose portraits of Hunt were startlingly and brilliantly grotesque, a wild mix of savagely surreal images. In the *Register* of 16 April 1831, the Preston Cock was hanging on to the bill like 'grim death!' One could almost see his teeth in it, as he sank back upon his haunches 'pulling with all his might and *staring* and *growling* at the same time.' Hunt was 'a political farthing candle,' that could see in the reform bill the chambermaid striding towards him with 'an *extinguisher in her hand* and with her *eye fixed on him!*' It was only human nature, Cobbett continued, 'to recoil at the manifest approach of *eternal extinguishment.*'

In this same issue, Cobbett re-published a newspaper article which referred to Hunt as looking very thin and complaining of ill health. A few pages later, Cobbett mockingly described Hunt as a 'great, impudent, hulky oaf!' who was at last to be forced to work for a living 'and by the help of a stone-cracker or a shovel, send a little sweat out of that great hulky carcass.'

On 21 May 1831, Hunt was 'this great, hulky, stupid, malignant oaf'. It was disgraceful, Cobbett ranted, for men of sense 'to *huzza* the roaring thing.'

As the months passed, Cobbett fine-tuned his technique. In the *Register* of 20 August 1831, he twisted the picture so that he appeared to blame the reporters who were quoting Hunt. 'Reporthers', wrote Cobbett in his pen's best mock Irish accent, were much given to 'LYING'. Whenever they decided to publish a lie that was at once '*glaring, cowardly* and *fool-like*', they always did it under the name of Hunt. 'The name of this HUNT seems to engender lies, as some unhappy bodies engender lice'. Cobbett's turn of the pen transformed Hunt into a visually horrible disease that corrupted the pens of the reporters, making them, willy nilly, write lies. There was an added level of horror to Cobbett's spectacular prose. Cholera was sweeping through the country and killing thousands of people. Cobbett's references to eternal extinguishment and dead bodies also conjured up the ever-present threat of death and linked it with Hunt. Hunt was the incarnation of the deadly disease.

By March 1832, as Cobbett had boasted to his family, he could rely on the fact that his readers would now recognise Hunt immediately from the catch-phrases in the *Register*. In the issue of 24 March, Cobbett backed the radical Birmingham schoolmaster and writer, George Edmonds, who was to stand as a parliamentary candidate for Birmingham. Edmonds based his campaign around the fact that he was among the reformers to have been imprisoned as a result of the Six Acts. Cobbett proclaimed his support for Edmonds by contrasting him with the distorted picture he had built up in the *Register* of Hunt. Cobbett did not have to name Hunt at all. He did it through the catch-phrases and nicknames that he repeatedly used. He also ruthlessly quarried the personal and family references that regularly appeared about Hunt in the newspapers, much of which was untrue.

It was a devastating attack against Hunt. Having been a victim of 1819 (like you know who), Cobbett mused, was not sufficient recommendation to get elected as an MP. That alone would not prove a man's fitness to be trusted because 'a man may *change*'. Although he may have acted rightly for a while, he may never have had a good motive. In fact, he may have possessed all the vulgarity of rural life and felt the stupid pride of the aristocracy. He may have squandered away the savings of his father, and spent not only his own fortune but also that of his brothers and sisters, even of his own children. Unable to get his wife to give up hers, he may have abandoned her and taken up with another. So, reduced to insolvency, he may have turned '*patriot*'. He may have become '*a tool in the hands of the people's foes*'. Out of need arising from his own laziness and vanity, he may have sold himself to the haters of reform. He may, by 'BRAZEN LIES', encourage the haters of reform to oppose it. He may be a 'BRAINLESS FOOL,' so illiterate, of such beastly vulgarity, so notorious a 'LIAR,' that even '*truths*' come blasted from his tongue. He may '*under a head as grey as a rat*,' present the '*fooleries of childhood*' mixed with '*malignity*,' which it had required half a century to mature. He may be the most '*bragging bully*,' and at the same time a '*coward*' so consummate and so often '*chastised*,' as to know by the feel, a stick of ash from one of hazel. George Edmonds, Cobbett continued smugly, was, of course, precisely the opposite of 'this loathsome picture'. He was always steady as a rock to the principles with which he started, independent, capable with pen and tongue, in the prime of life and, in short, industrious, able, frank, courageous and not greedy of gain (in total contrast to you know who).

The following week, with a wicked smile, Cobbett re-published a piece of news about Hunt that had been leaked to *The Times*. He headlined it 'Amusing Correspondence!' Hunt had been served with a notice to pay a debt of £57.5s 10d by Messrs Underwood and Chalk. The bill brokers had addressed the demand to H. Hunt Esq MP. Hunt had shot back the following answer:

Gentlemen – I have received your elegant epistle and I duly appreciate your impudent threat, which is couched in the true Change-alley slang. I have deposited it in my box of curiosities, as a genuine specimen of cockney ignorance and insolence.

Could Cobbett have been thrilled that Hunt had been publicly accused of a debt after so often dragging Cobbett's debts before the public gaze, or was he secretly amused at Hunt's stylish reply?

It was altogether a devastating campaign against Hunt the politician. Cobbett also waged a public war on the personal front. The pair's old fight over Cobbett's beloved Indian corn resumed with a vengeance. As the debate over parliamentary reform continued, the two men, unbelievably, squabbled and fought over 'Cobbett's Corn'. Cobbett sent samples of his corn to people all over the country, both for personal use and for distribution amongst poor labourers, and published a list of their names in the *Register*. Hunt spotted the list and wrote letters to all of them, making use of the free House of Commons franking stamp to dispatch them. Some of the letters were re-directed back to Cobbett. It can be surmised from various outraged references in the *Register* that Hunt had claimed that the corn was the greatest fraud that had ever been practised upon the public, and had questioned Cobbett's 'moral reputation'. Cobbett's pen quivered with fury. He raged about the selfishness, stupid vanity and malignity of the 'LIAR' and his desire to live upon the labour of others. (Hunt's Breakfast Powder based on Cobbett's recipe obviously still rankled.) Hunt, he wrote in the *Register* of 11 June 1831, had been 'animated by feelings somewhat like those which Milton puts into the bosom of Satan, when he took his first peep into Paradise.'

Cobbett pounded off to visit the people who were growing his 'fine, beautiful and most excellent corn' to check out for himself how it was doing. Hunt followed hot on his heels to check up on what they had told

Cobbett. Reams were written about who said what to whom, who denied this, and who alleged that. In the *Register* of 3 September 1831, Cobbett triumphantly informed his readers that one gentleman, who had a neighbourhood of labourers with fine crops in their gardens, had a rod in soak for the great 'LIAR'. Cobbett had reminded him that it was not a question of '*rods*' but of broom-sticks at the very least, because ten bull hides had to be penetrated.

Corn and Hunt, the two subjects obsessed Cobbett. In November 1831, in one short article commenting on newspaper reports about Hunt's political doings, Cobbett used the word 'liar' twelve times to describe Hunt. In the middle of the tirade was a burst of fury about Hunt's belittling of Cobbett's precious corn. 'His LIE about the CORN shows what a fool it [Hunt] is', wrote Cobbett. The following month Cobbett advertised his book, *The Woodlands*, which informed people about the best way of growing trees. His mind flew to Hunt and he berated the 'FOOL-LIAR' who had sent out his circulars to proclaim 'Cobbett's Corn' a fraud upon the poor. Would he now do the same with his book on trees, Cobbett wondered.

Cobbett's pen was constantly busy inventing ways to insult and belittle Hunt. In the spring of 1832, he suddenly remembered in the *Register* of 14 April, that 'the fellow' was so monstrously ignorant, he had once told his audience: 'I have lautely bin in Normany, Genmun; a great *forren country* in Vrance, Genmun.' This outburst came after Cobbett described his corn lyrically as the sort 'the disciples ate as they were going up to Jerusalem on the Sabbath-day', the corn the 'FOOL-LIAR' had called 'A FRAUD' in letters franked by the House of Commons.

There was another even more insidious way by which Cobbett attacked Hunt through the pages of the *Political Register*. He undermined Hunt's friends and praised his enemies. In December 1831, Cobbett wrote an article headed 'Cholera Morbus and Charley'. The 'Charley' referred to was the radical London lawyer, Charles Pearson, a close friend of Hunt. The cholera epidemic was sweeping down from the north. As chairman of the City of London's health committee, Pearson was in charge of efforts to minimise the impact of the disease in the capital. Cobbett was (wrongly) sceptical about the extent of the cholera threat, and also of the role played by 'Charley'.

With withering scorn, Cobbett referred to Pearson's circulated advice on how to take precautions against cholera as 'Charley's Rescript'. Cobbett could not think of moving an inch without it, he wrote ironically. It was at once a 'HOMILY' and a 'Sanitary Vade Mecum'. The paternal exhortations to scour water-courses, whitewash walls, scent floors, change linen and keep hands and faces clean and heads combed, all those lovely precepts were somehow overpowering, wrote Cobbett. Charley, Charley, Charley. Cobbett endlessly repeated the name, diminishing and mocking Charles Pearson and by extension, Hunt.

Cobbett did the reverse with Hunt's enemies. Suddenly they were Cobbett's best friends. On 4 February 1832, the *Register* mentioned a dinner held in Cobbett's honour at the town hall in Salford. Cobbett casually slipped in a mention that among the diners was Joseph Johnson. He was the radical brushmaker with whom Hunt fell out after Peterloo and whose anti-Hunt letters Cobbett had advertised in the *Register.* Cobbett must have known that the casual reference to Johnson would have burned into Hunt's eyes as he scoured his copy of the *Political Register* to see what Cobbett had written about him. In the *Register* of 25 February 1832, Cobbett casually added a line about how Johnson had shown him around a meat market in Manchester during his visit.

Cobbett did something similar using the reformer, Sir Charles Wolseley. The latter had been Hunt's blacking business partner in France, but the pair fell out when the business failed. Towards the end of 1832, Cobbett made sure he repeatedly mentioned Sir Charles in the *Register*, and how often he, Cobbett, stayed in his splendid country mansion, Wolseley Park House, near Rugeley in Staffordshire. How impressed Cobbett was with the baronet's fruit. Wolseley was one of the most skilful gardeners Cobbett had ever known. Cobbett would back Sir Charles as MP for Westminster any day. He was a man of 'sound understanding, steadiness of purpose, perseverance, courage and unconquerable attachment to the well-being of the common people' – and his strawberries were simply fabulous.

Hunt must have laughed sardonically when the names of both men were repeatedly misspelt in the *Register*. Johnson turned into Johnstone and Wolseley became Wolsley. It rather spoiled Cobbett's effect.

It was an unprecedented public attack, an avalanche of childish, manic and disproportionate abuse from the very man who should have been standing shoulder to shoulder with Hunt at such a moment in history. Throughout his term as an MP for Preston, Hunt tackled all the subjects that Cobbett considered to be his own, the barbaric flogging of servicemen, the vicious Game Laws, the Corn Laws that kept out cheaper foreign corn, the restrictions on the press (stamp tax and the fear of prosecution), the scandalous working conditions of children in the factories of Cheshire and Lancashire, and the Dead Bodies' Bill which permitted the bodies of people who died in workhouses or hospitals to be sold for medical purposes. Hunt also tried, fruitlessly, to get an inquiry into the Peterloo Massacre. His dignified performances in the House of Commons merely infuriated Cobbett further and he ignored Hunt's speeches, including those on the inadequacies of the reform bill.

Yet by 21 May 1831, Cobbett himself had begun to worry about the bill's provisions, especially the distribution of seats. He remained brazen: 'let the reader clearly understand, that, for my part, I will never *cavil* at the bill, *though none of these alterations take place*. It contains so much good that I shall always receive it as a real blessing.' By 29 October 1831, however, Cobbett was seriously concerned about how the bill was going to be modified and altered to try to get it through parliament. If so, what exactly were the plans and were they worthy of the people's confidence, and if they were not, why did they not say so, he asked. By December 1831, on his own electoral campaigns in Manchester, Cobbett listed what he would fight for as an MP. His list included the abolition of tithes, placemen and sinecures, a reduction in taxation and reform of the economy. There was nothing about a detailed reform of the parliamentary system. A great many people had mistaken the reform bill for reform itself, he explained laconically. It had been a very great mistake.

In the issue of the *Register* published on 7 January 1832, Cobbett conceded that the bill was a deception and a sham, a mere thing with which to cheat the people. A few weeks later, the *Manchester Courier* quoted Cobbett as saying that the reform bill meant nothing in itself any more than a cookery book meant victuals. By 14 April, Cobbett did not want the bill at all for the sake of a theory. The bill was necessary, he wrote, to get rid of the taxman so he would be able to make his own malt, grow his own hops, turn his own fat into soap, keep what horses he liked and have as many windows as he chose. He wanted a reform bill, he said, so that people's wages would be enough to buy meat and bread, instead of just potatoes. In short, the government should do what Cobbett had always advised it to do and restore happiness to the country by reviving, cheering and cherishing all that was good.

Hunt bitterly accused Cobbett of betraying him and the cause. After *The Preston Cock's Reply*, Hunt withstood Cobbett's slings, arrows and cock crowings until October 1831, when he seized the opportunity of the parliamentary recess to retaliate in a series of public *Addresses*. He called them *Addresses from Henry Hunt, Esq. M.P. to the Radical Reformers of England, Ireland and Scotland, on the measures of the Whig Ministers since*

'Insnaring the Preston Cock'
A cock with the head of Hunt in profile stands on a dunghill beside a building inscribed 'Preston Farm Ho(use).' The Tories are trying to entice him with corn to their side as Cobbett and the 'reptile' press alleged.
C J Grant, 1831
© *The Trustees of the British Museum*

they have been in place and power. There were thirteen of them. Hunt used them to justify his position and also to correct the press reports of his speeches in the House of Commons and at his political rallies across the country, many of which had been re-published in Cobbett's *Political Register.* The *Addresses* also gave him the opportunity to peck right back at the Kensington Dunghill, 'the hollow old Weathercock of the Register', who was, Hunt wrote, one of 'the most foul and the most cowardly assailants that I have had against me'. The dates on some of the *Addresses* show that Hunt wrote them on the same day that a particularly coruscating issue of the *Register* was published. They were read by the public with rapt attention, just as the Ilchester series of *Addresses* had been. This was a cock fight worth watching.

In his *Address* of 29 October 1831, Hunt challenged the concept of a radical reformer who was not fighting for universal suffrage, annual parliaments or voting by ballot. 'The Prince of Liars' of the *Political Register* was, of course, included. He, with the rest was ready to assassinate anybody who had the honesty and courage to resist and expose the infamous attempts to portray the reform bill as satisfactory. What could have induced the 'wretched old monster' to desert all the professions and principles he had so strenuously advocated for years? It was to improve his circulation of the *Register* of course. Had he stuck to his guns, sales would have dropped along with profits. Hunt compared 'the sly old dog' to a pickpocket whose cleverness enabled him to pick pockets more adroitly. This 'very clever writer' was able to persuade people that black was white one day and white was black another. Hunt had predicted that 'the Register Liar' would do this. Why, he, Hunt, could write a volume about the infamies of the fellow. If it amused people to read his *Register,* they should do so, but they should not believe what they read. 'He never wrote a line about himself or his family that was not false', wrote Hunt. 'He owes me most mortal hatred because I know him to be a villain.' He also hated him because Hunt had been elected by the people of Preston while he himself had been rejected in 1826. 'There's the rub,' crowed Hunt.

Right through this entire diatribe, Hunt did not refer to Cobbett once by name –another leaf out of the master's book.

Another *Address* hit the streets smoking just a few days later on 3

November 1831. It was written from Manchester. Hunt looked back to
the declaration of 1829 in which he and Cobbett had together laid out the
principles of reform by which they would stand or fall, live or die. He
remembered the ringing phrases coined by Cobbett:

We are of the opinion that great efforts will now be made to practise delusion upon you,
to betray you into an assent to measures bearing the name of reform, but having, in fact,
no object in view other than that of prolonging oppression ... Listen not to those who may
tell you that it is better to *get a little* than to get nothing ... It can only deceive, only enthral,
only prolong your degradation.

What do you think, my friends, Hunt asked rhetorically, of the conduct
of the man who had abandoned every sentiment and every principle
contained in that solemn contract? Here, Hunt used Cobbett's name,
mocking it as it had been written at the bottom of the declaration together
with his own:

Those who have read the *Register* must know that WM COBBETT has abandoned every
principle and falsified every protestation made in that declaration; and they must know
that HENRY HUNT has not in one instance deviated from those principles.

There were more *Addresses* from Hunt over the following weeks. An
unexpectedly friendly reference to Cobbett crept in to No 6, published on
18 November 1831, like a chink of light. It came in a re-published article
from the *Leeds Patriot* on Hunt's visit to Leeds. Amidst the choking dust
of the cock fight, Hunt had forgotten himself and publicly paid
unconscious tribute to the man with the most powerful pen in the world,
the man who could coin a phrase or a nickname like nobody else. It
happened as Hunt was addressing the crowds from the window of the
Scarborough Hotel and was assaulted by the editor of the *Leeds Mercury*,
Edward Baines. After the scuffle Hunt called on his audience to put up
their hands if they thought Baines was 'the great liar of the north' as
'Cobbett' called him.

It was an aberration. Cobbett's name did not appear throughout
Hunt's *Addresses*. Hunt was as colourful and inventive in his prose as
Cobbett. The latter was an old griping wretch, a *Gripum*, a base liar, the
prince of puffers, an old bone grubber, a cunning crafty shifting old fox and
the weathercock of the *Register*. He was the fellow who had done more to

deceive, delude and betray the 'working classes' than anybody else. Hunt had to save them from the deadly grasp of his horrid fangs, although he knew that the old dotard's rage was as impotent as the scolding of a fish woman and his shafts of malice would fall blunted and harmless to the ground.

Hunt repeated himself endlessly in his *Addresses*, hitting, kicking and biting, his pen flailing in fury, just as Cobbett's did against him. Cobbett's Corn loomed large. Hunt hit out at the '*fraud*' and '*humbug*' of the wretched '*maize*', the worst sort of '*maize*', which the old trickster of the *Register* was puffing off as '*his corn*'. In his *Address* of 3 December 1831, Hunt wrote that he would never forget Cobbett thrusting his tongue into his cheek and with a significant wink of the eye saying: '*Never you mind that, Hunt, so that I can sell it.*' How often had Hunt heard Nancy Cobbett mocking her husband about his schemes with the phrase she repeated so many times: '*Billy's geese are all swans*', she would say. It was the same with 'Mr Coles' TRUSS', Hunt informed his readers. (Cobbett had ruptured himself as a young man and wore a supporting truss for the rest of his life.) The only reason Cobbett declared that Mr Coles' TRUSS was a '*subject of the greatest importance* to the nation' was to get back at Mr Egg. It was Mr Egg who used to supply Cobbett with 'wonderful trusses' until Cobbett owed him so much money, Mr Egg refused to sell him any more until the debts were paid. Hence Cobbett's allegiance to Mr Coles!

This accusation was well and truly below the belt. Cobbett got his own back at the end of the issue of the *Register* exactly a week later, on 10 December 1831, by advertising Griffiths and Turner's Penny Blacking. It was so good, so convenient and so cheap, all the world would use it. The formula came from a well-known chemist in Cheshire and had been brought to London by Griffiths and Turner. There had been no fewer than fifteen imitations of it.

King William IV assented to the reform bill, though pointedly not in person, in the House of Lords on Thursday, 7 June 1832. In the issue of the *Register* two days later, Cobbett rejoiced: 'I have been fighting this hellish THING for 30 long years ... At last I have fairly beaten it.' He threw a party in the village of Sutton Scotney in Hampshire to celebrate.

Hunt, by now bruised, battered and depressed, with one of his legs slightly affected by a minor stroke, continued to fight on in the Commons. On 15 August 1832, the final day of the old unreformed parliament, he presented a petition from the Reform Association of Manchester. It called for the whole of the bill to be repealed except the clause that disfranchised the rotten boroughs. Hunt then left the House of Commons forever.

Cobbett may have got wind of the petition. That same day he was at his desk in his office in Bolt Court off Fleet Street to pen the lead article for his next *Register*. While the bill was passing through parliament, he had paid little attention to most of the details, he wrote. He had not realised that instead of around ninety rotten boroughs, each with a handful of inhabitants, the country was going to get one hundred and fifty rotten boroughs with populations of around 30,000 to 150,000 people. In each borough, only one to two hundred people would have the vote. (This had been Hunt's constant message.) Cobbett had also failed to realise that most of the former county voters would lose their right to vote and would end up the tools of the aristocracy more than they had ever been. 'I never imagined that the parts of the bill which provided for the *exercise of the franchise* would, in effect, defeat the apparent intentions of the bill', he said. (This was exactly what Hunt had continually told the House of Commons.)

When he had read the provisions of the Act with attention, Cobbett informed his readers, he had clearly discovered that it could never result in its professed principles of reform. Therefore, he had sent a petition to Daniel O'Connell on 17 July 1832 for presentation to the House of Commons. The petition had called for the whole of the Act to be repealed, except those parts relating to the abolition of rotten boroughs and the enfranchisement of the big towns. It requested the House to pass an act to introduce one man one vote, voting by ballot and elections on one day. The petition had been presented on 19 or 20 July, Cobbett said airily, he forgot which. (His petition was, in fact, presented on 18 July 1832. There was no mention of it in *Hansard* but *The Times* published a short report. It quoted Hunt telling the House of Commons that Mr Cobbett was a man of high ability and of the most powerful talent – so far as he was capable of 'turning short round from one side of a question to the other'.)

Half way through this issue of the *Register* of 18 August 1832 came a brief note from Cobbett. 'Since writing the above,' he had just read a report in the *Morning Chronicle* of a 'conversation' in the House of Commons on the last day of parliament about the number of people who qualified to vote under the new Act. He was re-publishing 'the report of this conversation' for the benefit of his readers.

He did so, but nobody reading the article as it appeared in Cobbett's *Register* would have had any idea that the 'conversation' had been sparked off by the Manchester petition, nor would they have known that Hunt had presented it to the House of Commons. Those details were missing. Cobbett carefully left out the first crucial paragraph that would have informed his readers of the fact.

17
Reaction

Let us not seek to satisfy our thirst for freedom by drinking from the cup of bitterness and hatred. We must forever conduct our struggle on the high plane of dignity and discipline.

Martin Luther King

Neither man won the battle. In fact few, apart from the middle-class property owners, the landed and the moneyed, won anything either. The Chartists, who followed in the footsteps of Cobbett and Hunt, continued the battle for reform between 1838 and 1848. Their charter included demands for annual parliaments, universal male suffrage and voting by ballot. They were ridiculed, intimidated and harried out of court. It took decades to get further parliamentary reform. It was not until 1918 that one man one vote was achieved. It was only in 1928, nearly a hundred years after the Reform Act of 1832, that men and women aged twenty-one got an equal vote. Today, owing to the first person past the post system, governments are still elected against the will of a majority of the people. If Cobbett and Hunt were alive today, they would probably be campaigning for proportional representation and the abolition of the whipping system in the House of Commons. That would be another story.

The question is, if Cobbett and Hunt had been united and working together in the run up to the 1832 Reform Act, could the course of electoral history have run more smoothly? Could the whole miserable process have been speeded up? Whatever the answers might be, their cock fight on the dunghill of politics is a searing example, repeated endlessly throughout history, of what goes wrong when jealousy gets in the way. And everybody, of course, knew it at the time. All the reformers argued and squabbled bitterly amongst themselves but Cobbett and Hunt, with their extraordinary relationship, towered above the rest. Their names were linked together as casually as salt and pepper or fish and chips. Whether they were the best of friends or whether they were arguing like cat and dog, the term 'Cobbett and Hunt' was a shorthand phrase for radical politics, used universally by their friends and foes alike. The writer Jeremy Bentham wrote acidly about the pair in a letter to Daniel O'Connell on 13 September 1828: 'Hunt and Cobbett I contemplate with much the same eye as the visitors of Mr. Carpenter, the optician, contemplate the rabid animals devouring one another in a drop of water.' The poet Byron was worried that his friend, John Cam Hobhouse, would be associated with 'Hunt and Cobbett'. He wrote in a letter to Hobhouse from Ravenna in March 1820 that the pair were 'infamous scoundrels' no better than Jack Cade or Wat Tyler (medieval English rebels). The following month, Byron referred to 'Bristol Hunt and Cobbett'. They should trample on 'such unredeemed dirt, as the dis-honest bluntness, the ignorant brutality, the unblushing baseness of these two miscreants', he wrote.

Even as the cock fight raged, Cobbett himself had no hesitation about re-producing in the *Register* in November 1831 the shouts at a meeting in

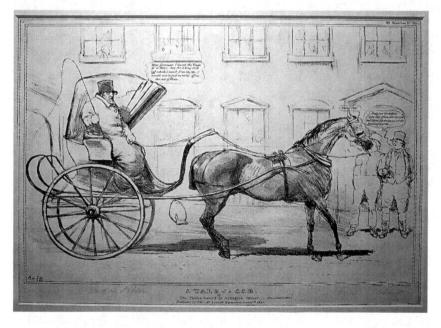

'A Tale of a Cab or The Tables turned in Arlington Street'
Cobbett and Hunt prepare to use the services of a former aristocrat, turned cabman, to take them to the House of Lords.   H.B. 1831
by permission of People's History Museum

Norwich when the Norfolk radical reformer, Sir Thomas Beevor, presented himself to the audience. There was an instant cry of 'We want no Cobbett or Hunt here!' It was the worst insult the hardline audience could think of to insult Beevor, who was given 'three groans'. Cobbett's pen almost twinkled as he described it all. He added that the last laugh would be when real reform came. Sadly, he was wrong.

The portrait painter and caricaturist John Doyle (grandfather of Arthur Conan Doyle), who worked under the name 'H.B.', produced at least two pictures of Cobbett and Hunt in these momentous years. One lithograph dated 1831 is catchlined 'Leapfrog on a Level', with the sub title: 'Going headlong to the devil'. Members of the government are playing a game of leapfrog as the devil waits at the finishing post. Hunt is leaping over the back of Earl Grey and Cobbett over the back of Sir Francis Burdett. In *A Tale of a Cab*, produced by Doyle in the same year, the Earl of Sefton is reduced to a hackney cab-man. Cobbett and Hunt, approach arm in arm: 'Hullo! Cab!' says Hunt. 'Suppose we take a ride out of the old Jarvy and tell him to drive us to the House of Lords.'

The 'base hireling' press exploited the Cobbett and Hunt show for all it was worth, using it to undermine both men. The radical press mourned and deplored it as tactfully as it could. The publications of Henry Hetherington, radical son of a London tailor, reveal how the lack of unity between Cobbett and Hunt at the eleventh hour embarrassed and upset the radical reformers. They found the fight distasteful and at first tried to overlook it, though that became impossible to do. This can be seen in Hetherington's political newspaper, the *Poor Man's Guardian*, which appeared weekly from July 1831 to the end of 1835, despite his frequent spells of imprisonment. His was the most successful of several hundred 'unstamped' anti-establishment penny newspapers published around this time. The term, 'unstamped', meant that the owners did not pay the newspaper stamp duty. This was not necessarily a reason for prosecution. The famous *Penny Magazine*, produced by the Society for the Diffusion of Useful Knowledge (founded by Henry Brougham), thrived with its diet of conventional facts and comfortable figures or, as the *Poor Man's Guardian* put it, 'a pack of nonsensical tittle tattle about forks and spoons and smock frocks, bridges, waterfalls and a thousand other things ...

utterly useless.' The *Penny Magazine* was held up as a beacon of light by the establishment. The radical unstamped press, however, laid itself open to prosecutions for criminal libel – writing which could be considered likely to cause a breach of the peace. Publishers, printers, distributors and poor street sellers were bundled into prison wholesale. Thus Hetherington's spells behind bars.

As soon as it launched, the *Poor Man's Guardian* linked Cobbett and Hunt together. The newspaper wrote that in the event of the success of the reform bill, Mr Cobbett and Mr Hunt would be invited to represent Manchester. Both would be certain to succeed, commented the newspaper with extreme optimism. (Hunt later observed sardonically in the House of Commons that Cobbett was as likely to be returned for the University of Oxford as for Manchester. Only rich merchants or men of large property, he said, could be sure of taking the two seats Manchester stood to gain from the reform bill.)

To begin with, Hetherington's *Poor Man's Guardian* attempted to be tactful in the way it handled the appalling public conflict between the two men. On 19 November 1831, it noted that 'Poor Hunt' had been 'terribly abused by all the legitimate papers'. (These were the newspapers and journals that paid stamp duty, and included Cobbett's *Political Register*.) No endeavour had been left untried to vilify him: and what was Hunt's great crime? Why, it was for remaining true to his principles. Hunt was, in fact, entitled to everybody's warmest support, wrote the *PMG*. It then moved on to 'our friend Cobbett' in the following paragraph. Cobbett had been too easily betrayed into supporting the reform bill. He had not liked to risk further accusations of inconsistency by suddenly altering his opinions, the newspaper suggested diplomatically. Cobbett had now returned to the cause and was ably proving that the reform bill was a mere delusion.

The following week, however, the newspaper, *Radical Reformer*, which was also published by Hetherington, included a coruscating article about the feuding and fighting between the reformers. It did not name anybody but it was obvious that the criticism was directed largely at Cobbett and Hunt. One of the principal amusements of some of the most popular and influential radical writers, observed the *Radical Reformer*, appeared to be calling each other nicknames, as if they were playing in a game of battledore and shuttlecock. One celebrated person called another a 'weathercock'. The 'weathercock' replied and called his adversary 'the great liar of the North'. (Cobbett called Edward Baines, editor of the *Leeds Mercury*, the latter name, while he called Hunt 'the great liar of the South.') The fighting was dividing the reformers and injuring the cause of reform, complained the newspaper:

It is really deplorable that the most competent Radical Reformers of England should degrade themselves by indulging in paltry, personal squabbles which merely serve as a handle for the abuse of the enemies of Reform. It is inconceivable how the opponents of Radical (or real) Reform chuckle at the contemptible petty dissensions of influential Radicals ... The whole Radical community is denounced as a set of quarrelsome fellows.

People should not classify themselves 'under the names of Cobbetites and Huntites', the *Radical Reformer* continued. They should be 'Universal Suffragites' and make principles their guide.

Just two weeks later, on 10 December 1831, there was a despairing note in the *Poor Man's Guardian*. Their party would be ruined by conflicting opinions and by different interests, it mourned. People were following names, not principles. 'Why not think for yourselves? Why not unite for the common good? Why enter into the paltry disputes of your "leaders" and your "orators?"' asked the newspaper. Some people sided with Hunt, others with Cobbett. 'Why enter into all the petty and disgraceful differences which exist amongst those individuals, with such unnecessary violence?' Such bickering compromised the success of 'our glorious cause'. People should not listen to Hunt but to the liberal principles he supported. The same went for Cobbett. There was a despairing note in the newspaper's pragmatic words:

We accept of co-operation and assistance, however trifling it be, from whatever quarter it come, whether from a Hunt or a Cobbett or a Carpenter or a Carlile or a Brougham or a Wellington or even a Bishop. We have no party spirit ... Alas! how differently do other persons feel! Party spirit runs so strong between them, that, though their object is the same, they look upon each other with the most virulent hatred and the consequence is ... a house divided against itself, falls to the ground!

The appeals to good sense and compromise were fruitless. The mainstream press exploited the row and made repeated references to the quarrels and the division into camps. On one occasion in 1833, for example, *The Times* published a letter from a reader who observed that one of the radical liverymen of the City of London had switched to Cobbett's camp:

Mr Nicholson is a coarse, stout, vulgar man, of stentorian voice, who imagines that all knowledge and integrity is concentrated in his own person. He was the 'bull-dog' of Henry Hunt, but when that great politician quarrelled with Mr Cobbett, Mr Nicholson adhered to the gridiron register, which is his Bible.

There was some sympathy for Hunt among the reformers as he endured the bitter and repetitive onslaughts by Cobbett that undermined his performance in the House of Commons and confused the people. Hetherington's *Poor Man's Guardian* mentioned the arrival on the unstamped scene of *The Patriot* and listed the subjects it was due to cover in its next issue. They included 'Cobbett's opinion of Hunt in 1812 and 1831.' It was obvious *The Patriot* was going to recap on the glowing praise, support and applause Cobbett showered on Hunt during the Bristol election, and contrast his writings then with what he was now heaping over Hunt.

In mid December 1831, Hetherington himself wrote a strong defence of Hunt. The headline was in bold type; the words were ironic: '"INFAMOUS CONDUCT" OF MR HUNT.' Hetherington listed all the propositions Hunt had raised in the House of Commons. They included an amnesty for the rioting labourers and a reduction in public spending on the army, the civil list and the royal family as well as changes to the reform bill and the repeal of the Corn Laws. (A Cobbettian list of demands.) Yet every stamped newspaper 'without exception' was traducing him, snorted Hetherington. There was no mention of Cobbett by name. It was not necessary. It was obvious from Hetherington's choice of words that Cobbett was included. If people believed exactly the '*reverse*' of what the newspapers said about a man, Hetherington continued, they were sure to know his true character: 'If, for instance, they call a man a fool, a scoundrel and a liar; you may conclude he is an intelligent, upright honest man, who abhors a falsehood – and you will draw an unerring conclusion.'

All those insults were indeed used by the mainstream press, but they were also words used repeatedly and obsessively by Cobbett in his *Register* against Hunt.

Some of the public sympathy offered to Hunt was extreme. Throughout 1832, a series of weekly articles was published in Hunt's constituency of Preston. The articles were entitled '*Addresses from One of the 3730 Electors of Preston to his Fellow-Townsmen.*' The number 3730 referred to the number of people who voted for Hunt as their MP in December 1830. The *Addresses* made compelling reading. The first issue, published on 31 December 1831, said that abuse had been heaped upon Hunt's character, enough 'to provoke the gentleness of the lamb into the ferocity of the wolf.' The tone had heated up dramatically by 4 February 1832 after the news that Cobbett was planning a visit to the town to give a lecture. The 'old buck or rather the old Bone Grubber' was going to enlighten the people of the town was he, sneered the writer. Look at the rings he pretended to make from Tom Paine's hair. Look at how he paid his work-people, not with money but with old bacon. Were the people of Preston really going to hear 'that man, that infamous old l—r, to use one of his own expressions ... who in defiance of common decency, turned his backside in a most insulting manner on a large and respectable body of the inhabitants of the town.' (Cobbett! mooning!?) Could any man with any regard for his own moral character be seen in Cobbett's company until he had cleansed his blemished reputation from the charges laid against him by his own 'WIFE.' If Cobbett had regard for his own character, he would never rest until he had cleared himself from the dark and foul calumny. The self-styled 'Monarch' of the press should go elsewhere.

The following week, another pen described how Cobbett came and addressed the people from a window of the town's Castle Inn. He advised them, said the writer with a tone of disbelief, to remain united and not allow '*private quarrels and bickerings*' to divide them.

As the weeks passed, one contributor reminded readers of the *Addresses* how Hunt had once been Cobbett's 'beloved and most faithful friend', and how Cobbett had addressed him as 'my dear Hunt'. Another seized on Cobbett's support in the *Register* for the Birmingham schoolmaster, George Edmonds, as a parliamentary candidate, who was all-good in comparison with the all-bad Hunt. Cobbett had 'degraded his columns by a coarseness of vituperation unworthy of his talents', roared the Hunt loyalist: 'When his passions are roused, the spleen of his heart gets into his mind's eye and makes him see the object of his wrath through a mist of malignity which at once blackens and magnifies it a hundredfold.'

These Preston *Addresses* also mined the pair's corn fight for ammunition. How could Cobbett write about his satisfaction at seeing his own Indian corn growing in Preston and the neighbourhood? It was the first time they had ever heard of Cobbett's corn growing locally, except at Sir Thomas Hesketh's Ruffard Hall. If it were so successful, why had they not seen it growing elsewhere in Preston? Who had any pigs that had been fattened by it? It was one more proof that Cobbett was entitled to 'the name of LIAR.' Readers were urged to support Hunt and buy his excellent roasted corn and his Matchless Blacking. The homosexual sex scandal of 1829 was also quarried for material. One of the Preston voters used the subject to compose a grotesque poem. All these years later, it still makes nasty reading. 'Thou *jealous reptile!*' said one of the milder verses:

We have not forgot
How thou didst strive a Patriot's name to blot;
But HUNT'S consistency defied thy scorn
And, match'd with thy *forever-changing* life
So *fraught with guile, with villainies so rife!*
He hardly seems an erring *mortal-born.*

In the middle of this hideous criticism of Cobbett by Hunt's supporters, there was a real message. It was all done, wrote one of the 3730, in the hope that Cobbett's pen would in future be employed 'not to *divide* but to *unite* the friends of freedom'. When Cobbett did not respond, alternative tactics were tried. Two weeks after the passing of the Reform Act, one of the writers of the Preston *Addresses* published a private letter that Cobbett had written to Hunt twenty-seven years previously. (This must have been done at Hunt's suggestion.) The letter had been written by Cobbett to his 'dear Hunt' on 29 August 1815, in those halcyon days when the pair were taking the county meetings by storm and their relationship was flourishing. Hunt was still unwell after his collapse at the end of the July. Cobbett wrote that he remained uneasy about Hunt's health: 'I have a sort of lurking uneasiness about <u>your illness</u>, but, I hope, my fears are groundless.' He hoped they would be seeing Hunt soon, because he was needed to teach Cobbett's sons to be bold in field sports, although 'you will believe me sincere when I say, that it is <u>your company</u> that is welcome to me'. If Hunt thought that Cobbett had been labouring away in a way that merited a reward, he could give him 'the reward that I value more than any other, namely – your company for a week ... bless you in all manner of ways, Wm Cobbett.'

It was a deeply emotional blast from the past. The depth of the personal friendship between these two men was once again unfolded before the public gaze. The letter appeared in the Preston *Address* of 23 June 1832. It must have been sheer coincidence or a trick of fate that after eighteen months of ferocious attacks against Hunt, the issue of the *Register*, which was published on that very same Saturday, was enthusiastic about a speech he had given in the House of Commons a few days beforehand. Hunt had introduced a motion calling for the suspension of flogging and spoken at length in support, reading out letters and documents which vividly illustrated the horror of what was in effect the public humiliation and torture of men in the services. Flogging was a subject dear to Cobbett's heart, and he first of all reminded his readers how he himself had been imprisoned in Newgate for two years after criticising the flogging of a group of soldiers in Ely. He then re-published a report of the debate in the House of Commons as published in *The Times*. In the commentary that followed, Cobbett took a deep breath and inched his way towards acknowledging Hunt's eloquence.

At first, he avoided addressing Hunt under his own name, but used the horrible third party '*reporther*' technique. 'The *reporter,* whom I have had so often to call LIAR, *new-negro*, and *beast,* has at last put forth a publication which really does make atonement for a considerable part of his enormous sins', wrote Cobbett. The paragraphs he had given them 'under the name of Hunt' were excellent and well-timed. 'The result was such as to earn for this *reporther* a great deal of sensible and well-founded praise, which I give, not only ungrudgingly, but with great pleasure.' And then, miracle of miracles, Cobbett went on to use Hunt's name properly and in a civilised way. He referred to 'Hunt' three times and chuckled over how John Cam Hobhouse had been almost ready to go upon his knees to get Hunt to withdraw his motion. 'HUNT stuck to his motion and insisted upon a division,' wrote Cobbett appreciatively.

It is difficult to explain Cobbett's sudden burst of oblique sunshine towards Hunt. *The Times'* reporter got the voting figures for the motion the wrong way round, giving the impression that Hunt's motion was passed by the House. In fact, it was thrown out. Cobbett made his comments about Hunt's performance <u>before</u> knowing this. When he realised the error, however, it did not alter his view. It had been a great mistake to have supposed that the House could ever vote for the abolition of flogging, Cobbett wrote the following week. Yet the debate had drawn forth statements and arguments which had produced a great impression upon the public, and none of which had been at all invalidated by the falsehood of the 'reporther'. (He meant *The Times* this time.)

Was this a change of heart or was it all self-interest on Cobbett's part? Even a bit of both? Three weeks later, Cobbett continued to campaign for a seat in a reformed parliament through the pages of the *Register.* In the issue of 21 July 1832, he informed his readers that he would prefer to sit first for Manchester, secondly for Oldham – and thirdly for Preston. He made this announcement despite the fact that Preston's Political Union had said it would have nothing to do with him, and despite the battery of *Addresses* that were pouring out of Preston poisonously attacking him. Cobbett made no direct reference to the Preston voters' *Addresses.* He phrased everything very carefully. He thought the people of Preston ought to elect him as one of their MPs, he wrote. He did not want to obtrude his opinions with regard to anybody else on them. Nothing done towards him by anybody had ever, for one single moment, diminished the real regard and affection he had for them. He had not forgotten the wonderful manner in which they had taken leave of him after his defeat in Preston in the 1826 election. What was more, nothing that any of them had said of him since had made him in the least angry. And then Cobbett wrote these incredible lines:

I pray them to take from me this observation, that it is true as holy writ, that he who is the *last* to consent to be reconciled is generally the *most in fault* ... he who has been the *least* in error is generally the *first* to forgive. Injuries are sometimes so deep that reconciliation on the part of the offended would be baseness, but these are not injuries of that sort.

These lines were ostensibly written to the people of Preston, but they were surely directed at Hunt, who had, as everybody knew, refused a reconciliation. Cobbett knew very well that Hunt had been asked repeatedly to name somebody with whom he would be prepared to stand in Preston at the general election for the first reformed parliament, but he had kept silent. Had Hunt's performance on the flogging issue in the House of Commons made Cobbett forget his jealousy and realise what a valuable political partner Hunt would make, just as he had once been? Was Cobbett stretching out his hand, both to the people of Preston – and to Hunt? His next words in that article for the *Register* strongly suggest he was. The injuries had not been deep, had they, Cobbett asked:

Let me therefore hope, that in this day of the dawn of our restoration to liberty, no cloud of contention will be found to hang over Preston. This is a matter very near to my heart and I hope that what I have said may tend to produce the desired reconciliation.

Whatever hopes or thoughts Cobbett might have had in his head, there was to be no reconciliation with either the Preston people or Hunt. The weeks went past. There was no reply. Hunt did not send for Cobbett, and nor did the people of Preston.

On 11 August 1832, Cobbett re-printed an article from the *Preston Chronicle* about a meeting of electors with a candidate, a Mr C. Crompton, who got a grilling over questions about the economy. A supporter in the crowd shouted out that poor Crompton was being asked questions that nobody could answer, not even Mr Hunt, who was the cleverest man in the House of Commons. Cobbett took great relish in coming up with all the answers.

A week later, in the *Political Register* of 18 August 1832, as has already been described, Cobbett's *Register* made no mention of the fact that on the last day of the last unreformed parliament, Hunt had presented a petition from Manchester calling for the Reform Act to be repealed. That same day, Saturday, 18 August, Hunt told the cheering crowds at an election rally in Preston that he had been pressed many times to select somebody who would pledge him support, stand by his side and fight the Preston people's battles in the House of Commons. His answer had always been that he did not know anybody suitable. Now he did, and Hunt triumphantly presented his friend, Captain Forbes from the royal navy, as a suitable candidate to stand side by side with him in the next election.

A month later, Cobbett was campaigning for a seat in Oldham. He was staying with Sir Charles Wolseley (Hunt's estranged business partner) who still had the finest strawberries Cobbett had ever seen in his life. Wolseley was one of the most skilful gardeners Cobbett had ever known, indeed skilful in the whole range of agricultural science. Cobbett, meanwhile, was absolutely sure of getting a seat in the first reformed parliament as MP for Oldham. 'I have led the *happiest life* of any man that I have ever known. Never did I know one single moment when I was *cast down*; never one moment when *I dreaded the future*', he informed his readers.

There was to be no reconciliation. Yet in October of this year, 1832, Hunt spoke at a meeting in Birmingham called to form a Midland Union of the Working Classes. A report was published in the *Poor Man's Guardian*. Out of the blue, in the middle of his speech about how the government paid the press to peddle its views, Hunt had referred to one newspaper which 'a certain gentleman called "the bloody old Times."' Hunt had no need to refer to Cobbett, but he did. His audience laughed. One suspects Hunt did too, although he may have done so a little wryly. Were there any regrets? We can only wonder.

18
The Chimes at Midnight

Too late, too late!
Alfred Lord Tennyson

The 'certain gentleman' achieved his heart's desire of a seat in the House of Commons on 13 December 1832, when he was declared a member of parliament for the new constituency of Oldham. The town had been allocated two seats in the House of Commons under the Reform Act. Cobbett's fellow MP was the progressive, wealthy cotton manufacturer, John Fielden. Cobbett missed the voting. He was in Manchester where, despite the odds, he was also standing as a candidate. There is no doubt that Cobbett would have preferred to have won a seat at Manchester, a much bigger and more important town – and the site of Peterloo, but the Oldham victory was all done and dusted on the first day of polling. Cobbett visited briefly to meet the cheering crowds, but unusually declined to be chaired or take part in a public procession. He despised ostentation, he said, and hurried back down south. He reported his victory in the *Register*: 'Let me first, in imagination at least, *shake hands with you all*. Let me have a laugh with you: let me imagine that I hear you all exclaim, "There! They have got him in then, at last."'

But there was not much laughter. Strangely, Cobbett did not even return to Oldham for the post-election victory dinner, possibly because he was busy moving his family from Kensington into a house at 21 Crown Street, four hundred yards from Westminster Hall, and overlooking St James' Park. (Like Duke Street, Crown Street long since disappeared.) In this moment of triumph in his life, Cobbett chose not to attend the dinner to shake hands properly with the people who helped to vote him in. He sent his son John in his place. It was not the triumph it could and should have been. It can be seen from the last *Register* of the year that on Christmas Day, 25 December 1832, Cobbett was busy working away in his office premises at 11 Bolt Court off Fleet Street.

Incredibly, it was Hunt who was in Oldham the night of the post-election dinner. He lost his seat at Preston owing to the combined efforts of the Whigs and Tories. Despite the passing of the Great Reform Act, it was business as usual. The two political parties used their funds to bribe voters and to hire gangs of ruffians armed with stout sticks, who terrorised those brave enough to turn out to vote for Hunt and Captain Forbes. There was also the small detail that many of the people, who would have voted for Hunt, had been disfranchised by the muddled and incoherent Act. Hunt started the journey back to London, stopping off in towns along the way to be greeted by crowds, flags, music and all the applause he needed to soothe his spirits. A deputation from the Oldham Political Union invited him to town to meet the people and give a lecture. The date was the very night of the dinner held to celebrate the successful election of Cobbett and Fielden.

Chance, coincidence, fate or design? Whatever it was, Hunt was greeted by a 'multitude' in Oldham market square, and his lecture in the theatre that evening was a sell-out. The *Poor Man's Guardian* described how both the theatre and the stage were 'crowded almost to suffocation'. This, observed the newspaper, was despite the fact that the friends of Mr Cobbett and Mr Fielden were dining together that same evening at the Swan Inn. The stage was so packed with people that Hunt barely had elbow room and he had difficulty keeping his feet. Although the stage had been hastily reinforced beforehand, it collapsed with an enormous crash. Hundreds of people fell to the floor with Hunt among them. He got away with 'a few slight bruises'.

If only things had been different. If only Cobbett and Hunt had been at that dinner together, as two members of the brave new parliament, celebrating their wins in triumph, side by side as in the old days. But things rarely turn out the way they should.

As it was, early on 29 January 1833, Cobbett marched into the House of Commons. Defying convention, he took his seat on the Treasury Bench (today's front bench), the historic preserve of ministers. When the chancellor of the exchequer and leader of the House, Lord Althorp, arrived, he had to sit down on the bench next to Cobbett. The artist John Doyle sketched the scene: Cobbett sitting next to a disconcerted Althorp, shoulders hunched, his top hat low over his eyes, one leg nonchalantly crossed over the other and ignoring the furious looks he was getting from all sides. It was to become Cobbett's familiar posture in the House of Commons. He was not going to be intimidated and he certainly did not suffer from nerves when addressing his fellow MPs. Decades of public speaking meant that he had already perfected his technique. The writer George Gilfillan described the way Cobbett addressed his audiences around this time: 'Quiet, clear, distinct and conversational and the fury and the fervour of the demagogue alike were wanting. The most sarcastic and provoking things oozed out at his lips like milk or honey.' At last Cobbett could challenge the THING face to face and he did so in the first words of his maiden speech in the House of Commons: 'It appears to me that since I have been sitting here I have heard a great deal of unprofitable discussion', he informed the House.

Cobbett was to need all the resources he could muster. After finally winning a seat in parliament, he would find it a tasteless victory. He was to be a very lonely man in the reformed House of Commons and experience all the opposition, the 'yells, groans and hootings' that Hunt had faced. Even before he got into the chamber, he wrote in the *Register* of 12 January 1833 that MPs were mere 'men of straw', expected to be 'nothing more than so many furze fagots, each tied round with a hazel withe'. When he got there, many of his observations and comments about the conditions, the way of parliamentary life and the opposition he faced echoed everything that Hunt had said.

It did not take Cobbett long to discover what life was like as a beleaguered individual in the House of Commons. By 2 February 1833, he was reporting in the *Register* how inaccurate the reptile press was in its reports of parliamentary proceedings. He told his readers that he had come to an arrangement with the new radical evening newspaper, the *True Sun*, published by William Carpenter, to correct any inaccuracies in reports of his parliamentary speeches. (The latter was Cobbett's friend and ally. Carpenter had bitterly attacked Hunt in very Cobbettian language during his time as an MP, and Hunt was in the middle of suing the *True Sun* for libel.)

By 2 March 1833, Cobbett was describing with horror, just as Hunt had complained, about the unhealthy conditions of the overcrowded chamber of the House of Commons, 'this sort of *hole*' with its insufficient seating and inadequate standing areas. Why were they squeezed into so small a space? Cobbett asked. Why did they live in such a hubbub? It was absolutely impossible that there could be calm and regular discussions. He was appalled by the 'everlasting trampling backward and forward on the floor', the constant interruptions, the incessant calls of 'order, order.' 'All these absolutely distract men's minds and render it impossible for them to do that which it is their duty to do and which they wish to do', he wrote. An Englishman, he said, would blush to compare the Commons with the House of Assembly of any one of the states of America, let alone the Congress of the United States.

The conditions were intolerable, with scores of men crammed together in St Stephen's Chapel. The smell of perspiring bodies was often superseded by the far worse stink rising up from the polluted River Thames flowing outside the windows. It had all disgusted Hunt, and so it did Cobbett. He brilliantly described the scene, the close packing of men upon the uncomfortable benches, the filling up of all the escape routes, squeezing one another, treading on each other's toes and running and scrambling to get a seat, just as people did at a public dinner at the Crown and Anchor. At least a hundred people had to be disturbed if a member wanted to get out of the chamber for any reason. Moving out of the pit in the middle of a theatre was nothing like getting out of the House of Commons. Cobbett was also appalled by the crowds constantly milling around the Speaker's chair. It was impossible for the Speaker to act with dignity even if he wanted to, he observed. The Speaker was constantly pestered by men poking forward to whisper in his ear and tease him about something or other, presenting him with bits of paper and pulling him from side to side.

During both Hunt and Cobbett's period in parliament, the Speaker was the Tory, Charles Manners Sutton, one of the most popular and long-serving speakers of the House of Commons. Sutton ended up holding the post from 1817-1835. At the end of the last unreformed parliament in August 1832, MPs voted to award Sutton, who had announced his retirement, a large pension in acknowledgment of his record of service. Hunt had reluctantly voted with the rest because, he said, he agreed that

Sutton had done a good job. At the time, Cobbett was scathing in his criticism. How could the only radical in the house justify giving to that man more than the wages received by two hundred miserable hand weavers of Preston, he asked in the *Register*. Did Hunt not remember that Sutton had been Speaker at the time of the Manchester massacre and that his father had awarded Parson Hay the lucrative living of Rochdale '*immediately after that bloody day?*'

When it became known at the beginning of 1833 that, despite his retirement, Sutton was to be re-appointed Speaker for the reformed House of Commons as a safe pair of hands, Cobbett devoted much of the issues of the *Register* denouncing the plan. MPs should be allowed a vote, he wrote. Sutton was part of the Tory old guard. He was an enemy of parliamentary reform. 'The pensioner' had been receiving public money in some shape or form since his infancy. His pockets were 'crammed with the people's money'. All pensions and abuses of the system should be abolished. (At the time of writing this, the Speaker of the House of Commons is still offered a pension on retirement.) There were pages of the stuff. The subject practically took up the whole of Cobbett's maiden speech. It was all wonderfully Cobbettian, but there was an obsessive note about it. Cobbett did not mention or blame Hunt. It is not too great a leap, however, to infer that Cobbett's overwhelming interest could have been fuelled by an association of the subject with Hunt.

Hunt could have thought so too. He seized a pen and replied via the pages of the *Poor Man's Guardian* the following week in the issue of 9 February 1833, pouring scorn on 'a precious deal of twaddle and humbug' that was spoken. The reformers in parliament wanted the Whig MP, Edward Littleton as Speaker, Hunt wrote. Yet he was one of the most haughty aristocrats in the House and biggest spenders of public money. 'This is pretty well for the first act of the Reformed Parliament', snorted Hunt with irony. 'If the sack is like the sample, the Lord have mercy upon us!'

By the beginning of March 1833, Cobbett was beginning to stagger under the pressure. He was a few days short of his seventieth birthday and had been in parliament for just over a month. His pen scratched wearily over the paper for the issue of the *Register* of 2 March 1833. It required perfect health and great bodily strength to sit in the House of Commons, he wrote. The hours were long and the sittings during the night extremely tiring. 'Birds of ill-omen – bats – toads – and all noxious things, do their work at night,' he told the House of Commons grimly during one of his many protests about having to sit past midnight. By the end of the month, he was complaining about the huge number of petitions flooding onto his desk, sent from all over the country. One from Huddersfield measured 130 feet long – more than twice as long as the House, passage and all, he said. He had by then received at least 120 petitions. They were 'quite as much as a stout boy can carry,' he wrote. He had staggered with them to the House for a fortnight without being able to present them.

Cobbett must have conveniently forgotten his stinging words and jeers when Hunt had complained of the volume of work faced by a conscientious MP. No doubt Hunt remembered as he read Cobbett's *Register*. The life of an MP, which brought with it long, unsocial hours, mostly overnight, and unhealthy working conditions, was taking its toll. Cobbett was by now very stout and no longer a boy. The journalist James Grant described him around this time:

He could not have been less than six feet, while his breadth was proportionately great. He was, indeed, one of the stoutest men in the House. His hair was of a milk-white colour and his complexion ruddy ... What struck you most about his face was his small, sparkling, laughing eyes. When disposed to be humorous himself, you had only to look at his eyes and you were sure to sympathise in his merriment. When not speaking, the expression of his eyes and his countenance was very different.

Cobbett put a brave face on in the House of Commons but his health was not good. His heels and ankles were swollen and he was often short of breath. His regular winter cough and cold had been far worse than usual. He was under pressure and desperately lonely. On 7 April 1833, he wrote a note to his friend Silvester Sapsford. It was a Sunday morning. Cobbett was not at home with his family in Crown Street. He was in his gloomy office premises at Bolt Court. The letter's few lines tell the story: 'I am here all this day alone. For charity's sake come and dine with me at 2 o'clock. I beseech. I implore. I supplicate!'

Cobbett must have felt that every man's hand was against him – including that of Hunt, who continued to snipe away at Cobbett from the columns of the *Poor Man's Guardian*. On Saturday, 13 April 1833, the newspaper published a letter from Hunt to his old political ally, John Knight, Oldham radical and veteran of Peterloo. What had they been struggling and risking their lives for, Hunt asked rhetorically. The people had lost their principles, and who was it that had deluded them and led them away from those great and unerring principles for which they had suffered and bled? Hunt wanted the questions to be put to the people of Oldham. He had seen the frivolous petitions which were being presented to parliament on their behalf. They were nothing to do with equal rights, political justice or a repeal of the Corn Laws. Could Knight tell him why the members for Oldham had not been in the chamber to vote against a motion to delay the Factory Bill. If they had, the motion, which was prolonging the torture of the helpless factory children, would have been lost. (Hunt was quite right. The motion to set up a commission of inquiry into the proposed Act, thus delaying it, was won by just one vote. Had Cobbett and Fielden voted, the motion would have been defeated.) Where had the old sergeant major (Cobbett) been when a motion was introduced for abolishing the torture of flogging in the army? Hunt continued. It appeared he had been there but did not vote. (Cobbett had indeed been in the House earlier that evening.) 'What has become of all the mighty promises and professions of Cobbett? What has become of the "12 propositions" which he promised the men of Manchester that he would not only move but carry, or he would resign?' It might be said that Cobbett had been busy exposing the inequality of the stamp duties. 'Pshaw, what has that to do with relieving the labouring poor or giving them political rights?' wrote Hunt. Now it was his turn to pile heaps of fiery coals on Cobbett's head.

Cobbett himself may have been feeling some loss of confidence. In yet another coincidence, on that very same Saturday in April 1833, Cobbett's *Register* included the following defiant lines: 'By this time, at any rate, even my bitterest enemies must be convinced of my sincerity, my zeal and devotedness to my country.' Despite the presence of other reformers in the House of Commons including John Fielden, George Faithfull, Joseph Hume, Thomas Attwood, Daniel O'Connell and the future Chartist leader, Feargus O'Connor, Cobbett was a lonely man on the bench. Just as Hunt had, Cobbett badly needed a loyal ally, as he revealed the following week in the *Register* of 20 April:

What is wanted in the House is this: ten men, who care not one single straw for all the noises that can possibly be raised against them; who would be just as insensible to the roarings and the scoffings as they would be to the noise of a parcel of dogs howling at the moon; who would preserve their good humour in spite of all the cheerings drawn forth by attacks upon them and, above all things, who would constantly, steadily and boldly persevere into looking scrupulously into every grant of the public money, however small.

The reader, Cobbett wrote, could have no idea of what it was like to get up on his feet and face hundreds of men, nearly all of whom were waiting for the opportunity to pick 'some little hole or another' in what he had to say, and who cheered a government minister as soon he began speaking against him. Scores of men had been so beaten down by it all, they pretended to convert to the other side rather than try to carry out their duty, Cobbett continued. It was easier for a camel to go through the eye of a needle than for a man to do his duty by the people in the House of Commons. 'If you have persons on whom you can rely, you do things that you *never would attempt to do without it*', he wrote. It would make all the difference in the world. Of course, he, Cobbett, was not going to give up but, 'oh God!' how different it would be if he had others with him. If only he had at least one of his sons there, he sighed. (Cobbett's son John stood for Coventry, this year, 1833, but failed to win a seat.)

The man Cobbett really needed sitting by his side in the House of Commons was Hunt – and Cobbett probably knew it. It was Hunt who could have ignored the roarings and scoffings, who would have been able to preserve his good humour and who would have had all the experience necessary to examine the expenditure of public money. It can only be wondered whether Cobbett was aware of the unfortunate resonance of the words he wrote. Did he remember how his pen had eaten into Hunt during his short time as an MP, undermining and betraying him when he had needed Cobbett's support so badly? This was one of the great missed opportunities in history. Cobbett and Hunt could have been a formidable team in these crucial years, both in the run up to and in the aftermath of the 1832 Reform Act. They could surely not have beaten the system, but they could have given it a far rougher ride, cheered on by millions of disaffected and disappointed working class people throughout Britain. Hunt would have been Cobbett's perfect partner in these difficult years.

As it turned out, Cobbett was on the verge of a nervous breakdown. The crisis was precipitated at the beginning of July 1833 when he was made a member of a select committee to investigate the activities of the police spy and *agent provocateur*, William Popay. This was a triumph for Cobbett. He had presented a petition to the House of Commons about Popay's dirty deeds against the Political Union of Camberwell and Walworth just a few days previously. Cobbett jubilantly returned to his house in Crown Street at 2 o'clock in the early hours of 3 July – to be bitterly disappointed. He described what happened in a long and miserable letter to Sir Thomas Beevor, how he found nobody to welcome him home, no drink of warm milk prepared, nor a fire. And when he finally climbed into bed, Nancy gave him hell: 'That <u>tongue</u>, which, for more than twenty years has been my great curse and which would have worried any other man to death, suffered me not to have one moment's sleep, after my long fatigues and anxious labours'. He knew it was just the beginning of a month of it, Cobbett wrote. Nancy would be breakfasting in bed every day, lounging on the sofa and exercising in the park 'to provide strength of lungs and the power of sustaining wakefulness at night'. As soon as dawn came, he told Beevor, he left the house and sought sanctuary in Bolt Court.

Cobbett never returned to his family. In January 1834, he advertised the Crown Street house for rent, and his wife, sons and daughters moved into 10 Red Lion Court, surprisingly close to Cobbett's premises in Bolt Court. An anonymous article, published after Cobbett's death, revealed that after September 1833 and until his final illness, despite their close proximity, he did not speak to his wife or children except his eldest son, William, and Cobbett only spoke to him until April 1834. For the rest of his life, Cobbett lived either at Bolt Court or at his rented Normandy Farm with its 160 acres in the village of Normandy in Surrey, just a few miles from his birthplace at Farnham. (The farmhouse overlooks the now tiny village common. Every so often people drop by wanting to dig in the garden for Tom Paine's bones.)

Six months after that miserable night with Nancy, Cobbett told his public in the issue of the *Register* of 28 December 1833 that 'a scheme' had been on foot for a considerable time '*by a crafty, round-about, hidden, damnable process, to crush the Political Register and to drive me from my seat in Parliament!*' The reader would stare with astonishment but wild and monstrous as it might seem, Cobbett knew it to be true. The scheme had become apparent around the first of July. From that date to this, he wrote, his object had been to blow the conspirators to atoms. It had been his sole occupation. He blamed the London lawyers or 'THE MONSTERS' at their dens, called the Inns of Court. The crocodiles on the banks of the Nile were not so ferocious. They were putting stories around that his children had written or contributed to a large part of Cobbett's publications, and that he, Cobbett, was an '*impostor*'. Doctor Black (John Black, editor of the *Morning Chronicle*) had warned Cobbett that his '*exit from public life*' was at hand. That was why he had been penned up at Bolt Court for the past few months, Cobbett explained. He had not thought it safe to leave the building for more than thirty-six hours at a time. 'This is the seat of war. It is here that the battle must be fought and I am resolved not to quit the spot until that battle be over', he told his readers.

Those who knew Cobbett well would have known that 'the monsters' included Cobbett's own sons, John and James, both of whom were barristers with chambers at Clifford's Inn. Cobbett specifically excluded his children in his article, but with a telling bitterness. He would make no complaint against them, he said, nor would he reproach them for never having earned anything for him; he had always taken pleasure in working to support them.

It was clear that Cobbett's state of mind had become seriously disturbed. There was no mention of Hunt, but he was surely there, lurking in Cobbett's nightmares. There had been more from Hunt in the *Poor Man's Guardian* of 9 November 1833. The Reform Act, or the 'Grey and Russell hoax,' as it was by then being referred to, had turned out exactly as he had warned the people it would, wrote Hunt. He had been 'abused and misrepresented by the interested tools of government and by the public press,' for doing so. They said he had been bribed to desert the people. He could now ask them what they thought of his struggle to expose 'this mighty humbug?' He reminded the readers of 'the principal persons, who, as tools to the Whigs, acted as false guides to the people', and who were 'the very men who are now disgusting the country with praises of their own prophetic wisdom.' Hunt named and shamed them all, including 'old Cobbett, who was a thick and thin tool of the Whigs,' eternally bellowing for 'the Bill, the whole Bill and nothing but the Bill.' Now, sneered Hunt, 'the old trickster' was working hard to 'delude his dupes' into believing that he sympathised with the people 'whom he so grossly assisted to mislead and to betray.'

The *Poor Man's Guardian* offered to publish the replies of anybody of those Hunt alluded to, 'should they have anything to offer in justification or extenuation of their conduct.' Cobbett, holed up in Bolt Court, did not take up the offer.

Two weeks later, Hunt took another swipe through the pages of the *Poor Man's Guardian*. Let the people beware of following the advice of those who were the foremost in telling them that the reform bill would benefit the working classes, he wrote. 'The paltry and hollow excuse that they were deceived themselves, is only an additional reason why they should never be trusted again as guides or leaders of the people.'

Throughout this year, 1833, Hunt also used the run up to a court case as an excuse to wield his stick and beat Cobbett. After his defeat in Preston, Hunt had begun an action for libel against the *True Sun*. This was the newspaper that had agreed to correct inaccurate press reports of Cobbett's speeches in the House of Commons. Hunt was furious that the *True Sun* had copied a story about himself from the *Liverpool Journal*, while knowing that it was a lie. The story claimed that Hunt had incited the mob at the end of the Preston election to murder one of his political opponents, and that a coroner's inquest had brought a verdict of wilful murder against him. The *True Sun* added the word 'Fudge!' at the end to show that it did not believe the story. This was not enough for Hunt. He said the *True Sun* had acted maliciously, and he wanted damages and a printed apology.

As it happened, Cobbett had also threatened several newspapers with court proceedings for having claimed that he was an undischarged bankrupt and therefore ineligible to sit in the House of Commons. This, too, was a lie. Cobbett had been promptly and officially discharged from his bankruptcy in 1820 – although it is unlikely he ever managed to pay off all his debts. The *Morning Herald* noted with thrilled amusement that Hunt and Cobbett, both 'admirers of the Liberty of the Press', were both pursuing prosecutions against newspapers at the same time. Hunt furiously fired off a letter to the *Herald* and copied it to the *Poor Man's Guardian*, which published it on 26 January 1833. Mr Cobbett, Hunt stormed, was filing 'Criminal Informations' against the newspapers. This meant they would not be able to appear in court to plead justification. Hunt, by contrast, had filed a civil action for libel against the *True Sun*. This meant that the newspaper would have to face him in court and justify what it had written. Hunt could therefore be liable to pay the defendant's costs.

Hunt was making a mountain out of a molehill. The case got to court in early December 1833. The lawyer of the *True Sun* argued that Hunt only brought the action because he was jealous that he was being represented in the newspaper 'in an unfavourable light as contrasted with Mr Cobbett.' What was more, said the *True Sun* lawyer, Hunt had already recovered damages against other newspapers.

Hunt was awarded damages of one farthing.

Around this time a curious poem popped up in the monthly publication, *Cobbett's Magazine*. This had been launched by Cobbett and two of his sons to coincide with his entry into the House of Commons. The poem was called 'The Devil's Visit'. It was part of a genre of verse that began in the early nineteenth century with 'The Devil's Walk'. This was variously attributed to the Greek scholar Richard Porson and the poets Coleridge and Southey. Other poems followed, including one by Byron. All were based around the theme of the devil returning to earth. The poem that appeared in *Cobbett's Magazine* was along similar lines. The devil decided to disguise himself and pay a visit to mankind to organise a second fall. He found that he blended in well. Nobody realised he was telling lies because everybody else was, including the preachers. The devil laughed with pleasure at the corruption and horror he saw all around him. They were all doing his work for him. While visiting the Law Courts, the devil thought he had descended back into Hell. The last verse ran as follows:

With ecstatic delight, he to Hell took his flight,
  Lest his presence should mar his own plan;
For he found that in feat of all sorts of deceit,
  He was vastly inferior to man.

It was a punchy poem with a dark message. It is difficult to say that any of the verses were casting insults against Hunt specifically, although Cobbett had endlessly portrayed Hunt as the devil. In this poem, the devil is vastly inferior to man and all his works. Cobbett, sunk in misery in his seat of war at Bolt Court, was depressed by the whole idea of mankind. Man was outclassing the devil; it was man who was bringing about a second fall to make a hell on earth. But could Hunt have been lurking in Cobbett's thoughts? Could it possibly have been Cobbett's answer to Hunt's attacks in the *Poor Man's Guardian* published, in particular, on 9 November 1833? The timing was right. While on the one hand presenting a dark picture of mankind, did Cobbett also want the devil paraphernalia and the whiff of sulphur to conjure up the image of Hunt? Cobbett's devil was relatively ineffectual, but a devil nonetheless. Did Cobbett want his readers to make an automatic connection with Hunt – as Cobbett once boasted to his daughter that he had taught them to do? Whatever the answers, the *Poor Man's Guardian* re-published the poem on 14 December 1833, without comment.

19
THE SPARKS FLY UPWARDS

On one thing I am resolved, namely that, unless snatched away very suddenly, I will not *die* the MUZZLED SLAVE OF THIS THING!

William Cobbett

He did not and nor did Hunt. Both of them continued to fight the Thing until the very end, Cobbett within the portals of parliament, Hunt outside them. It can only be hoped that Cobbett would not have objected to the use of his marvellously defiant words to embrace them both. This is the most difficult chapter to write, the one in which the two men die and are buried, just four months apart. Thanks to what they wrote, however, and with the help of what others have written about them, their spirits spark eternal, their battles for democracy, justice and human rights as relevant today as they were in the early part of the nineteenth century.

Despite Hunt's criticism, his own deteriorating health and increasing loneliness, Cobbett battled away on his bench in the House of Commons and managed to keep his publishing business going, even though he was experiencing a desperate lack of money. He never had any leisure, he wrote in the *Register* of 17 May 1834. He was always either at work or asleep, although, he assured his readers, he could see anybody at any time upon any business whatever, except sometimes on a Wednesday or a Thursday. He continued to fight on all the issues that he had written about for so many decades in his beloved *Political Register*, promoting the rights and happiness of the people and attacking the greed and corruption of the establishment. He began to sound suspiciously like the Jacobins he despised when he told his fellow MPs half way through 1833:

If we go on at this rate, the people will have a right to oppose us by every peaceable and constitutional means in their power; and if they shall be unable to bring us back to reason by peaceable means, they will obtain at length the right of resorting to absolute resistance.

At the end of the year, Cobbett informed the House: 'The man who is compelled to work all the hours that he is awake, is, whatsoever name he may choose to bear, to all intents and purposes a *slave*.' At the beginning of 1834, an advertisement for a copy of Tom Paine's *Rights of Man* slipped into the *Register*. It claimed to be the cheapest edition of Paine's work ever offered to the public. Just six months before his death, Cobbett wrote the following lines: 'I used to be very forward in saying that I was for a government of *King, Lords and Commons*. I do not know how it is, but I have always looked shy at these words, *since the passing of the Poor-law Bill*!'

Cobbett repeatedly condemned the Poor Law Amendment Act of 1834. The Poor Laws needed reforming, but what was put in their place was equally horrible. The Act established the monstrous prison-like union workhouses into which the poor were herded like cattle to be starved and ill-treated. The sexes were segregated and families broken up. There were cruel penalties for having an illegitimate child. It was practically impossible to get out of the system once you were in it. The Act effectively made it a crime to be poor. Cobbett called it 'that monster of all monsters of a measure'. MPs needed at least a year to read the voluminous and costly reports of Commissioners, he wrote, yet they voted for the provisions without reading them first. He challenged a shocked House of Commons about why the crime of bastardy was confined to the poor. Were there no bastards to be found in high places, no bastards on the pension list, he asked, like the Duke of Richmond, for example, who seemed to have forgotten that he was only noble 'because he had sprung from a bastard.'

Although critics say Cobbett's *Register* lost some of its sparkle in these final years as Cobbett devoted his energies to his parliamentary work, there were many marvellous and cogent lines. 'When members *of political parties unite, the pillage is greater*', he informed his readers. On the widespread misery in Ireland: 'Now the Ministers either know of this distress or they do not. If they do not, they are too ignorant or too lazy to be entrusted with public authority'. Then there were his comments on the plan to introduce Sir Robert Peel's organised London police force elsewhere in the country. Cobbett, still furious over the Popay police spy scandal, was absolutely opposed to the idea. He did not want to see Peel's 'Bourbon police force as disgraced the metropolis' introduced into any of the new boroughs where they would be 'a set of spies going sneaking about in coloured clothes.' (Cobbett's disdain and mistrust of the Metropolitan Police would have been reinforced had he been alive in the 1840s when they controlled the Chartist demonstrations, arresting activists and breaking up public meetings.)

As the shadows lengthened, what about Hunt in all of this? Even as Hunt criticised Cobbett's parliamentary performance, was the old friendship still in Cobbett's mind? Did Cobbett pause to muse over the golden years? The answer seems to be yes. In the *Register* of 26 October 1833, Cobbett re-published his lengthy and accusatory public letter to William Wilberforce, the man whom both he and Hunt had so despised. The letter dated back to 1817 and was written during Cobbett's exile in America. Cobbett decided to republish it in 1833 when a subscription was launched to raise money for a monument to Wilberforce's memory. The letter was a stinging resume of Wilberforce's dirty deeds while in the House of Commons, how he had been a member of the infamous green bag committee after Spa Fields and how he had voted for the suspension of the Habeas Corpus Act. Once again, Cobbett's belief that the affair of Spa Fields was hatched 'principally with a view of getting at the blood of MR HUNT', was presented to the public. There was no need for Cobbett to include the details about Hunt, but he did.

The following year, much of the Palace of Westminster, including the House of Commons, burned down in the fire of 1834. (Westminster Hall was saved.) Cobbett was on a tour of Ireland when he heard the news. In the *Register* of 1 November 1834, he listed the laws and Acts that had been passed 'in this same HOUSE' which had plundered and oppressed the people. Among many other things, he wrote, it was the place in which Sidmouth and Castlereagh had suspended Habeas Corpus and where the Six Acts had been introduced. It was also the place where members of parliament had voted 'that the House would *not inquire* into the massacre at Manchester'. It was no wonder, Cobbett wrote, that the people of London rejoiced as they watched the Houses of Parliament burn to the ground.

Just a week later in the *Register* of 8 November 1834, Cobbett suddenly once again remembered the events of 1816 when 'Mr Hunt' got the better of the Scottish lawyer Henry Brougham at the meeting in Westminster's Old Palace Yard, and the dinner Brougham failed to attend afterwards 'because of the presence of Mr Hunt'.

It is very likely that in the gloom of Bolt Court off Fleet Street, ill, beset by financial difficulties, struggling to set up an annuity for his wife, Nancy, whom, in a fierce letter to Silvester Sapsford, Cobbett accused of having done all she could to ruin and disgrace him, Cobbett bitterly missed his former partner on the dunghill.

Hunt remained obdurate and unmoved. In these final years, he was also in poor health and struggling to survive financially. He was working hard to keep up his blacking business. An advertisement appeared in the *Poor Man's Guardian* in 1833 for Hunt's Matchless Blacking bottles. They cost 4/8 and 1/- and, to prevent fraud, the labels were to be inscribed with the words: 'Equal Laws, Equal Rights, Annual Parliaments, Universal Suffrage and the Ballot.' Hunt lost no opportunity to support the cause and proclaim how right he had been in his persistent criticism of the reform bill. He also offered as much support as he could to the emerging political and trade unions and continued his battles against the guzzling and gormandising in the City of London. But Hunt was a saddened and disappointed man. On 12 February 1833, he sat down at his desk in his London home at 36 Stamford Street and wrote a letter to John Foster of the radical newspaper, the *Leeds Patriot*. The newspaper had been forced into bankruptcy. Hunt's writing was tired and spidery. He told Foster that his health had been ruined by 'the infernal air and late hours of the humbug and hypocritical House of Commons.' He despaired of recovering his former good health. It was vain to look back, he said. He simply had to struggle on. 'You and I of all men now living are an example of disinterested patriotism and a pretty reward we have had', Hunt wrote bitterly. Around these years, he wrote a private letter, possibly to his Blackburn friend, Gilbert Martin, expressing similar emotions:

The fact is this, I am abandoned, hated and feared by every pretender to patriotism, who has not the courage or the honesty to follow my example ... I really begin to doubt my physical power to sustain it much longer. I grow old. I want rest and peace and quietness, for I have no one to call my political friend, no one to whom I can hope for help in the hour of need.

In February 1834, Hunt was so crippled with rheumatism, he had to be carried into a committee room of the House of Commons to give evidence into an enquiry into the official costs of running elections before and after the 1832 Reform Act. Hunt had plenty to say. After losing his Preston seat, he had petitioned the House of Commons and demanded an inquiry into the 'hellish proceedings' in the town during the election. Nothing happened. Instead, the returning officer presented him with a huge bill for election expenses or, as Hunt described it in the *Poor Man's Guardian* on 1 March 1834, the money that had been spent by the town's officials 'in order to extinguish the last remaining vestige of the freedom of election for that borough.' He complained bitterly about the lack of interest in his petition from MPs. He belonged to neither the Tories nor the Whigs, 'nor mock Radicals', Hunt wrote. That was why not one voice had been raised in the House on his behalf.

There was no mention of Cobbett's name, but Hunt's finger was surely pointed accusingly straight at him. The lines ring with the same bewilderment and upset that ate into him in Ilchester Bastile as he bewailed his abandonment by Cobbett then.

The following month, to add insult to injury, Hunt lost his case against the returning officer's unfair demand for money and was faced with a bill including costs of nearly £250.

The *Poor Man's Guardian* reported on Hunt's last great northern tour in March and April 1834. It took in a final visit to Manchester and 'the blood-stained field of Peterloo'. Hunt was saddened to see that the area of land was being swallowed up by new development. He addressed the thousands of people who had gathered to hear him, but he felt so unwell, he had to cut short his speech and go to a nearby inn to recover. Afterwards, he was accompanied through the main streets of Manchester. The next day he managed to attend a dinner for two hundred gentlemen in Oldham – Cobbett's constituency.

Hunt arrived back in London in April 1834. He had to take to his bed because he was so ill. Nevertheless, he continued to write his political articles. In a letter published in the *Poor Man's Guardian* on 26 April 1834 and addressed to 'the Productive Classes of Lancashire' (including those in Oldham), he wrote:

Be of good cheer, my friends; but above all things, be UNITED! Let *Union* be your *motto*, *Universal Political Rights* your *principle*, and trust to time and events for the result ... Let the working classes be but united and steady to their purpose, and their oppressors must give way.

The following month, the Hebden Bridge Political Union passed a unanimous resolution that Henry Hunt, who had 'done and suffered more than any man in the United Kingdom', was a steady and incorruptible advocate of people's rights, whatever his detractors might say. The resolution was published in the *Poor Man's Guardian* on 3 May 1834:

We hereby express our admiration at his firmness, resolution and perseverance in the cause of the people, notwithstanding the slanders which have been circulated by the public press, denouncing him as a turncoat and a traitor. But their lies and malice have fallen upon their own heads and their evil designs have been frustrated.

In November 1834, Hunt's sixty-first birthday was celebrated all over the north of England. Just over two months later, he was on a business trip in the south of the country. He stopped off in New Alresford in Hampshire, the pretty Georgian town which was then on the main road between London and Winchester. As he got down from his chaise, Hunt suffered a stroke. It left him unable to speak and paralysed his left arm. He recovered the use of his voice but lost the movement in his arm. Undaunted, he battled on. Two weeks later he was again passing through New Alresford on business. As he got down from his phaeton outside the George Inn, he suffered another stroke and was taken to a private room. As soon as Catherine Vince received news of Hunt's illness, she hurried down south. The newspaper reporters, who went to knock on her door in Stamford Street in London, found the house dark and empty.

Hunt died a few days later in New Alresford on Friday, 13 February 1835, surrounded by his family and friends. The *Observer* reported that he maintained 'a composed and even cheerful demeanour throughout.' *The Times* wrote that just before he passed away, Hunt uttered these words: 'I die at peace with all mankind. Oh God have mercy upon me.'

Cobbett happened to be at Normandy Farm close to Farnham in Surrey at the time of Hunt's death. It would have been a relatively easy ride to the village of Normandy from New Alresford. There is a laconic entry in Cobbett's diary on Saturday, 14 February, the day after Hunt died: 'Mr

Arkall came; he left on 16th. Mr Martin came.' It is unclear who Mr Arkall was, but there are several possibilities for the identity of Mr Martin. Both Hunt and Cobbett were well acquainted with a Mr and Mrs Martin. In one of his furious diatribes against Cobbett, Hunt alluded to what Nancy Cobbett had told 'Mrs Martin'. This Mr Martin could have been Joseph Martin of Lincoln's Inn. He is mentioned in the *Political Register* in 1826 in connection with the arrangements for the subscription raised for Cobbett to fight the Preston seat that year. There was also Gilbert Martin from Blackburn who was a close friend of Hunt. He could have hurried to Hampshire as soon as he heard of Hunt's final stroke and so would have been able to make the journey to Normandy. Another possibility is that Cobbett's visitor was a relative of old Mr Martin, the Scottish gardener, who, decades earlier, had lived near the Cobbetts in Farnham and argued with Cobbett's father over the rights and wrongs of American independence. It cannot be known for certain who the two men were that visited Cobbett over that February weekend, nor can it be known whether they went to inform Cobbett of the news of Hunt's death, but I like to think they did.

In the issue of the *Political Register* of 21 February 1835 is a piece dated Saturday, 14 February. It had been written at Normandy Farm the day after Hunt's death. At some point during the day, Cobbett made a list of the precious bags of seed he was offering for sale. Each bag cost 10/6. The seeds were for a variety of vegetables ranging from asparagus to savoy cabbage, kidney beans, parsnip and parsley, turnips and radishes, mustard, onion and Cobbett's Corn. Was it a coincidence or is it possible that Cobbett did hear the news of Hunt's death that day and had chosen to immerse himself in the green tasks he and Hunt had loved so well – and remembered their ridiculous fights over roasted corn.

When Cobbett had compiled his seeds list, he added an N.B. He had no Cis-Alpine Strawberry Seed, but he did have packets of alternative 'fine plants', at 2/6 a packet, which would bear great crops that year. It is impossible to say whether these 'fine plants' had sprung from cuttings from the gardens of that greatest of all strawberry growers, Sir Charles Wolseley, Hunt's former business partner and the man Cobbett embraced to spite Hunt. If they did, this time Cobbett chose not to mention Wolseley by name.

Hunt was buried in the churchyard of St Peter's Church in Parham Park near Storrington in West Sussex on Saturday, 21 February 1835. *The Times*, which had not until then reported the news of Hunt's death, chose to print on the Monday after the funeral an account from the *Devizes Gazette* of Hunt's early years in his home county of Wiltshire. The following day, *The Times* published its own lengthy report of the funeral and recapped on the events leading up to it.

Hunt's burial was as controversial as his life had been. Today, Parham Park is a popular tourist destination. People enjoy visiting the fine Elizabethan house set in acres of parkland with a fine view of the church. The medieval village that once clustered around St Peter's was cleared away at the end of the eighteenth century to give the owners of Parham more space and a better view of the church from their south-facing main rooms. It was a curious place, therefore, for the setting of Hunt's funeral. The connection was that Parham belonged to the Bisshopps, the wealthy family of Catherine Vince. The Bisshopps had owned Parham since 1601. (They sold it in 1922, although their portraits still grace the walls, including those of Sir Cecil Bisshopp, sixth baronet, and his wife, Ann, the handsome grandparents of Mrs Vince.) The church of St Peter's, where Hunt was buried, had been largely rebuilt by Cecil Bisshop, Catherine's cousin and eighth baronet, in the early years of the 1800s.

This was the link, but it still does not explain why Hunt was buried there. Given Hunt's notoriety as a dangerous radical, it is unthinkable that the mainstream Bisshop family would have willingly allowed him to be buried at St Peter's Church in full view of their huge front windows. *The Times* reported that Hunt had expressed a wish for many years to be buried at Parham and that he was interred in 'Colonel Vince's vault'. The 'reporther', as Cobbett would no doubt have called him, must have made a mistake, however. In fact, he made several mistakes in the article, including putting Parham into Hampshire and mis-spelling Storrington. The mention of 'Colonel Vince's vault' was also an error. Catherine Vince's husband, Henry Chivers Vince, had no connection whatsoever with Parham. The reporter for *The Times* may have confused Catherine's husband with her father, Colonel Harry Bisshopp.

Despite the scandalous behaviour of Colonel Bisshopp in producing

St Peter's Church, Parham, 2008
Burial place of Hunt.

Spa Fields, painted by C A Matthews from memory about 1830-1840. Merlin's Cave Tavern is at the top of the hill.
City of London, London Metropolitan Archives

several illegitimate children before marrying their mother, and the subsequent coolness with which his family regarded him, Catherine's father had been buried at St Peter's Church in Parham in 1821. Before he died, he may well have given permission to his daughter Catherine for Hunt to be buried in their own family vault, whatever the aunts, uncles and cousin Bisshopps felt about it. Colonel Bisshopp would have expected that Catherine, despite her illegitimacy and scandalous separation from her husband, would also be buried in Parham in the bosom of her immediate Bisshopp family, side by side with Hunt. This would be a reasonable explanation of why Hunt was buried in the heartland of the enemy. There is no official record of Catherine Vince's burial at Parham. It is possible that when she later died and was buried next to Hunt, the Bisshopp family leaned on the vicar not to include her name in the church list of burials. They would have been ashamed of her life and association in death with Henry Hunt. For this reason, there is also no mention of or monument to Hunt at Parham. Visitors today would not know that Henry 'Orator' Hunt of Spa Fields and the Peterloo Massacre lies buried in the churchyard there.

According to *The Times*, the funeral procession set out for Parham on the morning of the day before Hunt's funeral. It attracted a crowd of people, many of whom had known Hunt. They accompanied the cortege as it slowly moved forward until an order was given to speed up the pace of the horses. At this point, it is unclear from the newspaper report where the procession was. *The Times* said it had passed through 'the village'. This could have been the village of Rackham just before Parham Park. It is quite possible that the Bisshopp family, furious that Hunt's coffin was heading into Parham, gave the order to speed up the horses so that the *hoi polloi* at least would be shaken off. It is also unclear what happened next. *The Times* says that the hearse moved into Parham Park on Saturday morning. Robert Huish claimed in his 1836 biography of Hunt that the Bisshopp family opposed Hunt's burial at Parham right up until the eleventh hour. He also claimed that Hunt's coffin lay for a night beforehand in Horsham parish church because of the Bisshopps' objections. Huish was notoriously shaky in his facts. He even managed to get the date of Hunt's death wrong. Horsham was a long way away and in the wrong direction.

It is likely, however, that Huish was correct about a last-minute row over the place where Hunt was to be buried.

Whatever did happen, Hunt's funeral took place on Saturday, 21 February 1835 at St Peter's Church in Parham. A relatively small number of people gathered in the churchyard. The group included Hunt's elder son who was the chief mourner. Henry junior stood side by side with Hunt's great friend, the London lawyer, Charles Pearson, the man Cobbett had so often jeered at in the *Register* as 'Charley'. *The Times* only mentioned male mourners. Conventionally, women did not attend funerals. It is possible, however, that the unconventional and independent-minded Mrs Vince and her equally unconventional daughter, Catherine Maria, were close by. In a sensational twist, Catherine Maria Vince had become Mrs Hunt just over two months earlier, when she had married Henry junior at the church of St Martin in the Fields in London.

The Rev. George Palmer, rector of the parish, read the funeral service, and the lead coffin, which was enclosed in a wooden one of 'prodigious size', was lowered into the vault. The coffin was so large, some of the brickwork at the entrance to the vault had to be removed. On the coffin's splendid silver plate were the words:

Henry Hunt, Esq; late M.P. for Preston,
Departed this life on the 13th day of February 1835,
In the 62nd year of his age.

The weekly *Poor Man's Guardian* loyally led on the news of Hunt's death at the first opportunity. The day happened to coincide with his funeral. The newspaper began the issue with these words: 'It is our lamentable duty this week to record the death of one of the best and bravest friends the working classes ever had – the death of HENRY HUNT.' Hunt's career was too well known and too well appreciated by their readers to render necessary a posthumous eulogy, the newspaper continued. During the thirty years or so that Hunt had taken a prominent part in the struggles of his country, he was never known to desert a cause he had adopted, nor to have adopted a bad one. Whatever he said he would do, he had done; if he had not always been successful, the fault lay with others, not with him. The *Poor Man's Guardian* continued:

His spirit was ever the same, the spirit of a brave Englishman, who loved justice for its own sake and hated tyranny, because tyranny caused the misery of his fellow-citizens ... Faults of temper he had, like most men, but they were mainly the result of the repeated persecutions and treachery he had experienced as a public man ... As the friend of justice and 'equal laws,' we see few that we could conscientiously pronounce his equal.

Hunt did not get anywhere near as many obituaries as Cobbett would get a few months later. Although Cobbett was reviled and excoriated by the establishment, his greatness as a political writer was always acknowledged. Cobbett is still celebrated today. Hunt, by contrast, was scorned by the establishment as a demagogue and largely dismissed by historians. He had to wait until almost the end of the twentieth century for his political biographer, John Belchem, to rescue him from oblivion. Belchem stripped away the image of the violent, vain demagogue to reveal the person whom Cobbett loved beyond all others, a gentleman of honour, good humour, loyalty and integrity and with a passionate desire to achieve the rights of man.

Cobbett ignored, at least publicly, the death of his former friend and political partner. There was nothing about Hunt's death or funeral in *Cobbett's Political Register.* Sadly, at the end, Cobbett withheld his powerful pen. He was back in the House of Commons when parliament resumed on 19 February 1835. In the issue of the *Register* that happened to be published on the day Hunt was buried, Cobbett told his readers that there had been a vote, once again, for the re-appointment of Sir Charles Manners Sutton as Commons' Speaker. He had not been able to vote for him, Cobbett explained, 'without an abandonment of the principle that a pensioner ought not to be the first Commoner of England'. He had also declined to vote for the other candidate because he had supported the Poor Law Bill. So Cobbett had walked out of the House without voting at all. (Surely Hunt's shade walked by his side.)

By 7 March 1835, Cobbett was complaining that his winter cough and hoarseness were so bad, he had the 'excruciating torment of sitting silent, at times when I am bursting to speak'. In the Commons three days later, he was unable to speak on a motion to repeal the malt tax (another of his pet hates which he had campaigned against so often with Hunt).

Cobbett retreated from London to his farm in Normandy village and put his frustration on paper. His words might have had no effect in the House, but they would have had an effect '*out of the House*', he told his readers.

Cobbett was now convinced that there was no hope of a restoration of freedom and good living in England coming from within parliament. It could only come through '*pressure from without*', he wrote in the *Register* of 21 March 1835, and here, Cobbett analysed life without a king. The government was not a '*monarchy*', he argued. It was a government of the three estates, the King, Lords and Commons. The *Morning Post* had written that if there were to be an end of the kingly branch of the government, anarchy, military despotism, confusion, bloodshed, carnage and republicanism would prevail. Was this really the choice on offer? Cobbett asked. Was it to be either a King or a republic? Must they have the pension list or a republic? Did they have to have the Poor Law Bill and big workhouses or a republic? Did they have to have a Popay-police or a republic? Maybe a republic was not such a 'hellish sort of thing' after all. There was only one republic in the world (America). When the revolution happened, there had been no anarchy or confusion, nor the rivers of blood they had all been warned about in England. There had been no military despot. The country now had trade, commerce and a navy nearly equalling those of Great Britain. The people there were the most free and happy in the world. What was more, there was no 'established domination of the few over the many'. The question was how could such a government be introduced into England? It was the very question that he would like to answer fully and frankly and '*without any disguise*', but he did not like to do so at that moment (and he never did).

On this issue, Cobbett trailed Hunt who had uttered similar thoughts on 16 June 1832, at a meeting of the National Union of the Working Classes in Pendleton. His words had been published in the *Poor Man's Guardian* on 30 June. He was of the opinion, Hunt said, that there could be no cheap government under a monarchy. In America, by contrast, there was a republican government which did things cheaply. He wanted a government that was cheap and good, so: 'If we cannot get this in a monarchical government, why then I would say, let us have a republican government.'

On 4 April 1835, Cobbett confided to his readers (as if they did not know): 'I seldom do things by halves; very seldom half love, half hate or half anything.'

As the end approached, Cobbett became increasingly retrospective. Some of his writing is superb. Reading it nearly two hundred years later, it is as if we are sitting with him watching his eyes sparkling, his mirth turning to anger and as quickly back again, as he takes us into his confidence. In the issue of 18 April 1835, Cobbett remembered Lord Castlereagh, the man whom he (and Hunt) had so hated, and who had committed suicide, much to Cobbett's undisguised joy: 'I used to tell him that he argued as if *he* was the country. I used to tell him that he was not the country, that I might like the country and hate him, which I did; that he might die (which he did, you know), and that the country would still live.'

In the *Register* of 23 May 1835, Cobbett announced his intention to set up an evening newspaper. It was to be called *Cobbett's Evening Journal* and owned by men 'inaccessible to corruption'. It would not be led by those who 'tuck their dirty cheeks into their filthy paws and snore out the fumes of the gin while those important matters, the estimates of the public expenditure, are before the House'. Then there was the next comedy he planned to write, to be called 'Bastards in High-Life'. He was also planning his autobiography about 'the *Progress of a Plough-boy to a seat in Parliament'*. It would tell how he began his career driving the rooks and magpies from his father's pea-fields and his mother's chicken-yard, and how he ended up 'endeavouring to drive the tithe and tax devourers from the fruits of the labour of his industrious countrymen'.

Cobbett's last speech in the House of Commons on 25 May 1835 was on the Poor Law Amendment Act and what it had brought to the people. A spaniel dog would be given more food than was allocated to a man in the workhouse, he said, and reminded his fellow MPs that the weekly 'bill of fare' for paupers in Sussex had been drawn up by none other than the Duke of Richmond. (The bastard!)

Cobbett did not go gentle into that good night. He had always been determined that the light, which had shone so strongly and brightly, would not go out 'twinkling down in the socket.' It did not and nor did Cobbett die 'THE MUZZLED SLAVE OF THIS THING!'

The next day, Cobbett, a sick man, left London for the last time and went home to die at Normandy Farm. An account of his final days was published in the *Political Penny Magazine* more than a year later in 1836. The article was written anonymously. The author said that despite his increasingly frail state, Cobbett managed to pen the material for what would be his last *Register*. He did so while sitting in his little garden at the front of the farmhouse. From there he could look over Normandy Common and see right across his fields as far as the hill called the Hog's Back. The pages included one final blast against the new poor law, or, as Cobbett described it to those around him at the time, the '*Grey-Althorpian damnable bill*'. The last words he wrote for his beloved *Register* were, 'let no one expect that we shall not finally succeed in all our lawful and laudable undertakings.' They echoed the optimistic lines Hunt had written in 1834 in which he declared that the people should trust to time and events for a result and their oppressors would have to give way.

As the days passed, Cobbett's health worsened. His secretary sent for his eldest son, William, and his publisher. The latter took it upon himself to send word to Cobbett's family at Red Lion Court. Cobbett was not amused. The anonymous author reported his words: '"Humph" said Mr Cobbett, "who told you to do *that*?"'

On Sunday, 14 June 1835, Cobbett was able to sit in a chair in his garden and talk cheerfully about the fields, the crops he could see across the common, his lettuces and cauliflowers and his corn growing at the back of the house. That night, he became delirious and talked about the cruelty of his family towards him. John and Anne arrived, and Cobbett agreed to see them on the Tuesday, but there was to be no forgiveness, no reconciliation. Lear-like, he told Anne that because of her 'cruelty' towards him, he no longer considered her to be his daughter. (Poor Anne. She had adored her father and had worked and supported him so closely for so many years. She was the one who would continue his publishing business after his death.)

On Wednesday, 17 June, Cobbett asked to be carried around his fields.

He was helped into an easy chair fixed into a wheelbarrow, and was carried across the common and around his fields for two hours to view his crops for the last time. He managed to summon up the energy to give some of his labourers fresh orders about what they should be doing. In the course of the day, he was told that his wife and his other children wanted to visit him. Cobbett sat down and wrote his last letter. He had no 'insuperable objection' to seeing any of his children at the farm, but it would be on the express condition that none of them attempted to sleep there, that no order was given to any of his servants and that they would not interfere in any of his affairs. Regarding the presence of his wife, Nancy, Cobbett was likewise obdurate. He had no objection to her going into the house in the day-time, but she was not to stay there over night. Moreover, 'night or day, she shall never have the power of commanding, or giving an order to any human being in my house.' (Had he read those words, Hunt might have felt vindicated.)

As Cobbett deteriorated, the doctor was summoned in the early hours of Thursday, 18 June. The writer of the article for *The Political Penny Magazine* described the scene. Cobbett had obviously not lost his acid sense of humour. Very cautiously, the doctor asked Cobbett whether he might wish to write anything down: '"Not," continued he, "that there is any *dainja*," – (danger).' As he prepared to leave the room, the doctor happened to cough. Cobbett 'with much apparent gravity and in the same affected drawl' asked him whether he was taking anything for it:

'No! Sir,' replied Esculapius. 'Then,' continued Mr Cobbett, 'I think that you should;' and, looking very archly, he added – 'not that I think there is any *dainja*.' The doctor looked rather blank at this humourous sally; and as he was leaving the bed-side, Mr Cobbett added, with one of [his] arch and laughing winks of the eye – 'there, take that, my buck!'

Nancy Cobbett was allowed in to attend to her husband later that day. She helped to bathe his temples and moisten his lips, but it was too late. Cobbett showed neither joy nor displeasure at her presence and appeared not to know that his wife was even there. There was no reconciliation with the woman he had loved so tenderly and without whom, as he had once written in the *Register*, he would have been 'just a middling sort of fellow'. At ten past one in the afternoon, Cobbett stretched out his hand, as if bidding farewell. Then, leaning back and closing his eyes as if to sleep, he died 'without a gasp.'

The 'Bloody Old Times', against which Cobbett had fought throughout his career, disgraced itself by publishing a nasty little piece the day after Cobbett's death:

A report prevailed last night in the House of Commons ... that 'William Cobbett was dead.' We know not whether we should confine ourselves to the simple expression of regret or ... whether we might not speak of his decease as matter of congratulation to himself; that after a life of incessant change and tumult, he had at last come to a state of tranquillity and permanence.

In the article, *The Times* referred to Cobbett as 'Poor fellow!' and mentioned what it called 'his followers' who, it said, were of 'a coarse intellect and mentally circumscribed'. (Hunt!?) But the newspaper must have had a re-think because it had another go the following day. This time *The Times* paid full, albeit reluctant tribute to the man who had filled column after column of the *Register* for decades with insults against it. The obituary began:

Take this self-taught peasant for all in all, he was perhaps, in some respects, a more extraordinary Englishman than any other of his time ... Birth, station, employment, ignorance, temper, character, in early life were all against him. But he emerged from and overcame them all ... By masculine force of genius and the lever of a proud confident and determined *will*, he pushed aside a mass of obstacles, of which the least and slightest would have repelled the boldest or most ambitious of ordinary men. He ended by bursting that most formidable barrier which separates the class of English gentlemen from all beneath them and died a Member of Parliament representing a large constituency.

Cobbett was buried on Saturday, 27 June 1835 in Farnham, the town of his birth, in the graveyard of St Andrew's Church next to his parents and grandfather. He was seventy-two years old. Hundreds of people joined the funeral procession as it wound its way along the country lanes from Normandy village to Farnham about six miles away. In the town, spectators filled every window of every house. Coaches passing through Farnham delayed their departure so that passengers could pay their respects. At least eight thousand people, nearly double the population of the little town, attended the funeral. Cobbett's four sons, his fellow MP,

John Fielden, and the Irish MP, Daniel O'Connell led the crowds. John Cobbett wept so hard, he had to be supported by his brothers. It poured with rain that day and there were no speeches. After the ceremony, the leading mourners adjourned to the Bush Inn in the High Street (now the Bush Hotel). The Cobbetts returned to what must have been a sad and silent Normandy Farm.

The Cobbett family tomb, enclosed in iron railings, is outside the main porch of St Andrew's Church in Farnham. Nancy Cobbett was buried with her husband when she died thirteen years later. The words on Cobbett's tomb are still clearly legible. The year of his birth is given as 1762 although it is now generally accepted that he was born a year later in 1763:

Beneath this stone lie the remains of WILLIAM COBBETT, son of George and Ann Cobbett. Born in the parish of Farnham March 9 1762. Enlisted in the 54th Regiment of Foot in 1784, in which regiment he became Sergeant Major in 1785 and obtained his discharge in 1791. In 1794 he became a political writer, in 1832 was returned to Parliament for the borough of Oldham and represented it till his death, which took place at Normandy Farm in the adjoining parish of Ash on the 18th June 1835.

There was an avalanche of obituaries. One of the best retrospectives was written nearly a century later by G D H Cole, who spent years amassing his Cobbett collection, which is now in The Library of Nuffield College, Oxford. This was Cole's conclusion at the end of his *Life of William Cobbett*:

The history of William Cobbett is, in plain language, the spiritual history of the common people of his day – of their uprooting from the land of their fathers, of their unease and maladjustment under the new conditions thrust on them by the torrential flow of economic revolution. It is a history not of ideas, but of facts and feelings ... He kept to the end, as the greatest possession of his spirit, his abounding faith in the common rightness of the common people.

There was no mention of Hunt in any of Cobbett's obituaries. It is interesting, however, to read part of an article written at the time by the *Morning Advertiser*. In it, the newspaper referred to what it described as Cobbett's merciless enmity and generous friendship:

He never failed in driving his opponent from the field, divesting him of his armour and exposing the nakedness of his figure to scorn and derision. His sarcasm was biting and unmerciful. He laughed with a fiendish joy at the discomfiture of his opponent and rioted with savage delight over the mangled remains of his victim. With equal enthusiasm, however, be it also remarked – nay, with equal exaggeration – did he glory in those whom he admired. In them all perfection was centred – from them all good emanated – from their approbation only could honour flow – by their exertions only could the country be benefited and saved.

Cobbett certainly had many friends and foes and deployed his formidable arsenal of weapons against many of them, but those words from the *Morning Advertiser* applied to Hunt more than to any of the others.

The year after the deaths of William Cobbett and Henry Hunt, Robert Huish published his biographies of both men and made interesting comparisons between the pair:

Cobbett saw in Hunt a formidable rival in acquiring that influence over the people, which it was his wish to engross to himself, and although in vigour of mind, the former surpassed the latter, yet, perhaps no man has existed in England, who knew how to work upon the feelings of a mob with greater success than Hunt. In this respect, he was far the superior of Cobbett, although as a writer, he never could compete with him. Cobbett sought to accomplish his object by downright main force, he dealt his arguments around him with the power of the sledge hammer, whereas Hunt adopted a freer or more conciliating tone and he won his way to the hearts of his audience by the most apt illustrations and a display of wit and humour which Cobbett would not condescend to use or which more properly speaking, he did not know the use of.

These words by Huish provide posterity with the best contemporary explanation of what sparked Cobbett's destructive rivalry and jealousy against Hunt.

Two weeks after Cobbett's funeral, the deaths of both men were mourned and commemorated in a letter published in the *Poor Man's Guardian* on 11 July 1835. It not only positively remembered the two men in the heyday of their political struggle, it was also a tribute from those who would help to carry the torch of reform into the future. The letter was written by one of the future leaders of the Chartist movement, the Bradford radical, Peter Bussey. It was very singular, he wrote, that within the space of a few months, they should lose 'two of the most staunch Reformers this country ever produced – Henry Hunt, the consistent and uncompromising advocate of equal rights, and the Member for Oldham.'

The pair had stood the test for years, braving 'the storm of Whig and Tory vengeance.' They fought and conquered the 'demon-like power' of Castlereagh, which had oppressed the country. 'The base minions in power trembled beneath their castigations', and the people were awoken from their slumbers. Cobbett and Hunt raised their 'gigantic powers,' and governments turned pale.

Epilogue

The old barn-door or dung-hill cock appears to be extinct ... I well remember when a boy you could not go out, but you heard them all crowing in all directions, each on his own dung-hill, challenging each other and their shrill clarion-like sound echoed through the valley ... The sort they have now are so hoarse and dull in their crowing that there is nothing to attract attention, nothing agreeable in the sound and not loud enough to be heard by one another, so there is no answering each other. In my boyhood the whole valley would ring with them.'

Small Talk at Wreyland
by Cecil Torr
letter, 7 October 1852

Bibliography

Main Sources:
Cobbett's Weekly Political Register, January 1802 - June 1835, 88
    volumes;
Cobbett's Evening Post, 29 January - 5 April 1820;
Cobbett's Advice to Young Men, 1829;
Cottage Economy, William Cobbett, 1822;
Rural Rides, William Cobbett, 2 volumes;
A Year's Residence in America, William Cobbett, 1818 and 1819;
Observations on the Emigration of Dr. Joseph Priestley, William Cobbett,
    1794;
The Political Censor, William Cobbett, 1796;
(Both of the above can be found in *Porcupine's Works* in 12 volumes,
    1801)
Memoirs of Henry Hunt, Esq. Written by himself in his Majesty's Jail at
    Ilchester, three volumes, 1820-1822;
*Addresses to the Radical Reformers of England, Ireland and Scotland 1820-
    1822*, Henry Hunt, 1820-1822;
*Addresses from Henry Hunt, Esq. M.P. to the Radical Reformers of England,
    Ireland and Scotland, on the measures of the Whig Ministers since
    they have been in place and power*, 1-13, 1831-1832;
The Preston Cock's Reply to the Kensington Dunghill, 1831;
The Times;
Poor Man's Guardian 1831-1835, four volumes, pub. The Merlin Press
    1969;
Parliamentary Debates, Hansard;

Main Secondary Sources:
William Cobbett: The Poor Man's Friend, George Spater, two volumes,
    1982;
'Orator' Hunt, John Belchem, 1985;

Libraries and Record Offices:
British Library in St Pancras (including the Francis Place Collection on
    microfilm);

British Library Newspapers, Colindale, (including *The Weekly Free Press of Trade, Manufactures and Commerce*, which began as *Trades newspapers and Mechanics Weekly Journal*, 1828-1832. M10633/4);
British Museum, The Department of Prints and Drawings (including the Stephen-George collection);
The Library of Nuffield College, Oxford (including the Cole Collection and all 13 of Hunt's *Addresses* 1831-1832);
Bristol Library (including microfilm of *Felix Farley's Bristol Journal* and other local newspapers);
Chetham's Library, Manchester;
Public Record Office, Kew;
Adelphi University Library, New York (including Cobbett's letters to Henry Hunt, copies of which are also in the Nuffield);
University of Chicago Library, Special Collections Research Center (including Henry Hunt Collection, Ms563);
Columbia University, New York (including *The Political Penny Magazine*, 29 October 1836 No. 9;
Yale University Library (including Stevens-Cox Collection);
Lancashire Record Office (including *A Collection of Addresses, Squibs, Songs pub. during the Contested Election for the Borough of Preston 1826* and *Addresses from One of the 3730 Electors of Preston to his Fellow Townsmen from 31 December 1831*);
Somerset County Record Office;
West Sussex Record Office;
Wiltshire and Swindon History Centre;

Selected Sources, Historical Background and Reference:

Aspinall, Arthur, *Politics and the Press 1780-1850*, 1949;
Bamford, Samuel, *Passages in the Life of a Radical*, 2 volumes, 1844;
Baines, Edward, *The Life of Edward Baines*, 1851;
Bentham, Jeremy, *The Works of Jeremy Bentham*, ed. John Bowring, 11 vols, 1843;
Biddell, Barbara, *The Jolly Farmer? William Cobbett in Hampshire, 1804-1820*, 1999;
Blanche, Lesley, *The Game of Hearts, Harriette Wilson and her Memoirs*, 1957;
Bovill E.W., *English Country Life 1780-1830*, 1962;
Broughton, Lord, (John Cam Hobhouse) *Recollections of a Long Life*, ed. Lady Dorchester, 6 volumes, 1909-1910;

Bryant, Arthur, *The Age of Elegance 1812-1822*, 1950;

Bush, Michael, *The Casualties of Peterloo*, 2006;

Byron, *Lord Byron's Correspondence*, ed. John Murray, 2 volumes, 1922;

Byron, *The Life, Letters and Journals of Lord Byron*, ed. Thomas Moore, 1875;

Cecil, Lord David, *Melbourne*, 1954;

Cobbett, Anne, *Account of the Family*, pub. The William Cobbett Society, 1999;

Cole, G.D.H., *The Life of William Cobbett*, 1924;

Dictionary of National Biography;

Evans, Eric J., *The Forging of the Modern State, Early Industrial Britain, 1783-1870*, 1983;

Gilfillan, George, *A Second Gallery of Literary Portraits*, 1850;

George, M Dorothy, *Catalogue of Political and Personal Satires*, 1952;

Grant, James, *Random Recollections of the House of Commons*, 1836;

Greville, Charles, *The Greville Memoirs*, 7 volumes, 1938;

Gronow, Rees Howell, *The Reminiscences and Recollections of Captain Gronow*, 1892;

Ham, Joan, *Storrington in Georgian and Victorian Times*, available in Storrington public library;

Hammond, J.L. and Hammond, Barbara:
    The Town Labourer 1760-1832
    The Village Labourer 1760-1832
    The Skilled Labourer 1760-1832
    1911-1919;

Hastings, Maurice, *Parliament House*, 1950;

Hazlitt, William, *The Spirit of the Age*;

Holland, Lord, *Memoirs of the Whig Party during My Time*, ed. Henry Edward Lord Holland, 2 volumes, 1852-4;

Holmes, Richard, *Shelley the Pursuit*, 1994;

Hone, William, *The Riots in London, Hone's Full and Authentic Account of the events in the Metropolis on Monday 2nd December 1816*;

Hope-Jones, Arthur, *Income Tax in the Napoleonic Wars*, 1939;

Horwood, Richard, *A to Z of Regency London*, 1985;

Huish, Robert, *The History of the Private and Political Life of the late Henry Hunt, Esq. MP for Preston*, 2 volumes, 1836;

Ingrams, Richard, *The Life and Adventures of William Cobbett*, 2005;

Johnson, Joseph, *A Letter to Henry Hunt, Esq.* and *A Second Letter to Henry Hunt, Esq*, both published 1822 (I found them in *Political Tracts 1816-1823* in the British Library);

Jones, Christopher, *The Great Palace, The Story of Parliament*, 1983;

Keats, John, *The Complete Poetical Works and Letters of John Keats*, ed. Horace Scudder, 1899;

Longford, Elizabeth, *Wellington Pillar of State*, 1972;

Marlow, Joyce, *The Peterloo Massacre*, 1970;

Melville, Lewis, *The Life and Letters of William Cobbett in England and America*, 2 volumes, 1913;

O'Connell, Daniel, *The Correspondence of Daniel O'Connell*, ed Maurice O'Connell, 8 volumes, 1972;

Paine, Tom, *Rights of Man*;

Patterson, William, *Sir Francis Burdett and His Times*, 1931;

Pearce, Robert and Stearn, Roger, *Government and Reform: 1815-1918*, 1994;

Pearl, M.L., *William Cobbett: A Bibliographical Account of His Life and Times*, 1953;

Priestly, J.B., *The Prince of Pleasure*, 1969;

Pugh, Martin, *The Evolution of the British Electoral System 1832-1987*, 1988;

Shelley, *The Letters of Percy Bysshe Shelley*, ed. Roger Ingpen, 2 volumes, 1912;

The Devil's Drive, Lord Byron;

The Devil's Walk, Richard Porson, (I found this in the Prints Room of the British Museum);

The Real Devil's Walk not by Professor Porson, 1830;

Thompson, E.P., *The Making of the English Working Classes*;

Townsend, William, *The Lives of 12 Eminent Judges*, 2 volumes, 1846;

Wallace, Graham, *The Life of Francis Place*, 1898;

White, R.J., *Life in Regency England*, 1963;

William Cobbett Society, *Cobbett's New Register*, published annually;

Wilson, Ben, *The Laughter of Triumph, William Hone and the Fight for the Free Press*, 2005;

Index